EDGE OF THE SWORD

Courtesy of Mary Twitchell

EDGE OF THE SWORD

THE ORDEAL OF
CARPETBAGGER MARSHALL H. TWITCHELL
IN THE CIVIL WAR AND RECONSTRUCTION

TED TUNNELL

LOUISIANA STATE UNIVERSITY PRESS

Baton Rouge

Designer: Amanda McDonald Scallan
Typeface: Janson Text
Typesetter: Coghill Composition
Printer and binder: Thomson-Shore, Inc.

Library of Congress Cataloging-in-Publication Data
Tunnell, Ted.
Edge of the sword : the ordeal of carpetbagger Marshall H.
Twitchell in the Civil War and Reconstruction / Ted Tunnell.
p.   cm.
Includes bibliographical references and index.
ISBN 0-8071-2659-4
1. Twitchell, Marshall Harvey.   2. Reconstruction—Louisiana.
3. Politicians—Louisiana—Biography.   4. Louisiana—Politics
and government—1865–1950.   5. United States. Bureau of Refugees,
Freedmen, and Abandoned Lands—Officials and
employees—Biography.   6. United States. Army. Vermont Brigade,
1st (1861–1865)—Biography.   7. Townshend (Vt.)—Biography.   8.
Red River Parish (La.)—Biography.   I. Title.
F375.T87   2001
976.3′06′0924—dc21
00-012116

For Letitia and our children, Alexander and Sarah

And there was a day when his sons and his daughters were eating and drinking wine in their eldest brother's house: And there came a messenger unto Job, and said, The oxen were plowing, and the asses feeding beside them: And the Sabeans fell upon them, and took them away; yea, they have slain the servants with the edge of the sword; and I only am escaped to tell thee.

—Book of Job

CONTENTS

Acknowledgments   *xiii*

Abbreviations   *xv*

Introduction   *1*

ONE
Vermont
8

TWO
The Vermont Brigade
21

THREE
The Virginia Peninsula
37

FOUR
First Sergeant
59

FIVE
Valley of the Shadow
72

SIX
A Troubled Beginning in Sparta,
Louisiana
92

SEVEN
Marshall and Adele
109

EIGHT
Rough and Tumble Politics,
1867–1869
119

NINE
The Father of Red River Parish
138

TEN
Death and Hard Times
169

ELEVEN
The Knife to the Hilt
184

TWELVE
Twitchell under Siege
211

THIRTEEN
The Stranger in the Green Eye
Goggles
232

FOURTEEN
Condemning the Victim
251

FIFTEEN
The Last Battles of Coushatta
272

SIXTEEN
Kingston
292

Bibliography   308
Index   319

ILLUSTRATIONS

Frontispiece
   Marshall Harvey Twitchell

Following page 86
   Harvey David Twitchell
   Elizabeth Scott Twitchell
   Sergeant Marshall Twitchell, Fourth Vermont
   Captain Marshall Twitchell, 109th USCT

Following page 160
   "The First Vote"
   Adele Coleman Twitchell
   Lisso & Bros. notice
   Clark Holland, Homer Twitchell, Bert Holland, Homer King,
      Monroe and Helen Twitchell Willis, George King
   Members of 1868 Louisiana convention and assembly
   Carpetbagger cartoon
   "The War of Races"
   Battle of Canal Street; Democrats being expelled from Louisiana
      House of Representatives

Following page 247
   Marshall Twitchell, American consul, ca. 1880
   Marshall and Henrietta Day Twitchell, with their sons
   Marshall Twitchell, ca. 1900

Maps

Page 91   Map 1 Northwest Louisiana Parish Boundaries after
                          the Civil War
Page 137   Map 2 Northwest Louisiana Parish Boundaries, late
                          1870
Page 183   Map 3 Louisiana's Alluvial-Electoral Y

Acknowledgments

I have accumulated many debts in the writing of this book. The writing and research was substantially aided by a summer stipend from the National Endowment for the Humanities and by a research and publication grant from the Louisiana Endowment for the Humanities. Michael Music guided me through the complex, sometimes arcane, filing systems of Old Army Records in the National Archives. Mary Lynn Wernet offered invaluable assistance at the Cammie G. Henry Research Center in Natchitoches, Louisiana. The archival staff of Prescott Memorial Library, Louisiana Tech University, has turned over several times since I started my research; but the respective members were invariably cooperative. Equally cooperative was the staff of the Vermont Historical Society. My graduate research assistant Kristin Thrower helped enormously with the research in northern newspapers. I am indebted to *Vermont History, Louisiana History,* and *Louisiana Cultural Vistas* for permitting me to reprint portions of articles and to Louisiana State University Press for allowing me to reuse passages and documents from chapter 9 of *Crucible of Reconstruction: War, Radicalism, and Race in Louisiana, 1862–1877* (1984). My thanks to the Baker Library at the Harvard Business School for permission to quote passages from the R. G. Dun & Co. Collection. Peggy Twitchell generously allowed me to use her family scrapbook. Mary Twitchell has been consistently helpful with documents and photographs. My wife, Letitia, made countless corrections of the manuscript, as well as drawing two of the maps. She also tolerated—with only occasional complaint—my research notes taking over the second floor of our home. My friend and colleague James T. Moore read most of the manuscript and made many editorial corrections. Another friend and colleague Alan Briceland performed Herculean labors on the manuscript, greatly improving it. Such faults as remain are, of course, my own.

Abbreviations

AAG	Assistant Adjutant General
AG	Adjutant General
AGO	Adjutant General's Office
BRFAL-LA	Bureau Refugees, Freedmen, and Abandoned Lands, Louisiana, Record Group 105, National Archives
CV	Ted Tunnell, ed., *Carpetbagger from Vermont: The Autobiography of Marshall Harvey Twitchell* (Baton Rouge, 1989).
DAB	*Dictionary of American Biography*
HRS	Historical Record Survey
JDR	Justice Department Records, National Archives
JSH	*Journal of Southern History*
LH	*Louisiana History*
LHQ	*Louisiana Historical Quarterly*
M	Microfilm
MHT	Marshall H. Twitchell
NA	National Archives
OR	U.S. War Department, *The War of the Rebellion: A Compilation of the Official Records of the Union and Confederate Armies*, 128 vols. (Washington, D.C., 1880–1901). (Unless otherwise indicated all references are to series 1.)
RG	Record Group
SDR	State Department Records, National Archives

USCT	United States Colored Troops
VCW	George G. Benedict, *Vermont in the Civil War*, 2 vols. (Burlington, 1886)
VHS	Vermont Historical Society

EDGE OF THE SWORD

INTRODUCTION

On a summer day in 1868, a Yankee planter in a black frock coat walked down a steamboat gangplank at Coushatta Landing on northwest Louisiana's upper Red River. His name was Marshall H. Twitchell, formerly Captain Twitchell of the Union Army and the Freedmen's Bureau. It was an election year, the beginning of Radical Reconstruction, and political passions were hot. A Republican candidate for parish judge, Twitchell was returning from political business in New Orleans. His home was twenty-five miles distant—in the village of Ringgold, in Bienville Parish. The Knights of the White Camellia monitored his arrival at Coushatta Landing. The White Camellia was close kin of the Ku Klux Klan, which terrorized neighboring states in those years. While Twitchell rented a mule, White Camellia spies rode ahead to set up a forest ambush. As the mule jogged north, Twitchell became distracted or perhaps fell asleep in the saddle. Just before entering the forest, a side road forked off to the west on a six-mile detour before rejoining the main road. With its rider preoccupied or asleep, the mule took the side road, bypassing the ambush. Twitchell, whose career resembled in some respects the proverbial cat with nine lives, had used up two or three fighting with the Vermont Brigade in Virginia; now, reaching Ringgold safely, he was unaware that he had just used up another.[1]

In the lexicon of the day, Twitchell was a "carpetbagger." According to the mythology of Reconstruction, the carpetbaggers were archetypi-

1. *CV*, 120.

cal villains, lowbred northern adventurers who descended like vultures on the conquered South. Since about 1960, historians such as John Hope Franklin, Otto H. Olsen, Lawrence N. Powell, Richard N. Current, Eric Foner, and others—myself included—have been refuting this hoary stereotype. Legend notwithstanding, modern scholarship suggests that Twitchell was more or less typical of the breed. A young ex-Federal soldier, he chose to remain in the South after Appomattox. He was comparatively well educated, had a little capital to invest, and when he first settled in north Louisiana, had no thought of going into politics. In 1868 his white neighbors began denouncing him as a carpetbagger before he had done much of anything, good or bad.[2]

Not surprisingly, much of America has managed to overlook the revisionist historiographical watershed of the 1960s. Modern writing about Reconstruction has come almost exclusively from academic historians who teach in universities. By comparison, the legend of the "Tragic Era," which historians call the Dunning tradition, was a grass-roots history that permeated every level of American society and that remains embedded in the national psyche—witness the "carpetbagger" accusations leveled against modern politicians.[3] Generations of white southerners grew to adulthood believing that Yankee vindictiveness and the evils of Negro-carpetbag rule were unimpeachable historical facts, as authentic as the New Testament. Southern writers such as Thomas Nelson Page, Thomas Dixon, and Margaret Mitchell exploited these themes in best-selling novels. This literary tradition in turn produced two landmarks of the American cinema, *The Birth of a Nation* (1915, based on Dixon's *The Clansman*) and *Gone with the Wind* (1939, based

2. The accepted definition of a carpetbagger is a white northerner who moved to the South during or after the Civil War and became a Republican. John Hope Franklin, *Reconstruction: After the Civil War* (Chicago, 1961), 93–98; Otto H. Olsen, *Carpetbagger's Crusade: The Life of Albion Vinegar Tourgée* (Baltimore, Md., 1965); Kenneth Stampp, *The Era of Reconstruction, 1865–1877* (New York, 1965), 158–59; Richard N. Current, *Those Terrible Carpetbaggers* (New York, 1988); Eric Foner, *Reconstruction: America's Unfinished Revolution, 1863–1867* (New York, 1988), 294–97; Ted Tunnell, *Crucible of Reconstruction: War, Radicalism, and Race in Louisiana, 1862–1877* (Baton Rouge, 1984); Ruth Currie-McDaniel, *Carpetbagger of Conscience: A Biography of John Emory Bryant* (Athens, Ga., 1987); Russell Duncan, *Freedom's Shore: Tunis Campbell and the Georgia Freedmen* (Athens, Ga., 1986). Tunis Campbell was a black carpetbagger.

3. The examples of Robert F. Kennedy and Hillary Clinton, both candidates for the U.S. Senate in New York, come to mind.

on Mitchell's novel of the same name). So influential was the latter film that for decades after its screening, any motion picture that portrayed the postwar South—such as *Red River* (John Wayne), *Three Violent People* (Charlton Heston), or *The Undefeated* (John Wayne and Rock Hudson)—was certain to employ its carpetbagger stereotypes. Except for *Birth of a Nation*, these films remain staples of contemporary television movie channels. A vignette from my graduate-student days at the University of California shows the impact of such fare. About 1975 I attended a revival of *Gone with the Wind* in downtown Berkeley. The film's images of gaudily clothed carpetbaggers thronging the streets of Atlanta immediately after the war make an indelible impression. (Never mind that it could not have happened this way.) Sitting behind me in the theater that night was a married couple with their two children, by all appearances a typical American family. When the overdressed Yankees appeared on screen, the little boy asked his mother what a carpetbagger was. Without a moment's hesitation, she said a carpetbagger was "a political adventurer from the North." I have often reflected that had the child asked his mother about a populist or a progressive—or even a Puritan—at the very least she would have paused before answering.

Surely, our popular culture is full of myths, stereotypes, and misinformation. What is the harm? Does this quibbling over carpetbaggers make any real difference—except to a few professors? My answer is, yes, it does matter. What millions of people believe about the past influences their understanding of the present, hence their conduct. For three-quarters of a century, as Dan Carter writes in his book on the Scottsboro case, the "dark days" of Negro-carpetbag rule were "the alpha and omega of Southerners' attempts to justify their treatment of the Negro"—of lynching, segregation, and economic serfdom. The carpetbagger images in *Gone with the Wind* go hand in hand with the film's offensive, racist images of blacks. Most of the blacks depicted on screen are stereotypical "darkies," slow-witted, passive, and loyal to their white masters. (Malcolm X wanted to "crawl under the rug" when he first saw the film as a teenager.) Uppity blacks, those who aspire to a loftier station in life than house servant or field hand, are the ones depicted in the company of greedy carpetbaggers.[4]

4. Dan T. Carter, *Scottsboro: A Tragedy of the American South*, rev. ed. (Baton Rouge, 1979), 109.

Although caricatured, *Gone with the Wind*'s linkage of black aspirations and carpetbaggers is rooted in fact. The carpetbagger stereotype did not evolve over decades in stories told by bards, to be transformed into literary epic by Thomas Dixon and Margaret Mitchell. Instead, the carpetbagger stereotype sprang to life full blown with the advent of Radical Reconstruction. Which is to say: at the exact moment black men began to vote and hold office, at the exact moment southern state constitutions began to guarantee African Americans some of the same rights that whites enjoyed, southern politicians and editors created the carpetbagger image as a counter-Reconstruction symbol. The carpetbagger image is more a creation of propaganda, or disinformation, than of legend.

Modern historiography notwithstanding, it is hard to write about a carpetbagger without periodically sensing the ghosts of Claude Bowers and other historians of the Dunning School peering over one's shoulder, shaking their heads in disapproval. The writer is tempted to dwell on the discrepancies between the facts, as revealed in the documents, and the mountain range of untruths that have built up around the subject. The dilemma easily lures the writer into what some scholars have called the "Rehabilitation School." The problem with rehabilitation is that it is a defensive mode of writing. In refuting the notion that Twitchell, or some other figure, was a minion of the Prince of Darkness, the author risks defining his subject in terms of what he was not, rather than what he was.[5]

I did not conceive this book as an exercise in carpetbagger rehabilitation, although I certainly will be pleased if that is one of the results. What has kept me interested in Twitchell over many years is the conviction that his is one of the great stories of Reconstruction, a story never fully told and indeed largely unknown outside the purview of specialists. Twitchell belongs to what historian Carl Degler has called the "Other South," the South of dissenters—among whom were critics of slavery; Unionists in the Civil War; carpetbaggers, scalawags, and black politicos in Reconstruction; and still later, readjusters and populists. These "other" southerners were, for the most part, neither saints nor heroes.

5. Howard N. Rabinowitz, ed., *Southern Black Leaders of the Reconstruction Era* (Urbana, Ill., 1982), xiv–xvii; Thomas C. Holt, "Georgia Carpetbaggers: Politicians without Politics," *Georgia Historical Quarterly* 72 (1988): 72–86.

Some of them, like Twitchell, became mavericks more or less serendipitously. Nonetheless, they explored new trails over rugged historical terrain. The history of the South would be less marred by tragedy if those trails had been followed. No monuments commemorate this "Other South" on Monument Avenue in Richmond, on Georgia's Stone Mountain, on courthouse squares in small southern towns, or in Lee's Circle in New Orleans. The people and institutions that erect monuments generally like to pretend that this alternative South never existed.[6]

In the 1870s, the names of Twitchell and his family members became familiar to newspaper readers from California to New England. Within a few years of his retirement from politics, however, Twitchell's fame (or notoriety) faded, and he was largely forgotten. Standard histories of Reconstruction written in the first half of the twentieth century do not mention him. He is not even discussed in Ella Lonn's *Reconstruction in Louisiana after 1868*. Then, in the early 1960s, Jimmy Shoalmire, a student at Louisiana Polytechnic Institute in Ruston, listened to his mother-in-law's stories about Twitchell and Coushatta. In April 1965, Shoalmire, by then a graduate student, discovered that Twitchell's grandson, Dr. Marshall Coleman Twitchell, a middle-aged ophthalmologist who taught at the University of Vermont, was living in Burlington. Out of the blue, he phoned Dr. Twitchell, inquiring whether his grandfather had left any papers. Dr. Twitchell was at first reluctant to talk to the stranger, but his wife persuaded him to cooperate. There were letters, newspaper clippings, and most important, a 245-page typescript autobiography.

Shoalmire wrote a Ph.D. dissertation, "Carpetbagger Extraordinary: Marshall Harvey Twitchell, 1840–1905." Dr. Twitchell graciously gave his grandfather's papers and a photocopy of the autobiography to the Prescott Memorial Library at Louisiana Polytechnic (now Louisiana Tech University). Although Jimmy Shoalmire never revised his dissertation for publication, his rediscovery of Twitchell has made the Vermont Yankee among the best-known carpetbaggers of the era. He appears in the works of Joe Gray Taylor, George Rable, Lawrence N. Powell, Eric Foner, Joseph G. Dawson, and in my own *Crucible of Recon-*

6. Carl N. Degler, *The Other South: Southern Dissenters in the Nineteenth Century* (New York, 1974).

struction: War, Radicalism, and Race in Louisiana, 1862–1877. In 1989 I edited Twitchell's autobiography as *Carpetbagger from Vermont: The Autobiography of Marshall Harvey Twitchell*. Excerpts from the latter work have recently been reprinted in *Voices from the Reconstruction Years, 1865–1877* (edited by Glenn M. Linden).[7]

Although Twitchell's autobiography is one of the most valuable documents of its kind, both as history and literature, it suffers from serious flaws. Twitchell was not a polished writer and never revised the work to get it into anything like publishable form. In places, his organization is dreadful, almost as if his typist had scattered the pages on the floor and then stuffed them back into a binder in the wrong order. Even with new chapter organization and notes, unless one already knows a lot about the subject, it is tough going. As history, it lacks context. People appear and disappear in his pages without analysis. On the other hand, he got most of his facts straight. As the papers in the Prescott Library at Louisiana Tech attest, he had kept a documentary record of his Louisiana career. Rather than relying on memory, it was a standard practice for him to more or less copy documents in his possession directly into the autobiography. Without the factual skeleton of the autobiography, this book could not have been written.

A word or two about the Civil War chapters: Writing and teaching in Richmond, Virginia, the war is never far from my mind. Each morning, en route to my office at Virginia Commonwealth University, I drive past the imposing equestrian statues of "Stonewall" Jackson, "Jeb" Stuart, and Robert E. Lee on Monument Avenue. Virginians, if they think of it at all, give scant regard to Vermont's role in the great conflict. (One still hears references to the War of Yankee Aggression.) When I first began work on this book some years ago, I requested G. G. Benedict's *History of Vermont in the Civil War* through interlibrary loan. I vividly remember the VCU librarian, staring wide-eyed at the two fat volumes, saying she had no idea Vermont was so involved in the war. Most people, North and South, are probably equally surprised to learn of Vermont's role in the conflict. In fact, Vermont's soldiers suffered the heaviest proportional losses in the Union army.

Marshall Twitchell was very proud of his Civil War service. To the

---

7. Jimmy Shoalmire died tragically young of a heart attack.

end of his days he believed that he and his fellow veteran volunteers had saved the Union and made history. Contemporary Civil War historians such as James M. McPherson and Reid Mitchell generally agree with him. Twitchell's Reconstruction career, moreover, grew naturally out of his Civil War service. He went from the Fourth Vermont Regiment—part of the elite Vermont Brigade—into the United States Colored Troops (USCT), into the Freedmen's Bureau, and then into planting and politics. Before he was a brave, tough man in Red River Parish, he was a brave, tough man in the Fourth Vermont. Thus, the first part of this book is about the experience of a sergeant in the ranks.

Disease accounted for two out of three deaths among Civil War soldiers, and disease accounted for most of the deaths in Twitchell's regiment (even though it saw heavy combat). Such facts, of course, are well known to Civil War scholars. The human side of Civil War medicine, however, too often receives short shrift from military historians, who are inclined to devote a few paragraphs to soldiers' health before rushing on to the battles, where their real interest lies. For the men in the ranks, it was otherwise. Prior to 1864, even battle-hardened veterans like Twitchell engaged in combat only a few days a year. They struggled against their microbiological enemies every day of the year. The military papers of the Fourth Vermont record the terrible toll the struggle took. It cast its shadow across every man in the regiment, even those like Twitchell who proved remarkably resistant.

In private correspondence, Marshall Twitchell, Adele Coleman, and most of the other people quoted in this book were less than punctilious about spelling and punctuation. They tended to write *dont* for *don't* and *cant* for *can't*. They misspelled words, *solger* instead of *soldier*, *penitant* instead of *penitent*. They put commas where there should be periods and vice versa. Sometimes they ignored punctuation altogether. To mark each error would needlessly clutter the text with *sic*s. Thus I have used *sic* sparingly.

I believe my fellow scholars will find much that is fresh and exciting in this biography. I have tried to write, however, with a broader audience in mind than those specialists who teach and write about the Civil War and Reconstruction. The notion of carpetbaggers as unprincipled scoundrels, one and all, is as dated as the "darkie" images in *Gone with the Wind*. It is time that our entire culture, not solely academic historians, looks at men like Twitchell and knows them by their deeds.

ONE

VERMONT

IN the southeastern corner of Vermont, the West River tumbles down from the Green Mountains and cuts through the rugged hill country of Windham County. About ten miles above its juncture with the Connecticut River at Brattleboro, the West River winds through the village of Townshend. With its old houses, covered bridges, and spacious commons, Townshend is a lovely place. Birch, beech, and maple trees blanket the surrounding hills, and every October the red and gold leaves splash a brilliant canvas over the landscape. Like the other townships in the region, Townshend's story dates back to a troubled time before the American Revolution when Vermont was a disputed frontier between the colonies of New York and New Hampshire.

In those days, the royal governor of New Hampshire was an unscrupulous opportunist named Benning Wentworth. In 1749 Wentworth began deeding New Englanders large tracts of land west of the Connecticut River, land claimed by New York. The governor's dubious largess stirred up a land quarrel with New York that festered for decades and shaped the early history of the region. For many years Vermont was known simply as the New Hampshire Grants, or the Grants. Townshend, one of the original Wentworth grants, was named after the governor's friend in England, Charles Townshend, author of the Revolutionary-era Townshend Acts.[1]

In the early 1770s, Ethan Allen, Vermont's greatest hero, emerged as the champion of the New Hampshire land claimants. As described by historians, Allen "was a swaggering and blustery giant," with an ego to match his physique. "Here was a man," legend claimed, "who had strangled a bear with his giant hands . . . who could run a deer to death without getting his wind up, and fell an ox with a single blow of his massive fist." Paradoxically, this oversized "Davy Crockett in a tricorne" was a forest philosopher who wrote more books than Thomas Jefferson, including the first American treatise on Deism. To Herman Melville, the Connecticut-born Allen seemed not a New Englander at all: "He was frank, bluff, companionable as a Pagan, convivial, a Roman, hearty as a harvest. His spirit was essentially Western."[2]

Allen led the Green Mountain Boys, a frontier militia, in a long fight to evict New York settlers from the New Hampshire Grants. Operating out of Catamount Tavern in Bennington, the Green Mountain Boys specialized in crude but effective mob violence. They terrorized New York officials, drove Yorker settlers off their claims, and intimidated wavering New Englanders. New York's royal governor dubbed them the "Bennington mob" and put a price on their heads.[3]

Allen's career peaked in the early days of the American Revolution. In the chill of a May morning in 1775, the Green Mountain Boys surprised the British garrison at Fort Ticonderoga on Lake Champlain. When a dazed English officer burst from his quarters, challenging Allen's authority for the attack, the hero reportedly shouted, "In the name of the Great Jehovah and the Continental Congress." Others remembered him saying more prosaically, "Come out of there, you damned old Rat," and still others, "Come out of there you sons of British whores, or I'll smoke you out." Whatever the words, he took the fort,

1. Michael A. Bellesiles, *Revolutionary Outlaws: Ethan Allen and the Struggle for Independence on the Early American Frontier* (Charlottesville, Va., 1993), 27–32; Charles T. Morrissey, *Vermont: A Bicentennial History* (New York, 1981), 78–81; Abby M. Hemenway, ed., *Vermont Historical Gazetteer* 5: 532–33.

2. Morrissey, *Vermont*, 73; Bellesiles, *Revolutionary Outlaws*, 4; Charles A. Jellison, *Ethan Allen: Frontier Rebel* (Syracuse, N.Y., 1969), 42; Herman Melville, *His Fifty Years of Exile (Israel Potter)* (1855; reprint, New York, 1957), 212.

3. Jellison, *Ethan Allen*, 39–60; Morrissey, *Vermont*, 80–85.

and it was the first statement that went into the history books. Generations of Vermont youth, one native recalled, grew up believing that Ethan Allen and the Green Mountain Boys, pulling together as equals with General Washington and the Continental Army, had defeated the British and won American independence. In truth, only a few months after Ticonderoga, the British captured Allen at Montreal, clapped him in irons, and shipped him off to England. Thereafter, his contribution to the Revolution was his *Narrative of Colonel Ethan Allen's Captivity*, an immensely popular book portraying the British as merciless fiends.[4]

In 1791, after a brief history as an independent republic, Vermont joined the Union, the first state admitted after the original thirteen. Its population soared, jumping from 85,000 at statehood to nearly 218,000 in 1810. The lure was not the richness of the soil nor a salubrious climate. Except for the fertile Champlain Valley, rugged hills and mountains covered virtually the entire state. The topsoil was thin and rocky, the growing season short and unpredictable. "A Vermont year," the saying goes, "is nine months winter and three months of damn poor sleddin'." In a bad year, the state seemed almost to slip back into the Pleistocene ice. No one, for instance, ever forgot 1816: "eighteen hundred and froze to death," the natives called it. There was snow and frost in July and August, livestock died, crops perished, and many farmers survived on wild berries and weeds. All this notwithstanding, in the early days of the Republic, when farming was well nigh the universal American occupation, the land most available to the multiplying sons and daughters of New England was in the Vermont hills. So stoically they came on, and among them, albeit arriving later than most, was a young farmer from an old New England family named Twitchell.[5]

In the early 1630s a Puritan yeoman named Benjamin Twitchell and his older brother Joseph emigrated from Buckinghamshire in England to the Massachusetts Bay Colony. Joseph died without male heirs, but Benjamin had two sons, and by the 1790s some three hundred Twitchells were living in New England, among them a certain Daniel Twitch-

4. Jellison, *Ethan Allen*, 116–19, 157–63; Bellesiles, *Revolutionary Outlaws*, 118, 149–51, 163; Stewart H. Holbrook, *The Yankee Exodus: An Account of Migration from New England* (New York, 1950), 2.

5. Morrissey, *Vermont*, 106–7; Ray Bearse, ed., *Vermont: A Guide to the Green Mountain State*, 2d ed. (New York, 1966), 28–29; Harold A. Meeks, *Time and Change in Vermont: A Human Geography* (Chester, Conn., 1986), 15.

ell and his wife Eunice, who lived in Winchester in the southwestern corner of New Hampshire.[6] In 1806 their fifth and last child, Harvey Daniel, was born. About 1824 Harvey Daniel's older brother Jonas crossed the Connecticut River and settled in West Townshend. A few years later Harvey Daniel joined his brother. In 1839 he married Elizabeth Scott and settled down to the life of a hill country farmer outside Townshend, just down the road from his brother. Eleven months later, on 29 February 1840, the couple's first child was born, a son they named Marshall Harvey.[7]

When the baby was a year old, the family moved to Franklin County near the Canadian border in the mountains of northwestern Vermont. For the next seven years they lived in a log cabin near the village of Montgomery. Harvey Daniel may have continued farming, but more likely he worked in one of the small plants manufacturing wooden butter tubs, sap buckets, or cheeseboxes. A second son was born in 1843, but he lived only a year. A daughter named Helen Elizabeth came in 1845, followed a year later by another daughter, Isabelle Hannah. In 1848 Homer Jonas was born. It was Marshall who suggested the new baby's first name, and his reason for choosing "Homer" opens a window into his boyhood world.[8]

Mountainous Franklin County offered poor farming but splendid fishing. The Twitchells lived near Trout River. A frequent visitor to Trout River was a certain up-and-coming young lawyer-politician named Homer Royce. The angler enjoyed little Marshall's company,

6. Just before the American Civil War, the Reverend Abner Morse, a member of the New England Historical and Genealogical Society, claimed the family was of noble lineage. The Twitchells, originally Tuchels, Morse wrote, had been Spanish vassals of William the Conqueror. Numerous members of the family, including the subject of this book, naively embraced these findings. In the 1920s, a less credulous member of the line exploded the myth. Ralph Emerson Twitchell—Santa Fe mayor, president of the New Mexico Bar Association, authority on New Mexico history—labeled the Reverend Morse's work "random speculation." Although such "theoretical, even imaginary, ancestries" had become popular in America, he advised the Twitchell family to avoid them. "A sturdy yeoman pedigree," he said, was both more American and "far more in keeping with our ancestral ideals and the character of our Puritan ancestors." *Genealogy of the Twitchell Family* (New York, 1929), ix–xii.

7. Ibid., xlvi–xlvii, 1–2, 145–46, 250–51.

8. Ibid., 251–52; *CV*, 19; Lewis Cass Aldrich, *History of Franklin and Grand Isle Counties* (Syracuse, N.Y., 1891), 557–59.

freely giving him lines and hooks and probably allowing him to tag along. We can imagine the eight-year-old boy worshipfully trailing his hero along the bank, brimming with delight at each small gift. Thus, the new baby was called Homer. (Years later Royce became chief justice of the Vermont Supreme Court).⁹

About 1849 Harvey Daniel became involved in a venture—Marshall remembered it only as a "manufacturing enterprise"—and moved the family across the Canadian border to Bedford, Quebec. Within two years, however, the family had returned to Townshend, where Harvey Daniel purchased a 150-acre farm just west of the village. Here in 1854 Harvey Daniel and Elizabeth's last child was born, a daughter named Kate Francis. And here in a spacious farmhouse that still stands at the base of the north bluff overlooking the West River, their eldest son would grow to manhood.¹⁰

The Twitchell farm bordered on subsistence agriculture. Owning horses, pigs, cows, and chickens, the family produced its own milk, butter, cheese, eggs, and most of its meat. Elizabeth and her children sold or bartered the surplus butter and cheese. With teams of oxen, Harvey Daniel worked the rocky bottomland below the house, raising wheat, corn, oats, and potatoes. In a good year, there would be surplus corn and potatoes for market. The cash crop was maple syrup, Townshend's chief export, the sap harvested from the surrounding forests. The Twitchell farm produced about three hundred pounds a year. Although many of their neighbors raised sheep, Harvey Daniel owned only one, which probably yielded enough wool to keep the family in winter socks and sweaters.¹¹

Beyond these meager facts, little is known of Marshall's boyhood. In all probability, though, his life differed only in detail from that of most other farm boys who grew up in the region. This we know: hill-country farmers worked hard and so did their sons. "Being the older son of a poor and hardworking farmer, struggling to pay off the debt incurred in buying his high-priced farm, and to support his increasing family, I was early made acquainted with labor," recalled Horace Greeley, who

9. *CV*, 19–20.
10. Ibid.; Federal manuscript census, agriculture, 1860.
11. Federal manuscript census, agriculture, 1860.

grew up in the neighboring New Hampshire hills. Frequently up at daybreak, young Greeley tended the animals, rode the ploughhorse ahead of the oxen, dug up wireworms and grubs, chopped wood, shoveled snow, burned charcoal, carted rocks, and a hundred other tasks. The rocks were especially irksome: "Picking stones is a never ending labor on one of those rocky New England farms. Pick as closely as you may, the next ploughing turns up a fresh eruption of boulders and pebbles, from the size of a hickory-nut to that of a tea-kettle; and, as this work is mainly to be done in March or April, when the earth is saturated with ice-cold water, if not also whitened with falling snow, youngsters soon learn to regard it with detestation."[12]

Although the Twitchell farm was small, Marshall's family still ranked nearer the top than the bottom of Townshend's economic hierarchy. After all, Harvey Daniel was a landowner, not a tenant or farm laborer. Including livestock, farm implements, and buildings, he owned $2,375 in real and personal property, well above the median property ownership in the region. He was, moreover, the brother of Jonas Twitchell, who with $11,200 in property was one of the town's wealthiest citizens. Uncle Jonas served in every office of town government and even went to the legislature; he eventually became president of the Windham County Savings Bank.[13]

The Twitchells were members of the First Congregational Church in Townshend. Founded about 1790, it was the oldest church in the village. Painted white with green trim and displaying a steep roof with an elegant steeple, it followed the typical New England two-story design. The church stood on the village commons, flanked by comfortable whitewashed houses, across from the town hall and the seminary. The Reverend John Wood, Marshall recalled, "was one of the old school." Possibly, "he could smile but I never saw him. He was accustomed to read three long, dry sermons to us every Sunday, no variation in his voice, no gestures, nothing to disturb you if you chose to sleep." Twitchell remembered Wood's parishioners as being strongly antislavery. This was doubtless true, even though few, if any, of them had ever

12. Horace Greeley, *Recollections of a Busy Life* (1868; reprint, Miami, 1969), 38–39.
13. Federal manuscript census, population, 1860; Hemenway, *Vermont Historical Gazetteer*, 5: 547.

seen a slave. Most of them, in fact, had probably never seen a black person. The 1860 census counted only thirty-three free blacks in Windham County. Ten years earlier the census had counted none.[14]

Across from the Congregational Church, on the southeast side of the Townshend commons, stood a two-story brick school with a wooden tower. Founded by Baptists, Leland Seminary was one of the oldest secondary schools in the state and the most important in Windham County until after the Civil War. Marshall's parents held education in high esteem, and Leland was the one of the main reasons they had moved back to Townshend. (Uncle Jonas was a founder and lifelong trustee of the school.) The academy organized its curriculum into two basic branches: the English Department and the Classical Department. All students enrolled in the English Department, which offered instruction in literature, rhetoric, and composition; history and geography; math, science, and modern languages; drawing, painting, and music. The school's most talented youth, about 25 percent, also entered the demanding classical program. In 1853, at age thirteen, Marshall entered Leland's classical program. He studied Greek and Latin grammar and read the works of Homer, Caesar, Cicero, and Virgil, as well as the Greek New Testament. Within the English Department, the curriculum distinguished between "Common English" and "Higher English." As a more advanced, or Higher English, scholar, Marshall would have studied such texts (or subjects) as "Johnston's Chemistry," "Dana's Mineralogy," "Adam and Gray's Geology," and "Cutter's Anatomy." Marshall also engaged in public forensic debate every other week in the school's lyceum. At the end of the winter and spring terms, a panel of teachers conducted oral examinations open both to trustees and the general public. Although religious studies played a lesser role in the curriculum than in colonial New England, Marshall and his classmates still attended devotional services each morning and were expected to attend church with their parents on Sunday.[15]

A majority of Marshall's classmates were women. For most of these,

14. *CV*, 21; *Seventh Census, Population, 1850; Eighth Census, Population, 1860.*

15. *CV*, 19–20; Howard Walden Cutler, *History of Leland and Gray Seminary* (Bellows Falls, Vt., 1927), 14–24. Founded in 1834, the school was named variously Townshend Academy, Leland Classical and English School, and Leland and Gray Seminary. From early 1848 on, the trustees called it simply Leland Seminary. *Catalogue of the Officers and Students of Leland Seminary* (Bellows Falls, Vt., 1859).

Leland was a finishing school, where they learned correct English and penmanship, practical math, a smattering of history and literature, painting and music, and perhaps some French or German. A minority of the women, however, traveled a different road. Roughly a third of the students in the Classical Department were women. One of these was a minister's niece named Henrietta Nancy Day. Her uncle, the Reverend C. L. Cushman, with whom she lived, replaced the Reverend Wood as the Congregational minister in late 1859. Marshall liked the new minister and admired his niece even more. He and Henrietta fell deeply in love. Beyond that, little is known, except that one day she would become an important figure in his life.[16]

Leland followed the cycle of the seasons and reflected the labor needs of an agricultural community. In the fall, the peak period, more than a hundred students enrolled. Attendance dropped to about thirty in the winter, picked up again in the spring, and declined to about a dozen in the summer.[17] Marshall attended two terms a year until his sixteenth birthday. Thereafter until he was twenty, he enrolled only in the fall. In the winter he taught school in neighboring villages for twelve dollars a month. The remaining six months of the year he worked on his father's farm.[18]

Teaching school in the hill country tested a young man's character. Marshall was only seventeen the winter he taught at Wardsboro, a mountain hamlet west of Townshend. Barely average in height and build, he quickly encountered discipline problems. Some of the boys were both older and bigger than he was and had a well-earned reputation for running off teachers. He considered quitting, but his pride was at stake and he rejected the idea. After considerable thought, he employed a strategy of divide and conquer. He won over some of the tougher boys, then used them to keep the others in line. His success was evidence of his own growth and maturity.[19]

Two years later he applied for a teaching post in the mountain village of Winhall. To understand his Winhall experience, we need to examine the little that is known of his reading habits. "In my father's

16. *Catalogue . . . Leland Seminary*, 1859 and 1860.

17. *Ibid.*, 1860.

18. *CV*, 20. Marshall's name first appears in the 1853 Leland catalogue; thereafter, he is listed as a student in every extant catalogue (three are missing) through 1860.

19. *CV*, 20.

house," he recalled, "there were very few novels with which I could waste my time, weaken my memory, and destroy my taste for other books." He probably read Mason Locke Weems's *Life of Washington* and other accounts of the Founding Fathers. He doubtless read Daniel Pierce Thompson's *The Green Mountain Boys*. Although fiction, Vermont youth of that era would have been apt to see Thompson's saga of freedom-loving woodsmen as true-life adventure. What is certain, though, is that Marshall was fascinated by Napoleon and had memorized the main events of Bonaparte's life.[20]

Marshall had to undergo an oral examination by the district school superintendent, a Mr. Gorden, before being hired by the Winhall school board. On a crisp winter Saturday, Marshall rode to Winhall. To his surprise, townspeople packed the schoolhouse to witness his exam. The reason soon became apparent. Superintendent Gorden wanted the teaching slot for himself. The school board, however, had made a commitment to Marshall, which could not honorably be broken—*unless* he failed the exam. The exam began with questions about American history, and the answers were more than satisfactory. The superintendent then moved on to European history. A member of the school board objected that this was not a required area. After some discussion, the questions were allowed. Unfortunately for his cause, Mr. Gorden made the mistake of quizzing his young rival about Napoleon. Within minutes, spectators were applauding the underdog youth's composure and knowledgeable answers. The superintendent gracefully accepted defeat and passed the young man.[21]

In his last term at Leland, fall of 1860, Marshall became involved in a teacup tempest over school discipline. Midway through the term, some of his younger classmates began taking walks in violation of evening study hours, earning themselves a reprimand at chapel from superintendent George E. Lane. Although not initially a member of this "young and wild party," Marshall wrote a verse essay expressing sympathy for their cause. His intervention affected the end-of-term honorary elections. The dissidents voted as a bloc and elected Marshall valedictorian. The honor carried the responsibility of delivering a valedictory address to an audience of students and parents from all over Windham

20. Ibid., 22.
21. Ibid., 22–23.

County. Feeling unworthy and probably a bit guilty about his election, he approached Mr. Lane about resigning. The principal, who evidently bore his young critic no ill will, advised him to accept the honor and simply do his best. Marshall titled his address "Christianity: Its Effects upon Society." It was well received. In later years he would reflect on his election as a demonstration of the power of an organized political minority to defeat a disorganized majority. It was also the first sign of a talent for intrigue that he was to display so coolly during Reconstruction.[22]

In the Vermont of Marshall's youth, the common institutions of society—family, schools, churches, governance, a shared Puritan heritage—all conspired to produce an ethos that would always be associated with New England character. It was an attitude toward life that valued honesty, grit, diligence, temperance, education, and discipline of mind—all traits associated with the Puritan ethic. Above all, it was a value system that honored work, the harder the better, and material success. Work was a virtue unto itself, and its practitioners were rewarded in this life. *The Farmer's Guide, or Practical Hints for Every Day Life*, for example, stressed: "When morning comes, chores can be done while breakfast is in progress. After breakfast let all hands go to work, especially the head of the family. Instead of telling about your rheumatism and 'business to town,' go to work." In a similar vein, a Vermont storekeeper told his clerks to "put your whole mind, during business hours, upon business and business—only business alone. Tell no stories, listen to no stories. Talk about nothing but business in business hours." Marshall would often have received similar advice.[23]

Parents took great pains to instill these values in the young. A father in Windsor presented his young daughter with an account book. Without fail, he advised her, "put down *every* cent you receive—of *whom* and *when* and *every cent* you pay out . . . *be sure* to date every writing—*Never* sign a writing without *reading* and *understanding* it *perfectly*—*always count* and *reckon* your money *yourself*—*never* trust to other peoples count." He further admonished her: "*Never* delay the work of today for tomorrow—it may never come—and be at *all times conscious* that the *eye of God* is watching *every action, word,* and thought." Another schoolgirl penned

22. Ibid.
23. Morrissey, *Vermont*, 151–55.

an essay on the virtues of hard work and industry, concluding that there was a world of wisdom in the old saying: "Take care of the minutes and the hours will take care of themselves."[24]

New England enterprise was a precious national resource. Antebellum America was changing faster than people could comprehend. In 1800 the United States was a nation of five million inhabitants residing mainly on the eastern seaboard. Most Americans of that day lived in a preindustrial mode, surviving by subsistence agriculture and handicraft. By the time Marshall graduated from Leland, however, Americans numbered thirty-one million, their borders spanned the continent, and they were in the throes of a commercial and industrial revolution. The growth was fueled by a high birth rate, a surge of European immigration, advances in transportation and communication, huge acquisitions of territory, and above all, by the enterprising, modernizing spirit of Americans. New England Yankees blazed that modernizing trail.[25]

When the U.S. Patent Office first opened for business one morning in 1790, Samuel Hopkins of Vermont claimed patent number one, a new way of making potassium carbonate, or pearl ash. In ensuing decades, New England invention astonished the world: the cotton gin, interchangeable parts, the power loom, the cookstove, the straw hat, the electric motor, the Concord coach, vulcanized rubber, the submarine cable, the typewriter, the lead pencil, the sewing machine, barbed wire, artificial ice, the telegraph, the friction match, and many more. According to students of American invention, between 1790 and 1860, New Englanders developed 42 percent of the most important inventions in the United States. (In 1825, only 16 percent of Americans lived in New England.) In the world of business, the region's role was even greater; more than half of nineteenth-century America's most innovative business leaders were natives of New England. It was also New England education reformers such as Horace Mann—and a legion of Yankee schoolmasters—who pioneered the public schools that made Americans the most literate people on earth. As a geographic area, New England lost power and influence when the nation's center of gravity shifted west, but the sons and daughters of the Puritans were cultural coloniz-

24. Ibid.
25. James M. McPherson, *Ordeal by Fire: The Civil War and Reconstruction*, 2d ed. (New York, 1992), 1, 13–14.

ers of amazing versatility. As late as 1950, the states with the most natives per population in *Who's Who in America* were Vermont, New
Hampshire, Maine, and Massachusetts. Connecticut stood sixth on the
list and Rhode Island eighth.[26]

As this narrative will show, New England stamped Marshall Twitchell's character indelibly. We need not speculate as to whose influence
was greatest on him—whether his father or mother, or Uncle Jonas, or
an unknown teacher or town official—the Yankee ethos was inhaled
with the crisp morning air of the hills.

After graduating from Leland Seminary, Marshall turned his back
on the only two occupations he had ever known—farming and teaching.
For nearly a decade he had helped his father scrape a living out of a
patch of rocky bottomland. He may have seen the work as "mindless,
monotonous, drudgery," as did another son of the hills, or simply as a
bad bargain—or possibly both. In any event, he began reading law with
a local attorney. It was a good choice, and he would have made a good
lawyer, but his personal plans, like those of millions of others, were
about to be swallowed up by events beyond his control.[27]

The previous November, while he and his Leland classmates had
been absorbed in their schoolbooks, an ominous cloud had gathered
over the American Union. In a bizarre four-way election, a hitherto
little-known Republican lawyer named Abraham Lincoln won the presidency. Lincoln's chief rival was a fellow Illinoisan, Democrat Stephen
A. Douglas. Vermont was Republican country, and every county in the
state went for Lincoln. In politics, though, Marshall and his family were
out of step with their neighbors. The Twitchells were traditional Jack-
sonian Democrats, and Douglas was one of Marshall's personal heroes.
He was too young to vote, but his sentiments may be gauged by his associations; John Roberts, with whom he chose to read law, was a well-
known Democrat. His father and Uncle Jonas almost certainly voted for
the Little Giant.[28]

26. Holbrook, *Yankee Exodus*, 297 n, 313–19; Roger Burlingame, *March of the Iron
Men: A Social History of Union through Invention* (New York, 1938), 468–76; McPherson,
Ordeal by Fire, 13–15, 17–18.

27. *CV*, 198; Greeley, *Recollections of a Busy Life*, 60; MHT interview, *Chicago Inter-
Ocean*, 9 October 1880.

28. W. Dean Burnham, *Presidential Ballots, 1832–1892* (1955; reprint, New York,
1976), 222, 246, 816; MHT interview, *Chicago Inter-Ocean*, 9 October 1880.

A month after Lincoln's victory, South Carolina seceded, and six more Deep South states followed her lead after the New Year's celebrations. In February, while northern New England endured a cold snap that dropped the mercury to thirty below, southern leaders in Montgomery, Alabama, organized the Confederate States of America and elected Jefferson Davis provisional president. That spring, as the snow melted in the Vermont hills, the two new presidents, Lincoln and Davis, came to loggerheads over Fort Sumter in Charleston Harbor. In early April, the New England states observed a special day of fasting and prayer for a peaceful resolution of the crisis. But it was war and not peace that the American ship of state was crowding sail to reach, and in the early morning darkness of 12 April, it heaved into its port of destination. The Confederate shore batteries belched smoke and flame. Thirty-four hours later, the Yankees in the harbor surrendered. President Lincoln now called up 75,000 state militia to put down an insurrection in the southern states. The president's appeal to arms sparked a second round of secession. Of the eight slave states still in the Union, Virginia, North Carolina, Tennessee, and Arkansas now lurched into disunion.[29]

Through the long secession winter and spring, Fort Sumter had become a symbol of the imperiled Union. To the generation of 1861, North and South, the guns of Sumter were as unforgettable as the bombs of Pearl Harbor were to a later generation. It was one of those evil moments—frozen forever in memory—when men and women remembered to the end of their days exactly where they were and what they were doing when they heard the news. In Vermont's White River Valley, a young man named Wilbur Fisk and his pals loitered about the Tunbridge post office, waiting for news. Abruptly, the postmaster, an elderly gentleman, stood before them, ashen-faced, fighting back tears. He said, "The war has begun."[30]

29. David Adams Yount, "Erastus Fairbanks: Vermont's First Civil War Governor" (master's thesis, University of Vermont, 1968), 40–41; Henry Steele Commager, ed., *The Blue and the Gray: The Story of the Civil War as Told by Participants* (New York, 1950), 38.

30. Emil Rosenblatt, ed., *Anti-Rebel: The Civil War Letters of Wilbur Fisk* (Croton-on-Hudson, N.Y., 1983), iii.

TWO

THE VERMONT BRIGADE

I
N July 1861, from their base on the Potomac, 35,000 Union troops
marched south into Virginia. The northern press, led by Horace Greeley's *New York Tribune*, cried "Forward to Richmond" and forecast the
imminent demise of the Confederacy. The *Brattleboro Vermont Phoenix*
reveled in the martial mood. It depicted the Federal advance as an epochal march of triumph that the Confederates were powerless to resist.
The ensuing Union defeat at First Bull Run was one of the profoundest
shocks of the war. The *Phoenix*, like other northern journals, found itself conducting a bitter postmortem. The bad news traveled swiftly up
the West River to Townshend. Ironically, the defeat spurred enlistments, and in the next three months 100,000 new men joined the Federal ranks, among them Marshall Twitchell and many of his boyhood
friends.[1]

To Twitchell's generation of northern youth, preserving the Union
of the Founding Fathers was a matter of sacred honor and duty. In Vermont the heritage of 1776 also meant bearing the escutcheon of Ethan
Allen and the Green Mountain Boys, "with all its historic luster." Patri-

---

1. *Brattleboro Vermont Phoenix*, 25 July 1861.

otism, though, blended with other motives. Men craved adventure and longed for escape from the tedium of daily life. For a few, slavery alone was cause enough to fight. "Thank God for the opportunity of preaching Abolitionism to slaveholders, and to slaves," a young Vermont abolitionist confided to his diary. Pay made military duty less burdensome. The federal government paid soldiers thirteen dollars a month, and the state of Vermont added seven dollars a month. Peer pressure was part of the equation, too. A Vermont youth whose parents were too ill for him to leave home expressed his frustration to a friend who had enlisted: "Oh how I wish i could go I can't hardly controll myself I here the solgers druming round. If you get your eye on old Jef Davis make a cathole threw him. I am agoing to join a training Company that they are getting up here so that I can realize a little of the fun that solgers have." In Twitchell's case, enlistment resulted from a combination of these factors. He was a patriot, without a family to support, and here was a chance to travel and see the country at government expense. His reading about Napoleon, moreover, suggests a fascination with things military. And, despite the lesson of Bull Run, he still believed the war would be short and painless.[2]

His decision to enter the army allows our first real glimpse into the inner life of his family. His mother, Elizabeth, and his older sisters, Helen and Belle, tearfully begged him not to go. Twelve-year-old Homer probably wished that he was old enough to go to war, too. His father remained silent until the day in late August when he hitched up the team to drive his son to the enrollment office. As the wagon wound up the West River Road to Jamaica Village, Harvey Twitchell broke his silence and pleaded with his son to stay home. Marshall was adamant, but as he walked out of the recruiter's office, he was struck by the pain etched in his father's face and the tears in his eyes. It was a patriarchal age, and hill-country fathers ruled their families with a strong hand. A daguerreotype of Harvey Daniel from just before the war reveals an imposing figure with silver-haired temples, a full gray beard, and the look of an Old Testament patriarch. The look was common to the age, and

2. James M. McPherson, *For Cause and Comrades: Why Men Fought in the Civil War* (New York, 1997), 16–23; Reid Mitchell, *Civil War Soldiers* (New York, 1988), 11–18; Rufus Kinsley Diary, 25 August 1862, VHS; Bell Irvin Wiley, *The Life of Billy Yank: The Common Soldier of the Union* (Baton Rouge, 1978), 37–40; *CV*, 24.

so was the awe and respect such fathers inspired in their sons. Marshall had never seen his father show such emotion, and in that moment arose his first suspicion that war might not be the frolic he imagined.[3]

In mid-September, Twitchell rendezvoused with the Fourth Vermont Regiment at Camp Holbrook outside Brattleboro. His enlistment papers reveal that he had a light complexion, hazel eyes, sandy-colored hair, and stood five feet, seven inches tall, a shade below the average height of Vermont troops.[4]

The infantry regiment was the clay from which Civil War armies were molded. Ten companies composed a regiment. I Company, Marshall's unit, had 104 soldiers: a captain, two lieutenants, five sergeants, eight corporals, and eighty-eight privates. The regiment was recruited from all over the state, but the men of I Company came mainly from the farms and villages of western Windham County. At this stage of the war, the men in the ranks elected company officers. I Company chose Leonard A. Stearns, a produce merchant, as their captain and company commander. When he first met Stearns, Twitchell could hardly have imagined the trouble he would have with this officer.[5]

The 1,006 enlisted men and thirty-six officers of the Fourth Vermont were mostly farmers or, more accurately, farmers' sons. Two-thirds of the men in Twitchell's company were farmers, and in one company, eighty-nine of one hundred men were farmers. The men were young. Nearly three-fourths were under twenty-five years of age, and nine out of ten were under thirty. An unknown but probably significant number were sixteen- and seventeen-year-olds who had lied about their age, claiming to be eighteen. Even most of the officers were young. Conversely, nearly every company had three or four men over forty. In ethnic makeup, the Fourth was a solidly Yankee outfit. Most were natives of Vermont, and nearly all the other recruits were from Massachusetts, Connecticut, New Hampshire, and New York. In an age of mass immigration from Germany and Ireland, less than 3 percent of the men were German- or Irish-born.[6]

The regiment mirrored the class structure of rural New England,

---

3. *CV*, 24; Twitchell Family Scrapbook, in the possession of Peggy Twitchell, Burlington, Vt.

4. MHT Compiled Military Service Record, RG 94, NA.

5. Fourth Vermont Regimental Books, RG 94, NA; Wiley, *Billy Yank*, 24–25.

6. Fourth Vermont Regimental Books.

too. Apart from the preponderance of farmers, the men in the ranks were overwhelmingly laborers, mechanics, teamsters, shoemakers, clerks, drummers, papermakers, harnessmakers, butchers, house painters, and other members of the rural working class. By contrast, the regimental officers were mostly business and professional men, as were the company commanders. The first lieutenants included three lawyers and the son of Vermont's governor-elect. In all, the regiment's thirty-six officers included only three farmers. There is no mystery here. Prominent citizens were more active recruiters than ordinary folk, and Americans have traditionally deferred to business and professional success in choosing leaders.[7]

The colonel was a twenty-three-year-old West Pointer named Edwin H. Stoughton. One of the first things that Twitchell committed to memory was Colonel Stoughton's Special Orders No. 1. These rules established a daily routine that governed camp life from before sunrise until well after dark. After breakfast was police call, then guard mounting, surgeon's call, company drill, orderly call, dinner (lunch), and so on through the day. Part of a recruit's education was mastering the jargon of such orders. Reveille was a brassy wake-up call, followed immediately by early morning roll check. Police call, or fatigue duty, was a time for cleaning up the camp. Retreat, in late afternoon, was regimental assembly, roll call, and inspection. Tattoo was company roll call, after which soldiers went to their quarters for the night. Taps was lights out. New soldiers learned to recognize the distinctive bugle or drum "calls" that announced each period of the day.[8]

After only a few days in camp, Stoughton doubled the amount of time devoted to drill. In the weeks and months to come, other changes would follow. What did not change, however, was the basic idea of Special Orders No. 1: that the daily life of soldiers was carefully regulated from morning to night. This principle would govern Twitchell's life for the next four years.[9]

Twitchell's first meal at Camp Holbrook consisted of a tin cup of coffee, a bit of bread, and a slice of meat. While some men complained, most, like Twitchell, were hungry and wolfed down the spartan break-

7. Ibid.

8. Ezra J. Warner, *Generals in Blue: Lives of the Union Commanders* (Baton Rouge, 1964), 482–83; Fourth Vermont Regimental Books.

9. Fourth Vermont Regimental Books.

fast. Sleeping on straw in conical Sibley tents, twenty men to a tent, one blanket per man, was also unsettling. Some of the soldiers groused that while one blanket might do for a pig, a man needed two blankets, one for the ground and one to cover up with.[10]

The Fourth was the first Green Mountain regiment issued regulation army uniforms—black hats, navy blue tunics, and light blue pants. Twitchell's unit was also fortunate to receive English Enfield rifles instead of the smoothbore muskets issued to earlier Vermont troops. The difference between the two weapons signaled a revolution in military technology. The smoothbore musket had been the basic weapon of foot soldiers for three centuries. It was not accurate beyond eighty yards, and at two hundred yards, soldiers might as well hurl imprecations. In the 1840s a French army captain invented the minie ball, an oblong bullet fired from a rifled gun barrel. The result was a heavy caliber rifle that approximated the range and accuracy, although not the rate of fire, of a twentieth-century weapon. In its Springfield and Enfield versions, it dominated Civil War battlefields.[11]

In the twilight of a September Saturday, Brattleboro turned out to see the regiment off. After several sweeps through the town, the men boarded the train. Like Twitchell, most of them knew little except Vermont. As the cars rumbled south down the Connecticut Valley in the night, their thoughts turned to family and home and speculation about the unknown war ahead. At New Haven, Connecticut, they transferred to a seagoing steamer that took them to Jersey City and another train. The people of Jersey City and Newark lined the tracks, cheering as the train jolted past. That night, Philadelphia welcomed them with a fine supper, enjoyed all the more because they had eaten little but dry bread since Brattleboro. Twenty-four hours later, the train pulled into Washington, D.C. On 24 September, after a night's stopover at Soldier's Rest, a reception center near the depot, the regiment pitched its tents on Capitol Hill.[12]

The men of the Fourth looked out on the famous city and saw an overgrown, overcrowded town. Despite the proximity of nearly 100,000 Union troops, their tents ringing the city and filling the open spaces

10. *CV*, 25–26.

11. *VCW*, 1: 158–59; McPherson, *Ordeal by Fire*, 196–98.

12. Timothy Kieley Diary, 21, 22, 23, 24, 25 September 1861; *VCW*, 1: 159–60.

within, Washington retained a distinctly rustic ambience, with cows and horses grazing within sight of the Capitol. It was malarial in summer and a muddy bog after winter rains. From Capitol Hill the view was splendid. The huge Capitol building towering before the Vermonters was unfinished; the marble wings lacked steps, and a scaffold and crane topped the structure where the dome would go. Looking west down the mall, they saw, a mile away, the Smithsonian Castle, and farther on, the partly completed obelisk of the Washington Monument. Apart from these, the only public structures in view were the Patent Office, the Post Office, and a cluster of small buildings around the executive mansion. The city's public edifices were so far apart that a disquieting emptiness seemed to fill the spaces between them. The idea of Washington as "a city of magnificent distances" was a subject of ridicule by European visitors. Losing oneself in the streets of Washington, Anthony Trollope wrote, was like getting lost in "the deserts of the holy land." The raw, unfinished city, to contemporaries and later historians, symbolized the unfinished state of the nation.[13]

The rude city could still inspire awe in Vermont farm boys. To a young soldier named Timothy Kieley, the capital, bearing the name of the American Cincinnatus, was a fountainhead of "sacred associations." "Me thinks," he wrote, that as General Washington "walks the Golden streets of Paradise, his proud spirits weeps as He sees the Happy Country which he fought for Now, standing in deadly array against each other and deluging the Continent with Blood and Misery. This Broad field, which once happy and prosperous, is now one vast camp of men."[14]

To Twitchell and his comrades, the encampment on Capitol Hill brought new and unwelcome experiences of army life. After pitching their canvas, they asked for straw for their bedding, only to be informed that the only available straw was reserved for the horses. A wagon lumbered up the hill with their first issue of army rations. The teamsters dumped a pile of maggot-infested bacon sides on the ground outside the commissary tent. An outraged Colonel Stoughton condemned the bacon as unfit for consumption and ordered it carted away. Alas, no new

13. Noah Brooks, *Washington, D.C., in Lincoln's Time*, ed. Herbert Mitgang (Chicago, 1971), 13–21; Margaret Leech, *Reveille in Washington, 1860–1865* (New York, 1941), 5–10.

14. Kieley Diary, 25 September 1861.

meat replaced it, and the regiment went hungry. "It was the first and the last time that the Fourth Vermont refused its rations," Twitchell recalled. Thereafter, "we always kept all we had and got all we could."[15]

In late September, after four days on Capitol Hill, the regiment packed up its gear and marched down Pennsylvania Avenue, through Georgetown, and across the Potomac on Chain Bridge. A few weeks before, Chain Bridge—the name notwithstanding, a solid wooden structure—had been the scene of a disturbing incident, especially to Vermonters. On 31 August, William Scott, a young private in the Third Vermont, had been posted as a guard on the bridge. An hour after midnight, the officer of the guard arrested Scott for sleeping on duty. Taking no account of his having stood guard two nights in a row, a court-martial the next day sentenced Scott to be shot. At this stage of the war, Washington was threatened on three sides, and many Union soldiers pitched their tents within cannon shot of Confederate batteries. On the 8th, the day before his scheduled execution, the commander of the Army of the Potomac, pretty clearly at President Lincoln's behest, pardoned Scott, sparing the youth the ignominy of being the first Union soldier executed for dereliction of duty.

In ensuing months, as the story of Scott's pardon was told and retold "in the watchfires of a hundred circling camps," it became legend. Then in early 1863, a war department clerk wrote *The Sleeping Sentinel*, a poetic rendering of the tale and one of the best-loved stories of the war. Dramatically read at the White House and in the Senate, the *Sleeping Sentinel* has Scott, shamefaced and manacled, standing before a firing squad awaiting the deadly volley, when "suddenly was heard the noise of steeds and wheels," and a dusty carriage rolled onto the field. Here was President Lincoln, come to stop the execution.

> And yet, amid the din of war, he heard the plaintive cry
> Of that poor soldier, as he lay in prison, doom'd to die!

In time, the *Sleeping Sentinel* made its way into the history books.[16]

Just beyond Chain Bridge, in the wooded hills of northern Virginia, lay Camp Advance and the tents of the Second, Third, and Fifth Vermont

15. *CV*, 26.

16. *New York Tribune*, 9, 10 September 1861; *VCW*, 1: 132–34; William C. Davis, *Lincoln's Men: How President Lincoln Became Father to an Army and a Nation* (New York,

Regiments. The October weather was cold and rainy, frustrating the officers who were anxious to train the men. For Twitchell, the Fourth's nearly two weeks at Camp Advance were eventful. He and his fellows gawked at their first sight of a soldier killed by the enemy—a cavalryman. Then there was a mysterious mail robbery to which Twitchell's name somehow became connected. Rumors abounded: he was in the stockade; he had been court-martialed and condemned to death, and so on. To refute the rumors, Captain Stearns published a letter in the *Brattleboro Vermont Phoenix*. Twitchell, he wrote, was not involved in the crime, nor had he been "arrested and shot." How the rumors got started the captain did not say. The whole affair remains obscure.[17]

Another bizarre event occurred the first night of picket duty. About midnight, a rumor made the rounds that a Confederate attack was imminent. Twitchell was on I Company's right when the moon came out, revealing what appeared to be a company of Rebels crawling forward over the crest of the hill. Twitchell alerted the captain, who quickly strengthened the line. The bluecoats then waited for the rising moon to reveal the intruders more clearly. A quarter-hour passed; then more minutes slipped by. Slowly I Company crept ahead. Twitchell heard rifle hammers cocking along the line: "Our nerves were strung to such a tension that it would be a relief when the enemy sprang to their feet, but they never rose." Finally, the Federals advanced into the ranks of the silent Rebels and found themselves standing amid the mounds of a cemetery. The event passed into regimental lore as "Captain Stearns's graveyard scare." To the end of his army days, Twitchell never mentioned his role in the affair.[18]

In early October the Union high command assigned Vermont troops a special place in the Army of the Potomac. The idea originated with General William F. "Baldy" Smith, a West Point graduate and a native of Saint Albans, Vermont. Smith proposed grouping the four Vermont regiments at Camp Advance (plus a fifth en route) into a single Vermont brigade. Like all Vermonters, General Smith was proud of

1999), 170–71, 191, 249, 276 n; Francis De Haes Janvier, "The Sleeping Sentinel," in *Patriotism in Poetry and Prose. . .* , ed. James E. Murdoch, (Philadelphia, 1866), 103–7; *VCW*, 132–33; Lorna Beers, "The Sleeping Sentinel William Scott," *New England Galaxy* 7 (1965): 3–14.

   17. *CV*, 26–28; *Brattleboro Vermont Phoenix*, 31 October 1861.
   18. *CV*, 27.

the revolutionary tradition of Ethan Allen. He doubtless believed that a unit made up entirely of "Green Mountain Boys" would have a special esprit de corps. The idea was controversial. The army was all for esprit de corps, but its leaders recognized the existence of a strong counterargument. In the event of military disaster, Vermont could suffer devastating losses in a single battle. For this reason, Union brigades almost always combined regiments from two or more states. In this instance, one of the few times, the army set aside its reservations and created the Vermont Brigade, assigning it to Baldy Smith's division. The brigade commander was Brigadier General William Thomas Harbaugh Brooks, a West Pointer from Ohio.[19]

For most of the war, the Vermont Brigade was in the Second Division of the Sixth Corps. The Army of the Potomac's official table of organization listed the unit first as Brooks's Brigade, then as Second Brigade (Smith's division). In practice, as Dr. George T. Stevens wrote in *Three Years in the Sixth Corps*, it was generally known as the Vermont Brigade.[20] Over the course of the war it earned a reputation as one of the Army of the Potomac's finest units, renowned for hard fighting, hard marching, and roughneck conduct. "I never saw such men," General Brooks confessed. "It is impossible to tire them out. No matter how far or how hard you march them at night they will be all over the country stealing pigs and chickens." General William T. McMahon, after a long and intimate association with the brigade as Sixth Corps chief of staff, echoed Brooks's praise. After a long march, when other outfits collapsed in weary silence, the Vermonters cavorted and "yelled like wild Indians," he said. Despite their lenient interpretation of regulations, their swaggering impudence and "patronizing Yankee coolness," McMahon believed they were the finest brigade in the army. They "fought as well as it was possible to fight," and showed on many

19. *VCW*, 1: 235–37; George W. Parsons, *Put the Vermonters Ahead: The First Vermont Brigade in the Civil War* (Shippensburg, Penn., 1996), 7–13. In contrast to the Federals, the Confederates often brigaded regiments from the same state together.

20. George T. Stevens, *Three Years in the Sixth Corps* (1866; reprint, Alexandria, Va., 1984). To this day, entries in standard Civil War reference works refer to the Vermont Brigade by its nickname. Only a handful of units in the Union and Confederate armies share this distinction, the Confederate Stonewall Brigade, the Union Irish and Iron Brigades, and a few others. (See Mark M. Boatner's *Civil War Dictionary* (New York, 1959) and the *Historical Times Illustrated Encyclopedia of the Civil War* (New York, 1986).

occasions that they could outmarch any brigade in blue. In the desperate fury of battle, said McMahon, "they made queer, quaint jokes and enjoyed them greatly. They crowed like cocks, they ba-a-ed like sheep, they neighed like horses, they bellowed like bulls, they barked like dogs, and they counterfeited, with excellent effect, the indescribable music of the mule. When, perchance, they held a picket line in a forest, it seemed as if Noah's ark had gone to pieces there." The "magnificent Vermont brigade," another officer wrote, were "most worthy successors of Ethan Allen and the Green Mountain boys." Fame and longevity came at a steep price. The reservations of the Union high command had not been entirely misplaced. According to William F. Fox's *Regimental Losses in the American Civil War*, "the greatest loss of life in any one brigade during the war occurred in the Vermont Brigade."[21]

In mid-October the Vermonters marched deeper into Virginia, to Camp Griffin on the frontier of Washington's elaborate outer defenses. The Rebel lines lay a few miles beyond, and a dozen miles to the southwest, the main Confederate army was deployed between Centreville and Manassas. "We are standing on the outer verge of all that is left of the American Union," one Green Mountain Boy mused. "Nothing but darkness and rebellion is beyond." The Vermont Brigade would spend the next five months here on the red clay soil of Smoot's Hill.[22]

At Camp Griffin, the brigade's officers finally found the time to turn Twitchell and his greenhorn companions into soldiers. By modern standards, simply firing and reloading a Civil War rifle was a complicated task. To load, a soldier had to tear open a paper cartridge with his teeth and pour black powder down the rifle barrel. He then rammed the bullet down the barrel with a ramrod. Finally, he pressed a copper cap on the nipple of the firing pan. The rifle could now be raised and fired and the process repeated.[23]

Civil War soldiers spent a lot of time in drill, and the Green Moun-

21. Frank Moore, ed., *The Civil War in Song and Story, 1860–1865* (New York, 1889), 335–36; Ira S. Dodd, *The Song of the Rappahannock: Sketches of the Civil War* (New York, 1887), 54; Thomas W. Hyde, *Following the Greek Cross: Or Memories of the Sixth Corps* (Boston, New York, 1894), 74; William F. Fox, *Regimental Losses in the American Civil War, 1861–1865* (1898; reprint, Albany, N.Y., 1985), 116.

22. *VCW*, 1: 237; Rosenblatt, *Anti-Rebel*, 7.

23. John J. Pullen, *The Twentieth Maine: A Volunteer Regiment in the Civil War* (New York, 1957), 33.

tain Boys probably received an extra quota, because West Pointers commanded four of the five regiments in the brigade. On a typical day, Captain Stearns drilled the company in the morning, then Colonel Stoughton put the regiment through its paces in the afternoon. Twitchell learned to respond instantly to such commands as: "Change front to the rear, on first company. Battalion, about—*Face*. By company, left half wheel. *March;*" or "Three right companies, obstacle. By the left flank, to the rear, into column. Double quick—*March*."

Rushing into a fight, Colonel Stoughton expected hundreds of men marching in a column of four to break on command left or right into a two-tiered line of battle. They had to be able to reform ranks, maneuver over or around obstacles, and move to another part of the battlefield. Failure to master the drills invited confusion and defeat. The complicated choreography could only be learned through unrelenting toil, and Twitchell and the men in the ranks came to hate it and the men who made them do it. Seeing his colonel drill his men to exhaustion day after day, a sergeant in a Maine regiment admitted that the men hated their commander more than the enemy: "I swear they will shoot him the first battle we are in."[24]

Twitchell remembered the long winter at Camp Griffin as one of the darkest times of the war. On Smoot's Hill, the Fourth Vermont met the deadliest enemy of Civil War soldiers: disease. Every morning the adjutant at regiment collected the rolls from the first sergeants in the companies and tabulated the results for Colonel Stoughton's morning report. Thirty days, thirty morning reports. These dry standardized forms, the very epitome of army red tape, tell a grim story. At the beginning of October, 31 men were unfit for duty because of illness; then day after day, the sick list grew longer, reaching 150 by November, soaring to 342 in early December. It fell after Christmas, but hovered around 200 for the rest of the winter. The afflictions ran the gamut from measles to consumption, but typhoid fever was the most dangerous malady. The probable cause was contaminated water. For two months prior to the regiment's arrival on Smoot's Hill, a thousand cavalry horses had occupied the slope above the stream from which the Fourth took its drinking water. By the first of the year, 28 men had died,

---

24. Ibid., 33–37; William J. Hardee, *Rifle and Light Infantry Tactics* (1855; reprint, Westport, Conn., 1971), 2: 155, 169.

mostly from typhoid. (In only one of the Fourth's battles in the war would that death toll be exceeded.) Many of the typhoid survivors never returned to duty. In a little over three months, without so much as a skirmish, the regiment's strength dropped from more than 1,000 men to only 660.[25]

On occasion, parents arrived in camp, hoping to save or at least comfort their sick sons. "I visited your Camp with a Gentleman from my native town in Vermont who had been summoned on account of his son's illness," a man wrote Colonel Stoughton in November. "He arrived to[o] late his poor boy was already dead and his body had been sent to his former home. This was the third death from one tent within a few weeks, and these three were all from the same town and neighbors."[26]

Death became so commonplace on Smoot's Hill that some officers neglected their duty. "The Commanding officer learns with deep regret," Stoughton wrote in November, "that there are in his command, Officers who are so unmindful of the observance and rights due to the unfortunate who fall in our midst, victims not to the missels [sic] of the enemy but to the unrelenting hand of disease, as that they allow those entrusted to their care by fin[e] friends and doting parents to be hurried to their last resting place on this earth with no drum to sound a last requiem nor chaplain to utter a last prayer for him whose loss is bewailed by as many and dear friends as those of us who are spared."[27]

Two weeks before Christmas, out of nearly 5,000 men in the Vermont Brigade, more than 1,000 were down sick with measles, pneumonia, bronchitis, typhoid, dysentery, diarrhea, and other afflictions. All the Union forces suffered appallingly that winter, but the Vermonters had the highest ratio of sick men in the army. It was one of the war's ironies that boys from the pure air of the Vermont hills were more susceptible to disease than those from the North's consumptive cities.[28]

Twitchell's generation blamed the epidemics that raged through both northern and southern armies on dirty, unsanitary army camps. It was a plausible explanation. As one soldier put it, "An army, any army

25. Fourth Vermont Regimental Papers, RG 94, NA; *VCW*, 1: 160–61.

26. H. A. Willard to Colonel Edwin H. Stoughton, 19 November 1861, Fourth Vermont Regimental Papers.

27. General Orders No. 11, 26 December 1861, Fourth Vermont Regimental Books.

28. *OR*, 5: 92, 108; *VCW*, 1: 237–38.

does poison the air. It is a city without sewerage, and policing only makes piles of offal to be buried or burned." The contemporary explanation, however, failed to comprehend the real danger. Dirt, or filth, in the common-sense usage of the words, contributed, but the real problem was microbiological contamination, something beyond the medical knowledge of the day. The revolutionary discoveries of Louis Pasteur and Joseph Lister belonged to the future. In 1861 medicine had one foot in the modern world and one foot in the Middle Ages. From the vantage point of World War I, a distinguished surgeon named W. W. Keen recalled his doctoring in the 1860s as though remembering his childhood:

> In the Civil War we knew absolutely nothing of "germs." *Bacteriology*—the youngest and greatest science to aid in this conquest of death—*did not exist!* . . . we were wholly ignorant of the fact that the mosquito, and only the mosquito, spreads yellow fever and malaria; and of the role of the fly in spreading typhoid fever by walking on the excreta of those sick of typhoid and then over our food and infecting it with the typhoid germs which we swallow with our food.

Surgery was equally primitive. Keen wrote:

> We operated in old blood-stained and often pus-stained coats, the veterans of a hundred fights. We operated with clean hands in the social sense, but they were undisinfected hands. To the surgeon, the spotless hands of a bride are dirty. We used undisinfected instruments from undisinfected plush-lined cases, and still worse, used marine sponges which had been used in prior pus cases and had been only washed in tap water. If a sponge or an instrument fell on the floor it was washed and squeezed in a basin of tap water and used as if it were clean.

Ignorance, in short, made it inevitable that disease organisms would triumph over the primitive medical science of the 1860s.[29]

In that first year of the war, there were, on average, nearly four bouts

29. *CV*, 28; Paul E. Steiner, *Disease in the Civil War: Natural Biological Warfare in 1861–1865* (Springfield, Ill., 1968), 3–17; W. W. Keen, "Military Surgery in 1861 and in 1918," *Annals of the American Academy of Political and Social Science* 80 (1918): 11–22.

of sickness for every Union soldier. It was then a statistical probability that Twitchell would have been ill at least once that grim winter on Smoot's Hill; but he remained healthy. His main concern that troubled winter was his relationship with Captain Stearns. Probably because of Twitchell's education, which was well above average, he became the company commander's clerk. Sometime in the fall he moved into the captain's tent, where he handled the company's official correspondence and wrote accounts for the newspapers back home over the captain's signature. Stearns, a young widower, asked his clerk to write love letters to a young woman in Stanstead, Quebec. "I was allowed to write these letters with no suggestions from the captain except that he wanted to marry her if he could," Twitchell recalled. Stearns and the lady were married in the spring.[30]

The friction between Twitchell and his captain arose over gambling. Twitchell, a stern Yankee moralist, did not swear, drink, or gamble. Camp life on Smoot's Hill, in addition to being deadly, was dull, and the men gambled to relieve the monotony. They played every game of chance known to nineteenth-century Americans: poker (or bluff), faro, craps, twenty-one (blackjack)—even games of their own devising. Visiting the Second Vermont one day, Twitchell found soldiers gaming with their muskets. Using blanks, they put their pieces on the ground and pulled strings to discharge them, wagering on the distance the weapons recoiled. Poker was the captain's passion. He proposed to teach his clerk the fine points of bluff and to get him promoted to lieutenant. The two of them could then play as a team against the other officers in the regiment, splitting their winnings. Twitchell rejected the captain's offer. Gambling, he told his superior, might seem a small matter in the army, but he feared the habit would be a liability when he returned to civilian life.[31]

From that moment, the relationship between the two men soured. Stearns had earlier promised to promote Twitchell to corporal. Yet, the weeks passed, December turned into January, and no promotion was forthcoming. Believing the captain possessed "only a small stock of gratitude and honor," the young man from Townshend took matters into his own hands. He waited until Stearns assigned him to write a spe-

30. Wiley, *Billy Yank*, 124; *CV*, 28–30; Leonard A. Stearns Pension File, RG 15, NA.
31. *CV*, 28–30.

cial letter. He composed the letter but at the same time wrote out his promotion. The captain rushed in from afternoon drill and found himself facing an ultimatum: no promotion, no letter. Stearns, furious, gave in, but soon afterward, Twitchell moved out of the captain's tent and returned to regular duty.[32]

He had no sooner sewn on his corporal's chevrons than he almost lost them—and his freedom. He had charge of a picket post on the Fairfax Road when a friend suggested they visit a southern woman who lived just beyond the Union line. Yielding to temptation, Twitchell and his companion left their post, slipped down a gully through the line and into the home of the hospitable woman, who offered to play the piano and sing for them. Leaving his friend alone with the woman, Twitchell stepped outside the house, only to discover Rebel horsemen galloping into view. "Rebel cavalry!" he shouted to his companion. There was no time to go up the ravine; the two soldiers reentered the Union line in a dead run. An officer caught them and ordered them to report to the captain of the guard under arrest. Twitchell avoided a court-martial only because the captain of the guard chose to overlook the incident. Indeed, he was twice lucky: had the Confederates caught him, he would have been a prisoner of war.[33]

After his escape, Twitchell determined to toe the mark. This resolve was shortly put to an unexpected test. Before the regiment left Vermont, the mother of Private William H. Miles, a schoolmate from Townshend, had charged Twitchell with the unwanted task of looking after her only son. One cold, rainy night when the company was on picket duty, the captain of the guard fell ill, and the task of making midnight rounds devolved on Twitchell. He approached Miles's post, where he should have been sharply challenged, but no challenge was forthcoming. A flash of lightning revealed his friend asleep on the ground. Despite the cold, Twitchell began to sweat. It was an agonizing moment. Regulations required him to take his friend's rifle—proof that he was sleeping on duty—and arrest him. A court-martial would subject Miles to the same penalty as William Scott, the sleeping sentinel at Chain Bridge. Twitchell reached for the weapon and lifted it. The wily Miles, however, had tied the rifle to his boot. He awoke and snapped to his feet. "Who comes there?" he challenged.

32. Ibid.
33. Ibid., 30–31.

"Grand Rounds," said a relieved Twitchell, releasing the rifle and stepping back. He warned his friend against any repetition and finished his rounds.[34]

Hours before sunrise on 10 March, reveille roused Twitchell and his comrades from their sleep. They had orders to pack their knapsacks and cook two days' rations. The regiment skipped out of Camp Griffin at dawn to the tune of "The Girl I Left Behind Me." The brigade was on the move. "It was an animating spectacle," wrote a soldier in the Second Vermont. "If the men had just been freed from prison their countenances would hardly have worn a more gleeful expression." They stopped a few days near Fairfax Courthouse and then headed for Alexandria in a cold, driving rain. After six hard months of drill, rain, mud, boredom, and pestilence, they were going to meet the enemy. The great Peninsula invasion of Virginia was underway. A week later, Twitchell boarded a transport for Fort Monroe.[35]

34. Ibid., 31–32.
35. Kieley Diary, 10 March 1862; Rosenblatt, *Anti-Rebel*, 11–12; *VCW*, 1: 161–62, 241–42.

THREE

THE VIRGINIA PENINSULA

LYING between the York and the James Rivers, the Virginia Peninsula is an eighty-mile finger of land, stretching from Hampton Roads to Richmond. Long before the Civil War, it was historic ground. Here the first English settlers planted Jamestown and the first African Americans came ashore to work in the tobacco fields. Here Patrick Henry defied King George and Cornwallis surrendered to General Washington. Here the great American paradox of slavery and freedom took root.

Fort Monroe at Old Point Comfort, the eastern tip of the Peninsula, was the largest stone fort in the country and the jump-off point for the Peninsula campaign. In March and April 1862, from Alexandria and Annapolis, the largest armada ever to sail North American waters, nearly 400 vessels of every description, carried 120,000 soldiers, nearly 15,000 horses and mules, 1,150 wagons, and a vast tonnage of supplies to the fort's wharves.[1]

The Peninsula campaign was the strategic brainchild of Major General George B. McClellan. Instead of attacking Richmond by the direct

1. *OR*, 5: 46; Stephen W. Sears, *To the Gates of Richmond: The Peninsula Campaign* (New York, 1992), 23–27.

route overland from Washington, McClellan's plan was to flank Confederate defenses, assemble the Army of the Potomac at Fort Monroe, and then advance up the Peninsula on the Confederate capital. In this way, the Union navy would safeguard the army's flanks and provision it.

Handsome and charismatic and only thirty-five years old, McClellan was a skillful organizer and administrator. The press called him the "Young Napoleon." His soldiers called him "Little Mac"—he was five-feet-nine-inches tall—and adored him. "I am to watch over you as a parent over his children; and you know that your general loves you from the depths of his heart," he told them. "I shall demand of you great, heroic exertions, rapid and long marches, desperate combats, privations perhaps. We will share all these together; and when this sad war is over we will return to our homes, and feel that we can ask no higher honor than the proud consciousness that we belonged to the Army of the Potomac."[2]

Like most Billy Yanks, Twitchell listened and believed. President Lincoln and the Republican Congress were more skeptical. McClellan had been in command for eight long months and only now, after much prodding, was pointing his troops south.

In the chill dawn of 25 March, Twitchell gazed at Fort Monroe from the deck of his transport. Turning his head, his vision swept a panorama of ships to the north and east as far as the eye could see. Anchored nearby was the ironclad *Monitor*. Two weeks before, this "Yankee cheese box on a raft" had fought the *Virginia* (formerly the *Merrimack*).[3]

The shoreline was pandemonium. Infantry and artillery, commissary and quartermaster trains, horses, braying mules, the rustle and creak of heavy equipment, sergeants and officers barking profanely—all mingled in martial cacophony. The Fourth Vermont went ashore in midmorning and camped near Newport News, where it remained for more than a week. The language of the local people intrigued Twitchell: "A woman told us that when 'youens' came in sight, 'weuns' jumped onto their 'critters' and left." In time, the dialect grew familiar, but that did nothing to weaken his conviction of New England superiority.[4]

2. Richard Wheeler, ed., *Sword over Richmond: An Eyewitness History of McClellan's Peninsula Campaign* (New York, 1986), 97.

3. Stevens, *Sixth Corps*, 26; *VCW*, 1: 161, 243–44; Herman Hattaway and Archer Jones, *How the North Won: A Military History of the Civil War* (Urbana, Ill., 1983), 129.

4. Stevens, *Sixth Corps*, 27–28; *CV*, 34.

On a cold, rainy day in early April, the Union host headed toward Richmond in two heavy columns marching on parallel roads a few miles apart. In the left column, Twitchell's unit slogged through marshy pine forests. Ahead lay the Warwick River, a sluggish stream that spanned the twelve-mile width of the Peninsula from the Revolutionary battlefield at Yorktown to Mulberry Island on the James River. It was a natural defensive barrier, along which the Confederates had built a string of fortifications. When the Federals first approached, though, the strength of the Warwick River line was largely illusory. Nearly half of its 13,600 defenders held the flanks at Yorktown and Mulberry Island, leaving fewer than 8,000 men guarding the interior line. With 55,000 men in his advance columns, McClellan could have smashed the Warwick line like rotten wood. Instead, his instinctive caution took over; he delayed days and then weeks. In the meantime, the enemy moved in reinforcements.[5]

In the center of the Warwick line, in a large clearing a mile upstream from Lee's Mill, three burnt-out chimneys of the Garrow farm stood as silent sentinels over the river. Across the way, the Rebels had built the first of a series of dams or causeways backing up the river's waters as barriers. A line of rifle pits was visible below the pond. More entrenchments and artillery redoubts lay concealed in the dense forest rising behind "Dam No. 1." In plain sight, a twenty-four-pound howitzer, dubbed the "one gun battery," nestled in a redoubt at the Rebel end of the dam. On 5 April, Twitchell's brigade first approached the Garrow farm and camped in the swampy woods near the river. For eleven dreary, rainy days, with thousands of others, they waited for orders. Twitchell caught glimpses of the butternut-clad defenders across the water and often heard their shovels and axes strengthening the fortifications. Periodically, the blue and gray pickets skirmished and artillery rounds crashed in the trees. For Twitchell the waiting was relieved by his second promotion, from corporal to third sergeant.[6]

5. Sears, *Gates of Richmond*, 35, 42–43, 51; *VCW*, 1: 245–49; Craig L. Symonds, *A Battlefield Atlas of the Civil War* (Annapolis, Md., 1983), 28–29. Exactly how many Confederate troops held the Warwick River line on 5 April is a matter of some speculation. Historians' estimates range from 11,000 to 17,000 men. Sears's calculation of 13,600 is most persuasive to this author.

6. *OR*, 11, pt. 1: 363–65; *VCW*, 1: 246–50; Sears, *Gates of Richmond*, 49–50; MHT Compiled Military Service Record, RG 94, NA.

McClellan decided to break the Warwick line near Yorktown, its strongest point. Still, the enemy works at Dam No. 1 troubled him like a swarm of gnats buzzing about his head. The result was the first real firefight of the Peninsula campaign. In the wee hours of 16 April, McClellan ordered General Erasmus D. Keyes and Baldy Smith to halt the Confederate work on the dam's fortifications. Within the hour, the Vermont Brigade formed for battle near the water's edge. There was just light enough to see as Twitchell's regiment crept into position in the pines above the dam. Mist and the melody of "Rosa Lee" drifted across the water. Colonel Stoughton himself slipped forward with the skirmishers to the swampy shore and about seven-thirty fired the first shot across the pond. Above and below the dam, supported by a New York artillery battery, the Green Mountain Boys laid down a brisk fire on the Confederates. The shooting lasted several hours.[7]

Just before noon, riding a beautiful black charger, General McClellan galloped up, trailing a cloud of staff officers and European observers. He ordered General Smith to capture the Confederate works but cautioned him against starting a major battle. McClellan and his entourage rode on, leaving the assault to Smith and his subordinates. As the plan unfolded, an unanswered question floated in the air: If the attack succeeded, what happened next?[8]

About three o'clock, battle flags flying, four companies of the Third Vermont formed in line of battle and marched to the stream below the dam. Estimates of the river's width vary, but the distance was at least seventy-five yards. A corporal named George Q. French described the attack: "Into the water we plunged, fixing our bayonets & capping our pieces as we went. On we pushed, climbing over logs, roots & every kind of impediment . . . firing as we had opportunity, until the channel of the creek was past, & the depth of the water began to diminish." Logs and debris and clouds of rifle and cannon smoke partially shielded the attackers. As the Vermonters waded ashore, the Confederates abandoned the front trenches and retreated into the forest. The Federals leaped into the abandoned works.[9]

7. *OR*, 11, pt. 1: 363–78; *VCW*, 1: 249–45.

8. *VCW*, 1: 253–54; *OR*, 11, pt. 1: 363–78.

9. *VCW*, 1: 255; Albert C. Eisenberg, "'The 3d Vermont *has won a name*': Corporal George Q. French's Account of the Battle of Lee's Mills, Virginia," *Vermont History*, 47 (1981), 223–31.

In the forest on the Union side of the river, Smith's whole division awaited orders to join the attack. Had it done so at that moment, the Warwick line probably would have been irreparably breached, York-town flanked, and the Confederates forced to retreat in haste up the Peninsula. Alas, neither Smith nor McClellan—who had returned to watch—gave the order.[10]

The fire from the Confederate line was intense. Captain Stephen M. Pingree, the company commander who spearheaded the attack, sent runners back to his colonel on the Union shore, asking to be reinforced or withdrawn. The better part of an hour slipped by without any reply to these urgent requests. More precious minutes passed. Although bleeding profusely from a wound in the hip and with his right thumb shot off, the valiant Pingree tried again. The order to retreat finally came—almost too late: a battle line of Johnny Rebs burst from the for-est. By now, many of the Vermont boys were either out of ammunition or had wet powder. "Something desperate had got to be done," a lieu-tenant named Erasmus Buck wrote. "A charge was our only show, and charge we did. We jumped the works and gave a loud yell. The rebels supposed a brigade was charging them and ran like sheep." The desper-ate charge won the bluecoats a few minutes respite to make their es-cape.[11]

If the trip over was exciting, the trip back was terrifying. Minie balls cascaded from the Rebel shore until the river churned like it was being pounded by hail. As Lieutenant Buck neared the water, he glanced back and saw lines of butternut-clad troops coming on. He plunged ahead, certain that he was dead man. He survived, but his instinct was not far wrong: casualties in the four companies that had waded the river were nearly 50 percent.[12]

Soldiers grabbed Captain Pingree, barely able to stand up, and helped him across the river. Some men were left behind, too badly wounded to rise. Forsaking the safety of the Union line, a sixteen-year-old drummer boy twice waded the river, each time carrying a wounded man bigger than himself to safety, a feat that won him the Congres-

---

10. *VCW*, 1: 255–56; Stevens, *Sixth Corps*, 41–42; Eisenberg, "'The 3d Vermont *has won a name*'," 227; Sears, *Gates of Richmond*, 55–56.

11. *VCW*, 1: 256–57 n; Eisenberg, "'The 3d Vermont *has won a name*'," 227; Ste-vens, *Sixth Corps*, 41.

12. *VCW*, 1: 256–58 n; Eisenberg, "'The 3d Vermont *has won a name*'," 227–28.

sional Medal of Honor. Perhaps the most poignant moment of the retreat was the action of eleven-year-old drummer boy Henry Davenport.
His father, Captain D. B. Davenport, was struggling toward the Union
side, blood spouting from his thigh. His son, heart pounding, eyes wide
with fear, broke cover, sprinted across the killing ground, leaped into
the river, and helped his father up the bank. After getting him to safety,
the boy returned to the stream to get his father a drink of water. A
minie ball knocked the cup from his hand.[13]

An hour before dark, Baldy Smith inexplicably ordered companies
of the Fourth and Sixth Vermont Regiments to make a second "recon-
naissance" of the Confederate position. The orders directed Twitchell's
company and three others to cross the dam and capture the "one gun
battery," while companies of the Sixth Regiment crossed the river
below the causeway. Predictably, the Confederates had rushed reinforcements to Dam No. 1; elements of three gray brigades now manned
the works.[14]

The men of the Fourth, bayonets fixed, moved out of the cover of
the trees on the double-quick, Colonel Stoughton in the lead, but they
did not go far. Met by flaming sheets of rifle and artillery fire, Sergeant
Twitchell and his men threw themselves to the ground. Twitchell had
seen wounded men before but not like this. One second, Stephen Niles,
a Halifax boy, was alive on the ground beside him; seconds later, he was
a corpse, his glossy blood and brain tissue staining the grass. Twitchell
bolted ahead of his company and fired his rifle from behind a gatepost.
As he dropped to reload, a shower of minie balls slammed into the gatepost. Another soldier, who had crawled up behind Twitchell, cried out
that he was hit. As Twitchell turned his head, he later recalled, "a bullet
grazed the post where my face had been, lifting the hair over my ear,
and passed on. I thought that I would try the other side of the post,
shifted my position, and putting my hand out, it was grazed by a bullet
just enough to break the skin." In the retreat, scrambling backward to
the safety of the trees, he was hit in the foot, a painful but not disabling
wound.[15]

The luck of many a Green Mountain Boy ran out that bloody after-

13. *VCW*, 1: 257–58, 263.
14. *OR*, 11, pt. 1: 364–77; *VCW*, 1: 259–61; *CV*, 34–35.
15. *VCW*, 1: 259–60; *CV*, 34–35.

noon. Nearly two hundred of them were casualties. The dead numbered forty-four and another twenty-one later died of their wounds. Among those who would never see home again was Private William Scott, the sleeping sentinel at Chain Bridge. He was fatally wounded in the first assault. His comrades carried his body back to the Federal side. Legend has it that with his dying breath he praised President Lincoln for allowing him the honor of a soldier's death. Honor was no empty word to these men. That night, despite his wounded foot, Twitchell helped dig earthworks, lest the dreaded words "cannon fever"—synonymous with cowardice—be whispered about him.[16]

Twitchell judged the Battle of Lee's Mill, as the fight at Dam No. 1 came to be called, a pointless sacrifice of good men. With more wit, another soldier called it a "Dam failure." The historian of Vermont soldiers, G. G. Benedict, was to be equally blunt: the bloody action was "one of the most useless wastes of life and most lamentable of unimproved opportunities recorded in this history." Reports of the battle caused consternation in Washington. The U.S. Senate subsequently investigated charges that General Smith was drunk that afternoon. To the extent that the general was incapacitated, his horse, rather than liquor, was found to be the cause. The high-spirited beast had thrown him twice, leaving him dazed.[17]

In most histories of the war, Dam No. 1 rates barely a footnote. Compared to Antietam, Vicksburg, or Gettysburg, it was an insignificant skirmish in a place no one remembered. Ordinary folk, however, measure events on a different scale than do historians. In the small state of Vermont in many a village and farm house, the dam above Lee's Mill was a place that ever after evoked infinitely more anguish than the more famous battles. The fight also tested the mettle of Twitchell and the Green Mountain Boys. It changed them from unblooded recruits into soldiers who had looked "Mr. Bullet" in the eye and "seen the elephant." It was no want of courage on their part that caused the defeat. That responsibility belonged to the generals, the "big dogs with brass collars." (In the case of General McClellan, the fight unerringly foreshadowed his command failures in the big battles to come.) Perhaps the best assessment of the Vermonters came from a soldier who had fought

16. *VCW*, 1: 262–64; *CV*, 35.
17. *CV*, 34; *VCW*, 1: 249, 264–66; Sears, *Gates of Richmond*, 56.

against them. Two days after the battle, Colonel William Levy of the tough Second Louisiana crossed the river under a flag of truce to talk about the burial of Union dead. He inquired about the regiment that had waded the river and stormed the rifle pits. "A detachment of the Third Vermont," an officer informed him. "It was lucky for us," Levy remarked, "that you did not send over many such detachments."[18]

The Warwick line held up the Army of the Potomac for a month. Then one night in early May, Rebel cannon pounded the Union line until after midnight, causing many Federals to expect a morning attack. But at first light at Dam No. 1, Yorktown, and all along the line, the west bank redoubts were empty. The Confederates had abandoned the river and withdrawn up the Peninsula.

Twitchell's brigade traipsed across Dam No. 1 after the retreating graycoats. That afternoon, the Vermonters marched point for General Keyes's columns. They covered ground at a pace that amazed Keyes and in time became legendary. "They had a long, slow swinging stride on the march," one officer recalled, "which distanced everything that followed them." As the day lengthened, they pulled away from the long blue columns. General Keyes summoned an aide. "If your horse has bottom enough to catch up with that Vermont brigade," he said, "I want you to overtake them and order a halt. Tell them we are not going to Richmond today."[19]

Ten miles west of the Warwick River, a second Rebel line stretched across the Peninsula. At Williamsburg, the old colonial capital, the advancing Federals battled the enemy's rear guard. Though not generally considered a major battle, more Union troops fought at Williamsburg and suffered higher fatalities than at Bull Run. The day after the fight, Twitchell surveyed the gruesome wreckage: splintered trees and huge gouges in the earth; busted artillery caissons and mangled horses buried in a lake of mud; mutilated human corpses strewn in odd, disjointed poses, some clutching faded photographs or scraps of letters; Union soldiers digging mass graves. Worst of all were the living. "I saw a man wounded in the head," a Vermont soldier wrote, "a clot of brains mark-

    18. Jay Monaghan, "Civil War Slang and Humor," *Civil War History*, 3 (1957): 125–33; *VCW*, 1: 265.

    19. *VCW*, 1: 268–69; Rosenblatt, *Anti-Rebel*, 23; Moore, *Civil War in Song and Story*, 336; MHT Scrapbook, MHT Papers.

ing the spot where he was hit. He was leaning back against some logs, in a partially upright position, still breathing, though apparently unconscious."[20]

An officer ordered Sergeant Twitchell to form a detail and report for duty at a field hospital. The hospital turned out to be a barn. Outside the door, the surgeons had pitched amputated arms and legs into a bloody pile. It reminded Twitchell of the stove wood stacked by his father's house back in Vermont. The doctor told him to search the battlefield, bury the dead, and bring in the wounded, but to leave men with clearly fatal wounds where they lay. The doctor did not explain the brutal necessity of concentrating on men who had some chance of living. Twitchell was shocked. He put his men to work under a corporal, but he returned to camp to denounce the surgeon to the adjutant. He would fight, but he would not work at the hospital, he said. Dam No. 1 and Williamsburg brought him face to face with his own mortality. It was all too easy to imagine his own torn body lying in this horrible place and someone standing over him saying, "Don't bother with this one, he won't last till sundown." The officer sent him to his tent and did not press the issue.[21]

The fifty-mile-long Chickahominy River rose northwest of Richmond, angled to the southeast, and emptied into the James River west of Williamsburg. Swampy and impenetrable, it was a formidable obstacle to the Army of the Potomac in 1862. "This creek," wrote a Vermont private, "is the most unpromising stream I ever saw to bridge. Like a city, its suburbs extend far back into the country on each side, and the whole valley, or plain, is one endless swamp." Another New Englander described the river's mile-wide lowlands as a dense jungle of moss-draped trees, clinging vines, swamp grasses, ferns, reeds, and thorn bushes. "Its stagnant water is poisonous; moccasins and malaria abound; flies and mosquitoes swarm; turtles and lizards bask; cranes and herons wade; buzzards and polecats stink; bitterns boom, owls hoot, foxes yelp, wild cats snarl and all nature seems in a glamor or a gloom."[22]

Three weeks after Williamsburg, lead elements of the Army of the

20. Wheeler, *Sword over Richmond*, 161–62; Rosenblatt, *Anti-Rebel*, 23–26.
21. *CV*, 36–37.
22. Rosenblatt, *Anti-Rebel*, 31; Steiner, *Disease in the Civil War*, 133.

Potomac pushed into the village of Mechanicsville on the north slope of the Chickahominy, six miles above Richmond. A few miles east the Sixth Corps held the Gaines's Mill area. Twitchell and the Vermonters pitched their tents on a farm above the river. Another Union corps occupied the low lying bluffs east of Gaines's Mill near New Cold Harbor, where the Union line bent at a right angle to cross the Chickahominy, and extend south toward Savage's Station and White Oak Swamp. The roughly 100,000 men of McClellan's army stretched over twenty miles. Because the Chickahominy bridges flooded easily, the army's division into two wings, one north and one south of the Chickahominy, was dangerous. The Confederate army defending Richmond numbered only about 65,000 men, but if the two wings of the Union force became cut off from one another, the Confederates could attack one or the other on even terms.

Rain had plagued the Army of the Potomac since its first days on the Peninsula. In late May it was torrential, and the Chickahominy basin filled like a lake. With the Union army cut in two, the Confederates struck. Cannon thundered and smoke billowed south of the river on a field variously called Fair Oaks or Seven Pines. Twitchell's brigade was under arms all day and through the night, expecting any moment to be rushed into the fight, and it probably would have been if the nearest bridges had been passable. The next morning, the division marched to the river's edge but was still unable to cross. Fortunately, the Union troops south of the river had blunted the attack, and the Confederates had withdrawn within Richmond's fortifications.[23]

A few days later, Twitchell's brigade relocated south of the Chickahominy on a hill called Golding's Farm, just six miles from Richmond. Over the next three weeks, enemy sharpshooters harassed them, but far deadlier than the marksmen was "Chickahominy fever." Like the "Potomac fever" of the previous winter, it was not a specific disease but a catchall term covering a host of ills afflicting the army: scurvy, diarrhea, dysentery, catarrh, bronchitis, jaundice, typhoid, malaria, and other maladies. Both the environment and the campaign were to blame. In *Three Years in the Sixth Corps*, Dr. Stevens wrote: "Day after day the men worked under a burning sun, throwing up the immense walls of earth, or toiled standing to their waists in water, building bridges.

23. *VCW*, 1: 277–80.

Night after night they were called to arms, to resist some threatened attack of the enemy. Their clothing and tents were drenched with frequent rains, and they often slept in beds of mud." Soldiers who were healthy and hardworking one day, he said, "would be found in the hospitals on the next, burning with fever, tormented with insatiable thirst, racked with pains, or wild with delirium; their parched lips, and teeth blackened with sores, the hot breath and sunken eyes, the sallow skin and trembling pulse, all telling of the violent working of these diseases." A fleet of hospital ships carried the victims from the overflowing field hospitals of Virginia to equally crowded hospitals above the Potomac: "Everywhere in the North, men were seen on cars and steamers, on the streets and in the houses, whose sallow countenances, emaciated appearance, and tottering steps marked them as victims of 'Chickahominy fever.'" As the weeks passed, Dr. Stevens came to see the sluggish Virginia river as a veritable "river of death," so deadly as to threaten the very destruction of the army.[24]

Twitchell's regiment had never fully recovered from its bout with "Potomac fever." At the end of its first month on the Peninsula, the Fourth Vermont had 730 men fit for duty and 121 down sick; then, over the next five months:

	Present for Duty	Sick
May	721	160
June	686	155
July	575	137
August	486	281
September	411	299

During this six-month period, the Fourth Vermont counted just 5 battle deaths and 43 men wounded; yet, 37 soldiers died of disease and 92 were discharged for disability due mostly to illness. Not until early 1863 did the number of sick drop below 200. Had replacements not started to come in, the regiment would have ceased to exist as a fighting force.[25]

Twitchell, however, remained immune to the pestilence. At Golding's Farm he was one of the few men who did not suffer from dysen-

24. Stevens, *Sixth Corps*, 74–75.
25. Monthly Returns, Fourth Vermont Regimental Papers; *VCW*, 1: 264, 300.

tery, an exemption he believed that came from his only drinking boiled water in coffee or tea. The explanation seems unlikely because later in White Oak Swamp, he recalled dipping and drinking "water so thick with mud and droppings from mules and horses that sucking it through our teeth, there was as much filth left in the cup as there was water which we had been able to drink." The man had an iron constitution. He did not report sick a single day during the entire war, a remarkable record of health.[26]

Rebel and Yankee pickets confronting one another at Golding's Farm often made private truces. The two sides kept many of these agreements, but others went the way of one described by Twitchell. He and his men lay concealed behind a low earthwork in the hot sun. He called out to the gray sentries for a truce, presumably so that they could all stand up, stretch their legs, and perhaps find some shade. The southerners agreed, and on both sides the boys stood up in plain sight of one another. One of the butternuts, however, shortly raised his rifle, and the Vermonters dived for cover. Laughter rose from the enemy position, and a voice asked if the Yanks doubted their word. Twitchell shouted back that traitors were capable of any kind of dirty trick. The truce was over.[27]

As the warm June days slipped by, word circulated in the Federal lines of a high-level change on the Confederate side. Robert E. Lee now commanded the Army of Northern Virginia. The new leader was something of an unknown quantity even in his own army. His first assignments had produced less than spectacular results. Some Richmonders ridiculed him as "Granny Lee" or the "King of Spades" (the latter because of his supposed reliance on earthworks). Unlike McClellan, however, he was aggressive by nature and willing to take risks. While the "Young Napoleon" inched closer to Richmond, Lee labored on a plan to bring reinforcements to the city and destroy the Army of the Potomac.

The distant rumble of musketry and artillery reverberated through the heat and haze of 25 June, forcing Twitchell and his companions to remain under arms all day. Late the next afternoon a cannonade of un-

---

26. *CV*, 38, 41; Carded Medical Records, Fourth Vermont Regiment, RG 94, NA; Carded Medical Records, 109th USCT, RG 94, NA.

27. *CV*, 38.

paralleled fury rolled down the Chickahominy from the direction of Mechanicsville. In the early afternoon of 27 June, from his perch at Golding's Farm, Twitchell watched the start of a big fight two miles across the Chickahominy bottom at Gaines's Mill. Holding good ground above a swamp, the Union Fifth Corps beat back ferocious assaults all afternoon. At twilight a last determined assault cracked the Union line and sent 35,000 bluecoats scurrying for the Chickahominy bridges.[28]

Late in the afternoon on Twitchell's side of the river, General Brooks ordered the Fourth Vermont to assist General Winfield Scott Hancock's brigade at nearby Garnett's Farm. The Fourth deployed on Hancock's right flank in a woods at the edge of a long wheat field, between the Fifth Wisconsin and Forty-third New York regiments. In the trees, about one hundred yards across the field, was the Georgia brigade of General Robert Toombs. In the center of the wheat field, running lengthwise, the ground rose to a low crest, partially shielding the combatants from one another. In Twitchell's sector on the Union edge of the field, the ground dropped off so that the forest floor was some four feet below the plain of the wheat. The Vermonters, in other words, held a position analogous to a sunken road.

Shortly before dark, the Rebels emerged from the trees and advanced to the center of the field. Thousands of rifles flashed in the twilight. Although separated by only about fifty yards, within seconds smoke and near darkness completely obscured the two sides from one another. The combatants fought on into the night in near total blindness. The muzzle flashes burst in the sulfuric summer darkness like giant exploding fireflies. Along I Company's line, a shower of leaves and branches, cut by the enemy's bullets, fell from the overhanging trees onto the men beneath them.[29]

That evening Twitchell decided his own captain was as much of a threat to his life as were the Georgians in the wheatfield. Amidst the larger story of the Peninsula campaign, a small, dark melodrama was unfolding in I Company between Sergeant Twitchell and Captain Stearns. Nearly four months before, Stearns had been hospitalized in Washington. After his release, he had traveled to northern Vermont to

28. Ibid., 38–39; Kieley Diary, 25, 26 June 1862; Rosenblatt, *Anti-Rebel*, 37.
29. *OR*, 11, pt. 2: 466–68, 476–79; *VCW*, 1: 283–87; *CV*, 38–39.

recuperate and to marry the woman Twitchell had wooed in his name. In the meantime, the company commander had missed the first months of the Peninsula campaign—the trip to Fort Monroe, Dam No. 1, Williamsburg, and the march up the Chickahominy. He had returned to I Company only at the end of May. Twitchell and Stearns had had little use for one another since their falling out on Smoot's Hill, and their reunion was not a happy one, especially since Twitchell had been made sergeant and was next in line to be first sergeant—theoretically, a company commander's right hand. On top of this, the unit Stearns returned to was a very different group of men from the one he had left. It was now a veteran outfit, while Stearns by comparison remained a greenhorn. Twitchell's attitude may well have been less than respectful, without actually being insubordinate.[30]

That evening at Garnett's Farm, Stearns posted himself behind a big tree and kept Twitchell moving up and down the line carrying messages. Fallen leaves and branches dogged the sergeant's every step. The contents of the messages seemed inconsequential. Some of the men speculated out loud that the captain was trying to get his sergeant shot. The same idea occurred to Twitchell: "I knew he was bad but did not think until then that he was mean enough to try and get me killed for the purpose of closing my lips." What Twitchell knew is unknown, but he doubtless did know things damaging to Stearns's reputation.[31]

The Union line held along the edge of the wheatfield. As the shooting died down, though, every Yank there, including Twitchell and the captain, had bigger things to worry about. The Confederate victory at Gaines's Mill broke more than the Union line; it broke General McClellan's nerve. He ordered the Army of the Potomac to fall back toward the James River. He called it a change of base, but it was a retreat, among the biggest and most important of the war.[32]

The day after Garnett's Farm, Twitchell's regiment packed its gear and headed southeast, arriving at Savage's Station, eight miles due east of Richmond, about noon. The station was a stop on the Richmond and York River Railroad, located in a large field ringed by heavy forest on

30. Leonard A. Stearns Compiled Military Service Record, RG 94, NA; Stearns Pension File; *Revised Roster of Vermont Volunteers, 1861–1866* (Montpelier, Vt., 1892), 135–38.
31. *CV*, 39.
32. Stephen W. Sears, *George B. McClellan: The Young Napoleon* (New York, 1988), 212–13.

every side except west toward Richmond. In this direction, brush and scrub timber flanked the tracks. More important to the Union forces than the east-west railroad, Savage's Station was on the main north-south road leading south from the Chickahominy bridges near Cold Harbor to the James River. The road was critical to the Army of the Potomac's retreat.[33]

Ordinarily a quiet country depot, Savage's Station had been turned into McClellan's forward supply depot. Long lines of troops plodded wearily by, caravans of wagons jammed the road, and trains clogged the station's sidings. The Union high command had shipped in huge quantities of provisions that now must be destroyed or abandoned to the enemy. Black acrid smoke rose from flaming piles of cheese, bread, sugar, coffee, flour, and pork, while other heaps—some as big as small barns—awaited the torch. Acres of uniforms, shoes, and other accoutrements littered the landscape. Hundreds of wild-eyed soldiers rummaged through them. Late that afternoon, an ammunition train was set ablaze and released unmanned downgrade. It roared north down the two-mile Chickahominy slope like a giant mechanical snake shooting off roman candles. Minutes later the engine leaped airborne from the burned Chickahominy trestle, burning cars in tow, and the entire train disintegrated in a series of massive explosions. A huge column of white smoke, visible for miles, billowed into the sky. The grimmest scene at the station, though, was the hospital. Some 2,500 sick and wounded soldiers lay in field hospital tents and makeshift shelters. When the last blue troops pulled out, they would become Confederate prisoners. Courageously, a handful of Union doctors remained behind with them.[34]

The Vermont Brigade was assigned to the Union rear guard. Its task was to hold Savage's Station until the last retreating unit had passed. The covering force formed a defensive line in the scrub forest west of the depot. The Vermont Brigade held the left flank, south of the Williamsburg road that paralleled the railroad tracks leading into the capital.[35] John F. Cook, a sergeant in the Third Vermont, wrote a colorful version of the ensuing fight:

33. Kieley Diary, 28, 29 June 1862; *VCW*, 1: 288–89.
34. Kieley Diary, 29 June 1862; *VCW*, 1: 289; Stevens, *Sixth Corps*, 96–98, 103; Thomas L. Livermore, *Days and Events, 1860–1866* (Boston, New York, 1920), 83.
35. *OR*, 11, pt. 2: 476–79; *VCW*, 1: 289–294.

At three o-clock p.m. the rebel skirmishers advanced from the woods on the opposite side of the field, and soon after their black columns came on, at double quick, yelling like demons, intending to take our guns. Not a shot came from our side, untill the rebels were to within about 100 yards of our batteries. Quicker than lightening, our guns were unmasked, and each laden with a double charge of canister they opened on their lines. Great God! . . . what a sight! they fell in heaps, and the way they put back to the woods, was a caution to see. But soon a heavier force came on again, but the same fate awaited them. For the third time they came on, fairly covering the field with their hordes, but this time they fared worse than before, fearfull was the slaughter wich our canister made in their crowded ranks, but as soon as they got up allmost to the mouth's of our guns, up rose our infantry and more than 10,000 rifles were emptied into their allready thined ranks.

After the battle . . . I went for a few minutes over the battle-field. The rebels lay there in rows, in some places three and four thick, legs and arms lay scattered in every way and the wounded lay groaning, covered with the dead, and unable to get out. There was a strong smell of rum, and picking up some of their canteens, I found that in most of them, was some rottgutt. The fact is . . . they were nearly all drunk, and this accounts for their boldness in walking up allmost to the cannons mouth.[36]

Sergeant Cook's notion that the enemy was "fighting drunk" was a common Civil War delusion. More important Cook saw only what was in front of him. Only a few hundred yards distant, beyond his view, a very different battle raged; and in this sector, the Fifth Vermont Regiment, not the Confederates, took the drubbing. The Fifth charged the enemy line, and "in less time than it takes to tell it," wrote G. G. Benedict, "the ground was strewn with fallen Vermonters." Of the Fifth's 400 men, 45 were killed and 158 wounded, the highest losses of any Vermont regiment in the war. In one company, six out of seven members of the same family were killed. Overall Union casualties, in fact, were much higher than Confederate casualties that afternoon. Despite the losses, the rear guard held the road open until the army had safely passed.[37]

36. George A. MacDonald, ed., "The Bloody Seven Days' Battles," *Vermont Quarterly*, n.s., 15 (1947): 230–35.

37. McPherson, *For Cause and Comrades*, 52–53; *VCW*, 1: 295–300.

Brigade headquarters held the Fourth Vermont in reserve during the Savage's Station fight. While the battle roared, Twitchell and I Company were busily employed destroying hospital supplies, mainly liquor. Whiskey and brandy were the "all-purpose medicine" of the Civil War, and field hospitals stored large quantities. Twitchell was one of the few men in the regiment who could be trusted to dump the stuff rather than drink it. Out of his sight, one of the men filled his canteen with whiskey. The next night the dehydrated soldier offered twenty dollars for a cup of water. In one hospital tent Twitchell found a patient, a member of his company, who claimed to be too weak to carry his heavy knapsack. On examining the bag, Twitchell discovered a big chunk of shell, and other war trophies. Discarding the dead weight, he sent the soldier to rejoin the regiment.[38]

In late afternoon, shell bursts from a Rebel battery halted the destruction. I Company broke for the rear, but unfortunately the men retreated in a bunch, making a tempting target for the butternut gunners, who quickly bracketed them with fire. Stearns dropped behind a stump, leaving it to the more vigorous and quick-thinking Twitchell to disperse the men. The shelling stopped because the enemy gunners could not afford to expend valuable powder and shot on lone Yankees. The work of demolition continued with Twitchell in command.[39]

After dark, the hospital detail found the regiment in an isolated woods preparing for a night march. Headquarters ordered Twitchell to form an eight-man night patrol and scout ahead. About a half-hour into the patrol, Twitchell saw the lights of a regimental bivouac through the trees: "Campfires were burning, cooks at work, camp guards in place," but the troops were absent. In the firelight, beneath the dark canopy of trees, gray and blue uniforms were virtually indistinguishable. Twitchell moved closer and coolly asked a sentry to identify his unit. "The 16th Georgia," replied the guard. The sergeant and his men casually moved away and reported back to headquarters. About ten o'clock the regiment moved out, avoiding the Georgians.[40]

As the rear guard withdrew that night from Savage's Station, mili-

38. *VCW*, 1: 293; *CV*, 39–40; Stephen B. Oates, *A Woman of Valor: Clara Barton and the Civil War* (New York, Toronto, 1994), 48.

39. *CV*, 40.

40. Ibid., 40–41.

tary order crumbled. Infantry columns, wagon trains, artillery, ambulances, horsemen, and stragglers snarled the road. Despite the confusion, the pace was brisk. Along the edges of the road, wounded men
hobbled on rifle crutches, trying to keep up. Groups of stragglers
dropped by the wayside and built fires, starkly illuminating the line of
march. Shortly after daybreak, Twitchell's regiment crossed White Oak
Bridge and climbed a low rise paralleling the southern edge of the
creek. The men moved into fields a few hundred yards east of the road
where, exhausted, they slumped to the ground and slept. Hundreds of
teamsters slept in their wagons on the rise above the bridge. When the
last men and wagons filed across, the Yanks burned the bridge.[41]

The next afternoon, thousands of men still lay sprawled asleep in the
fields near the burned bridge. Unbeknownst to them, General Stonewall Jackson, having observed the scene from across White Oak Run,
ordered his artillery batteries into the dense trees across the river.
Shortly before two o'clock, Jackson's thirty-one field pieces opened up,
and the sky fell on the sleeping Yankees. Wagons exploded and "rider-
less horses galloped madly to the rear," Dr. Stevens wrote. Officers
rushed about frantically, looking for men to command. A human head
tumbled through air twenty feet above the ground. On the crest of the
rise above the bridge stood a house where Baldy Smith had made his
headquarters. A cannon shot cut the elderly owner in half as he stood
in the doorway. Thousands of men bolted for safety. For the first time
in the war, blind panic gripped Twitchell. He raced for cover in the
nearby woods step for step with Captain Stearns. The sight of a man
cowering behind a stump, however, brought him up short. He turned
about and helped a lieutenant form a line of battle in the woods. The
shelling continued intermittently through the day. Twitchell led a patrol east along the swamp to see if the Confederates were crossing
White Oak Run on the Union flank. He found nothing.[42]

For the second night in a row, Twitchell's regiment marched from
midnight till dawn. The next morning, it joined the Vermont Brigade
in forming a line of battle on the far right of the Army of the Potomac.
The Green Mountain Boys did not fight but remained under arms all

41. Ibid., 41; *VCW*, 1: 303; Stevens, *Sixth Corps*, 103.

42. *OR*, 11, pt. 2: 476–77; *VCW*, 1: 304–7; Stevens, *Sixth Corps*, 104–5; Livermore,
Days and Events, 86–88; *CV*, 41–42; Sears, *Gates of Richmond*, 285–86.

afternoon while, a mile and half away, the Confederates dashed themselves against near impregnable Union defenses on Malvern Hill. For
the first time, the Union forces soundly trounced the Army of Northern
Virginia. Still, the withdrawal continued. Again, Twitchell's brigade
was under arms all night, covering the blue columns filing south toward
Harrison's Landing, General McClellan's new base on the James River.
The Vermonters waited until dawn to follow, when it started to rain.[43]

Though only seven miles, the "march from Malvern Hill to Harrison's Landing was," wrote G. G. Benedict, "the saddest and weariest
march of its length in the history of the brigade. The rain poured in
torrents; the wagons and artillery had poached the roads into canals of
mud; the stouter men could hardly drag one foot after another; and the
weaker fell out by hundreds, some to die of exhaustion, and others to
join the long caravan of stragglers." Along the way, "we lost our knapsacks and clothing and tents," one Green Mountain Boy wrote from
Harrison's Landing; and now "we have to sleep without any covering
at night, in a wet open field, and mud, mud, up to our knees. If we lie
down in it, we can hardly get up again." Twitchell was not even allowed
the luxury of lying in rain and mud; his company went on picket duty
within an hour of its arrival.[44]

Twitchell had survived what soon became known as the Seven Days'
Battles. Between 25 June and 1 July the contending armies fought on
seven successive days across a twenty-five-mile front. The seven days
broke the Army of the Potomac's grip on Richmond, doomed the Peninsula campaign, and prolonged the war. But to a sergeant in the ranks,
the epochal week of fighting was a dizzy blur of firefights, night
marches, cannonades, heat, rain, and mud. Years later, Twitchell would
reconstruct the sequence of events for his memoirs, but at the time he
remembered only the beginning and the end. In between, he said, "I
neither knew the day of the week or month, [or] hardly whether an incident occurred during the day or night."[45]

Captain Stearns, missing since the shelling at White Oak Bridge, rejoined the company at Harrison's Landing, claiming that he had been
ill. The verdict of Twitchell and most of the company, however, was

43. *VCW*, 1: 307–10.
44. Ibid., 310–11 n; *CV*, 42.
45. *CV*, 43.

"cannon fever." To Twitchell's relief, Stearns resigned his commission a few weeks later. With his departure, all of the company's original officers and sergeants were gone, in less than a year. Captain Daniel Lillie took over I Company.[46]

After six dreary weeks at Harrison's Landing, Twitchell's regiment headed back to Fort Monroe. President Lincoln had lost all faith in McClellan's Peninsula strategy and ordered the Army of the Potomac back to its base. Twitchell embarked at Hampton Roads on 22 August and two days later docked at Alexandria.[47]

The slow transit of the Army of the Potomac northward temporarily removed it from the military chessboard, and the Confederates seized the opportunity. The last of August, in a bloody two-day struggle, Lee decisively defeated a Union army under John Pope at the Battle of Second Bull Run. This victory, moreover, left Lee's army strategically placed to invade the North. On 4 September the southern commander pushed his columns across the Potomac into western Maryland. A decisive Confederate victory on Union soil increased the possibility of European intervention and foreign assistance to the South.

Thirty miles northwest of Washington, the parallel ridges of Catoctin Mountain and South Mountain bisect the Maryland panhandle. This mountain barrier screened the movements of Lee's army from the Federals. As the Army of the Potomac moved west in pursuit, the Vermont Brigade marched on the Union left flank. About noon on 14 September Twitchell's regiment entered the village of Burkittsville in the narrow valley between the two mountains. A mile up the road to the northwest, Rebel troops held Crampton's Gap, the southernmost pass across South Mountain. The Union forces outnumbered the butternut defenders, but rock fences, steep wooded slopes, ledges, and artillery made the enemy position formidable. Late in the afternoon, the Yanks attacked.[48]

As Twitchell started up the hill, a chunk of shell ricocheted off a fence and slammed into his calf, knocking him to the ground. His leg was "numb from the blow." Gingerly he put his finger into the hole the

46. Ibid., 43; Stearns Compiled Military Service Record; *Revised Roster of Vermont Volunteers.*

47. *VCW,* 1: 313.

48. Ibid., 219–31.

shell fragment had made in his new horsehide boot, fearing a broken leg, or worse. To his relief he found no blood. Nor were any bones broken. He credited the thick boot back with saving him from a serious injury.[49]

Three days later, shortly after sunrise, Twitchell marched in a long blue column heading west into the lush Potomac Valley. The din of heavy fighting arose from the little town of Sharpsburg, overlooking Antietam Creek six miles ahead. In midmorning, Twitchell's regiment took up a position near a stone bridge on the southern end of the Antietam battlefield. That afternoon, a deadly assault across the bridge would make it a Civil War landmark known ever after as the "Burnside Bridge" (after General Ambrose Burnside). The Vermont regiments, however, shortly pulled back and marched around to the right of the Federal line. Orders posted them behind a low crest where the battle lulled.[50]

In midafternoon, the Green Mountain Boys deployed for an attack on the north end of the battlefield. As Twitchell and his company waited for the signal, they beheld a field of strife that was to inspire a gallery of Civil War legends. Less than half a mile west was the road leading from Sharpsburg to Hagerstown. The road cut through one of the deadliest killing grounds of the entire war. On the left, heading toward Sharpsburg, was the Roulette farmstead, the Dunker Church, and the West Woods. In the center was the Corn Field and the East Woods. On the right, toward Hagerstown, was the North Woods. The carnage almost defied description. The Corn Field had witnessed waves of Union and Confederate attacks. Of the first Union attack at dawn, General Joseph Hooker wrote, "In the time I am writing every stalk of corn in the northern and greater part of the field was cut as closely as could have been done with a knife, and the slain lay in rows precisely as they had stood in their ranks a few minutes before." In the fields bordering the whitewashed Dunker Church, the Corn Field, and nearby woods, between sunrise and noon, a maelstrom of canister and lead had cut down 12,000 men.[51]

49. Ibid.; *CV*, 44–45.

50. *OR*, 19, pt. 1: 402–9; *VCW*, 1: 326–27; Stevens, *Sixth Corps*, 142–43.

51. *VCW*, 1: 328–29; *OR*, 19, pt. 1: 218; James M. McPherson, *Battle Cry of Freedom: The Civil War Era* (New York, 1988), 540–41; *CV*, 45–46.

The great battle of the morning was hours old, though. The vortex of the Antietam fighting had shifted from north to south. Only a few Confederate artillery pieces harassed the charging Vermonters that afternoon, and they easily captured ground earlier contested with ferocity. The entire Vermont Brigade suffered only twenty-five casualties on the bloodiest day, not only of the Civil War, but in all of American history.[52]

General McClellan failed to renew the battle the next day, and Lee's army slipped back across the Potomac into Virginia. Five days after Antietam, President Lincoln announced the preliminary Emancipation Proclamation. The war for the Union was now a battle for freedom. And although few realized it, the famous presidential decree was also the beginning of Reconstruction.

In the meantime, the Fourth Vermont camped at Hagerstown, Maryland, and in October, Twitchell became first sergeant of I Company. He had been a year in the army. Townshend, Leland, his father's farm—the world of his youth—must have seemed like another life. On the Peninsula, when he was a "strawfoot," or greenhorn, he had fretted, like young Henry Fleming in the *Red Badge of Courage*, over the decisions of the Union high command, fearing some general's blunder would get him killed. Such thoughts ceased to trouble his mind: "I had now reached the soldier stage of my existence and gave no trouble about what others did, confining myself strictly to carefully minding my own business." He was a cog in the machine.[53]

52. *VCW*, 1: 329; McPherson, *Battle Cry of Freedom*, 544.
53. *CV*, 44.

FOUR

FIRST SERGEANT

WHEN Rudyard Kipling described sergeants as the "backbone of the army," he expressed a military axiom of ancient lineage. A century before Kipling, Baron Friedrich von Steuben, General George Washington's Prussian inspector general, expressed the concept in practical terms. His *Regulations* (1779), or "Blue Book," was the first military training manual in American history. Officers must choose their sergeants (noncommissioned officers or NCOs) with utmost care, von Steuben wrote. An officer's career and the fate of his command hinged on whether he chose wisely or poorly. The sergeant major at regimental headquarters was the ranking NCO in an infantry regiment, but von Steuben devoted more attention to the company first sergeant.

The German modeled his American first sergeant after his Prussian army counterpart, the *Feldwebel*, "the mother of the company." Company discipline, "the conduct of the men, their exactness in obeying orders, and the regularity of their manners," he wrote, "will in great measure" be contingent on the top sergeant's capacity. The baron defined the first sergeant's role so definitively that it endured basically intact for the next century and a half.[1]

On 10 October 1862 Twitchell became I Company's first sergeant. Three inverted chevrons, a lozenge in the center, sewn above the elbow on each sleeve, signified the rank. With his clerk, under Captain Lillie's supervision, Sergeant Twitchell was I Company's principal record keeper. He kept the company books, logged orders, checked the roll, and accounted for every article of clothing and equipment issued by the army. After the style of British officialdom, many of the documents that crossed his desk were folded and tied with *red tape* (hence the origin of the term). Each day he prepared the morning report for the captain's signature and supervised the company's daily routine. He also groomed the company for weekly and monthly officers' inspections. He had direct authority over every enlisted man in the company, knew each man's name, background, and character. He was the company trouble-shooter. If another sergeant mercilessly bullied young replacements, it was Twitchell who reminded the erring NCO that his duty was to turn these boys into soldiers, not crush their spirits. In combat, the officers of the companies led the regiment's line of battle. Twitchell and the sergeants acted as file closers, preserving the order and cadence of the column. All in all, a good first sergeant needed to be hard working, literate, intelligent, brave, and a good judge of men, all for twenty dollars a month, seven dollars more than a private, twenty-five dollars less than a green second lieutenant.[2]

During a campaign, much of the routine of camp life was left behind. On a long march with battle impending, soldiers tended to leave regulations, along with excess clothing and accoutrements, dangling from scrubs and fence posts along the way. The conspicuous exception was roll call. Checking the roll "was inevitable as day and night," a sergeant named Ira Dodd recalled. "In storm or sunshine, in camp or on the march, before and after battle, the first thing in the morning and the last at night, we had to answer to our name." An efficient first ser-

---

1. Ernest F. Fisher Jr., *Guardians of the Republic: A History of the Noncommissioned Officer Corps of the U.S. Army* (New York, 1994), 31–37 (Kipling quote, 3); Joseph R. Riling, *Baron von Steuben and His Regulations* (Philadelphia, 1966), 129, 145–47; John R. Elting et al., *A Dictionary of Soldier Talk* (New York, 1984), 108–9, 323.

2. Riling, *Baron von Steuben*, 145–47; *Revised United States Army Regulations of 1861* (Washington, D.C., 1863), 525–26.

geant, like Twitchell, knew the names by heart and could go down the list in pitch blackness. As greenhorn recruits, the incessant roll calls had reminded Twitchell and other soldiers of their prewar schoolmasters, languidly intoning pupils' names before class. "But when exposure, toil, and battle began to thin the ranks," Sergeant Dodd wrote, "the roll-call gained a new meaning." It became a daily posting of important events, an intimate history of the company. It recorded the wounded and the dead, the sick and the dying; it told of men captured and men promoted and men who had fallen by the wayside on the march. "There were days when those of us who could answer to our names did so with a feeling of solemn thankfulness," Dodd continued. There were days, too, when a strange voice called the roll, because in the smoke and fury of battle, death stalked the sergeants.[3]

Regulations defined a first sergeant's duties, but not the spirit in which he carried them out. Among Civil War soldiers, writes James M. McPherson, two models of manhood contended: "the hard-drinking, gambling, whoring, two-fisted man among men, and the sober, responsible, dutiful son or husband." Twitchell clearly internalized the latter model, and it shaped his leadership. At Hagerstown, Maryland, just prior to his promotion, headquarters assigned him the task of training 109 replacements, the first to reach the regiment since it left Vermont. From the colonel down, officers and NCOs believed that coarse profanity was meat and drink to the men in the ranks. It was virtually an article of faith with them that soldiers would ignore orders unembellished with obscenities. "Never having been accustomed to profanity, I did not like to hear it," Twitchell recalled. "Many of our recruits were fine men, enlisting from the purest of patriotism, willing to suffer or fight, but resenting brutal and profane epithets." The young sergeant showed that men would obey orders without being abused with profanity. His solid performance earned him his first sergeant's chevrons. No doubt some officers and noncoms believed he was a bit of a prig, and perhaps he was. Nonetheless, his methods revealed a faith in the rationality and humanity of his men that much of the army assumed was nonexistent. His conduct also marked him as an inner-directed man willing to defy the conventional wisdom of his superiors and risk the ridicule of his peers.[4]

Twitchell's puritanical streak was relieved by a sense of humor. In-

3. Dodd, *Song of the Rappahannock,* 108–10.
4. McPherson, *For Cause and Comrades,* 26; *CV,* 48. See Wiley, *Billy Yank,* 247–49.

deed, his sense of humor helps explain how during the war and later he was able to command the loyalty and respect of men whose backgrounds and ideas were so different from his own. He took great delight, for example, in recounting the story of the soldier arrested for stealing a shell from the Lincoln gun and carrying it about in his vest pocket. The punch line was that the Lincoln shell weighed 484 pounds. At times, his humor took the form of practical jokes, which bordered on cruelty. While the Fourth was at Hagerstown, for example, a party of ladies—perhaps from the U.S. Sanitary Commission—inspected I Company's encampment. One of the company's older sergeants had gone into his tent, partially disrobed, and was picking the lice from his body. Lice, or "greybacks," were the constant companions of Civil War soldiers. Knowing the old sergeant's business, Twitchell directed the ladies to his tent, saying it was empty and a model of military order and cleanliness. The women marched down to the tent and opened the flap to enter. Their surprise and embarrassment—not to mention the old sergeant's—can be imagined.[5]

In November 1862 President Lincoln fired General McClellan and put General Ambrose Burnside in command of the Army of the Potomac. Like most of the army, Twitchell groused bitterly at "Little Mac's" dismissal. The men in the ranks knew little of Burnside or what to expect from him. For that matter, even senior officers had little notion of how he would perform as an army commander. "We had all known Burnside socially, long and intimately," Baldy Smith wrote, "but in his new position of grave responsibility he was to us entirely unknown."[6]

On 11 December the Army of the Potomac, 110,000-strong, crossed the Rappahannock and occupied Fredericksburg on the river's west bank. The Confederates held Marye's Heights just beyond the town. With artillery on the ridge and massed infantry below, shielded by a sunken road and a stone wall, the enemy position was nigh impregnable. Ignoring the odds, on the 13th Burnside hurled seven frontal assaults against the ridge, and seven times the veteran Johnny Rebs shot

5. *CV*, 33, 47.

6. *VCW*, I, 335; McPherson, *Battle Cry of Freedom*, 570; Robert Underwood Johnson and Clarence Clough Buel, eds., *Battles and Leaders of the Civil War* (1887–1888; reprint with new introduction by Roy F. Nichols, New York, 1956), 3: 133.

the charging Yanks to pieces. By dark, sacrificial heaps of Union dead littered the plain below Marye's Heights. The Vermont Brigade was posted on the Union left, a mile and a half below the town. Although the Green Mountain Boys remained out of the main action, they traded fire with the butternuts all afternoon. An hour or so before sundown, Twitchell's regiment moved up on the Second Division skirmish line. A bitter firefight developed in which the Fourth lost eleven men killed and forty-five wounded. Two nights later in another skirmish line, a sniper's bullet missed Twitchell by inches, cutting thirteen holes in the bedroll across his shoulder. In all, 13,000 Federal casualties at Fredericksburg gave the North its bleakest Christmas of the war.[7]

In mid-January 1863 the weather was fair and dry. Desperate to redeem himself, Burnside gambled on a midwinter campaign. He planned to march the army up the north bluff of the Rappahannock, cross the river above Fredericksburg, flank Lee's army, and force it back toward Richmond. On 20 January the Army of the Potomac loaded its gear and headed for Bank's Ford.

The storm clouds swept up in late afternoon. Near dark it began to rain, softly at first, then hard and cold, driven by the wind. It rained all night, and when morning came, the water fell in such torrents that the miserable bluecoats, their humor irrepressible, joked about Noah and the Biblical deluge. By midmorning, the roads were canals of mud. Mile upon mile of supply wagons, ammunition trains, artillery batteries, ambulances, and infantry inched forward in slow motion. The horses and mules floundered in belly-deep liquid earth, while the mud-caked feet of soldiers grew as big as shovels. Entire companies struggled to move a single wagon or field piece. Indescribable traffic snarls blocked crossroads. Still, Burnside pushed on. His miserable troops caught occasional glimpses of Rebel signs across the river: "Richmond this way."[8]

To Twitchell and the Vermonters fell the task of dragging the heavy pontoon boats down to the river at Bank's Ford for the army's crossing. It had been raining for twenty hours when they started and would rain for ten more. A hundred men dragged on the ropes of each pontoon. When their ordeal finally ended at dark, every inch of skin and particle of hair, every item of clothing down to their woolen underwear, was

7. *OR*, 21: 529–33; *VCW*, 1: 165; *CV*, 49–50.
8. Catton, *Glory Road*, 85–91; *VCW*, 1: 347–48.

soaked and stained with grime. Twitchell had been on the ropes as much as his men. "I do not think there was a man in the command," he recalled bitterly, "who did not fully understand that if there was any fighting done, it must be done by men who had not acted as mules the day before."[9]

The abortive three-day ordeal, bereft of battle, entered the annals of the Army of the Potomac as Burnside's "Mud March." It cost McClellan's successor whatever shred of credibility he had left. Within days, the Army of the Potomac had a new commander: Major General Joseph Hooker.[10]

Hooker moved quickly to restore morale. He fired crooked quartermasters, spruced up the camps, reorganized the medical service, supplied fresh meat and vegetables to the company messes, granted furloughs, and created corps and division insignia, which the men wore on their caps. Even the paymasters visited the camps on schedule. Twitchell most liked the improved diet. The brigade even built a bakery to supply the men with fresh bread. According to I Company's top sergeant, these improvements imparted "to every soldier the belief that the new general was looking out for his comfort."[11]

General Hooker's reforms allotted enlisted men two furloughs per company. Twitchell was one of those chosen from I Company. Jonathan Webster, his hut-mate, however, was a forty-year-old sergeant with a wife and two children. Entering his quarters, Twitchell found his friend crying softly, a letter from home in his hands. The first sergeant sought out Captain Lillie and gave up his leave to Webster. Twitchell never regretted his generous act. Webster was killed the following year.[12]

The army went into winter quarters on the north rise of the Rappahannock across from Fredericksburg. The Vermonters camped down river at White Oak Church. Knowing they would remain until spring, Twitchell and the men built "permanent" housing, crude log-canvas huts with indoor stoves. Life in this army shantytown was monumen-

9. *CV*, 50; *VCW*, 1, 347–48; Stevens, *Sixth Corps*, 176.

10. *CV*, 50; Peter M. Abbott to Friends at Home, 24 January 1863, Civil War Letters of Peter M. Abbott, VHS.

11. McPherson, *Battle Cry of Freedom*, 585; *CV*, 51; Peter M. Abbot to Friends at Home, 12 February 1863, Abbott Letters.

12. *OR*, 25, pt. 2: 11–12; Jonathan B. Webster, Compiled Military Service Record, RG 94, NA; Jonathan B. Webster Pension File, RG 15, NA; *CV*, 51.

tally boring. The men drilled, wrote letters, gambled, fixed up their huts, and foraged for firewood. After dark, guitar and accordion music drifted wistfully through the camps. On warm days the boys "assembled in the company streets," wrote Dr. Stevens, "and danced cotillions, and polkas, and jigs, to the music of violins"; they also played baseball. It snowed a lot, and the boys relished snowball fights. In late February the Twenty-sixth New Jersey, attached to the Vermont Brigade that winter, challenged the Third and Fourth Vermont regiments to a snowball fight. The New Jersey boys were fresh from home, and their full-strength regiment equaled the size of the two Vermont units worn down by hardship. A boisterous crowd gathered to watch the match and bet on the outcome. The regiments formed as if for battle, with skirmishers out front and officers mounted. The combatants surged forward, filling the air with snowballs, the crowd cheering lustily. At length, the Vermont boys claimed victory, capturing their opponents' headquarters. The big snowball fight became a minor legend that many soldiers remembered as vividly as a real battle.[13]

Soldier authors such as Twitchell also remembered the cruel practical joke played on Colonel A. J. Morrison, commander of the Twenty-sixth New Jersey, and some of his men. Being new to the front, the New Jersey boys had little experience foraging for food. The Vermont veterans showed the newcomers how to forage; explaining that what was stealing in civilian life was merely foraging in the army. The Jerseymen learned the lesson too well and were soon stealing from the Vermonters. To get back at them, soldiers in the Second Vermont captured Colonel Morrison's large Newfoundland dog, butchered the unfortunate beast, and hung it up in the Second Vermont quartermaster tent, where it resembled nothing so much as dressed mutton. Falling into the trap, the Jerseymen stole the carcass and served up the dog meat in their messes the next day. Word of the trick spread through the brigade, to the discomfiture of the New Jersey soldiers, who for weeks endured howling choruses of Vermonters barking like dogs wherever they went.[14]

Spring came and with it the hope that General Hooker would live up to his nickname "Fighting Joe," which he had earned as a division

---

13. Stevens, *Sixth Corps*, 183; *VCW*, 1: 353–54.
14. *VCW*, 1: 332 n; *CV*, 52.

and corps commander in the Peninsula, Antietam, and Fredericksburg campaigns. Alas, Hooker proved an even bigger fool than Burnside. At the battle of Chancellorsville in early May 1863, Fighting Joe self-destructed. His army numbered 115,000 to Lee's 60,000, but it was Lee who dictated the course of the battle and inflicted one of the worst defeats of the war on Union forces.

Twitchell and the Green Mountain Boys called the fight Second Fredericksburg. Hooker's order of battle sent the Vermont Brigade, part of the Sixth Corps, into Fredericksburg while the main Union forces circled west into a dense forest known as the Wilderness. On 3 May Twitchell's regiment helped storm Marye's Heights, much less strongly defended than the previous December when thousands of Billy Yanks had dashed themselves against the now famous stone wall. The capture of Marye's Heights threw the Confederates momentarily on the defensive. Twitchell's brigade now headed down the Orange Plank Road toward the Wilderness and the relief of Hooker's main body. Midway between Fredericksburg and Chancellorsville, the Confederates slammed the door on the Federal advance at Salem Church. Twitchell camped that night by a stream about a mile and a half west of Fredericksburg. The next morning while he was washing his face, a cannon shot plowed into the creek, showering him with muddy water. He and the other men gathered around the stream gaped at one another in astonishment. The shot came from the rear, in the direction of Fredericksburg. The Confederates had recaptured Marye's Heights in the night. The Vermont Brigade and the entire Sixth Corps were threatened with encirclement.

In the long day that followed, Twitchell fought in a series of confusing firefights in which, at times, the Johnny Rebs seemed to be shooting at him from "all points of the compass." Late in the afternoon he experienced a miraculous escape from harm while in charge of I Company's right wing. Deployed as skirmishers, he and his men warily approached the Confederate line, clearly visible over the crest of a hill. From the trailing Federal infantry, a messenger abruptly appeared with an urgent—and seemingly suicidal—command to advance on the enemy line. Twitchell looked off to his left where his company commander, Captain Lillie, led the rest of the company skirmishers. The captain seemed to be waiting for his top sergeant to advance. Twitchell reluctantly gave the command and his men dashed over the hilltop. Amazingly, the volley of butternut rifle fire that washed over them seemed "to pass all around," without hitting a man. A moment later Twitchell spied another messenger hurrying toward him, crying out "Left Flank! Left Flank!" The first messenger had become rattled and gotten the command reversed: they were ordered to fall back, not advance. Twitchell and his men slipped off the hilltop before the enemy could reload. After dark, I Company somehow became cut off behind the Rebel line. Captain Lillie and his top sergeant conferred. Because the butternut troops were facing away from them, Twitchell counseled an attack, which he believed, coming from the rear and in the dark, would produce a stampede. Lillie rejected the advice. Instead, I Company skirted the Confederate position and eventually made its way back to the regiment, which was guarding the high ground near Bank's Ford. Through the long night, the Vermont Brigade acted as the rear guard while the Sixth Corps retreated to the north shore of the Rappahannock. Early the next morning in heavy fog, Twitchell's regiment withdrew across the river.[15]

As he had done the year before after defeating Pope, Lee used his victory over Hooker as a springboard for invasion of the North. In late June, President Lincoln replaced Hooker with General George Meade. The day Meade took command, lead elements of the Army of Northern Virginia marched into Chambersburg, Pennsylvania. Panic gripped Washington. At Harrisburg, Pennsylvania, frightened officials and citizens loaded government records, antiques, paintings, and other valuables onto railroad cars for a quick getaway. Lee was in strange country, however, and almost by accident the Union and Confederate armies converged on the small Pennsylvania town of Gettysburg.[16]

These were tough times for the Green Mountain Boys. Long marches and frequent skirmishes had worn them down. After a particularly hard march in mid-June, only twelve men had answered Twitchell's roll call. "I was one of the two or three who were able to build a fire and make a little coffee for the rest." With amusement, he recalled his parents' prediction, two years before, that he was too "weakly and puny" to last long in the army.[17]

15. *VCW*, 1: 165–66, 361–74; *CV*, 54–56; Stephen Sears, *Chancellorsville* (Boston, 1996), 348–57, 376–89.

16. James M. McPherson, ed., *The Atlas of the Civil War* (New York, 1994), 116–17.

17. *CV*, 58–59.

When the Gettysburg battle opened on 1 July, the Sixth Corps was at Manchester, Maryland, over thirty miles away. In the previous four days, its soldiers had covered more than a hundred miles. In the late afternoon the men lay about in the shade resting or sleeping. During their northward trek, rumors had swirled about the column like leaves in the wind: Grant's army had been destroyed at Vicksburg; the Union Army of the Cumberland was about to meet the same fate; Lee was going to "gobble us up," one soldier said, and put "Jeff. Davis firmly on his thrown, so that no power on earth can disturb him."[18]

At dusk, bugles sounded and the men fell into formation. Up and down the line, the first sergeants could be heard singing out the rolls. Not until 10 P.M. did the column lurch forward. Each man carried a rifle and bayonet, knapsack, haversack with five days' rations, cartridge box with forty rounds, and canteen—more than forty pounds of equipment. The pace was slow, with wagons, ambulances, artillery, pack mules, and infantry clogging the road. They covered only about five miles that night. "Marching by rods is like dying by inches," one soldier complained.[19]

About dawn, the corps escaped Manchester's heavy traffic, and the Baltimore Pike to Gettysburg stretched ahead. Sedgewick ordered the Green Mountain Boys to the head of the column, and the Sixth Corps began to eat up the miles. It was a scorching hot day; men dropped by the wayside, some bone-weary, others suffering from sunstroke; but the dreaded words "cannon fever" kept most soldiers plodding forward. Farmers and their wives and daughters stood by the roadside, filling the men's canteens with water, praying for victory. Ambulances and carriages loaded with wounded men met the soldiers on the road, and hundreds of men with blood-stained clothes and bandages hobbled past, their eyes bright with fear. They kept glancing back up the road toward Gettysburg, as if expecting gray-clad demons to come thundering in pursuit. Some shouted dire warnings: "You fellows will catch it; the whole army is smashed to pieces."[20]

As Twitchell neared the battlefield, clouds of white smoke hung in

18. *CV*, 59–60; *VCW*, 1: 384–85; Stevens, *Sixth Corps*, 235–39; Rosenblatt, *Anti-Rebel*, 110–11.

19. *CV*, 60; Stevens, *Sixth Corps*, 239–40; *VCW*, 1: 385; Rosenblatt, *Anti-Rebel*, 114.

20. The command to "Put the Vermonters ahead" is among the most famous utterances in Vermont history. *VCW*, 1: 385–86 n; *CV*, 60.

the sky and the roar of battle echoed like thunder in the hills. About six o'clock, from General Meade's headquarters on the Taneytown Road, a reporter with mounting alarm watched the dust cloud kicked up by the advancing Sixth Corps. "Jeb" Stuart's cavalry had been missing for days. "Had Stuart suddenly gained our rear?" the reporter asked. Tense-faced junior officers trained their field glasses on the dusty column, which was closing fast. "It is not cavalry, but infantry," an officer cried at length. "There is the flag, it is the sixth corps!"[21]

After dark on the second day of battle, Twitchell's brigade camped east of Big Round Top on the extreme left of the army. The Green Mountain Boys had marched for over twenty straight hours, with only five- or ten-minute breaks each hour. They had covered thirty-five miles and led the Sixth Corps in its longest sustained march of the war, a feat that in time became enshrined in legend. Ironically, Twitchell's unit missed the epic fighting. The main enemy attacks on the Union left and right were over. Pickett's charge against the Union center on the third day completely bypassed their position. "All day we lay in line of battle," Twitchell recalled, "amusing ourselves as best we could while the battle was raging to our right."[22]

The scale of Gettysburg losses, both blue and gray, shocked even hardened veterans. Advancing into the abandoned Confederate lines, Twitchell saw dead men and horses and shallow graves littering the landscape. Barns, houses, and tents overflowed with the wounded. So vast was the suffering that it was hard for him to imagine at first that any part of the Rebel army had gotten away. Another Vermont veteran filed through a passage of craggy rocks and giant boulders into a macabre forest inhabited by corpses. Northern and southern dead "lay thickly together, their thirst for blood forever quenched. Their bodies were swollen, black, and hideously unnatural. Their eyes glared from their sockets, their tongues protruded from their mouths, and in almost every case, clots of blood and mangled flesh showed how they had died."[23]

21. VCW, 1: 387; Harry W. Pfanz, Gettysburg: The Second Day (Chapel Hill, 1987), 80–81.

22. Stevens, Sixth Corps, 240–41; OR, 27, pt.1: 675–76, 678; CV, 61; VCW, 1: 387–88; Edwin B. Coddington, The Gettysburg Campaign: A Study in Command (New York, 1968), 456.

23. CV, 62; Rosenblatt, Anti-Rebel, 115–16.

In the eastern theater, Gettysburg was the first decisive Union victory of the war. Fully 30 percent of Lee's army was killed, wounded, or captured in the three-day struggle. Unfortunately, General Meade, the new Federal commander, was as cautious as McClellan and fumbled the opportunity of hammering the reeling Confederates. The Army of Northern Virginia escaped across the Potomac to fight again on other fields. Thus, despite the great victory—and the fall of Vicksburg in the west—the war ground on.

As the last months of 1863 slipped away, a profound predicament troubled the Union government. Two years before, Twitchell and the Boys of '61 had volunteered for three years service, none of them dreaming that the war might outlast their enlistments. Be that as it may, the war was now two years old with no end in sight. Next summer, their enlistments would begin to run out. If Lincoln's veterans then shed their uniforms and went home, the war would be over and the Confederacy victorious. Southern soldiers had also enlisted for three years. Jefferson Davis's government, with no margin for error, solved the problem by forcing reenlistment. The U.S. Congress, on the other hand, treated the three-year enlistments as solemn contracts. Washington thus gambled that Twitchell and his peers would reenlist, "for three years or the war," of their own free will.[24]

For reenlisting, the War Department offered soldiers with two years' experience four hundred-dollar bounties, thirty-day furloughs, and special braided red and blue chevrons as emblems of service. Shrewdly, the army allowed regiments or companies in which three-fourths of the veterans reenlisted to retain their original organization and go home on furlough together. Although leniently interpreted, this feature of the plan subjected holdouts to intense peer pressure. Over a thousand veterans in the Vermont Brigade reenlisted. In all the Union forces, reenlistments totaled about 136,000. Roughly 100,000 refused.[25]

In Twitchell's regiment, 210 men signed up to finish the war. His own name topped I Company's 33-man reenlistment roll. Near Christmas, he escorted the company's contingent back to Vermont. He and I

24. McPherson, *Battle Cry of Freedom*, 719–20; *OR*, ser. 3, 3: 785.

25. *OR*, ser. 3, 3: 414–16, 785; Special Order No. 329, 21 December 1863, Third Vermont Regimental Papers, Box 4763, NA; *VCW*, 1: 410; McPherson, *Battle Cry of Freedom*, 719–20.

Company were a tiny part of the blue migration that rode the rails to every part of the Old Union. This veteran cohort to which Twitchell belonged scarcely realized the gravity of the hour. They had survived pestilence, bullets, bad food, mud marches, and incompetent generals—and still they refused to quit. In the words of one Vermont veteran: "The staunch patriots, who love their country and are willing to fight for it, are here yet, and will remain here till the regiment is sent home." They were the best, the irreplaceable best of northern manpower. The draftees and bounty-men who came after them were a lesser breed. The veteran volunteers, by contrast, had earned their braided red and blue chevrons and wore them proudly. In the terrible fighting ahead, this veteran legion was the glue that held the Union army together. In this most perilous moment of the nation's history, these farmboys, clerks, teamsters, teachers, and mechanics were the sword-edge of victory. They could not have prevailed without General Grant and President Lincoln, but neither could the general and the rail-splitter have triumphed without them.[26]

26. *CV*, 69; Muster and reenlistment roll, 15 December 1863, Fourth Vermont Regimental Papers, Box 4739; Wiley, *Billy Yank*, 342–44; Rosenblatt, *Anti-Rebel*, 59; Reid Mitchell, "The Perseverance of the Soldiers," in *Why the Confederacy Lost*, ed. Gabor S. Boritt (New York, 1992), 109–32.

FIVE

VALLEY OF THE SHADOW

IN January 1864, when he returned from his veteran's furlough, Twitchell learned to his dismay that he had been passed over for promotion to lieutenant. The particulars are unknown. Possibly his superiors in the Fourth simply believed another sergeant was better qualified. Most likely, though, the explanation for Twitchell's failure to win promotion lies in his relationship with his company commander, Daniel Lillie.[1]

Reading between the lines, there had been friction between the two men at Chancellorsville. At Gettysburg their strained relations produced an ugly incident. The day after Pickett's charge, the Fourth Vermont moved west of Big Round Top. On the skirmish line, with rain cascading from the sky, I Company probed the woods ahead. As at Chancellorsville, Captain Lillie commanded the company left and Twitchell the company right. A mile or so west of the Round Top, both

---

1. Captain Lillie had acquired the nickname "Tiger Lillie." William Monroe Newton, *History of Barnard, Vermont, with Family Genealogies, 1761–1927* (Vermont Historical Society, 1928), 1:105. While the unusual moniker most likely signified admiration, it could also have been used in a mocking spirit.

wings of the company came under heavy fire from the Confederate rear guard. Lillie ordered a withdrawal.[2]

The captain expected Twitchell's men to fall back, scurrying from right to left diagonally through the trees, joining his own men as they retreated. From the sergeant's vantage point, however, to do as Lillie wanted would mean leaving heavy forest cover and exposing his men to enemy fire in thinned-out woods. To avoid that, Twitchell led his men back by a longer but safer path, using the heavy forest as a shield. Crouching down in the rain, watching Twitchell's men hug the dense trees, the frustrated captain shouted out, "What is that fool doing with his company?"[3]

Twitchell, who heard the remark, was furious: "In all my army service, I had never before been called or spoken of as either a coward or a fool." Back in camp he headed for the Captain's tent. Lillie, he recalled, "met me, pulled me into the tent, and talked so fast that I had no opportunity to say a word." The captain apologized and pleaded with Twitchell to overlook the incident, because making an issue of it would only hurt company morale. Twitchell let the matter drop.[4]

If the incident raises doubts about Twitchell's competence, it raises equally troubling questions about Lillie's. Possibly Twitchell misjudged the situation or misconstrued his orders. Whether he was right or wrong, Lillie committed a major breach of military etiquette—not to say common sense—by ridiculing his first sergeant in front of the entire company. First sergeants, moreover, served at the pleasure of their company commanders. If Lillie was truly dissatisfied with Twitchell, he could have, and should have, replaced him.

Here follows a speculative explanation of the troubled relationship. To begin with, some degree of tension between a company commander and a first sergeant, the company matriarch, is almost inevitable, the more so if they do not see eye to eye. As in the case of his first company commander Leonard Stearns (with whom he had also had trouble), Twitchell's quick mind and self-assurance made him an intimidating

2. *CV*, 61, 69; *OR*, 27, pt. 1: 678; *VCW*, 1: 388; G. G. Benedict, *Vermont at Gettysburg* (Burlington, 1867), 20.

3. *CV*, 61; *VCW*, 1: 388–89.

4. *CV*, 61.

and, at times, irritating subordinate. On the one hand, Lillie, a farmer's son, probably yearned to be rid of him. On the other hand, a top-notch, veteran first sergeant was hard to replace. Twitchell, moreover, was liked and respected by the men, all of whom came from the same small corner of Vermont. Lillie resented his first sergeant too much to recommend him for promotion, but could not dismiss him without playing havoc with the company. The spike of the captain's resentment was probably sharpened by the knowledge that he needed Twitchell to run the company.

Twitchell was deeply aggrieved. He wanted out of I Company, even if it meant leaving the Fourth Vermont. The fruits of the Emancipation Proclamation, now a year old, offered him an exit. Lincoln's famous edict had authorized the recruitment of black soldiers "into the armed services of the United States." In the year that followed, over one hundred thousand runaway slaves and free blacks had joined the United States Colored Troops (USCT), and every month saw the formation of new black units. The government paid its black soldiers less than it paid white soldiers and insisted that white officers command the black units. The disparity in pay—which lasted until mid-1864—was egregious. A private in a white regiment earned thirteen dollars a month whereas a private in a black unit earned only seven dollars. Seven dollars, in fact, was the maximum monthly pay that any black soldier could earn. In the USCT, sergeants, even sergeant majors, received the same pay as privates.[5]

Still, there was method in the racism. The Emancipation Proclamation was the most controversial act of Lincoln's presidency, and his party suffered electoral setbacks as a consequence. The political reverses would doubtless have been worse had not the president shrewdly justified his action on the grounds of *military necessity*. Lower pay and white officers were part of the same expedient equation.

In late March 1864, Twitchell applied for a commission in the USCT. Lieutenant Colonel George P. Foster, the third and last com-

---

5. *A Compilation of the Messages and Papers of the Presidents, 1789–1897*, comp. James D. Richardson, (Washington, D.C., 1896–1899), 6: 157–59; McPherson, *Battle Cry of Freedom*, 563–64; Dudley Taylor Cornish, *The Sable Arm: Negro Troops in the Union Army, 1861–1865*, 2d ed. (New York, 1966), 192.

mander of the Fourth Vermont, supported his request. A few days later the War Department ordered him to Washington for examination.[6]

Five months after the Emancipation Proclamation, in May 1863, the War Department had created the Bureau of Colored Troops to supervise the recruitment of black soldiers and the white officers who would lead them. Officers' examination centers were set up in Washington, New Orleans, Saint Louis, and three other cities. Major General Silas Casey, the author of the Union army's standard work on infantry tactics as well as *Infantry Tactics for Colored Troops*, presided over the Washington board.[7]

In mid-April Twitchell appeared before the Casey board. His oral exam probably lasted an hour or so. The exact questions put to him are unknown, but the general criteria by which candidates were evaluated is reasonably clear. The army wanted quick-witted men of good moral character. The board looked for leadership ability and signs that the applicant was interested in the advancement of African Americans. Board members asked specific questions about military tactics, regulations, and organization. They inquired into a candidate's general level of education, his math skills, for example, and his knowledge of history and geography. Thus, a candidate might be asked about the Bible, Shakespeare, and famous men of antiquity. Several candidates recalled being asked: "What is the largest city in the United States?" Although rooted in a discriminatory policy, the Bureau of Colored Troops's screening generally produced good officers. Only one in four applicants earned a commission. Compared with the average run of volunteer officers, General Casey wrote after the war, "I have no hesitation in saying that . the officers of the colored troops, *who passed the board*, as a body were superior . . . physically, mentally and morally."[8]

Twitchell obviously performed well because the Casey board passed him and recommended him for the rank of captain first class, giving him priority on the promotion list. Still, it took time for army bureau-

6. USCT Register of Applications, 1863–1865, RG 94, entries 369, 370, and 382, NA; MHT Compiled Military Service Record, RG 94, NA.

7. Cornish, *Sable Arm*, 130–31, 209; Joseph T. Glatthaar, *Forged in Battle: The Civil War Alliance of Black Soldiers and White Officers* (New York, 1990), 41–59.

8. USCT Register of Applications, 1863–1865, entry 382; Glatthaar, *Forged in Battle*, 44–59; Cornish, *Sable Arm*, 208–12.

cracy to find assignments for the successful candidates. It was not until mid-June 1864, that the adjutant general of the army in Nashville, Tennessee, cut orders assigning Twitchell to Louisville, Kentucky, where the 109th Regiment USCT was being organized. In the meantime, Twitchell had returned to Brandy Station and resumed his duties as I Company's top sergeant. By the time his orders posting him to Kentucky caught up with him, the war and his own life would have dramatically changed complexion.[9]

The same month Twitchell applied to the USCT, the new general in chief of the Union armies, Lieutenant General Ulysses S. Grant, arrived in Virginia. Twitchell was initially unimpressed with the new commander. He described Grant "sitting upon his horse carelessly, cigar in his mouth, coat unbuttoned, hat pulled over his eyes," giving "more of the appearance of a cavalryman just in from a raid than the General of the Armies." The small man with the cigar, however, had captured Fort Henry and Fort Donelson, defeated the Rebels at Shiloh, and captured Vicksburg and Chattanooga. His presence in Virginia augured hard fighting. Just how hard, Twitchell and the Green Mountain Boys could scarcely have imagined.[10]

On 4 May Twitchell's brigade crossed the Rapidan River with the Army of the Potomac into the Wilderness, an expanse of dense, second-growth forest west of Fredericksburg. The air was still and muggy, and the land undulated with gentle rises and swales. Patches of oak, pine, ash, and walnut—choked with underbrush—alternated with impenetrable thickets, swamps, and knife-sharp grass. In places, skeletons, ghastly remnants of Hooker's ill-fated campaign, littered the forest floor. The roads were narrow. The overhanging trees blotted out the sun. Veterans eyed the terrain warily. If a fight started, the forest would burn out of control, as it had done the year before at Chancellorsville.[11]

The first firefights broke out about breakfast time the next morning. The discordant clatter of musketry swelled and rolled through the woods and thickets, at times seeming to come from all directions. In

9. USCT Register of Applications, 1863–1865, entry 382.
10. *CV*, 71.
11. Hazard Stevens, "The Sixth Corps in the Wilderness," *Papers of the Military Historical Society of Massachusetts* (Boston, 1887), 4: 187–88; Gordon C. Rhea, *The Battle of the Wilderness: May 5–6, 1864* (Baton Rouge, 1994), 51–52.

this verdant jungle were two critical crossroads. The first, near Wilderness Tavern, the Federals occupied the afternoon of the 4th; the other, two miles south of Wilderness Tavern, was where the Orange Plank Road intersected Brock Road. Both Union and Confederate commanders initially overlooked this second road juncture. Late on the morning of the 5th, however, its critical significance dawned on both sides: if the Confederates captured it, the huge Army of the Potomac would be cut in half.[12]

When the race for the crossroads began, the Vermont Brigade was at Wilderness Tavern, part of General George W. Getty's lead division of the Sixth Corps. Shortly before noon, an officer rode up with an urgent dispatch for Getty. Within minutes Twitchell and I Company moved out on the double-quick. The men knew something big was up, because, as Twitchell remarked, even the ammunition wagons, the "monarchs of the road," pulled over to let them pass. With Getty in the lead, the Federals seized the crossroads just as butternut skirmishers came into view down the road. The Vermonters took up positions to the left of the Orange Plank Road in a double line of battle. Twitchell and I Company were up front. Getty deployed his other two brigades astride and north of the road. A short distance down the Orange Plank Road, completely concealed by the forest, two enemy divisions waited. For the next two or three hours, except for skirmishers throwing lead, the crossroads was quiet.[13]

About three o'clock, perhaps a little later, the Federals advanced. "The ground was covered with brush and small timber," the Vermont Brigade commander Lewis A. Grant wrote in his report, "so dense that it was impossible for an officer at any point of the line to see any other point several yards distant." About three hundred yards into this tangled growth, a tree-lined swell, its base camouflaged by brush, rose perpendicular to the road. Behind it massed Confederate infantry waited in ambush. The skirmishers from the Fifth Vermont had not heard the order to advance; thus Twitchell's regiment plunged blind into what one soldier aptly described as "a wilderness of woe." I Company's first

12. *VCW*, 1: 420–21.
13. Stevens, "Sixth Corps in the Wilderness," 189–90; *VCW*, 1: 422–23; *OR*, 36, pt. 1: 676–77, 696–97.

sergeant and the men on either side of him were about seventy-five yards from the tree line when the enemy musketry exploded in their faces. They reeled back, gaping holes torn in their ranks.[14]

Recovering from the initial shock, Captain Lillie ordered his men to charge the tree line. A bullet ball knocked him down on the spot. Within seconds, every officer in sight was down. Twitchell repeated the order to charge. The company's forward surge was the last thing he remembered of the Battle of the Wilderness. A second later, a minie ball ripped the outer corner of his left eye, cut a groove along the left side of his skull, and exited behind the ear.[15]

As he lay unconscious, the fight spread across the road, engaging Getty's entire division. It raged all afternoon. The Vermonters loaded and fired, loaded and fired, huddling the ground. "The men's faces," G. G. Benedict wrote, "grew powder-grimed, and their mouths black from biting cartridges. The musketry silenced all other sounds; and the air in the woods was hot and heavy with sulphurous vapor. The tops of the bushes were cut away by the leaden showers which swept through them; and when the smoke lifted occasional glimpses could be got of gray forms crouching under the battle-cloud which hung low upon the slope in front." It was a long, long afternoon.[16]

As the day faded, the Vermonters fell back to the Brock Road near the intersection, dragging most of their wounded. In the brigade, four regimental commanders and fifty line officers had been killed or wounded. In Twitchell's entire regiment only three line officers escaped injury. In most companies, new voices called the roll that sanguinary night. Nearly a thousand men present at reveille that morning were gone. In I Company only twenty-one of fifty-three men answered the roll. Captain Lillie never recovered from his wound. In the Fifth Regiment, Captain David Davenport, whose son had pulled him from the bloody water of Warwick Creek, was dead. The battle around the crossroads resumed the next day on a massive scale. As on the previous day, the Vermonters bore the brunt of the fighting, and nearly two hundred

14. *OR*, 36, pt. 1: 696–98, 710–11; *VCW*, 1: 422–24; Carol Reardon, "The Other Grant: Lewis A. Grant and the Vermont Brigade in the Battle of the Wilderness," in *The Wilderness Campaign*, ed. Gary Gallagher (Chapel Hill, N.C., 1997), 205–12; Rosenblatt, *Anti-Rebel*, 215, *CV*, 73.

15. *CV*, 73–74; MHT Pension Records, RG 15, NA.

16. *OR*, 36, pt. 1: 697–98; *VCW*, 1: 424–25.

more of their number went down. Sergeant Webster, to whom Twitchell had given up his furlough the year before, was killed. In the two-day Battle of the Wilderness, the Vermont Brigade suffered the heaviest casualties in the Army of the Potomac. But when night fell on 6 June, the Union still held the crossing of the Orange Plank and Brock Roads.[17]

It was dark by the time Twitchell's comrades lugged him to a field hospital. His head was covered with matted blood and swelling badly. Looking at the ghastly wound, the surgeon told the men who carried him in that their sergeant was as good as dead. Only the pleas of a boyhood schoolmate persuaded the doctor to bandage the wound.[18]

When Twitchell regained consciousness the next morning, he was lying on the ground between two corpses. Some of the men from his company, less badly wounded, had put up a crude shelter to shield him from the sun. The attendants removed his blood-caked coat, washed it, and put it back on him. Later in the day they carried him into a tent with other wounded from his outfit. No one mentioned his condition. His head was grotesquely swollen. He read death in the eyes of all who looked at him.

He slipped back into unconsciousness. When he roused the next afternoon, the blue and gray armies were shifting southeast to Spotsylvania Courthouse, destined to be another bloody Civil War milestone. Traffic on the road outside was heavy. At twilight he asked an orderly when he could expect an ambulance to take him to Fredericksburg. He was shocked by the blunt reply; the last ambulance was gone and none would be returning: "There are no ambulances for dead men." Twitchell rebelled at the thought. The other mangled forms in this tent might be goners, he concluded, but he was still alive. After repeated efforts, he made it to his feet: "My face was so badly swollen that one eye was entirely closed and the other had to be pulled open with my fingers in order to see at all. Keeping my feet well apart and taking short steps, I moved out to the road, found the direction to Fredericksburg, and started." Exhaustion soon overtook him. He left the road and fell asleep between two saplings.

17. *OR*, 36, pt. 1: 695–706; *VCW*, 1: 424–36; *CV*, 74; Rhea, *Battle of the Wilderness*, 310–12, 436.

18. This paragraph and those that follow recounting Twitchell's hospital experiences and recovery are based on *CV*, 74–79.

The next morning, as consciousness seeped back into his body, he heard two men talking over him. "He's Vermont Brigade," said one, pointing to the unit badge on his uniform. "Put him into the ambulance." The lieutenant who gave the order was in charge of the First Vermont Cavalry's ambulance train. Had Twitchell been a New York or Ohio soldier, the officer probably would have left him where he lay. That night Twitchell's wound started to bleed. He called out, but no one heard his feeble voice. Had the blood not seeped through the ambulance floor, dripping onto the driver underneath and awakening him, Twitchell might have bled to death. The next day when Twitchell woke up, he was being carried into a Fredericksburg church, now converted into a Union hospital. The wounded lay in rows upon the floor, and Twitchell lay with them.

The hospital attendants were notably lacking in compassion. Some hours later Twitchell heard his name called and raised his hand. An orderly bearing a cup of beef broth walked up to him and knelt on one knee. "Here, damn you," the attendant swore, lifting Twitchell's head roughly, "drink this." Twitchell drank part of the broth and asked if the man lying next to him could have some. The attendant snapped, "Drink or I will pour it down you."

Drifting in and out of consciousness, Twitchell lost track of time. At some point, a doctor's voice called out that the wagon for Aquia Creek was leaving. The hospital ships from Washington docked at Aquia Creek. If he could get there, he had a better chance to live. A big man with a bad leg helped Twitchell to his feet; another soldier helped him make his way along the wall to the door. At the church door, an assistant surgeon looked at his infantry uniform and announced that the wagon was for cavalry only. Twitchell stepped back, took off his coat, waited a few moments and tried again. And again he was challenged. A trooper already in the wagon spoke up for him: "He belongs to my company." The surgeon waved him aboard. As the wagon bumped down a corduroy road—excruciatingly painful for injured men—Twitchell thrust the change from his pocket into the hands of a black woman in exchange for a pillow.

Handed a cup of coffee as he stepped down from the wagon at Aquia Creek the next morning, Twitchell drank gratefully. Never had coffee tasted so good or so warmed his body. Except for the coffee and a few swallows of beef broth, he had not eaten in four days. He staggered visibly as he approached the gangplank of the loaded transport. Just as he reached the entrance, the guard blocked the passageway with his rifle, announcing the boat was full. Coincidentally, at that moment an official of the Christian Commission and the son of a Vermont governor was leaving the boat. Without a word, he lifted the guard's rifle, allowing Twitchell to mount the gangplank. Lying down on the deck, within minutes he was asleep.

He awoke on clean sheets, in Armory Square Hospital in Washington, surrounded by dozens of sick and wounded men. But in the center of the room, seated at a desk, there appeared to be an attractive woman. Because he had been shot in the head, he was terrified of losing his mind. Frontline soldiers rarely saw a "lady." His first thought was that he was mad. Meeting his gaze, the nurse walked over and gently asked him how he was feeling. "Hours passed away before I fully realized I was in one of Uncle Sam's hospitals in my right mind," he said. The nurse in charge, he later pronounced, was "one of those grand representatives of her sex who had left the ease and luxuries of her Northern home to nurse back to life and strength the defenders of her country."

Armory Square Hospital aided Twitchell's convalescence. All the same, like most soldiers, as soon as he was up and about, he wanted to go home. He suspected, probably correctly, that complete recovery was more likely in the Vermont hills than in the steamy heat of a Washington summer. After a week or two he finagled his release and caught a northbound train, reaching Townshend by early June. His family and friends were relieved to see him, but a little puzzled. He had written his folks from the hospital that he was well. The same day this letter arrived, however, a neighbor showed them a letter from Virginia claiming that Twitchell had been killed at the Wilderness. Word of his demise spread far. In a Winhall shop one day, an old friend turned to look at him. The man dropped his tools, his face white. "My God," he burst out, "ain't you dead?"

His recovery was slow. His left eye had been injured. The first few weeks at home he lay in a darkened room. The bullet had also impaired his hearing. Periodically, Dr. Charles Clark, the family physician, removed bone splinters from his face, a dangerous procedure because of the risk of infection. Over the summer Dr. Clark wrote four notarized letters delaying Twitchell's return to duty. The last, dated 17 August, argued that his patient was in danger of being deaf in the left ear. Twitchell's eyesight and hearing were permanently impaired.[19]

While Twitchell convalesced, the war news grew grimmer. In only two months, May and June 1864, the Army of the Potomac had lost 65,000 men, killed, wounded, and missing. The figure almost defied belief; it exceeded the combined Union casualties of the Peninsula, Antietam, and Gettysburg battles. It far exceeded the total casualties of all previous American wars, plus the Spanish-American War. The news from Georgia was less bloody, but no more encouraging. Neither Grant nor Sherman had produced the breakthrough the northern public eagerly anticipated when the great campaigns of 1864 began. The stalemate continued.[20]

In late August, Twitchell's orders finally caught up with him, and he learned of his appointment as captain in the 109th Regiment USCT. A few days later he headed west by train. By the time he reached Louisville in mid-September, the 109th had moved nearly two hundred miles east to Louisa, Kentucky, on the border of West Virginia. The commander of the Louisville training depot was Colonel John Hammond. With black recruits pouring in from Tennessee and Western Kentucky, the understaffed Hammond conscripted Twitchell as a drill instructor. After a week training a company of black recruits, he was assigned another company. Twitchell quickly realized that if Hammond had his way, his departure for Louisa was apt to be delayed indefinitely. When Hammond disapproved a written request to join his regiment, Twitchell took characteristically bold action.[21]

Learning that the adjutant general of the army, Lorenzo Thomas, was docked at the city wharf, Twitchell called at the general's ship. Thomas remarked on his visitor's scarred face. When he learned the wound had been received at the Wilderness, he turned to his aide: "Give the boy what he wants, I like to accommodate such lads."[22]

In late September, Twitchell reported to Colonel Orion A. Bartho-

19. *CV*, 78–79; MHT Compiled Military Service Record, USCT, RG 94, NA; Regimental Papers 109th USCT, entry 354, RG 94, NA.

20. McPherson, *Battle Cry of Freedom*, 741–42.

21. MHT Compiled Military Service Record, USCT; MHT to Major Charles W. Foster, 10 September 1864, in AGO, Bureau of Colored Troops, Box 102, RG 94, NA; Cornish, *Sable Arm*, 249–50; *CV*, 79–80.

22. *CV*, 80–81.

lomew, commander of the 109th USCT, in Louisa and took command of H Company. The ninety-four men of H Company were, with a few exceptions, illiterate ex-Kentucky slaves. Discipline was lax. Looking younger than his twenty-four years and having spent the previous four months on convalescent leave, Twitchell probably looked soft. His fellow officers doubted that the "boy captain" was up to the job of disciplining his unruly men.[23]

Twitchell, however, quickly put his stamp on the company. He made a list of goldbrickers. Then each evening after dark, the men on the list reported to him with rifles and full equipment, and he led them on a starlight hike through the Kentucky countryside. In less than a week, the daily offenders dropped from a full squad to a couple of men. The latter in heavy gear paced back and forth in front of the captain's tent after dark. Within a month, H Company was one of the best-disciplined units in the regiment. The former slaves, properly trained, Twitchell later wrote, made "splendid and perfect soldiers."[24]

In October the 109th joined the siege of Richmond and Petersburg at Deep Bottom, Virginia. Two months later it merged with fifteen thousand other men to form the Twenty-fifth Corps, the only all-black corps in the Union army.[25] The Twenty-fifth Corps was the creation of Major General Benjamin F. Butler, commander of the Army of the James. Butler, a short, corpulent Massachusetts Democrat, was the last of Lincoln's political generals still in high command. Although inept as a battlefield commander, Butler was a talented administrator, who did more for black soldiers than any other major general in the Union army. In Butler's command, contrary to general practice, black soldiers received the best equipment and rations available, held critical points on the line, and were trusted to lead important assaults. The Massachusetts general sought the best white officers available. He severely disciplined or sacked those who were incompetent or abusive of their men. Aware of the army's prejudice against his "sable arm," USCT officers composed a majority of all court-martial boards involving his black soldiers.[26]

23. Regimental Papers, 109th USCT; *CV*, 81.
24. *CV*, 81.
25. Cornish, *Sable Arm*, 266–67, 281; Edward G. Longacre, "Black Troops in the Army of the James, 1863–1865," *Military Affairs*, 45 (1981): 2.
26. Longacre, "Black Troops in the Army of the James," 1–3.

Butler established regimental schools. "The men came to us ignorant of books," one officer recalled, "ignorant in manners, and with little knowledge of and less interest in anything outside their own little plantation world. Few could read their names. When the regiment was disbanded nearly all could read." Even more important, "they had learned self-reliance and self-respect."[27]

The winter of 1865 was the most severe of the war. During Twitchell's long convalescence in Vermont, the war in Virginia had turned into one of the great sieges of history. As the crow flies, thirty-five miles of trenches stretched from north of Richmond to south of Petersburg, foreshadowing the deadly trench warfare of World War I. The 109th spent the hard winter manning a portion of the trench line.

Even after the cold weather broke in February, Twitchell's regiment saw no real action. This was in big part due to General Edward O. C. Ord, who in early January 1865 replaced Butler as commander of the Army of the James. Ord was contemptuous of his black soldiers and rarely permitted them to fight. In the opinion of one of his subordinates, Ord evinced his prejudice by always spelling Negro with an extra g: "neggro." When Richmond fell in April, the Fifth Massachusetts Colored Cavalry and Twenty-fifth Corps infantry were the first Union forces into the Confederate capital. Ord halted the USCT units in the suburbs, allowing white troops to occupy the heart of the city. "You must get these damn niggers of yours out of Richmond as fast as you can!" Ord barked at a USCT general.[28]

After Appomattox, most of the Union soldiers in Virginia were quickly released from service and allowed to return to their homes. Most of the men in the Twenty-fifth Corps, however, including Twitchell and the 109th, were ordered to Texas. They were to be part of a fifty-thousand-man force being assembled along the Rio Grande under General Philip Sheridan. While North and South fought, Napoleon III had made the Archduke Maximilian of Austria emperor of Mexico. Although the men of the 109th had enlisted to fight Johnny Rebs, it now appeared they might be used to run the French out of Mexico. They resented being kept in service after hostilities.

The subsequent history of the 109th was marred by racial conflict.

27. Ibid., 3.
28. Cornish, *Sable Arm*, 282; Longacre, "Black Troops in the Army of the James," 6.

Twitchell's role in these later events, however, was tangential. Off Mobile Bay in early June, for example, 109th soldiers on board the *Thomas A. Scott* protested the punishment of two of their number and threatened to shoot their white officers. This so-called "mutiny" resulted in the courts-martial of fifteen black soldiers, eleven of whom were convicted and sentenced to forfeiture of pay and terms at hard labor. Twitchell had no part in the mutiny or the subsequent courts-martial, however, because he sailed to Texas on the *Clyde*, not the *Thomas A. Scott*.[29]

Even before the mutiny, racial tensions in the regiment had been aggravated by a long-simmering dispute over the regimental chaplaincy. Francis A. Boyd, the central figure in the story, was born a slave about 1843 in Lexington, Kentucky. He gained his freedom, and the first year of the war found him working as a house servant in Louisville. He was a member of the First Christian Church in the city, a white congregation, and highly esteemed by its members. In 1864 Boyd felt a calling to become a chaplain in the great black army being raised to save the Union. In June 1864, Colonel John Hammond, the same who had conscripted Twitchell as a drill instructor, induced the twenty-one-year-old Boyd to enlist in the 109th, assuring him that he would be the regimental chaplain. Alas, that September Colonel Bartholomew and his officers chose a white clergyman as regimental chaplain. Whether they were aware of the promise made to Boyd, army regulations put the decision in their hands, not Hammond's. Feeling betrayed, Boyd protested up the army chain of command, then to Presidents Lincoln and Andrew Johnson, respectively. The dispute spanned the entire history of the regiment. A good soldier and a forceful personality, young Boyd eventually won the admiration and respect of the 109th's white officers. At Indianola, Texas, in November 1865, the first chaplain having succumbed to illness, Colonel Bartholomew and his officers without a dissenting voice made Boyd the regimental chaplain. Unfortunately, the war department, citing bureaucratic rigmarole, vetoed the appointment. Boyd never received his chaplain's commission.[30]

29. Ira Berlin et al., eds., *Freedom, A Documentary History of Emancipation, 1861–1867,* Series 2, *The Black Military Experience* (New York, 1982), 465–71; Court-Martial Case Files, RG 153, MM-3244; Regimental Papers, 109th USCT, Box 54.

30. Francis A. Boyd, Compiled Military Service Record, USCT, RG 94, NA; AGO, Bureau of Colored Troops, Box 104, NA; Berlin et al., eds., *Black Military Experience,* 309, 350–54.

Twitchell's role in the Boyd episode, like so much of his USCT career, is speculative. The history of 109th USCT is much less fully pre-
served than the history of the Fourth Vermont. No survivor of the
Twenty-fifth Corps wrote anything comparable to G. G. Benedict's history of Vermont soldiers or Dr. Stevens's *Three Years in the Sixth Corps.*
Moreover, by the time the Boyd episode came to a head, Twitchell had
gone on detached duty with the Freedmen's Bureau. Like the 109th's
other officers, he probably started out opposed to Boyd, only to be
gradually won over to the young man's support. This is speculation,
however; his name nowhere appears in the files.

Deep summer in south Texas is a cruel season. At Indianola in late
August 1865, for the first and only time in his military service, Twitchell
reported ill. The cause was a toothache, a toothache that changed his
life. The post surgeon obligingly ordered him to New Orleans for
treatment. A few days later he sailed out of Matagorda Bay, bound for
the Crescent City where a new career and a new life awaited him.[31]

31. *CV*, 87–88.

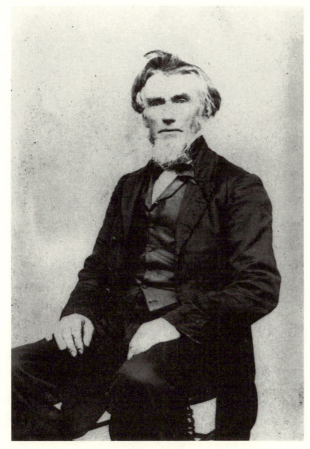

Harvey Daniel Twitchell.
Courtesy of Mary Twitchell

Elizabeth Scott Twitchell.
Courtesy of Mary Twitchell

First Sergeant Marshall Twitchell, Fourth Vermont Infantry.
Courtesy of Mary Twitchell

Captain Marshall Twitchell of the 109th United States
Colored Troops, fall 1864.
Courtesy of Mary Twitchell

Map 1—Northwest Louisiana Parish Boundaries after the Civil War
Letitia Tunnell

SIX

A TROUBLED BEGINNING IN
SPARTA, LOUISIANA

AFTER New Orleans fell to the Federals in 1862, southeastern Louisiana became the showcase for President Lincoln's wartime Reconstruction program. Although the president's "ten percent plan" failed, a host of northern military and civil officials worked in the city throughout the war, and many remained after Appomattox. Among these migratory northerners was the Reverend Thomas W. Conway, who became the director, the assistant commissioner, of the Louisiana Freedmen's Bureau.

In early September 1865, Twitchell walked into Conway's office looking for a job. Conway needed agents, and USCT officers were just the sort of men he was looking for. For his part, Twitchell wanted out of Texas and probably had some notion of helping the freedmen. Offered two choices, Twitchell chose Bienville Parish in the northwestern part of the state. Mid-October found him aboard a small stern-wheeler steaming up the Red River. In Alexandria, he saw a man point him out to others and caught the remark, "There goes one of our bosses."[1]

The great Red River raft had shaped much of the topography of

1. Circular No. 6, 9 August 1865, BRFAL-LA, M-1027, reel 26, NA; *CV*, 88–90 n.

northwest Louisiana. "Raft" was a misnomer. What settlers called a raft was a series of huge logjams, extending for nearly two hundred miles, backing up the Red River's waters and forming a veritable sargasso of bayous, swamps, and raft-lakes. Old maps of the region give the impression that it must have been once inhabited by giant Ice Age beavers. In the 1830s Henry Shreve cleared the raft with his "Steam Snag Boat," but it later reformed above the city that bears his name. During Reconstruction, the Army Corps of Engineers finally cut through the logjam, but no part of the upper Red River country escaped its impact.[2]

Bienville Parish, Twitchell's destination, formed a large irregular rectangle southeast of Shreveport. A twenty-mile-long raft-lake shaped most of its western boundary with Bossier Parish. In the rainy spring, Lake Bistineau was two or three miles across, its turgid waters dotted with cypress stumps. In the low-water months of late summer and autumn, it was transformed into a large swampy marsh, lazily pumping its dark waters through Loggy Bayou into the Red River. Expanses of alluvial soil were scarce, and so were big plantations. Before the war only eight planters had owned as many as fifty slaves, and none had owned a hundred. There were no cities, nor even any real towns, only villages and country crossroads. Cotton was the cash crop, but the inhabitants, six thousand whites and five thousand blacks, planted more corn than cotton. They also planted grain and potatoes and herded livestock. It was remote country, only a generation removed from the frontier. Beyond the reach of Federal forces, it had belonged to the trans-Mississippi South, the last part of the Confederacy to surrender.[3]

Sparta, the parish seat, straddled a sandy, forested ridge in the center of the parish. In the early twenty-first century, only a small African American church and cemetery remain, but from 1849 to 1892 it was a busy shire town. In the fall of 1865, it numbered two or three hundred

2. Fred B. Kniffen, *Louisiana: Its Land and People* (Baton Rouge, 1968), 63–65; *Coushatta Citizen*, 17 June 1938; Descriptions of Shreve's patent in Louisiana Vertical File, LSU Archives.

3. Samuel H. Lockett, *Louisiana As It Is: A Geographical and Topographical Description of the State*, ed. and introduction by Lauren C. Post (Baton Rouge, 1970), 67–68; *Eighth Census, Population, 1860*, 194 (figures are estimates because the census was either never conducted or lost); *Biographical and Historical Memoirs of Northwest Louisiana* (Nashville and Chicago, 1890), 153–54; Philip C. Cook, "Ante-bellum Bienville Parish" (master's thesis, Louisiana Polytechnic Institute, 1965), 110.

people. Its business district boasted a wooden courthouse, hotel, school, newspaper office, houses, and saloons. The town was laid out in blocks along a north-south thoroughfare, with the courthouse square in the center.[4]

The last week of October, leading a contingent of nine black soldiers from the Sixty-first USCT, Twitchell rode into Sparta. He set up his headquarters in the courthouse jury room and settled his men in a nearby house. At first, his strange surroundings produced a panicky sense of isolation. It was twenty-five miles through dense forest to the nearest military post at Minden, and New Orleans in good weather was a three-day journey. "In case of needing assistance," he later wrote, "I was without telegraph, railway, or water connection . . . I am free to confess that I known beforehand what my position was to be, I should have remained with my regiment."[5]

The first Freedmen's Bureau agent in the parish, Twitchell was the "symbol and substance" of the Union occupation. He was the man responsible for informing the region's people, black and white, of the North's expectations for a free-labor South. As he interpreted his orders, his duty was to acquaint planters and freedmen with "their changed relations from master and slave to employer and employee, giving them the additional information that it was the order of the government that old master and old slave should remain where they had been [and] work as usual in the harvesting of the crop." The new free-labor system was to be governed by yearly contracts negotiated under the bureau's watchful eye. If disputes arose over pay, working conditions, or punishment—the lash was prohibited—the agent would act as arbiter. Twitchell received unexpected help in getting his message out from the brotherhood of Freemasons, the fraternal order he had joined during the war. Crowds gathered at country crossroads to hear him explain bureau policy.[6]

His first public announcement, directed to both landowners and

4. J. Fair Hardin, *Northwestern Louisiana: A History of the Watershed of the Red River, 1714–1937,* (Louisville, Ky., and Shreveport, La., 1939), 2: 126, 133–34; Cook, "Antebellum Bienville Parish," 79–86; Bienville Parish Historical Society, *History of Bienville Parish* (Bienville, La., 1984), 30–33.

5. Special Order No. 17, 24 October 1865, Regimental Papers, Sixty-first USCT, RG 94, Box 41, NA; *CV,* 89–91.

6. *CV,* 47, 91–92.

freedmen, emphasized restoring agricultural production. The "hearty co-operation of the Freedmen's employer is earnestly requested," he wrote, in aiding the bureau with its tasks. He urged planters to recognize their former bondsmen as "free laborers, the employment of which the good of the parish demands." On the other hand, he warned blacks against the erroneous notion "that freedom from slavery implies freedom from work—a life of idleness and vagrancy must not be the result of their liberation." Twitchell's statement reflected the odd notion, widespread in the bureau, that the former slaves were unaccustomed to work.[7]

Freedmen in the parish, it is safe to assume, had expected more from the government. When Congress first created the bureau, the possibility existed that some blacks would receive homesteads on land seized by the government under the wartime confiscation and abandoned property acts. The government currently held 78,200 acres in Louisiana, 10,000 of which Commissioner Conway had leased to freedmen.[8] The freedmen's grapevine telegraph transformed this ray of sunlight into the legend of "forty acres and a mule." Even as Twitchell made his way into north Louisiana, however, orders from Washington quashed any hope of significant land reallocation. President Johnson removed Conway for coddling the freedmen and appointed General James S. Fullerton as his interim successor. A few days before Twitchell reached Sparta, Fullerton's "Address to the Freedmen of Louisiana" set a new tone of harsh realism: "Slavery has passed away, and you are now placed on trial. . . . It is not the intention of the officers of this Bureau to nurse and pamper you. . . . Some of you have the mistaken notion that freedom means liberty to be idle. . . . You must not believe the idle and malicious stories that have been told you by bad men as to what the Government intends to do for you. . . . Neither rations, nor clothing, nor mules, nor working implements will be given to you hereafter. . . . *No land will be given to you.*" Even though no land had been confiscated

7. John and LaWanda Cox, "General O. O. Howard and the 'Misrepresented Bureau,'" *JSH*, 19 (1953): 428; *Bienville Messenger*, 28 October, 25 November 1865.

8. LaWanda Cox, "The Promise of Land for the Freedmen," *Mississippi Valley Historical Review*, 45 (1958): 413–40; William McFeely, *Yankee Stepfather: General O. O. Howard and the Freedmen* (New Haven, Conn., 1968), 91, 97–100; Claude F. Oubre, *Forty Acres and a Mule: The Freedmen's Bureau and Black Land Ownership* (Baton Rouge, 1978), 32–37.

in Bienville Parish, the bureau's retreat on the land issue was a bitter blow to freedmen's hopes.[9]

Apprenticeship was another rough-edged area of bureau management. Bureau policy promoted the apprenticing of black orphans and minor children to white planters. The program addressed real needs, but both senior officials in New Orleans and field agents like Twitchell generally overlooked the potential for abuse. Twenty-eight child indentures bearing Twitchell's signature, for example, survive in the National Archives. Under slavery, bondsmen were commonly known by the names of their owners. In twenty-one of these documents, the surname of the child being bound is the same as the person defined as the "master" or "mistress." The names of certain "masters" appear repeatedly. Nineteen of the youths were bound over to just five individuals. In January 1866, for instance, a planter named Hodge Raburn signed six black children, all named Raburn, to apprenticeships ranging from six to thirteen years. In all, Raburn contracted for fifty-four years of unpaid labor from children who, a year before, had almost certainly been his slaves. In the twenty-eight agreements, the average term of service was eight years. Such lengthy indentures might have been justified if the youths had been taught skilled trades that prepared them for productive adult lives. The only occupations mentioned in these papers, however, were "house servant," "farmer," and "field hand." So defined, apprenticeship was merely a euphemism for child slavery.[10]

If freedmen were anticipating a messiah in blue, they doubtless found Twitchell a big disappointment. On the other hand, whites hoping for a pliant ally were to be discomforted, too. A case in point: In his first official action, Twitchell inspected the parish jail. The only prisoner was a young black female, a servant in the household of Ben Pearce, the ex-Confederate lieutenant governor of Louisiana and the town's most prominent citizen. Inquiring into the situation, the agent learned that the girl was likely Pearce's illegitimate daughter. He fur-

---

9. McFeely, *Yankee Stepfather*, 174–79; Donald G. Nieman, *To Set the Law in Motion: The Freedmen's Bureau and the Legal Rights of Blacks, 1865–1868* (Millwood, N.Y., 1979), 45–53; 20 October 1865, BRFAL-LA, M-1027, reel 26; *Bienville Messenger*, 11 November 1865.

10. Circular No. 25, 31 October 1865, BRFAL-LA, M-1027, reel 26; BRFAL-LA, entry 1896; Howard A. White, *The Freedmen's Bureau in Louisiana* (Baton Rouge, 1970), 82–83.

ther learned that when Pearce was out of town—as he was now—his wife Ann invariably found excuses to beat the girl and have her confined. Unable to find any formal charges, the agent took the bold step of visiting Ann Pearce. The lady declined to file a complaint, and he released the girl. No matter how delicately he approached Mrs. Pearce, neither she nor her husband, nor their neighbors, could have appreciated his intrusion in so sensitive an area.[11]

In his November monthly report, Twitchell expressed misgivings about newspaper reports that General Fullerton was closing bureau courts in the state and transferring freedmen's cases to the civil courts. Because the order had not officially crossed his desk, he continued to try cases himself, relying on his provost marshal's authority. In other instances, he turned matters over to justices of the peace, keeping an eye on the proceedings. He believed that Fullerton's order had increased black unrest in the parish. Even so, he wrote, "an equal number of free white laborers subjected to similar treatment, at work for the same pay, forced into a contract the contents of which in many cases were entirely concealed from or grossly misrepresented to them, would have given their employers and the authorities trouble much more serious than have the Freedmen." Black complaints convinced him that all labor contracts "should be in writing and read by an agent of the Bureau to the Freedmen." Few, if any, planters wanted Freedmen's Bureau agents reading and interpreting labor contracts to their hands. After local planters informed him of their intention to dismiss their "vicious and idle" workers, Twitchell investigated. "I find without exception their vicious and idle are those who have the largest families of small children, for many of whom I can only see starvation without government aid," he wrote.[12]

The daily life of a bureau agent was hard and physically demanding. Bienville Parish encompassed more than a thousand square miles. Even with an automobile and paved roads, Twitchell would have been hard-pressed to cover his territory; on horseback it was impossible. Long hours of letter writing and record keeping followed long days in the

11. *CV,* 91; *Biographical and Historical Memoirs,* 193.

12. Unfortunately, Twitchell's November monthly report is the only one that has survived. Marshall Harvey Twitchell to Absalom Baird, 1 December 1865, BRFAL-LA, M-1027, reel 13; Circular No. 24, 30 October 1865, BRFAL-LA, M-1027, reel 26; White, *Freedmen's Bureau in Louisiana,* 134–38.

saddle. "Everything must be recorded," a South Carolina agent wrote in similar circumstances. Each contract between employer and freedmen:

> must be entered alphabetically in the book of Contracts, with statement of employer's name, number of employees, date of signature, date of closure, and terms of agreement; letters forwarded must go in the book of Letters Sent, and letters received in the book of Letters Received; indorsements in the Indorsement Book; so with transportation; so with orders. If a document appeared in two books, each entry must be marked with reference numbers, so that the subject could be hunted from volume to volume. Along the margin there was a running index, by which every name might be traced from beginning to end. In short, the system of army bookkeeping is a laborious and complicated perfection.[13]

Another agent wrote, "My office is full from morning until night generally—I get nothing to eat from Breakfast until 5 or 6 o'clock p.m." After dark, there were other duties and "interminable Reports and Returns."[14]

A constant stream of aggrieved freedmen flowed through Twitchell's office, with the result that—for weeks at a time—he spent most of his waking hours arbitrating disputes. His most memorable case concerned a planter who had hit his black foreman. The freedman filed a complaint, and the agent convened a bureau court, summoning the foreman, the planter, and two black witnesses. The facts as presented by the landowner, the plaintiff, and one witness, were simple enough. The planter had struck his foreman with a stick because the foreman had repeatedly failed to keep the pigs out of the corn. The blow had principally injured the black man's dignity. The second witness, however, told a different story. "To my great surprise," the agent recalled, "he

13. John W. De Forest, *A Union Officer in the Reconstruction*, ed. James H. Croushore and David M. Potter (Hamden, Conn., 1968), 40.

14. Quoted in Cox and Cox, "General O. O. Howard and the 'Misrepresented Bureau,'" 430. See J. Thomas May, "The Freedmen's Bureau at the Local Level: A Study of a Louisiana Agent," *LH* 9 (1968): 5–19.

made out a case of such bad treatment that I think the plaintiff must have wondered that he was alive."[15]

An audience had gathered for the inquest, and blacks and whites alike eagerly awaited Twitchell's decision: "I told the plaintiff that the defendant had no right to strike him but that he had done him no injury, which was more than I could say for the corn crop." In the future, the agent advised him to follow his employer's instructions. Turning to the planter, Twitchell warned him against striking any of his workers again. Finally, the agent addressed the witness with the hyperactive imagination; he ordered him to "walk home and allow the plaintiff to ride his mule." The audience's open approval of this last ruling left Twitchell in a sanguine mood. One can only wonder if he would have been quite so pleased with himself if an employer had ever taken a stick to *him*.[16]

Most disputes brought before Twitchell involved physical abuse or wages. Complaints often arose over seemingly insignificant matters—a hammer, a bonnet, or a few scraps of bacon. Nor were all quarrels between whites and blacks; freedmen bickered among themselves. Twitchell considered the majority of complaints trivial, but dutifully took evidence and rendered decisions.[17]

The South of Presidential Reconstruction was a troubled land. Dark clouds of fear and violence rumbled on the horizon, and in December 1865, they unleashed their fury on Bienville Parish. From the day of his arrival, Twitchell worried about the tension between local whites and his black soldiers. In late November, seven soldiers from the Eightieth USCT in Shreveport replaced his original guard detail. Among the new men was a thirty-five-year-old private named Wallace Harris. An ex-

15. *CV*, 92–93.

16. Ibid., 92–93; MHT to Absalom Baird, 1 December 1865, BRFAL-LA, M-1027, reel 13.

17. De Forest, *Union Officer in the Reconstruction*, 29–30; *CV*, 93. Unfortunately, the specifics of these cases are lost. For the first half of 1866, most of the records of Louisiana local agents are unaccountably missing from the National Archives. During the ten months of Twitchell's bureau service only one of his monthly reports is extant (1 November1865). His performance in office is largely a record of mishaps, which generated paper trails outside of regular bureau channels.

Virginia slave, Harris had enlisted at Baton Rouge in 1863 and made sergeant before being demoted. He had a wife and newborn daughter living in New Orleans. The younger men called him Uncle, but his disposition was anything but avuncular.[18]

The soldiers resided across the street from a saloon owned by Robert B. Love, a prominent citizen, parish official, and deputy sheriff. The trouble started the Sunday before Christmas, while Twitchell was out of town. Some black men were wrestling in the street in front of Love's place. Private Harris and other bystanders, mostly black, wagered on the contestants.[19]

An argument erupted. The black man holding the stakes called Harris a "damned liar." Harris cuffed and kicked the name-caller, saying no man talked to him that way. From the veranda of his saloon, Robert Love injected himself into the fracas, taunting Harris by saying, "If you was a white man I would beat you and kick you till you got enough of it." Harris snapped back, "If you want to take this man's part come down and I will give it to you the same way." Love jumped down and grabbed him by the collar; the soldier knocked the saloonkeeper's hand away. Enraged, Love told a white onlooker to get the jail keys; he was going to get his pistol and "shoot this nigger." Harris thereupon pulled his own revolver and told the saloonkeeper to fetch his weapon. The other white man refused to get the keys, telling Love that "he had no business out there, with those colored boys." As Love was led away, Harris, by some accounts, stomped after him, brandishing his cocked revolver and threatening to shoot him.[20]

Private Narcisse Austin, left in charge by Twitchell, hurried Harris off the street. After dark, he and his companions saw armed whites milling about Love's store. When a black informant warned them that the townsmen were planning an attack, the frightened troopers slipped out of town and passed the night in a Negro farmer's corn crib.[21]

Twitchell returned the next day to find peaceful Sparta a smoldering

18. MHT to G. B. Furgeson, 29 November 1865, Military Division of Western Louisiana, RG 393, entry 1918, NA; Wallace Harris Compiled Military Service Record, RG 94, NA; Wallace Harris Pension File, RG 15, NA.

19. *Biographical and Historical Memoirs*, 154, 160; Hardin, *Northwestern Louisiana*, 2: 140; Harris Compiled Military Service Record.

20. Harris Compiled Military Service Record; *Bienville Messenger*, 23 December 1865.

21. Harris Compiled Military Service Record.

tinderbox. His soldiers were holed up in their quarters, rifles at the ready. Gun-toting whites strode about town. While Private Austin was making his report, Love entered Twitchell's office carrying a double-barrel shotgun. The storekeeper claimed that Harris "had threatened his life," and "he was afraid to go unarmed."[22]

When Austin finished, Twitchell ordered him to arrest Harris and confine him in the parish jail. Exactly what the agent had on his mind is unclear. He was probably thinking of returning Harris to his regiment in Shreveport; but his first priority was doubtless to get Harris off the streets and prevent a pitched battle between the townspeople and his black troopers. Love handed the jail keys to Private Austin, who then left to find Harris. Austin returned a few minutes later, reporting that Harris refused to submit to arrest. Twitchell strapped on his pistol and headed for the soldiers' quarters. As he passed the saloon, Love stepped out and proffered the loan of his shotgun, warning that Harris was dangerous. The agent declined the offer and walked on across the street into the men's house.[23]

He confronted Harris, who stood with rifle in hand, packed to leave. Challenging Twitchell's authority, the private said, "If I must be arrested I will go to my company and be arrested." Then, Twitchell later testified, "I told him to take off his equipments, lay down his gun, and follow me. He refused. I told him I should have to shoot him if he did not obey. He replied that I would have to shoot then, as he was going to his Regt. I laid down my revolver, and commenced to unfasten his equipments. He struck down my hands and run out the door." Grabbing his pistol, Twitchell rushed out the door after him, Austin a step behind.

Harris headed across the courthouse square. Austin, seeing a shotgun barrel protruding from the courthouse door, cried, "Look out Captain he is going to shoot uncle Harris."

"Halt! Stop right there!" Twitchell heard someone shout.

Flame belched from the courthouse doorway, and Harris slammed to the dirt, his head and upper body perforated by shot. The soldiers carried their bleeding comrade back into the house.[24]

22. Ibid.
23. Ibid.; *CV*, 95–96.
24. Harris Compiled Military Service Record.

When Twitchell entered, Harris cried out, "Go out of here. I dont want you to come near me. You caused me to get shot." The agent returned ten or fifteen minutes later only to hear the soldier's bitter words repeated. He found a conveyance, which carried Harris to the regimental hospital at Shreveport, where he died at ten o'clock that night.[25]

The next morning, a detachment of Federal soldiers arrested Love and took him to an army prison in Shreveport. Lieutenant Colonel Orrin McFadden investigated the shooting. McFadden interviewed Twitchell, Private Austin, and two other soldiers of the Sparta contingent. While the four witnesses generally agreed on what happened, the three privates identified with their fallen comrade and, like him, partly blamed Twitchell for the deadly outcome.[26]

McFadden concluded that the shooting was *"Premeditated Murder."* In line with this report, Colonel William S. Mudgett, the commanding officer of the Eightieth USCT, recommended that Love be bound over for trial. The recommendation was evidently rejected by higher authority, because Love was soon back in Sparta running his saloon. The chief obstacle to prosecution was doubtless the conduct of the victim. In the last two days of his life, Harris had struck a black gambler, drawn his pistol on a deputy sheriff, and physically resisted his commanding officer. At the moment of the shooting, he had a rifle in his hands and was willfully disobeying orders. For his part, Love claimed to be aiding Twitchell when he fired on Harris. The shadow of plausibility in this assertion further muddied the waters. Even if Harris had been white, Love probably would have gone free.[27]

Twitchell's handling of the incident dismayed General Mudgett. The Sparta agent's "conduct in this case," thundered Mudgett, "is highly culpable and demands a very close investigation if not his arrest and trial before a court martial." Although this seems a harsh judgment, Mudgett's displeasure is understandable. Putting Harris under arrest did appear to prejudge the case. The decision, moreover, failed to consider Harris's likely fate in Robert Love's jail, something Harris must

25. Ibid.; Harris Pension File.
26. *Bienville Messenger*, 30 December 1865; Harris Compiled Military Service Record.
27. Harris Compiled Military Service Record. There is no mention of a trial in the *Bienville Messenger*, which would have eagerly reported the event.

have thought about. On the other hand, without warning and with virtually no time for reflection, Twitchell had stepped into a situation that threatened to turn Sparta into a battlefield. From the instant he dismounted his horse to the moment Harris was shot, no more than sixty minutes appear to have elapsed. What made the predicament worse was the fact that Harris's antagonist, a deputy sheriff, was the duly constituted civil authority, to which bureau officials were expected to defer. Harris was not safe in jail; just as obviously he was not safe on the street. The best course was probably to get him out of Sparta immediately with a military escort. Whether the volatile soldier would have submitted to this is another question.[28]

Even as the events of the postwar Christmastide sputtered to their sad denouement, more trouble was heading in the Sparta agent's direction. Education was a vital part of the Freedmen's Bureau mission. Bureau officials assumed that literacy was essential for uplifting black people and preparing them for life in a free-labor society. In the fall of 1865, the Louisiana general superintendent of education, Captain Henry R. Pease, managed 126 freedmen's schools employing 230 teachers. Captain Pease wanted to increase the number, but the responsibility for founding schools resided with the local agents.[29]

In early December, Twitchell wrote Pease that there were 816 black children between the ages of five and sixteen in Bienville Parish. He believed that small schools could be started at Sparta and Mount Lebanon. He had in mind a well-educated young man of good habits named Dubois, from "one of the first families of the town," to serve as teacher in Sparta. Because of his social standing and knowledge of the local people, he "would give the schools a popularity which a stranger though ever so good a teacher could not." The agent's plan, however, could not be immediately acted upon.[30]

In February 1866 Twitchell met the bureau's traveling education agent Captain Charles A. Meyers in Shreveport. He asked for additional teachers. A few weeks later, Meyers sent him Mrs. Mary E. War-

---

28. Ibid.; Harris Pension File; *CV*, 95.

29. White, *Freedmen's Bureau in Louisiana*, 170–72.

30. MHT to Henry R. Pease, 2 December 1865, BRFAL-LA, M-1026 (education), reel 2.

dell and Mrs. Julia M. Thomas. Mrs. Thomas was an English woman. Mrs. Wardell was probably a Yankee "schoolmarm."[31] Both had taught in the Department of the Gulf's freedmen's schools during the war, where their relations with their superiors had sometimes been strained. Lieutenant Edwin M. Wheelock, supervisor of the Gulf Board of Education, had formally complained of lax discipline in Mrs. Thomas's classroom and of her habit of summoning the provost marshal to maintain order.[32] In a day when teachers were expected to administer liberal doses of corporal punishment, Mrs. Thomas was not up to the task. The chaplain, Wheelock wrote, "reports that you punished a child in his presence by giving it only a gentle tap upon the head; a punishment so slight and insufficient as to induce only laughter on the part of the child." Mrs. Wardell had also been the recipient of criticism from Lieutenant Wheelock.[33]

The two women had grievances of their own: unruly students, frequent transfers, and long periods without pay. "If it is convenient I should like to receive a little money," Mrs. Wardell wrote Wheelock in the spring of 1865. "When I came here in the autumn, I was, as I informed you, without funds. Since coming here, I have not received a dollar. As you may well imagine, I have suffered no little inconvenience during the winter for want of means." All in all, the two overworked and underpaid matrons were very likely heartily sick of men in uniform peering over their shoulders.[34]

In mid-March, Mrs. Thomas, her child, and Mrs. Wardell reached Shreveport, where they boarded the stage for Sparta. Exactly what befell them between Shreveport and Sparta is somewhat vague, but it was bad. They were set upon, insulted, and roughed up by thugs. Evidently the ruffians extorted what little money they had as ransom for their

31. A. G. Studer to A. F. Hayden, 11 June 1866, BRFAL-LA, M-1026, reel 1. The reason for believing that Julia Thomas was English is that her sister Agnes Maher arrived in New Orleans from England during the war. Agnes Maher to Board of Education, 21 January 1865, and Julia M. Thomas to Edwin M. Wheelock, 2 April 1865, BRFAL-LA, M-1026, reel 8. Mary Wardell could also have been a southern Unionist.

32. Edwin L. Wheelock to Julia M. Thomas, [?] April 1865, BRFAL-LA, M-1026, reel 1.

33. Edwin L. Wheelock to Julia M. Thomas, 5 May 1865, BRFAL-LA, M-1026; Mary E. Wardell to Wheelock, 20 January 1865, BRFAL-LA, M-1026, reel 2.

34. Mary E. Wardell to Edwin L. Wheelock, 27 March 1865, BRFAL-LA, M-1026.

baggage.[35] However noble in northern eyes, white southerners held Yankee teachers in low esteem. In time, the likes of Julia Thomas and Mary Wardell would occupy a special niche in the dark legend of Reconstruction. The "Yankee schoolma'am," Wilbur Cash writes venomously, was "generally horsefaced, bespectacled, and spare of frame, she was, of course, no proper intellectual, but at best a comic character, at worst a dangerous fool, playing with explosive forces which she did not understand."[36] Albion W. Tourgée, author of the classic Reconstruction novel, *A Fool's Errand*, has whites describe such women as "nigger schoolmarms" and "free-love nigger-missionaries of the female persuasion." One of the book's characters sums up the point of view of postwar whites: "we can't help thinking that any one that comes from the north down here, and associates with niggers—can't—well—can't be of much account at home."[37]

When the stage rumbled into Sparta, the women were broke, frightened, and dog-tired. There was worse to come. Twitchell was not expecting them, nor to their astonishment, did he welcome them. As he tried to explain, the political climate in the parish—witness their stagecoach misadventure—had taken an ugly turn in the weeks since he had asked for teachers. Except for two black orderlies, his soldier guards had been recalled to Shreveport. With only two men, he had no means of protecting teachers and as matters stood, even feared for his own safety. Nor was there any place for them to live. The local thugs threatened to burn out anyone who offered them accommodations. In short, Twitchell informed the two women that schools were no longer possible in the parish and they must leave. The ladies' reaction to this unwelcome news was volcanic. What nerve! What impudence! After all they had endured! How dare this officious man treat them this way. One of the pair addressed him as "General" and then, over a three-day period, demoted him down through the ranks to plain "Mister." Their protests

---

35. A. G. Studer to A. F. Hayden, 11 June 1866, BRFAL-LA, M-1026, reel 1; A. G. Studer endorsement book letter, 10 April 1866, BRFAL-LA, M-1026.

36. Wilbur J. Cash, *The Mind of the South* (New York, 1941), 137. See Sandra E. Small, "The Yankee Schoolmarm in Freedmen's Schools: An Analysis of Attitudes," *JSH* 45 (1979): 381–402; and Robert C. Morris, *Reading, 'Riting, and Reconstruction: The Education of Freedmen in the South, 1861–1870* (Chicago, 1981).

37. Albion W. Tourgée, *A Fool's Errand*, ed. John Hope Franklin (1879; reprint, Cambridge, Mass., 1961), 52–53.

availed them nothing, however. Twitchell gave them twenty-five dollars apiece and put them on the stage back to Shreveport. From there they made it to Natchitoches, where the resident bureau agent found them jobs.[38]

The matrons were not done with Twitchell, though. The Sparta agent hovered like a dark star on their horizon, flickering malignantly. Mrs. Thomas's letters, recounting his beastly conduct to bureau officials, lost nothing in the telling. She demanded that his pay be garnished to reimburse herself and her companion for their losses. One of her letters was so vitriolic that the new superintendent of education Major A. G. Studer responded: "For the future letters couched in such language as your last from you or any other person in the employ . . . of the Freedmen's Bureau, will receive no further notice except the summary dismissal of the writer." Despite his anger, Superintendent Studer and other bureau officials believed the two women had a case. Why had not Twitchell canceled his request for teachers if the situation was so bad, they asked. Why had he given the ladies only fifty dollars between them, a sum insufficient for their return trip? One agent even suggested that he was partly responsible for the women's mistreatment on the Sparta stage.[39]

Accounts of the teachers' misadventures put Twitchell's conduct in the worst possible light. The army expected its officers to adhere to high standards in protecting women's honor. The code stressed that ladies were chaste and delicate creatures who relied on gentlemen, especially gentlemen in uniform, for protection. It seemed impossible for those who were not present to reconcile events in Sparta with these archaic notions. Like General Ben Butler with his "woman order," Twitchell was no knight in blue.[40]

The Vermont agent's version of these events has largely been lost. Except for a brief excerpt, his official report is missing. The comments in his autobiography are short and incomplete. The hullabaloo over his

38. A. G. Studer endorsement book letter, 10 April 1866, BRFAL-LA, M-1026, reel 2; Studer to Julia M. Thomas, 19 May 1866, and Studer to A. F. Hayden, 11 June 1866, ibid; *New York Tribune*, 15 August 1866; *CV*, 97.

39. A. G. Studer endorsement book letter, 10 April 1866, BRFAL-LA, M-1026, reel 2; Studer to Julia M. Thomas, 19 May 1866, and Studer to A. F. Hayden, 11 June 1866, BRFAL-LA, M-1026, reel 1.

40. Paul Andrew Hutton, *Phil Sheridan and His Army* (Lincoln, Neb., 1985), 142–43.

alleged want of gallantry, however, overlooked a vital element of the story: namely, that Julia Thomas and Mary Wardell were sometimes hard to get along with, as bureau officials in New Orleans had reason to know. After Sparta, both women found employment as teachers in Natchitoches Parish. In August, Mrs. Thomas quit her job abruptly, forcing the closing of the Natchitoches town school. Mrs. Wardell resigned two months later. "During her period of service in the employ of this Office," the Natchitoches agent wrote, she "made herself extremely troublesome and her resignation was a great relief to all concerned."[41]

Chivalry aside, Twitchell's assessment of school prospects in the parish was doubtless correct. Moreover, even if it had been possible to safeguard teachers and pupils, the problem of financing parish schools would have remained. When Congress created the Freedmen's Bureau, it had neglected to appropriate money for its operations. Thus, however important education was in theory, the agency did not have the funds to carry out its goals. When Twitchell first proposed opening the Sparta and Mount Lebanon schools in December, nothing had happened because the Louisiana bureau, $80,000 in debt, was in the act of closing its schools until spring. Bureau schools had to be self-sufficient. Freedmen were expected to pay 5 percent of their wages as a school tax. The program worked best in large towns where there was a semblance of a black artisan class. There were no towns in Bienville, and most of its black farmers had not seen any wages since the war. Including Twitchell, five men served as agents in Sparta after the war, but when the bureau closed its doors in the village in late 1868, there were still no schools in the parish.[42]

Other agents in the region experienced similar difficulties. The Shreveport office, for example, encompassed the entire northwestern corner of the state—Caddo, De Soto, and Bossier Parishes. In November 1866, the resident agent Lieutenant Colonel Martin Flood reported only one school in operation and "that one was but a partial success." Flood's litany of woes included dirt-poor freedmen, high water and a poor cotton crop, and vicious whites. He dwelled on the mean-spirited

41. Monthly School Reports, Natchitoches Parish, 31 August, 31 October 1866, BRFAL-LA, entry 1768.

42. White, *Freedmen's Bureau in Louisiana*, 173–78, 181 n.

whites. The Texas-Arkansas border, he wrote, was notorious for toughs and lawless men: "Colored schools would have but furnished them with the opportunity for not only breaking up all such schools; but an excuse for commiting other depredations upon Freedmen." The planters were no help. They generally opposed Negro education and were unwilling "to protect either school or teacher from insult or personal violence." The truth was that the bureau's schools in Louisiana were in decline in 1866. When the year began, the agency had 150 schools, 265 teachers, and 19,000 students. Seven months later, only 66 schools, 76 teachers, and 2,239 students remained.[43]

Mrs. Thomas and Mrs. Wardell's complaints against Twitchell took time to work their way up the chain of command to Assistant Commissioner Absalom Baird. "Captain Twitchell has without doubt acted very badly," Baird wrote in May, "but under the circumstances, it will be impracticable to have him relieved."[44] In the meantime in February, the 109th USCT, from which Twitchell was on detached duty, had been mustered out of the army. In April, General Philip Sheridan, commander of the Gulf, cut a routine order for Twitchell's discharge. The order miscarried and because it did, Twitchell remained the Sparta agent through midsummer 1866. Had he left the bureau in April, he probably would have gone home to Vermont, never to set foot in Louisiana again. His last three months in Sparta, the result of a bureaucratic miscue, were to be his most important days in the bureau.[45]

43. Martin Flood to A. F. Hayden, 30 November 1866, BRFAL-LA, entry 1873; White, *Freedmen's Bureau in Louisiana*, 177.

44. A. G. Studer endorsement book letter, 19 May 1866, BRFAL-LA, M-1026, reel 2.

45. E. D. Townsend to Philip H. Sheridan, 13 April 1866, MHT Compiled Military Service Record; Sheridan to Townsend, 23 April 1866, George Lee to Absalom Baird, 5 July 1866, Sheridan to Townsend, 13 July 1866, in AGO, Bureau of Colored Troops, entry 1864, Box 102, RG 94, NA; Personnel Records, BRFAL-LA, M-1027, reel 34.

SEVEN

MARSHALL AND ADELE

ADELE Coleman was twenty, very attractive, and recently returned home from a South Carolina finishing school. About the first of January 1866, she was hired to teach music at Sparta Academy. She lived at the Mays Hotel, where many of the townsfolk, including Captain Twitchell of the Freedmen's Bureau, frequently dined. Within a month or two she and Marshall were taking meals together and engaging in animated conversation. They met almost every day, strolling about town or picnicking in the forest. The townsfolk were aghast. Adele's brothers, Cornelius and Augustus ("Gus") had fought for the South. Where was the girl's loyalty . . . her dignity? Had she no shame? The way Twitchell remembered it, Adele had taken the initiative. Possibly this was male vanity, but under the circumstances, he could not have made much headway without her encouragement.[1]

Adele's father, Isaac Coleman, traced his roots to a seventeenth-century Virginia planter named Robert Coleman, whose descendants had migrated into the Carolinas and Georgia. Isaac was born in 1812 in Fairfield County, South Carolina. He married Judith McShan, and by

---

1. *Bienville Messenger*, 6 January 1866; *CV*, 99–100; MHT Scrapbook.

1840 the couple had three children, a farm, and nine slaves. The family moved west to a small plantation in Choctaw County, Mississippi, where on 15 August, 1846, Adele and her twin sister Luella were born. At midcentury Isaac and his wife had seven children and owned seventeen slaves. In the early 1850s the family moved again, to a plantation in Brush Valley, Louisiana, eighteen miles southeast of Sparta. By the war, Isaac owned twenty-five slaves and had graduated into the planter class.[2]

Adele was a strong-willed, intelligent young woman much admired by local bachelors. One of Twitchell's rivals for her favor was J. M. Scanland, the young editor and publisher of the *Bienville Messenger*. When Twitchell first arrived in the parish, Scanland greeted him cordially: Captain Twitchell "seems be a gentleman in every particular, and I doubt not that he will do well by our citizens, if they will only receive him in the proper spirit." For the next two or three months, brief but favorable comments about the new agent graced the *Messenger*'s columns, and it routinely printed bureau circulars. But within two months of Adele's arrival in town, Twitchell and all news of the bureau vanished from the paper. For the duration of his bureau career, as far as the *Messenger* was concerned, the Freedmen's Bureau did not exist in Bienville Parish.[3]

Trouble started one evening in late spring. Marshall and Adele had been walking. They stopped near the hotel. Adele seemed distracted, and Marshall was somewhat annoyed. She abruptly asked him for his revolver. He hesitated, then reluctantly unholstered the heavy weapon and handed it to her. Brown eyes blazing, she cocked the pistol and fired a ball into the shrubbery along a nearby fence. Marshall grabbed the weapon, but not before a second shot went wild in the air. Like a flushed deer, a young man burst from the greenery and sprinted away, a trail of dust swirling in his wake. The eavesdropper was a rival for Adele's affections.[4]

2. J. P. Coleman, *The Robert Coleman Family: From Virginia to Texas, 1652–1965* (Ackerman, Miss., 1965), 39–41, 398–400; Federal manuscript census, population, South Carolina 1840, Mississippi 1850 (the 1860 census for Bienville Parish, Louisiana, does not exist); *Biographical and Historical Memoirs*, 153; Twitchell, *Genealogy of the Twitchell Family*, 414.

3. Adele Coleman Twitchell to Luella Coleman, 4 November 1866, MHT Papers; *House Miscellaneous Documents*, 41st Cong., 2d Sess., No. 154, pt. 2, p. 180.

4. *CV*, 99.

"I have since learned enough of the customs and ideas of the Southern people," Twitchell would later recall of the incident, "to know that had she hit the young man, it would have been pronounced an accident." The boy was from a good family, hence a gentleman who could not possibly have been spying on his lady love. By the same token, being a lady, Adele could not have meant to shoot him. "A certain pride and honor were of more importance than life to them."[5] Twitchell's jealous rival lost no time in telling Adele's family of her liaison with a Freedmen's Bureau agent. Two or three nights later in the hotel dining room, Adele passed Marshall a note telling him that her brother Gus had come to take her home to Brush Valley. Just before her departure, the next morning at breakfast, Marshall slipped her a letter with his picture enclosed.[6]

When her parents ordered her to stay home and cease all contact with Twitchell, Adele set up a secret courier system using a black family retainer. The loyal messenger worked in the fields by day, but three nights a week, mounted on a mule, he carried love letters between Brush Valley and Sparta, a thirty-six-mile round-trip. When inevitably word of the secret correspondence leaked, Adele's family was indignant. Friends urged Gus to kill the upstart Yankee.[7]

Late one evening, Twitchell's black orderly informed him that a young man was outside and wanted to see the captain. The soldier warned against going out, though. The rider was well-mounted, he explained, on "a fine white horse, acts very suspiciously, and will not allow me to come near him." Twitchell rose from his desk: "Cocking my revolver, I slipped it into the breast of my coat, keeping my hand upon it in such a manner that I thought I could shoot first, and walked out." Warily approaching the horseman who, in the dim light, looked like a young boy, he demanded: "What do you want?" A female voice answered, "Marshall, don't you know me?"

"My God, Adele!"

She told him to get his horse and escort her home.[8]

Gus had left Brush Valley for Sparta that morning, Adele explained.

5. Ibid., 100.
6. Ibid.
7. Ibid., 100–2.
8. Ibid.

He had some notion of goading Twitchell into a gunfight before witnesses and claiming self-defense. Learning of the plot—perhaps from the servants—she rode off in late afternoon, ostensibly to visit a girlfriend. Upon arriving at her friend's house, however, she borrowed a boy's clothes and a pistol, then after dark, set out for Sparta to warn her beau.

Twitchell and Adele rode leisurely back to Brush Valley, stopping several times to talk and doubtless to exchange caresses. The normally two- or three-hour trip took all night. At first light, according to Twitchell, Adele disappeared into the forest and changed into proper lady's clothes. Twitchell left her at her father's gate at sunup and headed home to Sparta. Predictably, the Coleman household exploded when the long-missing daughter marched in with the morning sun.[9]

In the meantime, Brother Gus, unaware that Adele had returned home, was in Sparta looking for her. Twitchell had made friends among Sparta masons, and one of them, an ex-Confederate officer, volunteered to accompany Gus to the bureau agent's quarters. After his all-night ride, Twitchell had gone to bed. It was midday before he awoke and Gus and his companion entered his quarters. Adele's brother demanded to know the whereabouts of his sister. Relieved to learn that she was safe at home, Gus nonetheless cross-examined Twitchell like an indignant prosecutor. He asked, Twitchell recalled, "whether I was going to steal her without her parents' consent or what I was going to do?" The situation had become intolerable, the brother said. Twitchell responded that he intended to conduct himself honorably. He added, however, that where he came from—enlightened Vermont—a twenty-year-old woman did not need her parents' consent to marry. This irrelevant comment, as well as other gratuitous remarks suggesting that Louisiana was still in the Dark Ages, terminated the meeting. Gus stormed off in a rage.[10]

The next night Twitchell heard a tapping on his window. Adele's messenger delivered a letter describing the stormy family scene that had transpired upon Gus's return home. Adele's parents had ordered her to South Carolina to stay with her sisters. She refused to go. She, in turn, demanded that Twitchell be invited to the Coleman home. If the family

9. Ibid.
10. Ibid.

denied this request, she threatened to take more midnight rides to Sparta. At length, her parents surrendered. Adele could invite her beau.[11]

Because there had been ugly talk in the community about a pasty-faced "Yankee plebeian" courting a Coleman daughter, Twitchell indicated that he would only accept the invitation if it came from Adele's mother, Judy, with all the proprieties. A day or two later, for the first time riding in daylight, the long-suffering courier brought Twitchell a formal invitation from the mistress of the Coleman house. The next afternoon, clad in mufti, Twitchell rode to Brush Valley to meet the Colemans. There were tense moments. Twitchell recalled with wry amusement the "studied efforts [of] Mistress Coleman and myself to express to each other the dislike we felt without being exactly impolite or uncivil." On the other hand, Marshall and Adele's father, Isaac, began a friendship that would last more than twenty years, until the old man's death. There remained, though, Isaac and Judy's four children who lived in Union County, South Carolina.[12]

Although chagrined, Adele's two older sisters and her brother Cornelius, a doctor, accepted the misalliance. Adele's twin sister, Luella, was another matter. Since early childhood the two girls had been close. They looked so much alike that outsiders could not tell them apart. Whether she returned home or merely wrote letters is unclear, but Luella vented her outrage until virtually everyone in Bienville Parish knew that she regarded Twitchell as a blackguard unworthy of her sister's hand. As the nuptials drew nigh, though, Luella had second thoughts. She doubtless realized that, with or without her approval, her sister was going to marry this man. If she persisted in her opposition, she would be estranged from her twin—perhaps for life. A few weeks before the wedding, she wrote Adele begging for forgiveness and extending a peace offering to the Yankee.

At Adele's urging, Twitchell accepted the olive branch. In a moving "Dear Sister Lu" letter, he confessed that her unkindness had hurt him badly. Still, her recent letter, so full of heartfelt contrition, had moved him deeply. He was willing to "forgive" and love her as a sister, but he warned against any backsliding: "I can never but once more change my

11. Ibid., 102–3.
12. Ibid.

feelings toward you. I have suffered to[o] much." He urged her not to let Adele doubt him. "I love her [and] it was not her fault that she gave you pain." With Luella's capitulation, the last hurdle fell away.[13]

The wedding day took place on 24 July at twilight. A violent thunderstorm ripped through Sparta in the morning, but the sky cleared by afternoon. Twitchell left for Brush Valley about three o'clock. Inexplicably, he took a wrong turn and arrived an hour late, his horse lathered, the wedding guests preparing to leave. Marshall and Adele took their vows in the parlor, she in white, he—at her insistence—wearing his blue uniform.

Twitchell attributed his late arrival to absentmindedness. But what he dismissed as inattention may have been subliminal ambivalence. On the one hand, he was infatuated with Adele, genuinely liked most of her family, and had made friends in Sparta. On the other hand, he had not forgotten his first love, the well-educated Henrietta, and his outburst to Gus about southern backwardness revealed his inner thoughts. Like most New Englanders, Twitchell assumed New England's cultural superiority to the rest of the country, especially the South.[14]

He had been in Bienville Parish for nearly a year, and his impressions were mostly negative. Illiteracy was rampant among both races, the Methodist minister and his wife smoked tobacco, and his landlady swore like an Irish drill sergeant. Having assumed that assignations between slaves and poor whites produced the mulatto class whose members were ubiquitous, he had discovered that the planters themselves were the culprits (clearly he had not read much abolitionist literature). He had assumed, too, that most planters lived in great mansions like the stately homes he had seen in New Orleans's Garden District, not oversized log cabins. This last belief died hard. After many disappointments, he had occasion to visit one of the wealthiest planters in the parish. Now surely he would see the great planter in all his glory. "We reached the place just at sundown," he later wrote. "It was a large one-story log house with the usual chimneys at each end of the outside and a broad piazza across the entire front, no better than the other planters' houses which I had visited. I at first thought it must belong to the overseer." Inside, the furnishings were crude, the floors uncarpeted, and the

13. MHT to Luella Coleman, [June or July] 1866, MHT Papers.
14. *CV*, 103–4.

shingled roof was the only ceiling. At supper he sat in a homemade chair and ate with an iron fork with only two tines: "I never afterwards attempted to find any realization of my boyhood fancies of Southern splendor."[15]

Yet, on that July afternoon, he married a southern woman. After a few months of married life, his bride wrote Luella a revealing letter, describing how she had ironed some shirts for her husband: "[W]hen I finished them I brought them in the room and put them on the bed. [H]e looked at them and asked me who ironed them I told him I did. he come to me and sit down and drew me down in his lap told me how he had been all along deceived in me thought that I was an idle worldly creature who cared for nothing but dress fashions and admiration, that he had been afraid we would not be happy together . . . but now he said all doubts were gone he knew I could make him happy." Such thoughts as these, one suspects, help explain Marshall's absentmindedness the day of his wedding.[16]

By this time, the orders for his army discharge had caught up with him. He planned to spend a few days with the Colemans, take Adele with him to New Orleans, and then carry her home to Vermont to live. It was a measure of the turmoil surrounding the marriage that Adele's parents—and possibly Adele herself—had failed to give serious thought to this possibility.

It provoked a family crisis. The Colemans argued hour after hour with their new son-in-law, trying to keep him and their daughter in Louisiana. The Colemans harbored a secret. At length, all else having failed, the painful words tumbled from Judy Coleman's lips. Adele had a sore spot on one of her lungs, which her doctor feared was consumption, tuberculosis, the great killer of the nineteenth century. Unlike modern heart disease or cancer, which generally attack people late in life, tuberculosis's victims were mostly young, especially young women. Taking Adele to Vermont, Judy Coleman argued, would be a death sentence.[17]

It was a nigh irrefutable argument. Vermont was notorious for the disease; it accounted for about a fourth of all deaths in the state. In one

15. Ibid., 93–97.
16. Adele Coleman Twitchell to Luella Coleman, 4 November 1866.
17. Ibid.; *CV*, 104.

town, in a two-year span, it killed seventeen young women. The South, on the other hand, had a reputation—however undeserved—as a consumptive health resort. Vermonters, it was said, migrated south either to become schoolteachers or recover from the "white plague." Postponing a final decision, alone Twitchell headed for New Orleans to muster out. He rode south to Coushatta Chute, where he caught a steamer, never dreaming of the significance that the name Coushatta would have in his future.[18]

A letter from Vermont awaited him in New Orleans, summoning him home to deal with family problems occasioned by his father's death two years before. He stayed away a long time. "How strange it seems for me to be preparing to keep house," Adele wrote her twin. "I have been married three months but during all that time I have been with Marshall only *eight days.*" Mistaking Adele's melancholy for some deeper discontent, Luella—perhaps even now not fully reconciled to the marriage—worried about her sister's happiness. Adele reassured her: "I am blessed with a husband I love *far* better than any thing else on earth, and am myself a worshiped wife. . . . I could tell you darling of little things, little acts of love . . . treasured in my heart." For example, Marshall never fails "to kneel with me at night by our bedside in prayer. Oh I feel this love will make me a better girl and him a better man. he says that I can make him good. Oh pray God Sister to help me, that this love so strong in us both will yet lead us to the feet of Jesus, humble and penitant."[19]

Twitchell was in Vermont so long that many of Adele's friends and neighbors began to suspect that he had deserted her. On his return, he heard the gossip long before he reached Brush Valley. He read the relief on his bride's face as she rushed to embrace him.

While away, he had made the only decision a caring, loving husband could have made: He and his wife would remain in the South. He had to make a living. Cotton farming in Louisiana was a much more appealing prospect than scratching out a living on a small farm in the Vermont hills. "Though farming is not to his taste," Adele confided to Luella,

18. *CV*, 104; Lewis D. Stilwell, *Migration from Vermont* (Montpelier, Vt., 1948), 129, 146–47, 165–66, 228.

19. *CV*, 104–5; Adele Coleman Twitchell to Luella Coleman, 4 November 1866, 1 July 1867, MHT Papers.

"he thinks he can make more money farming that at any other business." Within days of his return, he and Isaac set out on a land-scouting expedition that took them across north Louisiana and into Arkansas and Mississippi. In the end, though, Twitchell returned to familiar territory. In December 1866, with a $1,000 down payment, he bought a 420-acre plantation on the high east bluff overlooking Lake Bistineau in Bienville Parish. He had saved his money. The federal government and his hometown of Townshend had paid him $700 for his wartime reenlistment. For two years, the army had paid him $70 a month as a captain. Austere and disciplined—shunning tobacco, liquor, and gambling—he saved money as easily as other men spent it.[20]

Cotton planting was a risky business in these years. The dreaded army worm, a mustard-colored caterpillar, ravished north Louisiana cotton almost every summer. Because the levees had gone unrepaired during the war, large expanses of bottomland now flooded. Most planters suffered severe losses two and three years in a row.

Twitchell had much to learn. As one planter put it: "Cotton's a ticklish plant to raise. You've got to watch it mighty close." Even with the best of care, bad weather or caterpillars could destroy the crop. One of the advantages to remaining in Bienville Parish was Isaac Coleman, who purchased the plantation next to Marshall's. Together with Gus, the two men worked their lands jointly. With Isaac as his teacher, Twitchell learned the yearly cycle of cotton cultivation, beginning with winter plowing and spring planting, through the weeding and thinning of the plants, to picking in late summer and early fall. The crop was then shipped and marketed through a New Orleans factor. Lake Bistineau was navigable through to the Red River, and the Twitchell-Coleman plantations were near Pine Bluff Landing. Twitchell devoted himself to finance and labor, while Isaac concentrated on managing the crop.[21]

One of Adele's letters, dated mid-1867, gives a brief glimpse into the economic life of the Twitchell-Coleman plantations: "Pa and Marshall are crowing over a big rain they have just had. . . . They are both well pleased with their present prospect for a good crop (both cotton and

20. *CV*, 105; Adele Coleman Twitchell to Luella Coleman, 1 July 1867, MHT Papers; Deed, 22 May 1868, MHT Papers; *Statistics Relating to the Soldiers and Expenses of the Town of Townshend, Vt.* (Brattleboro, Vt., 1874).

21. Edward King, *The Great South*, ed. W. Magruder Drake and Robert R. Jones (1875; reprint, Baton Rouge, 1972), 298.

corn). . . . Pa himself says he can make more money now than when the negro was a slave Marshall works 12 hands, Pa 12 also and Gus works 2 and Ma has her little cotton patch and works her cook and another woman she hired."[22]

Despite Adele's optimism, the 1867 cotton crop was a disappointment. Her father was unable to pay his debts. Judy Coleman recognized her talented son-in-law's head for business. "You Yankees are said to be awful cute," she chided one day and suggested that he "might take Mr. Coleman's business and straighten it out." Twitchell accepted the challenge, on condition that his authority be absolute. When Isaac agreed, he sold off a parcel of unproductive land that put his father-in-law financially back in the black.[23]

In early 1868, Adele proudly wrote Luella that Marshall "has paid off all the land notes and $100 on the stock note, besides taking up an old note of Barretts against Pa. Gus and Marshall has paid all [Pa's] debts in Ringgold, and now you see there is not much more to pay. I can thank the Lord the plantation is paid for, 'every cent' and there will be no trouble about the balance that Pa owe's. Pa says he dont know what in the world he would have done with out his *Yankee* son-in-law to help him out." For the time being, she confided, she must live frugally because Marshall "has paid out all his money in paying Pa's debts but the day is not far distant when I can have any thing I want."[24]

Alas, neither money nor love could vanquish the harsh realities of nineteenth-century life. In 1869 Adele gave birth to a sickly son. She recorded his brief life inside the cover of her Bible:

> My poor little Harvy
> My sweet babe is better 12th Sept. –1869
> *Our precious boy still improving* Oct 3rd 69
> *My darling boy is dead* June 4 1870

In 1871 Adele bore a second son, a healthy boy named Marshall Coleman Twitchell. But the spot on her lung—about which her mother had warned—slowly grew larger.[25]

22. Adele Coleman Twitchell to Luella Coleman, 1 July 1867.

23. *CV*, 108.

24. Adele Coleman Twitchell to Luella Coleman, 30 January 1868, MHT Papers.

25. Bible in the possession of Mary Twitchell; Twitchell, *Genealogy of the Twitchell Family*, 558.

EIGHT

ROUGH AND TUMBLE POLITICS, 1867 ~ 1869

I N March 1867, the U.S. Congress enacted a sweeping Reconstruction Act that overturned Presidential Reconstruction and launched Radical Reconstruction. The Reconstruction Act divided the South into five military districts and mandated new state constitutions and new state governments. The ex-Confederate states were required to ratify the Fourteenth Amendment, which guaranteed blacks basic civil rights and disfranchised high-ranking Confederate military and civil officials. Most radical of all, the act imposed black suffrage on the South. Three weeks later, a supplemental law directed the commanding general in each military district to commence voter registration and supervise delegate elections for state constitutional conventions.[1]

The Reconstruction Act broke two and a half centuries of tradition. Since the founding of the Thirteen Colonies, the South—indeed the nation—had been a white man's country. Inherent in the slavery question that brought on the Civil War was the deeper issue of black people's future in America. After Appomattox, with the approval of Presi-

---

1. Walter L. Fleming, ed., *Documentary History of Reconstruction* (1906–1907; reprint, New York, 1966), 2: 401–3, 407–11.

dent Johnson, southern leaders from Virginia to Texas began crying
anew that the South was a "white man's country." Black suffrage challenged this bedrock principle. In the United States, voting was a symbolic as well as a temporal act. The ballot was a badge of membership,
an emblem of equality among the citizenry of the Republic. For this
reason, Radical Reconstruction was probably the most controversial
and far-reaching domestic program ever adopted by the U.S. government.[2]

News of the Reconstruction Act reached Twitchell in Ringgold. He
was preparing for spring planting and as a parish road overseer, super-
vising a gang of black road-workers. As he described the scene: "At my
last road working, when I dismissed the hands for the year, I informed
them that they (the colored men) would be allowed to vote and that
when the time came, they would be in great danger from two extreme
parties. One party would put them back in slavery if they could; the
other would crowd them forward into position so much faster than
their education and experience of affairs of government would justify
that the injury would be nearly as great." These moderate sounding
words were written years later when Radical Reconstruction had fallen
into disrepute. Twitchell's actual mood in March 1867, one suspects,
was less restrained.[3]

Louisiana and Texas constituted the Fifth Military District, commanded by General Philip H. Sheridan. Sheridan appointed voter registers in each Louisiana parish, and by June, registration was underway
all over the state. North Louisiana freedmen were eager to vote.
Twitchell assisted the Bienville registers and became upset when they
failed to enroll African Americans with appropriate seriousness. When
preposterous names appeared on the rolls, for example, "Alexander the
Great" and "Jeremiah the Prophet," Twitchell altered the names to
read simply Alexander and Jeremiah.

That summer, Bienville Parish was to choose a delegate to the Louisiana constitutional convention. Twitchell had never imagined himself
a statesman, but his support of the Reconstruction Act pushed him into
the public eye. Indeed, from one end of Dixie to the other that spring,

---

2. Stampp, *Era of Reconstruction*, 87, 122; Allan Nevins, *The Emergence of Lincoln* (New
York, 1950), 2: 470–71; Foner, *Reconstruction*, 276–78.
    3. *CV*, 108.

relative newcomers from the North woke up one morning to find that overnight they had acquired political availability. In Twitchell's case, experience in the USCT and the Freedmen's Bureau, not to mention his support of the Reconstruction Act, gave him standing with blacks. Many whites found him acceptable, too. He had married into a prominent local family and become a planter. His election, moreover, would allay any concerns as to the region's loyalty. At a public meeting, a Sparta merchant and German immigrant named John H. Scheen introduced Twitchell's name. The nominating committee—probably composed entirely of whites—pressed the argument that he was the only man in the parish with broad support from both races. Two weeks later, he accepted the nomination "with a prepared schoolboy speech which I presume gratified my hearers most when they discovered that I was through."[4]

In November, Twitchell joined ninety-eight other delegates in New Orleans. Nothing like this convention had ever been seen in the state or, before Reconstruction, anywhere in the country: fifty delegates were black; thirty-four, native white southerners; and fourteen, newcomers from the North. The dominant force in the convention was the black delegates, the majority of whom were members of southeastern Louisiana's old free Negro class, the *gens de couleur*. Twitchell had doubtless encountered *gens de couleur* in earlier visits to the Crescent City, but the convention marked his first intimate contact. They made a distinct impression on whites—especially northerners—encountering them for the first time. Whitelaw Reid, a reporter for the *New York Tribune*, left a vivid account of his first meeting with *gens de couleur*. Reid initially encountered a delegation of these "creoles of color" conversing in the library of a stately house. At first, he failed to recognize them as black people. Only gradually did it dawn on him that the "quiet well-bred gentlemen" were African Americans. They were almost white. Indeed, some of them were whiter than the white gentlemen who escorted him about New Orleans. "Every man of them was well educated. All spoke French fluently; the English of all was passable, of some perfect. Some of them were comparatively wealthy, and all were in easy circumstances." From the convention, Twitchell remembered "negroes of all complexions, from the bright octoroon to the full-blooded negro. With

4. Ibid., 108–9.

the exception of a few of the last class, all were well fitted for their position."[5]

The white southerners were largely old Unionists and, for the most part, professional men or businessmen—lawyers, physicians, editors, dentists, merchants, tradesmen. A few were planters. None fit the stereotypical scalawag image of "Tragic Era" legend. As Twitchell was to write, the group was "rich in men of experience, education, and ability."

Of the fourteen northerners, all but two were ex-Union soldiers. Four had been officers in the USCT. Two had been Freedmen's Bureau agents. Over half were now cotton planters. Imbued with northern concepts of governance, Twitchell wrote later, the newcomers "were a very necessary balance between" the black and native white contingents.[6]

The delegates deliberated all winter and in March 1868 produced Louisiana's path-breaking Reconstruction constitution. It was the first Louisiana constitution to contain a Bill of Rights, and Article 13 of the Bill of Rights was a hundred years ahead of its time. It decreed that all

5. Whitelaw Reid, *After the War: A Tour of the Southern States, 1865–1866*, ed. C. Vann Woodward (New York, 1965), 259–60; *CV*, 110.

6. For a discussion of the convention and the delegates, see Tunnell, *Crucible of Reconstruction*, 111–35, 231–38. According to tradition, accepted by earlier historians, the convention membership was equally divided between forty-nine blacks and forty-nine whites. See A. E. Perkins, "Some Negro Officers and Legislators in Louisiana," *Journal of Negro History* 14 (1929): 523–28; and Charles Vincent, *Black Legislators in Louisiana during Reconstruction* (Baton Rouge, 1976), 226–27.

At the start of his research, the present author assumed that the traditional count was correct, but after amassing data on each delegate, he discovered contrary facts. The most clear-cut concerns the delegate John Scott from Winn Parish. Perkins and Vincent assumed that Scott was white. The evidence that he was black, however, is incontrovertible. In the contemporary photograph of the convention delegates ("Extract from the Reconstructed Constitution of the State of Louisiana with Portraits of the Distinguished Members of the Convention and Assembly. A.D. 1868."), just to the right of the flag above Lieutenant Governor Oscar J. Dunn's head is a bearded black man named Scott. On key civil-rights roll calls, Scott voted with the other black delegates. How Scott, a native of New Orleans, managed to get himself elected as Winn Parish's delegate to the convention is puzzling, but no more so than how other blacks from New Orleans, James H. Ingraham and Caesar C. Antoine, managed to get elected from Caddo. As to how the traditional view got started, there is an explanation for that too: The *New Orleans Tribune*, an African American paper, was sensitive to white charges of "Negro rule," etc.; hence, it deliberately undercounted the black delegates.

people were to receive "equal rights and privileges" on railroads, steamboats, stagecoaches, in restaurants, theaters, bars, and in all businesses for which a state license was required. Another section of the constitution prescribed a mandatory oath for all public officials: "I . . . do solemnly swear . . . that I accept the civil and political equality of all men, and agree not to attempt to deprive any person or persons, on account of race, color, or previous condition, of any political and civil right, privilege, or immunity enjoyed by any other class of men; . . ."

In conformity with the Reconstruction Act, universal manhood suffrage was guaranteed. Article 135 called for the establishment of "at least one free public school in every parish." The constitution mandated that all children were to be admitted to these schools without regard to race or color. To avoid any misunderstanding, Article 135 explicitly forbade any public-supported schools based on race.

Next to civil rights, the most controversial feature of the constitution was Article 99, the disfranchisement clause. It exempted ordinary folk—common soldiers, farmers, mechanics—from loss of political rights, but disfranchised most Confederate officeholders (including local functionaries), guerilla leaders, signers of the ordinance of secession, and editors and ministers who espoused the Confederate cause. In order to regain their rights, these proscribed individuals had to confess publicly and in writing that the Confederacy was "morally and politically wrong." The article contained a loophole, however. Individuals who supported Radical Reconstruction, who had become Republicans in other words, were exempted.[7]

Twitchell supported the disfranchisement article, black suffrage, and the racial equality oath. He missed the final vote on Article 13, but earlier votes and frequent missed roll calls suggest that he opposed the public accommodation clause. He may have thought it was unenforceable. Although a fervent supporter of education, he voted against the education article. He perhaps agreed with W. Jasper Blackburn, another north Louisiana delegate, who argued strongly that Article 135 was misguided. The state badly needed public schools, but attempting to force black and white children into the same classrooms would undermine the legitimacy of public education at the outset. "I am a friend

7. *Digest of the Laws of the State of Louisiana, in Two Volumes* (New Orleans, 1870), 1: 8, 114, 129–30, 134–35.

of all men, and more especially of all children, regardless of race or color," Blackburn said, "but I desire and aim to be so upon a safe and *practicable* basis."[8]

Twitchell had another, even stronger objection to the education article. He saw clearly that "at least one public school per parish," in effect, meant only one school per parish. Given the primitive roads and the size of the parishes, most of the state's children would be denied access to a school. In the waning days of the convention, Twitchell proposed an amendment to Article 135: "All children . . . not residing within a convenient distance of any established public school, shall draw their portion of the public school fund." The delegates promptly tabled the proposal. A few days hence, Twitchell voted for the constitution but inserted into the record a written protest against the document's failure to insure an equitable distribution of school money among the state's children.[9]

Twitchell played a secondary role in the convention. To be sure, he did his work and attended seventy-three of the eighty-one sessions, but as "one of the youngest" members—his own words—he was diffident in the presence of so many experienced and articulate older men, black and white. His protest of the education article was his most forceful act.

The convention, its membership and its revisions of the state's organic law, alienated most of Twitchell's white neighbors. White Louisianians branded it the "Black and Tan Convention," the "mongrel Convention," the "Nigger Convention," the "Piebald Convention," and the "bastard convention." The *Bossier Banner* echoed the sentiments of whites from the Arkansas border to the Gulf: "We want no negro suffrage—nor negro jurors—nor negro governors—nor negro officers of any kind, State, parish, or municipal." This is "a white man's government." The newly enfranchised freedmen, the *Banner* asserted, were "semi-barbarians, ignorant, beastly, and besotted"; they were "BLACK VOMIT." The white delegates in New Orleans were thieves and scoundrels. Twitchell personally was a "perjured villain and notorious Radical Emissary."[10]

The carpetbag was a common article of luggage in the nineteenth

8. *Official Journal of the Proceedings of the Convention for Framing a Constitution for the State of Louisiana* (New Orleans, 1868), 201.

9. Ibid., 269, 277.

10. *Bossier Banner*, 12 October 1867, 18, 25 January, 2, 9 May 1868; *Alexandria Louisiana Democrat*, 11 December 1867.

century, so named because the shell of the bag resembled a cut-up section of carpet. It is safe to say that most well-traveled individuals on both sides of the Atlantic owned carpetbags. In the antebellum South, the term *carpetbagger* was sometimes used to describe unwelcome or suspicious strangers. During Presidential Reconstruction under Lincoln and Johnson, neither the word carpetbagger nor its pejorative cousin *scalawag* was part of the white South's political vocabulary. When Louisiana's radical constitutional convention first met in late 1867, Democratic newspapers variously denounced its white members as "renegades," "blackguards," "mongrels," "Jayhawkers," "loyal scum," "white niggers," and "radical pimps." Interestingly enough, the earliest references to scalawags usually pertained to the Yankee delegates, who were singled out as "imported scalawags," "Yankee adventurers," "political nomads," and "'poor white trash,' fresh from Yankee land." There was no mention of carpetbaggers.[11]

Carpetbagger first began creeping into the Democratic lexicon in late January and February 1868. The *Opelousas Courier* first used the term in a general reference to *all* the convention delegates. The first mention in the *West Baton Rouge Sugar Planter* in early March was an amalgam of prewar and emerging Radical Reconstruction meanings: "Mysterious. A stranger appeared in this parish yesterday whose attire consisted principally of a 'carpet-bag.' Is an election near at hand!" In Bossier Parish, just above Bienville, the *Banner*'s first use of the term in early April connected "Radical thieves" and "imported carpet-'baggers'" with "the work of this bastard Convention." By mid-April, however, the epithet was becoming ubiquitous in the Democratic press. Newspapers all over the state used it to discredit the convention and northern Republicans generally. No issue was seemingly complete without fulsome denunciations of this new species of villain.[12]

11. Franklin, *Reconstruction*, 93; *Alexandria Louisiana Democrat*, 20 November, 4, 11 December 1867; *Bossier Banner*, 23 November 1867, 28 March 1868; *West Baton Rouge Sugar Planter*, 11 January 1868. The term *imported scalawag* first appears in the *Banner* on 23 November and the *Louisiana Democrat* on 20 November. In Alabama, *scalawag* comes into use about the same time as in Louisiana, late 1867. The precise origin of the term is unknown. Sarah Woolfolk Wiggins, *The Scalawag in Alabama Politics, 1865–1881* (University, Ala., 1977), 2; Current, *Those Terrible Carpetbaggers*, 72.

12. *Alexandria Louisiana Democrat*, 29 January, 19 February, 25 March 1968; *Opelousas Courier*, 29 February 1868; *West Baton Rouge Sugar Planter*, 7 March 1868; *Bossier Banner*, 4 April 1868.

The emergence of the word *carpetbagger* as a potent political symbol—indeed, among the most potent such symbols in all of American history—coincided with mounting white fears over the April referendum on the radical constitution and the first statewide election of Radical Reconstruction. When the constitutional convention had first assembled the previous fall, the tone of the Democratic press had been largely contemptuous. Calling the proceedings a "ridiculous farce," Democratic editors had waxed ecstatic over the convention's financial embarrassments, ridiculing the race and social character of the delegates and predicting the assembly's bust-up. By late winter, however, ridicule had turned to alarm. Editors underscored the document's revolutionary features and exhorted whites to rally to its defeat. In January, moreover, the Louisiana Republican Party had nominated a slate of candidates for state office headed by Henry Clay Warmoth, an ex-Federal soldier from Illinois, for governor, and Oscar J. Dunn, a free man of color, for lieutenant governor. The referendum on the constitution and the general election were both scheduled for 17 and 18 April. The addition of the term *carpetbagger* into the broader lexicon of Louisiana Reconstruction coincided with this election to the month, almost to the week. In other words, at the exact moment when Radical Reconstruction was about to become a reality, Louisiana whites invented the carpetbagger as a counter-Reconstruction symbol. The opportunistic carpetbagger, the sum of his worldly goods stuffed in a tattered piece of luggage, became a stereotypical foil against northern demands that blacks be granted equal civil and political rights. Men like Warmoth and Twitchell became carpetbaggers before they were even in office. In the latter's case, apart from his year in the Freedmen's Bureau, his political history consisted of being elected a delegate to the constitutional convention, in which capacity he had voted for black suffrage and an equitable distribution of state school funds. Beyond that and marrying Adele and buying a plantation, he had no record, good or ill.[13]

At roughly the same time and in similar circumstances, Democrats in other states discovered the uses of the carpetbagger symbol. When Alabama's radical constitution failed to gain a majority in February

13. *Bossier Banner*, 12 October, 23 November 1867, 25 January, 28 March 1868; *Alexandria Louisiana Democrat*, 20 November, 11 December 1867, 1, 15 January 1868; *Opelousas Courier*, 23 November 1867.

1868, the *Montgomery Mail* gloated over the defeat of the state's "carpetbaggers and scalawags." With more wit, the Mississippi *Yazoo Banner* attacked a prominent northerner named Albert T. Morgan with new lyrics to a popular hymn:

> Old Morgan came to the Southern Land
> With a little carpet-bag in his hand.
> Old Morgan thought he would get bigger
> By running a saw-mill with a nigger.[14]

By mid-1868, the notion of carpetbagger infestation was becoming a Reconstruction legend, in the North as well as in the South. Northern reform editors such as E. L. Godkin of the *Nation* concluded that these so-called "carpet-baggers" must be a bad lot to have stirred up so much condemnation. That September the Democratic *New York World* pummeled the reputation of Louisiana's new Republican governor. Elected in April, Warmoth had only been in office a month when this bit of doggerel appeared:

> I am a carpet-bagger—
> I've a brother scalawag—
> Come South to boast and swagger
> With an empty carpet-bag,
> To rob the whites of Green-backs
> And with the blacks go bunk
> And change my empty satchel
> For a full sole-leather trunk.
> I'm *some* on constitution,
> For a late rebellious state,
> And I'm *some* on persecution,
> Of disloyal men I hate;
> I'm *some* at nigger meetings
> When white folks ain't about,
> And I'm *some* among the nigger gals
> When their marms don't know they're out.[15]

The carpetbagger tag would dog Warmoth, Twitchell, and their fellow northern migrants for their rest of their lives. In later years,

14. Current, *Those Terrible Carpetbaggers*, 72, 117.
15. Ibid., 92, 127.

Twitchell found himself attacked as a corrupt carpetbagger by Democratic newspapers in his home state of Vermont. "It has always seemed to me very strange," he reflected bitterly, "that the Northern people should so readily have believed their young men the infamous wretches which the South represented them to be, on the testimony of men reared under the demoralizing influence of slavery, traitors to their government for four years and then gamblers and barroom loafers." He conceded that some of the northern migrants behaved badly; but the larger portion, he insisted, "zealously worked for nearly ten years to substitute the civilization of freedom for that of slavery."[16]

The April 1868 Louisiana elections, which made an ex-Union soldier from Illinois governor and a free man of color lieutenant governor, saw another free man of color, Antoine Dubuclet, elected state treasurer. Republicans won majorities in both the house and senate. Seven blacks (18 percent) entered the senate and thirty-five (29 percent) the house. In Bienville Parish, Twitchell had stood for parish judge. Although defeated, his opponent was later disqualified under the disfranchisement clause of the constitution, and Twitchell assumed the office. His friend Edward Dewees, Bienville's last Freedmen's Bureau agent, went to the house of representatives.[17]

Louisiana's majority black electorate ratified the constitution, 66,152 votes to 48,739. Bienville Parish voted against the constitution, 780 to 635. Of the latter figure, 619 (97.4 percent) were black votes. Only Twitchell and fifteen other whites in the parish supported the constitution. Whites coerced ninety-two blacks into opposing ratification.[18]

In June 1868 the U.S. Congress readmitted Louisiana and six other states to the Union. A month later the Fourteenth Amendment became part of the U.S. Constitution. A new order was taking shape in the

16. *CV*, 18. One of the ironies of the carpetbagger story, largely overlooked, was the movement of "Confederate carpetbaggers" into the North. Daniel Sutherland estimates that in proportion to population there were probably more white southerners who moved to Yankeedom during Reconstruction than northerners who went south. *The Confederate Carpetbaggers* (Baton Rouge, 1988), 41–43.

17. Vincent, *Black Legislators in Louisiana*, 71; *CV*, 114–15; *Bossier Banner*, 9 May 1868, 17 April 1869.

18. Donald W. Davis, "Ratification of the Constitution of 1868—Record of the Votes," *LH* 6 (1965): 301–5.

South, one in which black people shared basic civil and political rights, voted, held office, sat on juries, and aspired to a better life. They dreamed of a southern homeland in which all men were treated with respect and dignity.

The white South spurned this revolutionary vision. At the very moment that Louisiana and most of the former Confederate states were coming back into the Union, a "Counter-Reconstruction" backlash was underway. The reaction focused on the 1868 presidential election. In May of that year the Republicans nominated Ulysses S. Grant for president. Two months later the Democrats chose former New York governor Horatio Seymour as his opponent. The northern Democratic Party had been proslavery, soft on the war, and was now anti-Reconstruction. Thus, to white southerners, a Seymour victory promised a retreat from Reconstruction.

The Ku Klux Klan first appeared in Pulaski, Tennessee, in 1866 as a Confederate social club. By mid-1868, the secret organization had spread into neighboring states. In Mississippi and other southeastern states that year, Klan nightriders conducted an organized campaign of violence and terror against the new Republican governments. Beyond rumors, solid evidence of the Klan's existence in Louisiana is fragmentary, but nightriders there were aplenty, and they mainly called themselves the Knights of the White Camellia. Organized in 1867, the White Camellia and kindred groups instigated vicious race riots in New Orleans, Opelousas, and the upper Red River parishes of Caddo and Bossier. In a three-week span, a Shreveport freedman named Solomon Thomas witnessed a parade of horrors. He saw armed whites capture four black men and a boy in a brickyard. The whites cut holes in the captives' hands with knives, then "ran [a] rope through their hands, [and] tied them together." The assailants dragged their victims across a bayou "half a mile to Red River, and there they shot them and shoved them in face forward." The bodies became caught in the river's back current. A month later they were still bobbing in the drift. Black bodies in the Red River became commonplace. Thomas personally claimed to have seen thirty, including "a woman with a child in her arms, both dead, floating down."[19]

19. *House Miscellaneous Documents*, 41st Cong., 2d Sess., No. 154, pt. 2, pp. 440–41; Franklin, *Reconstruction*, 150–69. Michael Perman reviews the literature on Reconstruction violence in "Counter Reconstruction: The Role of Violence in Southern Redemption," in *The Facts of Reconstruction: Essays in Honor of John Hope Franklin*, ed. Eric Anderson and Alfred A. Moss (Baton Rouge, 1991), 121–40.

William Meadows was an ex-slave and an ex-Federal soldier who had served in the constitutional convention with Twitchell. He lived with his wife and children on a farm in Claiborne Parish twenty miles north of Ringgold. One evening in early May, two white men killed him with shotguns as he and his son walked from the stable.[20]

Nightriders struck near Ringgold in late May, taking a black Republican named Moses Langhorne from his farmhouse and cutting off his head. The same night, vigilantes assaulted Massachusetts-born William H. Honneus, who had been the Republican candidate for sheriff a month before. A party of neighbors stopped at his house near Lake Bistineau about eleven o'clock and called out Honneus's name. "I looked out of the window to see who it was," Honneus later testified. "It was moonlight and I recognized the party, and did not think . . . my nearest neighbors, would do me any harm, so I went down to see what they wanted. One of them said, 'They want you down at the landing,' and at the same time raised his revolver and shot me right on top of the head and knocked me senseless." Pistol shots and shotguns blasts reverberated in the night. The assailants continued shooting even after Honneus's wife appeared on the balcony screaming for them to stop.

That same night, a party of horsemen stopped at Twitchell's gate and called out that they had a letter for him. Twitchell quickly dressed, grabbed his pistol and rifle, went out the back door, and made his way in the shadows to the front of the house. When Adele sent a black girl to fetch the letter, the riders became suspicious and rode off. Minutes later, a messenger arrived from Mrs. Honneus. Twitchell took a back path to his neighbor's plantation and found the lady nursing her wounded husband. Miraculously, most of the wounds were superficial. The next night, Twitchell, three blacks, and Adele, pistol in hand, guarded the Honneus house. The nightriders did not return. As soon as he was able to travel, Honneus packed up his family, abandoned his plantation, and moved to New Orleans.[21]

Twitchell and Honneus later testified about the episode before a U.S. House investigating committee. Such congressional investigations were a fixture of Reconstruction. Witnesses from every southern state

---

20. *House Executive Documents*, 44th Cong., 2d Sess., No. 30, pp. 264–67.

21. *Report of the Joint Committee of the General Assembly of Louisiana on the Conduct of the State Elections* (New Orleans, 1869), 155 (hereinafter *Conduct of the State Elections*); *House Miscellaneous Documents*, 41st Cong., 2d Sess., No. 154, pt. 1, pp. 656–57; *CV*, 116–17.

testified before House and Senate committees over a period of fifteen years. No state, it is safe to say, was the subject of more scrutiny than Louisiana. The first big investigation focused on the 1866 New Orleans riot; then three years later, Congress examined the 1868 election, about which Honneus and Twitchell testified. In the ensuing decade, almost on a yearly basis, Congress probed elections, Republican factionalism, the role of the army in Reconstruction, the New Orleans Customhouse, and the post-Reconstruction exodus of blacks to Kansas. The testimony runs to many thousands of pages and more or less constitutes an oral history of Reconstruction Louisiana. Sooner or later, just about everybody who was anybody appeared before a congressional committee. Although invariably partisan, the evidence had the great advantage of immediacy.

Twitchell testified five times over a span of eleven years. In his first appearance in May 1869, he described his three years in Bienville Parish and his part in the 1868 election. He had cast the only vote Ulysses S. Grant received in the parish. "I was compelled to advise the freedmen . . . not to vote," he informed the committee. "I knew from warnings which I had received and they had received that any black man who voted the Republican ticket would do so at the risk of his life." The congressmen thus inquired how it was that Twitchell had voted safely. For one thing, he explained, because he was the sole member of the board of registration who had not been scared out of Ringgold, he was the only person who could legally open the polls. He believed his property, his marriage into the Coleman family, and his status as a former federal official gave him a measure of protection that no freedman or scalawag enjoyed.

Moreover, while he refused to be "bluffed down," he had not exactly voted with impunity. The polls were in the middle of town. After dropping his ballot in the box, he spied "a well-known desperado" advancing toward him through the crowd, revolver in hand. Twitchell immediately exited the polling place, mounted his horse, and rode home. Earlier in the campaign, he avoided a White Camellia ambush only because he went to sleep on his mule and the mule took the wrong road. On another occasion, he slipped through a White Camellia cordon to New Orleans, there to read his obituary in the *Republican*.[22] A congress-

22. *House Miscellaneous Documents*, 41st Cong., 2d Sess., No. 154, pt. 1, pp. 62–66; *CV*, 119–20.

man asked him if he knew many of Bienville's black voters. "I do not think there is a man of them whom I am not acquainted with," he replied. He had registered most of them as voters.[23]

During the presidential campaign, for the first time since his marriage, Twitchell encountered social ostracism. Prominent Democrats, with whom he had been on good terms, stopped speaking and warned him to get out of the parish. Adele received hateful letters claiming her husband had been unfaithful. One morning in church Marshall and Adele listened in astonishment as their minister denounced Adele for marrying an outsider. Marshall retaliated by taking notes on the sermon, unsettling the clergyman. Badly frightened, the Colemans tried to persuade their son-in-law to withdraw from politics but to their credit, never turned their backs on him.[24]

Grant won the presidential election, but without Louisiana (or Georgia, which the Klan put in the Seymour column). The White Camellia and its ilk had a decisive impact at the polls. In April 1868 Warmoth received 65,000 votes for governor. Six months later Grant got only 33,000. Seven parishes recorded not a single vote for the hero of Appomattox; his combined total in nine other parishes was 19 votes. The Freedmen's Bureau reported that 297, mostly black, Republicans had been killed during the campaign. State officials, noting the incompleteness of the Freedmen's Bureau report, estimated 784 deaths and another 450 people wounded or physically abused. A congressional report put the number of dead at more than 1,100. The state report is probably nearest the mark, but whatever the exact number killed—and we will never know—it was enough to strike fear into every Louisiana Republican. As Twitchell told the House committee: "For the first time in all my living in Louisiana, I was compelled to keep [to] the house or to keep within the plantation. I never went near the woods . . . but always kept in the open ground."[25]

The 1868 presidential election profoundly influenced the whole history of Louisiana Reconstruction. From Governor Warmoth down, Republican leaders saw clearly that if the state elections had been set for

23. *House Miscellaneous Documents*, 41st Cong. 2d Sess., No. 154, pt. 1, pp. 63–65.

24. Ibid., 62–66; *CV*, 117–20.

25. *Conduct of the State Elections*, 301, 316–21; *House Miscellaneous Documents*, 41st Cong., 2d Sess., No. 154, pt. 1, p. 62.

November instead of the previous April, then Warmoth, Dunn, radical candidates for the legislature—and the constitution—would all have gone down to defeat with Grant's electors. Radical Reconstruction in Louisiana would have been crushed before it began. The election exposed the Republican regime's achilles heel: the vulnerability of the black vote to intimidation. Republican government in the state was only as strong as its ability to protect its black voting base. Thus over the next two years, the Warmoth administration enacted a program designed to forestall a repetition of the 1868 electoral debacle.[26]

The legislature reorganized the governments of New Orleans and adjacent parishes, giving the governor broad control over their affairs. The New Orleans Metropolitan Police Department was placed under the governor's direct supervision. New laws gave the governor broad control over elections. The lawmakers set up the state Returning Board to monitor election returns. After investigation, the Returning Board had the authority to overturn elections where it found fraud or intimidation. With the legislature's complicity, Governor Warmoth and his advisers increasingly found it expedient to bypass elections on one pretext or another, appointing formerly elected officials in New Orleans, Shreveport, Natchitoches, and other localities.[27]

On the upper Red River, Twitchell followed these events closely. Democratic complaints about the new election machinery, he wrote in an 1870 newspaper editorial, overlooked the cause: Democrats' own scurrilous epithets and violence. "Is it possible they thought Republicans would take no steps to avoid a repetition of 1868?" he queried. Could they believe Republicans had "forgotten the social and business ostracisms, the abuse and murders of the past two years?" Twitchell's logic was impeccable, but what he and others of his party failed to see was that the Republicans' centralized election apparatus raised a whole new set of issues. At the heart of Reconstruction politics was a question of legitimacy: Were governments based on black suffrage legitimate? Almost to a man, white Louisianians—indeed the white South—said no and registered their opposition with pistol and rope. Northern Democrats cast another no vote. The election machinery created by Louisiana Republicans—and by Republicans in other Reconstruction states—

26. Tunnell, *Crucible of Reconstruction*, 157–61.
27. Ibid.

addressed one wrongdoing with another. No political party could be trusted with a returning board empowered to discard election results at will. The abuses to which the system was prone would, in time, undercut the legitimacy of Louisiana's Reconstruction government almost as much as the tactics of the Democrats.[28]

The terrorism ceased after the 1868 presidential election, and Twitchell and his neighbors returned to peaceful pursuits. Twitchell's plantation sprawled on the 150-foot bluff above Lake Bistineau. It was a lovely place. Cypress rose from the lake, and tall pine, oak, and hickory trees, draped in heavy banners of moss, mounted the face of the bluff. From the crest, Twitchell could see beyond the lake an expanse of low forested hills stretching west toward Texas.

Lake Bistineau was Bienville Parish's gateway to the Red River and the outside world. Like most inland waterways, it needed constant clearing of stumps and debris, all of which had been neglected because of the war. In 1869 four Democrats from Minden introduced a bill in the legislature creating the "Lake Bistineau Navigation Company." The company was to receive $50,000 for clearing the lake, the money to be paid *after* completion of the work. In March, in the final stages of the bill's passage, Twitchell's friend and ally Edward Dewees, a member of the lower house, substituted Twitchell's name for one of the other incorporators. The measure passed both houses, but Governor Warmoth withheld his signature, regarding it as Democratic project. Because the measure passed in the last five days of the session, under Louisiana law the governor had until opening of the next session to make up his mind. In other words, the Lake Bistineau Navigation Company could remain in limbo until January 1870.

When news of Warmoth's action reached north Louisiana, the company's stock plummeted. Twitchell now sent his agent to Minden, and the agent proceeded to buy out the interests of the other incorporators. "As soon as my agent had left," he later wrote, "the town was filled with their boastings of how they had outwitted the Yankee." The boasting was short-lived. The Lake Bistineau Navigation Company was now a Republican project, and Warmoth signed the bill. Twitchell subcon-

28. *Sparta Times*, 26 November 1870; Tunnell, *Crucible of Reconstruction*, 160–61.

tracted the work to a steamboat captain who owned a clearing vessel. The energetic captain cleared the lake in a few months.[29]

The epilogue, however, was still to come. Twitchell's takeover of the lake-clearance project had made powerful enemies, and he had gone heavily in debt pushing it to completion. All of his work would be for nothing—indeed, he would be ruined—unless the state promptly reimbursed him. His Democratic enemies contrived a scheme to challenge the reimbursement in court. Win or lose, they figured the delay would crush Twitchell financially.

Despite Twitchell's Yankee accent and his abstemious personal habits, most southern males, politics aside, liked and respected him. Because of this, he developed an almost uncanny ability to get information about the plans of his adversaries. Learning of the plot to forestall state payment, he raced to New Orleans one day ahead of "the best lawyer in the parish." The state auditor and his clerks worked all through the night processing his claims—$48,600. The next day as he was leaving the auditor's office, he met the esteemed lawyer. The attorney said: "I dislike to do it on account of your wife's family, but a lawyer must serve his employers." Twitchell informed him that he was "six hours too late."[30]

The Lake Bistineau project made possible Twitchell's next move. In December 1869 he offered Colonel C. K. Gillespie and his wife, Carolyn, $21,000 for Starlight Plantation, located in a horseshoe bend of the Red River. Starlight encompassed 620 acres of the best bottomland in De Soto Parish. After some haggling, the Gillespies accepted the offer, $7,000 down and the balance within two years. In May 1870 Marshall and Adele moved about thirty miles from Ringgold to Starlight.[31]

For several years Twitchell had entertained the idea of establishing a Yankee colony in north Louisiana. William H. Honneus, run out of the Bienville Parish in 1868, had originally figured in the colony plan. "I proposed to form a settlement between myself and Mr. Twitchell,

29. *Acts of the State of Louisiana (1870),* 6 (the act is bound with the 1870 laws because the governor signed it in September 1869); *CV,* 121–22; *Senate Reports,* 46th Cong., 2d Sess., No. 388, pp. 1089–90.

30. *CV,* 121–22; *Senate Reports,* 46th Cong., 2d. Sess., No. 388, pp. 1089–90.

31. *CV,* 123–25; Louisiana Supreme Court, *Caroline Gillespie et al. v. M. H. Twitchell et al., Louisiana Annual Reports,* 34: 288–300; Starlight Plantation Documents, MHT Papers.

who is there yet," Honneus told a House committee, referring to his land above Lake Bistineau. "We had several others who were going to settle in our neighborhood." These others probably included Twitchell's kin, because in 1870 to 1871, Homer Twitchell, Marshall's three sisters and their husbands, and Marshall's widowed mother, Elizabeth, all moved from Vermont to Starlight. Then in mid-1870 Twitchell sold a half-interest in Starlight to his friend Edward Dewees. Dewees and his brother Robert, together with their wives, joined the Starlight nexus. Over the next few years, other northerners settled in the vicinity—Frank Edgerton, John W. Harrison, William S. Mudgett, Henry Scott—most of them in the small river town of Coushatta, two miles from Starlight on the east bank of the Red River.[32]

32. *House Miscellaneous Documents*, 41st Cong., 2d Sess., No. 154, pt. 1, p. 657; Starlight Plantation Documents; *CV*, 123–25. The lives of Twitchell and Edward Dewees intertwined over a ten-year period, yet Dewees remains an enigmatic figure. No Dewees manuscripts survive, and contrary to a statement made earlier in this work, he was a somebody who never testified before a congressional committee. Dewees later sold his half of Starlight back to Twitchell.

Map 2—Northwest Louisiana Parish Boundaries in Late 1870
Letitia Tunnell

NINE

THE FATHER OF RED RIVER PARISH

O N opposite shores, Starlight Plantation and Coushatta Chute lay in an isolated stretch of the Red River Valley midway between the river towns of Shreveport and Natchitoches. Citizens of the region had long wanted political boundaries redrawn and a new parish created. A new parish would mean increased representation in the legislature and more convenient local government. In order to pay their taxes or transact legal business, farmers across a vast distance had to visit the parish courthouse. In a day in which most of them rode mules, drove wagons, or walked, a trip to the parish seat was a major expedition. In good weather with dry roads, the *Sparta Times*, observed, "it takes two days for the citizen of Loggy Bayou to ride to Natchitoches to pay his taxes . . . while in high water time, he has to take passage on a steamboat or not go at all." In 1870 Twitchell won election to the state senate as a champion of the new-parish plan. In January 1871 he introduced his "Warmoth" Parish bill in the senate. The name was controversial, and he accepted an amendment changing it to "Red River" Parish.[1]

1. *Natchitoches People's Vindicator*, 21 December 1878; *Bossier Banner*, 29 January 1870; *New Orleans Republican*, 11, 27 January, 3, 14 February 1871; *Sparta Times*, 11 February, 22 April 1871, MHT Papers.

Twitchell's bill met stiff opposition from the towns of Natchitoches and Mansfield, the parish seats of Natchitoches and De Soto Parishes. The merchants, lawyers, and functionaries of these courthouse towns benefited from the status quo. Twitchell had made the Natchitoches trip himself. "I had first to go on horseback, and then on foot," he told the senate. "It cost me five dollars down, three dollars a day while there, and five dollars back." Another argument in favor of the new parish was enhanced law enforcement. Thieves and murderers often escaped punishment because the machinery of law enforcement was so remote. Twitchell cited an instance in which a murderer took the time to pack his household belongings and put his affairs in order before fleeing to Texas.[2]

Twitchell steered the Red River bill through the senate, while his business and political partner Edward Dewees managed it in the house. The pair skillfully outmaneuvered the opposition and pushed the bill to passage. Because both the young carpetbaggers were Warmoth supporters, the governor promptly signed the law.[3]

The Red River act directed Governor Warmoth, with the senate's "advice and consent," to appoint parish officials: a sheriff, justices of the peace, a tax collector, and police jurors. The appointees would serve until the first general election. The subsequent law incorporating Coushatta contained similar provisions. In practice, Twitchell chose the nominees, which the governor approved.[4]

Warmoth and the Republican majority, however, had more in mind than simply accommodating Twitchell and his constituents when they created Red River Parish. It was only one of eight parishes created during Radical Reconstruction. In each instance, the governor appointed entire slates of local officials, allowing the Republicans to seize and consolidate strategic footholds. As events in Red River and Grant Parish, twenty miles downriver, would later show, it was a risky strategy, but the risk must have seemed remote when Twitchell headed home to Starlight that spring.[5]

2. *Sparta Times*, 11 February, 22 April 1871, MHT Papers.

3. *CV*, 127.

4. *Acts Louisiana, 1871*, 86–88; *Acts Louisiana, 1872*, 74–78.

5. HRS, "County-Parish Boundaries in Louisiana" (New Orleans, 1939), 79–87; Lawrence N. Powell, "Centralization of Local Government in Reconstruction Louisiana: Democratic Contradictions and Republican Factionalism" (paper presented at Louisiana Historical Association meeting, March 1989); *New Orleans Republican*, 27 March 1873.

Twitchell, Dewees, and their kinsmen dominated the early political history of Red River Parish. Twitchell was president of the police jury (the county court) and president of the school board. Homer Twitchell was the first parish recorder, then later the tax collector. Belle Twitchell's husband, George A. King, became chief constable, a police jury-man, and mayor of Coushatta; he subsequently served terms as tax collector and sheriff. Twitchell's brothers-in-law Monroe C. Willis and Clark Holland were also officials—as were several of his friends and political allies.

Twitchell's influence extended into neighboring parishes. He and Dewees held positions in De Soto Parish as well as in Red River. Dewees's brother Robert was tax collector and supervisor of voter registration in De Soto. Marshall's wife's family, the Colemans, held important posts in Bienville. Indeed, Red River became the "Republican Stronghold" of northwest Louisiana.[6]

The Twitchell organization was a political ring, and people professed to be shocked. Ring politics, however, was a fixture of nineteenth-century local government from Maine to California, and Louisianians were no stranger to it. Nor was the Twitchell regime especially corrupt. After Reconstruction, the redeemer-controlled legislature dismissed the charges of alleged malfeasance against the carpetbagger and his allies. Considering that by this time, Twitchell's enemies controlled the parish government and all its records, these charges surely would have been validated if they had been true.

The creation of Red River Parish carved off prime pieces of De Soto and Natchitoches real estate. It also included a corner of Bienville and the panhandle tips of Caddo and Bossier Parishes. From Loggy Bayou to Bayou Lumbra, as the crow flies, a twenty-three-mile strip of Red River bottomland, four to six miles wide, cut lengthwise through the western third of the parish. East to west, the parish extended nearly twenty miles from Black Lake Bayou to Bayou Pierre. Although larger than a half-dozen parishes along the lower Mississippi, Red River was the smallest parish in north Louisiana.[7]

The parish's alluvial bottomlands were among the best cotton land

6. State Commission Books, 1868–1877, Louisiana State Archives, Baton Rouge; MHT White League document [1875], in the possession of Mary Twitchell.
7. *Biographical and Historical Memoirs*, 209; Lockett, *Louisiana*, 66–67.

in the state. There was good farmland in the uplands and verdant forests of shortleaf pine, oak, gum, hickory, and black walnut. In the northwestern hills near Lake Bistineau, the hum of small sawmills foreshadowed the rise of a timber industry. The parish's demographics were especially important. The first federal census in 1880 counted 6,007 blacks, living mainly in the bottomlands, and 2,506 whites, living mainly in the hills. Most people in the region clearly wanted the new parish. The citizens in northwestern Natchitoches and southern Caddo approved it by referendum, 383 to 13. All the same, one cannot help but wonder how many whites considered the future governance of a parish nearly three-fourths black, fathered by a Vermont carpetbagger.[8]

At Coushatta Chute, the Red River Valley narrows to a width of two miles. When Twitchell first saw it, only a warehouse and a country store stood on the bluff overlooking the river. The road east of the landing dipped low across Coushatta Bayou. A mile inland, it climbed a gentle slope into the village of Springville. Springville's location made it safer from yellow fever than Coushatta Chute. The disadvantage of the location, though, was increased shipping costs. Before the coming of the railroads after Reconstruction, the Red River was northwest Louisiana's "Main Street." Springville merchants had to haul cargo back and forth across Coushatta Bayou on an unpaved road.

In December 1868 a small group of business leaders, led by Thomas W. Abney, Mrs. Elizabeth A. Carroll, Marks and Julius Lisso, John F. Stephens, and several others, commissioned a town plan for the riverfront at Coushatta Chute. A year later the lots were selling and the town of Coushatta was going up (Chute was gradually dropped from the name). By 1871 most of Springville had moved to the river. During this same period, Twitchell planted his Yankee colony at Starlight and entered the state senate.[9]

Coushatta's street plan resembled a backward *F*. Along Front Street, bordering the river, rose the two-story office building of Abney & Love, and the stores of Abney & Co., Lisso Bros., Mrs. Carroll, and other merchants. Saloons and billiard parlors, the post office, and the

8. Lockett, *Louisiana*, 66–67; *Tenth Census, Population, 1880*; *Sparta Times*, 27 May 1871, MHT Papers.

9. *Coushatta Citizen*, 17 June 1938; "Plan of Town Lots," 18 December 1868, MHT Papers; *House Reports*, 43d Cong., 2d Sess., No. 261, pp. 489–90.

newspaper offices of the *Citizen* and the *Times* were also on Front Street. A block over on Abney Street were Fannie Pickens's school, the McLemore Building, and private homes. Carroll Street, the shank on the backward *F*, was perpendicular to the river and intersected the north ends of Front and Abney Streets. Along its length stood residences, Abney and Love's Coushatta Hotel, a livery and saloon, Prudhomme's general store, a "cheap" store, and other businesses. The town also had one or more groceries, doctors, a dentist, a confectionery, and a ten-pin alley. As the town filled up, new streets appeared—South Street, Main Street, and even Twitchell Street (long since disappeared).[10]

Just above the town, the river curved sharply to the west for more than a mile, then doubled back on itself in a horseshoe (almost an oxbow) bend. The western shoreline of the bend was all part of Starlight Plantation. South of the bend on the first rise of the bluff lining the valley, Twitchell's large, comfortable house stood in a clump of oak and hickory trees facing east. From the house he could see Coushatta in the distance. In late summer a plain of fleecy white cotton stretched from his front yard to the levee, which blended with the town's profile on the far shore, shimmering in the heat. The Yankee planter was among the chief speculators in the town, shrewdly buying and selling lots as business grew.[11]

At the start of the 1870s, considerable rapport existed between the carpetbagger clan on the Starlight side of the river and Coushatta whites. Because he was a Republican, Twitchell had been able to bring the dream of a new parish to fruition, with Coushatta as the parish seat, something no Democrat could have accomplished. During the legislative fight, Coushatta merchants had contributed more than $1,500 to a slush fund, which their new senator had used for lobbying and entertainment. In spite of his politics, Twitchell had earned a reputation as a hardworking, honest businessman. He and Adele went to church with their white neighbors, entertained them at Starlight, and were in turn invited to Coushatta homes.

Twitchell had been careful to give native-born whites a role in the

10. "Plan of Town Lots"; *Biographical and Historical Memoirs*, 215–16; Red River Parish Conveyance Records, Red River Parish Courthouse, Coushatta, La.
    11. Starlight Plantation maps, MHT Papers.

parish government as justices of the peace, parish judge, clerks of court, city councilmen, and so on. While some of these appointees were Republicans, others remained Democrats. Some whites were shocked that so many prominent men would accept office in a Republican administration. "My greatest objection to this country," a Coushatta woman wrote her sister, "is that there [are] so many radicals and they have supreme controll of every thing." Individuals, she added, "once looked upon as men of thorough-bred southern principals are now (for the sake of money) holding radical offices and voting with them."[12]

Twitchell's governance was a localized example of what one historian has called the "politics of convergence," in which Republicans, by playing down their differences with Democrats, tried to capture the political center. It imitated Governor Warmoth's strategy and that of other centrist Republicans from North Carolina to Texas. Twitchell used the patronage to try to build a base of white support and establish the legitimacy of Republican government. The lesson of 1868, in the Red River country as in the state, argued that Reconstruction was vulnerable as long as it depended upon a huge mass of black voters led by a tiny handful of carpetbaggers and scalawags. The legitimacy issue was personal as well as political. Like Warmoth, Twitchell wanted respectability. He sought a reputation as a solid businessman and community leader who was welcome in the homes of the "best people."[13]

Economic progress was another aspect of Twitchell's centrist strategy. With his plantation properties, town lots, and other investments, he stood among the inner circle of Coushatta's business elite. He had married into a southern family and had helped to restore its fortune. He was a business-minded modernizer who would remake Red River in the image of Yankee thrift and industry. He recognized, however, that for the near future, economic growth depended mainly on whites who possessed the wealth and the business know-how to use it. In time, through education and the acquisition of property, blacks would claim a greater

12. *New Orleans Republican*, 21 March, 4 May 1872; *Sparta Times*, 22 April, 17 May 1871, MHT Papers; *Biographical and Historical Memoirs*, 211, 213, 215; Etta M. McKinnie to Bessie Roach, 12 July 1871, Roach Collection, Cammie G. Henry Research Center, Northwestern State University of Louisiana, Natchitoches.

13. Michael Perman, *The Road to Redemption: Southern Politics, 1869–1879* (Chapel Hill, N.C., 1984), 24–25, 30–35, 42–46, 51–52.

share of society's economic bounty, but as the new stores went up on Front Street, that day of black fulfillment remained far off.[14]

An inevitable consequence of Twitchell's governance was that blacks, though 70.5 percent of the population and the backbone of the Republican Party, received a lesser share of the patronage than their numbers warranted. A contributing factor was the scarcity of blacks who could read and write, because to function effectively as a public official meant keeping records. With its 450 mostly white inhabitants, Coushatta was far and away the largest community in the parish. There were no *gens de couleur* here and little to attract the kind of literate blacks who lived in New Orleans and the larger towns.

Not surprisingly, the documentary record of black people's role in Red River Parish is much thinner than that for Twitchell and his family. Almost no African American correspondence has survived, and only a few editions of Coushatta's two newspapers, the Democratic *Citizen* and the Republican *Times*, are extant. The Red River Police Jury minutes and most other parish documents have also been lost. Whether the destruction of so many records was accidental, or a consequence of post-Reconstruction purging, is unknown. This much is clear: the few records that have survived show that black people's role was substantive.

Twitchell recruited a coterie of able black lieutenants, the most important of whom was Andy Bosley. Born a slave in 1837, a carpenter and engine mechanic by trade, the literate Bosley had lived in the Coushatta area all of his life. In 1861 he married Martha J. Brooks, who like her husband was a light-skinned mulatto. The 1870 census-taker listed both as white. The 1880 census-taker appears to have made the same error but then corrected it on the form. (Several prominent white families named Bosley lived nearby.) Because slave marriages were not recognized by law, in 1874, after Martha's death, Bosley signed a legal declaration—formally witnessed by Twitchell—attesting that he and Martha had lived together as man and wife and that their daughter, Mary, was a legal heir. Bosley remarried a black woman still in her teens named Ida Johnson. Over the next few years he became the head of a large extended family: three small children with Ida, his daughter Mary,

14. For comparison, see Ibid., 32–34, 44–45, 67–68.

Ida's mother, two sisters-in-law, and a brother-in-law—all living together in one house.[15]

In Red River's Reconstruction government, Bosley was coroner, a justice of the peace, a Coushatta city councilman, and Twitchell's chief link with the black community. Other black Republicans held comparable posts. P. E. Roach was a member of the police jury, a constable, and a deputy sheriff. For most of Reconstruction, William Peck, a school teacher from Rhode Island, was the parish recorder. Other black officials were Jerry Tooke (justice of the peace), Prior Porter (police juror and constable) and his brother Henry (constable), and Benjamin Perrow (police juror), a preacher. No African American was sheriff, tax collector, president of the police jury, or mayor of Coushatta.[16]

The exclusion of black leaders from top positions of authority was deceptive. The police jury was the key institution of parish government. Traditionally in Louisiana and the South, membership on this county court, as it was called in other states, was confined to a community's most respected citizens. (In their day, George Washington, James Madison, and Thomas Jefferson had all served on county courts.) The police jury's decisions affected schools, levees, taxes, roads, and law enforcement. On a day-to-day basis, the police jury was more important in the lives of people than the state legislature in New Orleans. Of the fifteen men who served on the Red River Parish Police Jury between 1871 and 1874, seven (46.6 percent) were black. The absence of a single white juror, as occurred on 16 May 1873, meant that the police jury had a black majority. A similar pattern developed with the justices of the peace. These local magistrates, in the words of one scholar, were "an important cog in the machinery of the administration of justice." Justices of the peace enforced parish ordinances and levee laws. They had jurisdiction over civil cases where the debt or fine did not exceed one hundred dollars (roughly one thousand dollars in current value). They could summon the sheriff or his deputies to enforce their rulings. When first organized, none of the Red River Parish justices of the peace were black, but in the years 1873 and 1874, two, and possibly three, of

15. *House Reports*, 44th Cong., 1st Sess., No. 816, pp. 709–11; Federal manuscript census, 1870, 1880; Red River Parish Conveyance Records.

16. State Commission Books.

the five justices of the peace were black. In parishes with black majorities, such as Red River, when whites complained of "Negro rule," they
usually had in mind the parish government, not the state government.
After Reconstruction, within a year of Twitchell's departure, there were
zero black members of the Red River Police Jury and *zero* black justices
of the peace.[17]

The jury panel was an institution of local government in which Red
River Parish blacks were represented in numbers roughly equivalent to
their population. In mid-1874, the *Coushatta Times* printed the complete parish jury list—both grand and petit. Of the one hundred names
on the list, seventy-eight have been identified from the census and other
records. Fifty-one of the names, 65 percent, belonged to black men.
The presence of so many black farmers and laborers on juries—along
with black justices of the peace and members of the police jury—had a
good deal to do, one suspects, with the low incidence of crime against
freedmen of which Twitchell later boasted to a congressional committee. Here again, when Red River's redeemers took control of the parish,
they reversed the trend. By the fall of 1877, the number of blacks on
the jury panel had dropped to eighteen, less than 20 percent. This was
still too many prospective black jurors for the Democratic *Coushatta
Citizen*. The upcoming meeting of the district court, the newspaper
predicted, "will draw a large crowd of freedmen to the courthouse,"
further delaying farmers' efforts to harvest what little cotton had survived the recent heavy rains. In all probability, the paper said, "every
day during Court there will be a hundred or so field hands loafing about
the courthouse, waiting a chance to get on the jury for a dollar a day in
parish script, or about sixty cents in green backs." How unfortunate
that black people were more concerned with politics and jury duty than
with honest labor, the newspaper concluded.[18]

As far as is known, Red River black leaders did not protest Twitchell's division of the patronage loaves and fishes. They may have been
suspicious of his efforts to bring whites into the Republican ranks, but
they had ample reason for accepting their lot without complaint. Red

17. Ibid.; R. L. Carleton, *Local Government and Administration in Louisiana* (Baton
Rouge, 1935), 45–57; *Coushatta Times*, 24 May 1873.

18. *Coushatta Times*, 1 August 1874; *Coushatta Citizen*, 17 June 1938.

River planters were a hard-bitten bunch, and the hills on either side of the valley were peopled with hostile white farmers. It was not by chance that Harriet Beecher Stowe chose the upper Red River as the locale for the brutal ending of *Uncle Tom's Cabin*. Along with East Texas, the upper Red River had been the slave regime's rawest frontier, with a well-earned reputation for murder and mayhem. Frontier violence lingered in the valley after the war like a deadly virus, afflicting the local population and attracting outlaws, gamblers, and other predators from Texas, Arkansas, and the Indian nation. During Reconstruction most whites in the region viewed one black man in office as the beginning of "Negro Rule," and each additional black official only added to their stock of fear and resentment. A study of violence in neighboring Caddo Parish in the two decades after the Civil War has documented 652 homicides. In the great majority of these killings, the victims were black males, usually casualties of white males acting in groups. About 10 percent of the adult black males in Caddo Parish under the age of forty-six died violent deaths in these years. A disproportionate number of the victims were black leaders. The murders, in other words, were not random, but a systematic method of race control.[19]

As a trouble spot, Red River was only a step behind Caddo. The first two sheriffs of Red River exited office via gunshot wounds, and one of the pair exited life. The early tax collectors suffered similar fates. Whatever Twitchell's motive for making Andy Bosley coroner instead of sheriff, the decision allowed Bosley to survive Reconstruction and grow old with his family. Whether this outcome was part of a reasoned strategy on Twitchell and Bosley's part is impossible to know, but neither man was stupid.

Education was another area in which Twitchell protected the interests of his black constituents. Schooling was a vexing statewide problem for Republicans. Before the war, Louisiana's public schools, like those of her sister southern states, had lagged far behind the North's. Inadequate funding, planter hostility, public apathy, and the opposition of the Catholic Church had undermined the ambitious public school act of 1847. In 1861, with a school-age population of 96,522 whites and

19. Gilles Vandal, "The Policy of Violence in Caddo Parish, 1865–1884," *LH*, 32 (1991): 164–67.

revenues of about $620,000, fewer than 40,000 Louisiana children, most of whom lived in New Orleans, attended schools at state expense.[20]

Determined to do better, the Republicans nonetheless faced nearly insurmountable odds. In 1873, with a school-age population of 272,334 black and white children, state school funds totaled a mere $678,473, a fractional increase over prewar spending, with nearly three times the number of children needing schooling. The Republican government relied upon a two-mill state school tax, expecting that parish school boards would raise the additional money needed for new buildings, teachers, desks, and other improvements. Alas, local authorities generally failed to raise the extra money. The reasons were numerous. Thomas W. Conway, the first state superintendent of education, tried to enforce the constitutional provision requiring integrated schools (Article 135). Most whites opposed using tax dollars to educate black children under any circumstances, much less in racially mixed schools. Many whites opposed school taxes even for the education of white children. Corruption was another cause. Public officials, Democrat and Republican, black and white, stole school money. Black state senator David Young could not explain the disappearance of $31,000; a white Republican senator embezzled $85,000. Beyond all this, even in the best of times, most of the state's people were poor and would remain so for decades. During the first eight months of 1874, hard times closed schools all over the state. Republican officials agonized over the situation but were unable to change public opinion, stop the corruption, or raise the price of cotton on the world market.[21]

Twitchell succeeded far better than most Republicans. Negroes "were in a degraded state on account of their ignorance," he believed, but they were eager to learn. In 1871, as president of the school board, he set about organizing schools in Red River Parish. Ignoring the state constitution, he proposed two primary schools in each ward, one for blacks, one for whites. Nonetheless, most of his white supporters broke

20. Raleigh A. Suarez, "Chronicle of Failure: Public Education in Antebellum Louisiana," *LH* 12 (1971): 117–22; *Annual Report of the State Superintendent of Education*, 1874, x; Taylor, *Louisiana Reconstructed*, 453.

21. *Annual Report of the State Superintendent of Education*, 1874, x; Thomas W. Conway, circular to school directors, 16 May 1870, HRS, State Department of Education Records, Louisiana State Archives, Baton Rouge; Taylor, *Louisiana Reconstructed*, 261–66.

ranks with him, wanting no part of educating "niggers." Hoping to
crack the wall of prejudice, he built a black school at Starlight and hired
his sister Helen, a Yankee schoolmarm, as teacher. When whites refused to budge, Twitchell acted on his own, implementing his two-
school program. Ominous rumors circulated that the black schools
would soon be burned. Twitchell announced that if any black school
was destroyed, the teachers in the locality's white school would not be
paid. The threat worked, but the Vermonter used up a lot of political
capital.[22]

Red River Parish was in Louisiana's fourth school division. Encom-
passing the entire Red River Valley, the fourth was the largest of the
state's six school districts and one of the hardest districts to administer.
Starting in mid-1871, Twitchell managed to get four schools started,
and 161 students enrolled by Christmas. Of the three new parishes created in the fourth division that year, Red River was the only one in
which any schools existed at year's end. By 1873, of the fourteen parishes in the fourth division, Red River had the highest percentage of
school-age youth actually in school (36 percent); the average in the
other parishes was 23 percent. State officials lauded Twitchell's achievement. In his 1871 report, J. Sella Martin, the fourth division's black superintendent, observed that Twitchell and his brother, Homer, the
school treasurer, had demonstrated "their faith in the permanence of
the public school system by advancing their own money, not only to
pay teachers, but to erect schoolhouses." Only their "zeal," Martin
concluded, had gotten the system started. Two years later, State Superintendent Conway's black successor, William G. Brown, wrote: "It is
sufficient when speaking of this parish to state that the Hon. M. H.
Twitchell is connected with the board of directors. This gentleman is a
pioneer in the public school work of the State, and the founder of the
cause in Red River parish." Twitchell's achievement endured. In the
decade after Reconstruction, an average of more than 400 black students attended school each year in the parish, slightly outnumbering
their white peers.[23]

One of Red River's fourth division neighbors provided an example

22. *CV*, 128–29; Biographical sketch of MHT, Charles W. Smith Papers, Indiana
Historical Society, Indianapolis.

23. *Annual Report of the State Superintendent of Public Education*, 1871, 227, 236; Ibid.,
1873, 86–87, 212; *Biographical and Historical Memoirs*, 215.

of the mismanagement and corruption that plagued Louisiana's Reconstruction schools. In 1871 the district superintendent reported that Sabine Parish had failed to establish a single school. But two years later, parish officials reported the existence of twenty-nine schools with an attendance of 1,281, an astonishing 57 percent of school-age children. If correct, these figures made Twitchell and every other Republican educator in the state look like foot-dragging obstructionists. Alas, the figures were false. In March 1874, a resident named Valmont Byles wrote State Superintendent Brown asking why "we have not had a public school in this parish for twenty-two months?" Adjacent parishes had schools and teachers, and it was grossly unfair to him and his tax-paying neighbors that none existed in Sabine. Upon investigation, the state superintendent found that Byles's complaint was largely true. J. F. Smith, the school-board treasurer, responded to Brown's inquiry by demanding the name of the informer and denouncing him as a "worthless, lying, mischief-making dog." Smith conceded, however, that the earlier report was in error. Instead of twenty-nine schools, he now claimed only four. Superintendent Brown asked the logical question: What had Smith and his cronies "done *with the [18]73 school money?*"[24]

In the beginning Red River Parish fulfilled the expectations of its founders. Crops were comparatively good, and the new courthouse was indeed more convenient than was the long trip to Mansfield or Natchitoches. Red River's prosperity, Twitchell declared, was "the envy" of neighboring parishes, and Coushatta "was indisputably the most industrious and beautiful of the Small Towns of Northern Louisiana." Louisiana State Seminary professor David H. Lockett observed in his 1872 topographical survey that Coushatta "has but recently sprung into existence, but it is one of the prettiest and most enterprising small towns in the state. It has grown rapidly within the last two years and seems likely still to improve." Gilded Age novelist Mary E. Bryan, a close observer, lived in Springville from 1868 to about 1874. Her novel *Wild Work* fo-

---

24. *Annual Report of the State Superintendent of Education,* 1871, 237; *Annual Report of the State Superintendent of Education,* 1873, 101; Valmont Byles to State Superintendent William G. Brown, 14 March 1874, HRS, State Department of Education Records; J. F. Smith to State Superintendent William G. Brown, 13 April 1874, HRS, State Department of Education Records.

cuses on Coushatta and Twitchell (thinly disguised as "Cohatchie" and "Witchell"). While parts of her book are invented, her descriptions of places and people—and some events—are generally accurate. She admired the town's whitewashed cottages, modern brick stores, and "the cupola of the really handsome court-house." Coushatta, she wrote, "had the irregular appearance that marks a new place, but the bales of cotton piled before the warehouse, and the amount of freight in boxes and barrels which a steamboat, petulantly puffing at the landing, had just discharged, told of thrift and business." Even the rabidly antiradical *Shreveport Times* praised early Coushatta as a thriving community full of prosperous and industrious people.[25]

"A few young men of Northern Birth," Twitchell wrote, "ex-officers and Soldiers of the Federal army, possessors of both Capital and enterprise" had turned Coushatta, a burned-out river landing when the war ended, into a garden spot. These "early Northern Colonists," purchasers of "the most valuable property in the town and Parish . . . fostered nearly every industry and every public improvement," he claimed. He and his family contributed money for schools and churches, he told a congressional committee. They brought steam engines upriver from New Orleans and built Starlight Mills, a complex of cotton gins, lumber mill, grist mill, and cotton press. Starlight, Bryan wrote in her novel, had the ambience of a New England village, brimming with energy and industry. Its "well-stocked storehouse furnished customers, mostly the negroes belonging to the place and to neighboring plantations, with provisions and other merchandise." The plantation even had a printing press and a newspaper office. Subsidized by state contract, the *Sparta Times* was the official state journal for four neighboring parishes. Some two hundred or more people, mostly black, worked on Starlight and Twitchell's other properties.[26]

The prosperity of the parish, Twitchell told a congressional committee, "was noticeable by the most perfect stranger; you could almost tell when you would reach the parish line." The black people's sense of security, he said, was a major factor. The parish government vigorously

25. MHT White League document [1875]; Lockett, *Louisiana*, 66–67; *Shreveport Times*, 15 January 1873; Mary E. Bryan, *Wild Work: The Story of the Red River Tragedy* (New York, 1881), 130.

26. MHT White League document [1875]; *House Reports*, 43d Cong., 2d Sess., No. 261, p. 385; Bryan, *Wild Work*, 130–31; *Sparta Times*, MHT Papers.

prosecuted the Negro-baiting toughs that preyed on the freedmen. "Whenever a murder was committed, we would either arrest the party or force him out of the parish," said Twitchell. This sometimes meant "going ourselves as *posses comitatus*." Thus, he explained, blacks "came from Sabine and other parishes until we did not lack labor at all—we had abundance of it." (He might also have added that Red River had black schools and Sabine had none.) Twitchell perhaps exaggerated, but his boasting was not hollow. He had indeed created the most stable political economy in north Louisiana. Given the cruel constraints of postwar race relations and economics, to a remarkable degree he had made Reconstruction work in Red River Parish.[27]

Still and all, the Vermont carpetbagger overlooked vital forces. Across the South, nearly three years of unrelenting hardship followed the Civil War. In many places, whites and blacks battled starvation. In Louisiana, high water and the army worm devastated the cotton crops two years in a row. The year 1868 witnessed the first decent crops since Appomattox, ushering in a brief economic recovery. The creation of Red River Parish and Coushatta coincided with this economic upswing that peaked in Louisiana in 1870–1871. The building of Coushatta created jobs and inspired a growth psychology. Moreover, as the parish seat the town did, as predicted, bring in business that hitherto had gone to Sparta, Natchitoches, Mansfield, and other courthouse towns.[28]

The Red River was an important factor in Coushatta's growth. Old Red was a mile wide near its juncture with the Mississippi. Above Alexandria the river narrowed and turned and twisted in tortuous curves. It also grew more shallow. The most experienced pilots ran afoul of sandbars and snags even "in season," the period of high water usually lasting from October through early June. From July through September, the low-water season, pilots, shippers, and travelers fretted constantly about the river's depth. A trip from New Orleans to Shreveport that took three days in March could take three weeks in August—and the last leg of the trip by horseback.[29]

27. *House Reports*, 43d Cong., 2d Sess., No. 261, p. 385.

28. Taylor, *Louisiana Reconstructed*, 350–58; William C. Harris, *The Day of the Carpetbagger: Republican Reconstruction in Mississippi* (Baton Rouge, 1979), 274–90.

29. Lockett, *Louisiana*, 122–23; *Shreveport Times*, 18 August 1874.

The river swept through Coushatta Chute in a swift, narrow channel. Despite the current, Coushatta Bayou pumped a steady flow of silt into the river, creating mud bars. Just above the town at the mouth of the north branch of the bayou, the river curved sharply to the west. Here beneath the rippling dark water, stretched Coushatta Bar, the most formidable of the two bars bracketing the town. In those days, shippers and travelers followed the rise and fall of the river assiduously. Among the most read newspaper columns in the state was Colonel E. Mason's "River and Weather" report in the *Shreveport Times*. When the river was low, Colonel Mason devoted more space to Coushatta Bar than any other trouble spot between Shreveport and Alexandria. In deep summer, clearance at the bar sometimes dropped to fifteen inches of water. Old Red was unpredictable, too. In 1872 the period of extreme low water came in autumn instead of summer. For long weeks in October and November, clearance was barely seventeen or eighteen inches at Coushatta Bar. The builders of flat-bottomed riverboats designed them to float *on* the water, not—like the keels of deep-water ships—*in* the water. No riverboat, however, could negotiate less than two feet of water without help. Thus men and animals had to tow boats over the bar. Towing often meant lightening a steamer's load. In July 1874, even with nearly three feet of water, the *Belle Rowland* had to move 150 tons of cargo onto a barge before she could be pulled over Coushatta Bar. This jettisoning of cargo at Coushatta was so common a sight as to hardly excite notice. Small herds of cattle and sheep leaped into the water and waded ashore. The steamer *Bryarly* reached Coushatta at dawn on a Saturday to find two other boats already stuck on the bar. The *Bryarly* waited her turn and cleared the mud bank early Sunday morning.[30]

The river's treachery sometimes verged on the diabolical. The *Behan*, Mason wrote, "ran up on a snag just as she was blowing her whistle to make the landing at Coushatta." To stop her from sinking, her desperate captain threw "overboard a large portion of her cargo, including between 350 and 400 sacks [of] salt, a quantity of shot, six or seven casks [of] bacon, and other articles." Small wonder that the Cou-

---

30. J. Fair Hardin, "An Outline of Shreveport and Caddo Parish History," *LHQ*, 18 (October 1935): 102–5; *Shreveport Times*, 26 July, 5, 12, 18 August 1874.

shatta coast earned a reputation as the "steamboat grave yard." The wrecks of half-a-dozen ships protruded from the water like gravestones along that stretch of Old Red.[31]

The delays, so costly to shippers, benefited the town during the slack summer months. Coushatta Bar functioned like a toll plaza, local citizens levying taxes on each vessel that needed help over the bar, storage for unloaded cargo, fodder for animals forced ashore, food, lodging, and transportation for stranded passengers. The falls at Alexandria had a similar effect on that city's economy.

In sum, the newness of the town and its location boosted Coushatta's prosperity. The regional economic revival, however, was easily the most important influence. Without it, little that Twitchell did would have mattered. In the beginning, most residents of Coushatta, some begrudgingly, credited their carpetbagger senator with giving the locale a fresh start, but their gratitude was as thin as bayou ice. By late 1872, Coushatta's prosperity, like that of the rest of the South, was fading. The economic decline coincided with a disputed election, which threw the entire state into turmoil. The combination of economic and political woes led to a deep division among Coushatta's business elite.

The files of the Mercantile Agency, the pioneering New York credit company, allow an inside look at Coushatta's business community. The Mercantile Agency relied on a network of local agents, usually lawyers and merchants, to assess the acumen and creditworthiness of businessmen, not only in Louisiana and the South, but all over the country. The anonymous Mercantile agents tracked the fortunes of all businesses in Red River Parish, including the firms in Coushatta. The agents also kept tabs on Coushatta's lawyers, some of whom were also in business. There is, of course, a Twitchell file. It describes him as a creditworthy man of good character who owned large real estate and was making money. The file also describes him as "shrewd, sharp," and energetic. The credit reports never mentioned politics, but they clearly had political implications. Using the Mercantile Agency reports combined with other sources, it becomes possible to reconstruct the political economy of Coushatta and Red River Parish in the early 1870s.[32]

31. *Shreveport Times,* 5 August 1874; *Coushatta Citizen,* 17 June 1938.
32. Louisiana, 19: 3, R. G. Dun & Co. Collection, Baker Library, Harvard Graduate School of Business Administration. See James D. Norris, *R. G. Dun & Co., 1841–1900: The Development of Credit-Reporting in the Nineteenth Century* (Westport, Conn., 1978).

Initially, Twitchell's regime had broad backing from Coushatta's business elite, even though most of the town leaders remained Democrats. Within a year or two, though, Front Street began to sort itself into two factions. The nucleus of the pro-Twitchell faction was an influential family of German Jews led by Marks and Julius Lisso. While most of the town's merchants had contributed money to the fund that Twitchell used to get the parish created and the town incorporated, it was Marks and Julius Lisso who gave him carte blanche, Twitchell said, "to draw on them for whatever I needed." The first police jury met in the Lisso Bros. store, and Julius became parish treasurer. Most of Twitchell's business dealings involved the Lissos, including the financing of a parish courthouse. The carpetbagger needed a base of support on Front Street, and in turn, Lisso Bros., furnishing merchants, benefited from the trade of black Republican sharecroppers. While Twitchell socialized at some level with most of Coushatta's business leaders, it was with these German Jews that he was most comfortable. He and Julius Lisso became close friends.[33]

Jews were an influential minority in Louisiana, even though their exact number is unknown. The 1870 federal census, for example, counted 2,200 Jews in the state, *all* living in either New Orleans or Shreveport. Historians of southern Jewry, however, estimate that there were three or four times that many Jews in the state, giving it the largest Jewish population in the South. The census is incomplete. In *The Business of Jews in Louisiana, 1840–1875*, Elliot Ashkenazi finds evidence of Jewish businesses in thirty-seven of the state's forty-seven parishes. In the Red River Valley, the Mercantile Agency files document the presence of Jewish merchants in most river towns. Jewish merchants and peddlers were commercial trailblazers in the region.[34]

The Lissos were one of these pioneering Jewish families. A. Michael Lisso, the older brother of Julius and Marks, came to the United States in the early 1840s, when he was hardly more than a boy. In 1851 he opened a small country store at Coushatta Chute. For years it was the only store at the landing, and local people often referred to the place as

33. *House Reports*, 44th Cong., 1st Sess., No. 816, p. 652.
34. Ninth Census, *Population*; Elliott Ashkenazi, *The Business of Jews in Louisiana, 1840–1875* (Tuscaloosa, Ala., 1988), 8–9, 15; Stephen Hertzberg, *Strangers within the Gate City: The Jews of Atlanta, 1845–1915* (Philadelphia, 1978), 281 n.

"Jacob's Town." He married Pauline Wolfson, the daughter of another Jewish merchant. Julius and Marks followed their brother from the old country to Louisiana some time in the 1850s. They settled in Springville and learned merchandising in their older brother's store.[35]

The Lissos fit the pattern of Jewish migration described by Elliot Ashkenazi. The earliest Jews in Louisiana arrived in the eighteenth and early nineteenth centuries. Few in number, they were generally Sephardic (Iberian in ritual). Many of them, like Judah P. Benjamin, the best known, were from the Caribbean. The Lissos were part of a second and larger immigration of Ashkenazic Jews (central European in ritual) from France and Germany that occurred between 1830 and 1870. They came from the towns and villages of a precapitalist rural society, in which Jews were prohibited from owning land. Their fathers and grandfathers had thus been merchants and tradesmen. In important respects, the antebellum South resembled their homeland. Like Prussia, it was a rural agricultural society dominated by a landowning elite, which offered opportunity to a cohesive minority oriented toward commerce. "Jews filled a void in the feudal South," Ashkenazi writes, "as they had in many other settings around the world, through their minority status and their nonconformist religious and commercial practices."[36]

Marks was twenty-five when the Civil War broke out and Julius twenty-three. They lived in Springville with their older brother. Both were merchants and neither was married. Unlike many German immigrants in the South, the Lissos fought willingly for the Confederacy. Marks and Julius enlisted in A Company of the First Louisiana Infantry in the beginning days of the war. A later newspaper story accorded Marks the honor of "being the first Confederate volunteer" from the Coushatta Chute region. Marks and Julius fought in the Louisiana Brigade—"Lee's Tigers"—of the Army of Northern Virginia. Michael Lisso stayed home and served in the Louisiana Reserve Corps.[37]

35. *Biographical and Historical Memoirs*, 226; Louisiana, 7: 118, 134, R. G. Dun & Co. Collection; Receipts dated 23 November 1842, Misc. Box 8, Ellen L. Nachman Collection, Cammie G. Henry Research Center; Obituary, Scrapbook, 70: 141, Melrose Collection, Cammie G. Henry Research Center.

36. Ashkenazi, *Business of Jews in Louisiana*, 5–11; See Bertram Wallace Korn, *The Early Jews of New Orleans* (Waltham, Mass., 1969).

37. *Records of Louisiana Confederate Soldiers and Louisiana Confederate Commands*, comp. Andrew B. Booth (New Orleans, 1920), 3: 768; Scrapbook, vol. 72, Melrose Collection.

In the 1864 Red River campaign, Yankee cavalry burned Coushatta Landing. A few months after the war, Marks and Julius formed Lisso Bros. and rebuilt Coushatta Landing, putting up a log warehouse and country store. Michael moved to New Orleans. The credit reports of the Mercantile Agency chart the history of Lisso Bros. In the first year or two the brothers struggled with debt and nearly went under, but business gradually improved. In 1870–1871, the credit agents' reports praised them: "Good & safe. Old Merchants d[oin]g a large prosperous bus[iness]"; "Men of high tone"; "A No 1 in all respects, shrewd, calculating & prosperous"; "all the officers of the Red River Boats speak well of them and say they are w[orth] fully $20 [thousand]."[38]

The attraction between Twitchell and the Lissos had its own logic. Anti-Semitism was not as virulent in the South as in the North. The first Jew to serve in the cabinet of an American president was Judah P. Benjamin, who held three cabinet posts under Jefferson Davis. (The first Catholic cabinet officer was also in the Davis administration.) On the other hand, historians have repeatedly emphasized the isolation and loneliness of southern Jews, especially the first generation. A Jewish merchant in a small community like Coushatta, with his foreign accent, his mysterious religion, was "the eternal stranger." Although they were white, "or at least men who could pass for white," one scholar writes, Jews invariably remained "outsiders." There is ample evidence of such attitudes in the Mercantile Agency files. The only religious references in the credit evaluations come when agents describe Jewish merchants. It is from the Mercantile reports that we learn that Coushatta Chute was nicknamed "Jacob's town." In describing the Lissos, the credit agents used phrases such as "A Jew," "Good Jews," "Are Hebrews," "Although Jews," and "A real live active Jew mercht." While such comments do not appear to have prejudiced the agents' credit evaluations, they do at the very least suggest an ethnocentric perception of these Jewish merchants. The Lissos, in other words, like Twitchell won acceptance as businessmen and community leaders, but at the same time remained (in the inner social world of white, Protestant Coushatta) outsiders.[39]

38. Louisiana, 7: 118, 134, R. G. Dun & Co. Collection; Louisiana, 19: 8, R. G. Dun & Co. Collection.

39. Ben Kaplan, *The Eternal Stranger: A Study of Jewish Life in the Small Community* (New York, 1957), 8; Eli N. Evans, *The Provincials: A Personal History of Jews in the South* (1973; reprint, New York, 1997), 38; Louisiana, 7: 118, 134, R. G. Dun & Co. Collection; Louisiana, 19: 8–9, R. G. Dun & Co. Collection.

Such perceptions would have been reinforced by the tight-knit structure of the Lisso family. All three Lisso brothers married Jewish women. For many years, their business was strictly a family enterprise. When Michael Lisso moved to New Orleans, reportedly to provide for the education of his sons, Paul and Samuel, his brothers took over the Coushatta Chute business, probably with Michael as a silent partner. A few years later Paul and Samuel returned to Coushatta and worked as merchant apprentices for their uncles. In late 1872, at ages nineteen and twenty respectively, Paul and Samuel opened their own store on Front Street adjacent to Marks and Julius's furnishing store. The tight-knit structure of the Lisso family mirrored the tight-knit structure of the Twitchell family.[40]

Commercial values welded another bond between Twitchell and the Lissos. Whether the Lissos's entrepreneurial spirit was inherent in the Jewish religion is a scholarly controversy beyond the scope and competence of this book.[41] Whatever the reason, the Lissos were demonstrably an enterprising, entrepreneurial family. They worked long and hard, lived modestly, and reinvested their earnings. Their values found a companion spirit in Twitchell's Puritan ethic. On average, German Jews and Vermont Calvinists created and attained more wealth than other Americans wherever they settled in the South (or in the nation).[42]

Lisso Bros. was one of the two most important merchant houses in Coushatta. Marks and Julius formed the core of a small but influential group that remained Twitchell loyalists to 1874, a pivotal year in the story of Louisiana Reconstruction. Other members of the group were Thomas Paxton, Duke H. Hayes, Judge Orin S. Penny, parish attorney William Howell, Sheriff John T. Yates, and Mrs. Elizabeth Carroll. Yates, like Twitchell, was a carpetbagger, albeit from Missouri. Penny had come from Ohio before the war; he and Paxton started out in

40. Louisiana, 19: 10, R. G. Dun & Co. Collection.

41. This is the thesis of Werner Sombart, *The Jews and Modern Capitalism*, trans. M. Epstein (1911; reprint, New York, 1969). For a refutation of Sombart see Fernand Braudel, *Civilization and Capitalism, 15th–18th Century: The Wheels of Commerce* (London, 1982), 154–60, 165–67.

42. This conclusion is drawn from McPherson, *Ordeal by Fire*, 14; Ashkenazi, *Business of Jews in Louisiana*; Korn, *Early Jews of New Orleans*; Hertzberg, *Strangers within the Gate City*; Louise Matthews Hewitt, *Days of Building: History of a Jewish Community* (Shreveport, La., 1966).

Coushatta as law partners. Mrs. Carroll, one of the founders of the town, often did business with Twitchell. Mrs. Carroll and the Lissos excepted, what these people had in common was professional status (four of them were lawyers) without much professional success. After his partnership with Penny broke up, Howell formed a partnership with another attorney. The Mercantile file on him and his partner reads "not much pract[ice]." The Mercantile report on Hayes describes him as a man of good standing and integrity but "sm[all] means." Yates won the bid to build the new courthouse, but lacked the capital to carry through the project. None of these men were successful independent businessmen. They all took public jobs in the early 1870s. With the possible exception of Paxton, all needed public money to make ends meet. And Twitchell controlled the patronage. This radical coterie, in other words, was bonded by what the historian Lawrence N. Powell has called "the politics of livelihood."[43]

A second faction coalesced around Thomas W. Abney, Coushatta's other leading furnishing merchant. By most standards, Abney was the first man of the town. Born in Alabama about 1831, he had grown to manhood in Bossier Parish, where his father was a small planter. During the war he had served as a company commander in the Twenty-eighth Louisiana Regiment, rising to the rank of major. In 1866 he opened a country store in Springville and three years later, as the partner of Mrs. Leander E. Love, became a founder of Coushatta. Judged by his property interests on Front and Carroll Streets, he was the wealthiest man in town. In early 1873, a Mercantile agent reported that Abney and Love had cleared $15,000 the previous year and invested it all in real estate.[44]

Mrs. Love retired from the firm in 1872, and her husband, Leander, took her place. John L. Stephens joined the partnership that year, too. Where Abney, Love, and Stephens led, most of Front Street—store owners, saloon-keepers, blacksmiths—followed, down a path that ultimately led to the White League. Unlike many of Coushatta's leading

43. Lawyers Book, Louisiana, 1: 99–100, R. G. Dun & Co. Collection; Lawrence N. Powell, "The Politics of Livelihood: Carpetbaggers in the Deep South," in *Region, Race, and Reconstruction: Essays in Honor of C. Vann Woodward*, eds. J. Morgan Kousser and James M. McPherson (New York, 1982), 315–47.

44. Louisiana, 7: 139, R. G. Dun & Co. Collection; Louisiana, 19: 6, 17, R. G. Dun & Co. Collection.

citizens, Abney never flirted with scalawagism. He never held any public office in Red River's Reconstruction government.[45]

Abney denied the notion that Yankee enterprise and northern capital created Coushatta's prosperity. "I don't think Captain Twitchell ever added anything to the prosperity of the town of Coushatta," he said. Rather, he argued, it was local people such as himself, John F. Stephens, and the Lissos that built the town.[46]

He had a point. The building of Coushatta started before Twitchell moved to Starlight. Moreover, though he became the third largest taxpayer in the parish, neither the carpetbagger's town lots nor his Starlight investments had much of a multiplier effect on the overall parish economy. On the other hand, Abney conveniently overlooked the economic significance of Twitchell's politics. Eventually, another lawmaker might have pushed a new-parish law through the legislature and made Coushatta the parish seat, but it was Twitchell who actually did it, after others had tried and failed. And it was the security created by Republican governance that attracted black labor to the parish. With some justification, the man from Vermont believed he had fathered the parish's prosperity. For all his business and political acumen, however, Twitchell never squarely confronted a basic question: What lay ahead for him and his family if the political and economic climate changed?

45. Ibid.
46. *House Reports*, 43d Cong., 2d Sess., No. 261, pp. 490, 496.

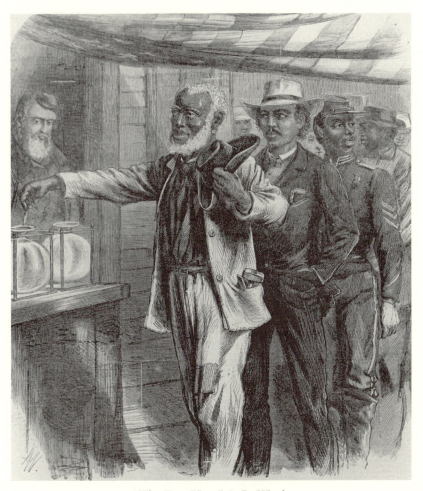

"The First Vote," A. R. Ward.
The Historic New Orleans Collection

Adele Coleman Twitchell
Courtesy of Mary Twitchell

Office of **LISSO & BROTHER,**

Coushatta Louisiana, December 15, 1873.

NOTICE

Is HEREBY GIVEN to all persons indebted to the firm of Lisso & Bro., that the undersigned, charged with the liquidation of the partnership affairs, is prepared to make settlement of all accounts, notes &c., due to said late firm, Debtors are requested to call at once and settle the accounts due by them. Relying upon the mutual confidence and kindly relations which have heretofore existed between the members of the firm and customers, PROMPT SETTLEMENTS AND SATISFACTORY ARRANGEMENTS ARE EXPECTED AND RELIED UPON.

JULIUS LISSO,
Liquidator for the Firm of
LISSO, & BROTHER.

Clark Holland.
Courtesy of Mary Twitchell

Homer Twitchell, holding his
nephews Bert Holland, left, and
Homer King, right.
Courtesy of Mary Twitchell

Monroe Willis and Helen
Twitchell Willis.
Courtesy of Mary Twitchell

George King.
Courtesy of Mary Twitchell

Members of the 1868 Louisiana constitutional convention and assembly.
The Historic New Orleans Collection

PLATE XI.   THE CUNNING FOX WHICH JOINS THE COON.

In the 1873 Comus parade during Mardi Gras, this satirical fox
represented Yankee carpetbaggers.
The Historic New Orleans Collection

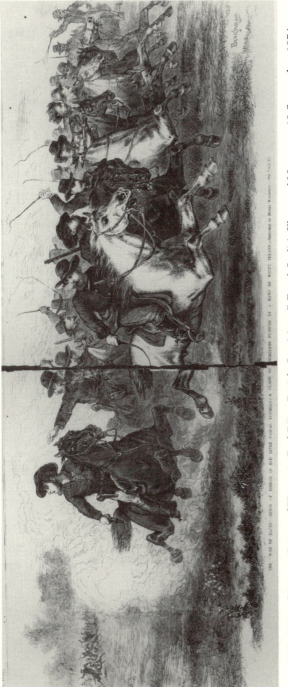

"The War of Races—Reign of Terror in Red River Parish, Louisiana," *Frank Leslie's Illustrated Newspaper* 19 September 1874.

The Library of Virginia

Battle of Canal Street, 14 September 1874.
The Historic New Orleans Collection

Federal troops expel Democrats from the Louisiana House of
Representatives, 4 January 1875.
The Historic New Orleans Collection

TEN

DEATH AND HARD TIMES

IN 1872 Louisiana plunged into a time of troubles from which it would not emerge until after Reconstruction. Political upheaval, racial violence, economic panic, and natural disasters hammered the state relentlessly. As we have seen, the Warmoth government, in reaction to the 1868 Democratic terror campaign, responded with a program of centralized governance and force. It created the state Returning Board, put the New Orleans Metropolitan Police under the governor's control, and resorted to government by appointment. This "policy of force," however, was only half of Warmoth's strategy. The other half was a "policy of peace," through which the governor attempted to conciliate white Louisianians. Depicting the Republicans as the party of prosperity, Warmoth invited old Whigs, yeoman farmers, and German and Irish immigrants to enter the Republican fold. He used patronage to bolster white support. But every job Warmoth bestowed on a former foe robbed a loyal Republican of employment.

Times were hard, jobs were scarce, and Warmoth's party, its ranks composed of former slaves, was poor. How poor were the Republicans? Consider: during the whole of Reconstruction, the Mercantile Agency files on Red River Parish contain not a single entry on any black person.

In other words, not a single black man or woman in the parish owned enough property to warrant a credit rating. Nor has the author ever seen a credit report for a black person in the Bienville Parish files. Can there be any doubt that most of the parishes in the state would yield the same results?[1]

Warmoth's peace policy not only failed to conciliate white Louisianians, it tore his own party apart, triggering a factional brawl that destroyed his administration. Republican opposition to the governor was centered in the New Orleans Customhouse. From the security of their federal offices, the "Custom House faction" attempted to wrest control of the party. The infighting consumed the last two years of Warmoth's governorship (1871–1872). Republicans in neighboring Arkansas, Texas, and Mississippi—as well as their brethren in the southeastern states—engaged in similar fights and for many of the same reasons, but the Louisiana infighting produced the longest and most acrimonious intraparty struggle of the era.[2]

The 1871 Republican State Convention became known as the "Gatling gun convention." On the pretext that hooligans planned to attack the meeting, U.S. Marshal Stephen B. Packard, a leader of the Custom House faction, asked for federal troops to protect the site of the convention. In San Antonio, Texas, far removed from the scene, General Joseph J. Reynolds, commander of the Fifth Military District, complied with the request. But the so-called hooligans turned out to be Governor Warmoth and the delegate majority. When the governor and his supporters arrived at the customhouse, they found the building guarded by bluecoats with Gatling guns.[3]

Five months later in January 1872, the Louisiana legislature met in New Orleans. Its proceedings read like opera *buffa*. To prevent a quorum, more than a dozen anti-Warmoth senators went sailing along the Gulf Coast aboard a U.S. revenue cutter. In the house, rival Republicans physically fought over the speaker's chair like a gang of street

1. Tunnell, *Crucible of Reconstruction*, 157–72; Powell, "Politics of Livelihood," 315–47.

2. Carl H. Moneyhon reviews the extensive literature on Republican factionalism in "The Failure of Southern Republicanism, 1867–1876," in *Facts of Reconstruction*, 99–119.

3. Henry Clay Warmoth, *War, Politics, and Reconstruction: Stormy Days in Louisiana* (New York, 1930), 115–18; *New Orleans Republican*, 8, 11 August 1871.

thugs. In an attempt to gain the upper hand, Marshal Packard arrested Governor Warmoth and eighteen other state officials. Warmoth, after posting bail, ringed the statehouse with militia and Metropolitan Police. News of the breakdown of constitutional government in Louisiana shocked the entire country. Heretofore, most Americans associated such shenanigans only with South American juntas.[4]

The Custom House faction's ace in the hole was President Grant, whose loyalty to friends and relatives was often as tenacious as it was misplaced. The New Orleans collector of customs was the president's brother-in-law. No matter how much his brother-in-law and his cronies abused their positions, Grant refused to remove them. In the battle for control of the state Republican Party, the Custom House faction gradually gained the upper hand over Warmoth. As it did, the governor veered toward a fusion alliance with Louisiana Democrats.

At first, Twitchell had remained loyal to Warmoth. In August 1872, however, when it was clear that the governor's fusion politics were apt to put a Democrat in the Louisiana governor's office, Twitchell broke with him.[5]

The fratricidal feud came to a head in the 1872 elections. Warmoth bolted the regular Republican Party and President Grant, running for reelection, to support liberal Republican Horace Greeley for president. In the Louisiana governor's race, he backed Democrat-fusionist John D. McEnery against William Pitt Kellogg of the Custom House faction. Warmoth's apostasy meant that the Republicans' election apparatus—controlled by the governor—was now turned against them. The results were bizarre. The state Returning Board split in two, one board Republican, the other Democratic. The Republican Returning Board proclaimed Kellogg the winner while the Democratic board awarded victory to McEnery. On 9 December, with only a month left in Warmoth's term, the Louisiana House of Representatives impeached him for unspecified high crimes and misdemeanors, automatically suspending him from office. Three days before the impeachment vote, empowered by a "midnight order" from a federal judge, Marshal Packard

4. Warmoth, *War, Politics, and Reconstruction*, 125–34; Tunnell, *Crucible of Reconstruction*, 169–70.

5. *New Orleans Republican*, 10 August, 24 September 1872.

seized the statehouse with federal troops. The senate never tried Warmoth, but the impeachment made P. B. S. Pinchback acting governor
for the remaining weeks of the term.[6]

In January 1873, Twitchell stepped to the speaker's rostrum in the
general assembly and announced the Republican Returning Board's
tabulation of the election: Republican Kellogg 72,890 votes, Democrat-
fusionist McEnery 55,249. This vote tally also gave the radicals solid
majorities in both houses of the legislature. In truth, to this day no one
knows who won the 1872 election, nor does it matter. The real story,
reported nationwide, was the election itself—the farcical returning
boards, the "midnight" court order, the bayonets. Republican Louisiana was becoming an embarrassing "Albatross" for President Grant and
the national Republican Party.[7]

The Democrats, refusing to concede defeat, erected a shadow government. The day Kellogg took his oath of office, the Democrats inaugurated McEnery across town. Republican representatives and senators
took their seats in the statehouse; Democrat-fusionist lawmakers met in
Odd Fellows Hall. Thus, during the winter and spring of 1873, Louisiana had dual governments. The rival parties contested control of no
fewer than seventeen parishes, eight of them bordering the Red River.
In the entire valley, the Democrats conceded defeat only in Twitchell's
Red River Parish.[8]

All over the state, Democrats cursed the name of "Kellogg the
Usurper." "We are completely under the rule of ignorant and filthy negroes scarcely superior to the orang outang," a New Orleans Democrat
wrote. "The Republic of Greece had their solons, we have Sambo."
With more detachment, a modern scholar has written that the Democrats used Warmoth to try to steal the election and then grew indignant
when the Republicans stole it back. In March, white mobs assaulted
Metropolitan Police stations. In retaliation, the police seized Odd Fellows Hall.[9]

6. The Democratic Returning Board was actually a succession of three separate
boards. Taylor, *Louisiana Reconstructed*, 241–49.

7. *New Orleans Republican*, 8 January 1873. Warmoth, *War, Politics and Reconstruction*,
209–12; George Rable, "Republican Albatross: The Louisiana Question, National Politics, and the Failure of Reconstruction," *LH* 23 (1982): 109–30; William Gillette, *Retreat
from Reconstruction, 1869–1979* (Baton Rouge, 1979), 133–35.

8. Tunnell, *Crucible of Reconstruction*, 171, 178, 189.

9. Taylor, *Louisiana Reconstructed*, 248, 254–55.

Outside the capital, guerrilla war spread across the state. The worst trouble occurred in Grant Parish, named after the president, fifty miles below Coushatta. Colfax, the parish seat, was not much to look at, just some old plantation buildings on the east bank of the Red River. The courthouse was a converted brick stable. Through the winter of 1873 Republicans and Democrats feuded over the courthouse. In late March the Republican sheriff took possession of the building and swore in black deputies to protect it. Gangs of armed whites were soon lingering about the village. On 5 April one of these bands murdered a black farmer who was peacefully building a fence. The murder and ominous rumors of more violence to come led about 400 blacks, farmers and their families, to congregate at Colfax for protection. Some of the blacks had rifles and shotguns, but the great majority was unarmed. The whites flocking to Colfax were much better armed and had no women or children to worry about.[10]

On 13 April, Easter Sunday, three hundred armed whites besieged the black defenders of Colfax. Christopher Columbus Nash, a veteran of the Louisiana Tigers and the leader of the white mob, demanded the surrender of the courthouse and of all the weapons in the village. When the blacks rebuffed the demand, the whites attacked. The whites remained beyond shotgun range while firing their rifles into the compound. Nash's men had taken a four-pound cannon from a steamboat and mounted it on a wagon. They maneuvered the cannon, loaded with chunks of iron, in close to the compound. The cannon's blasts "created consternation and panic among the negroes," who fled down the riverbank or into the courthouse. The whites torched the old stable, trapping more than sixty blacks inside, bullets pouring into the building as it burned.[11]

The trapped men improvised white flags and tried to surrender. According to witnesses:

> The firing ceased then, and some of the white people came up and shouted to the negroes that if they would lay down their arms

10. Joel M. Sipress, "The Triumph of Reaction: Political Struggle in a New South Community, 1865–1898" (Ph.D. diss., University of North Carolina at Chapel Hill, 1993), 93–99; *House Reports*, 43d Cong., 2d Sess., No. 261, pp. 409–11.

11. *House Reports*, 43d Cong. 2d Sess., No. 261, pp. 411–12; *Christopher Columbus Nash: A Tribute by Milton Dunn*, Judge R. B. Williams Collection, Cammie G. Henry Research Center.

and come out they would not hurt them. A condition of panic . . . existed inside the building, and the door was opened at once, and the negroes, unarmed, rushed out, to be met with a volley the moment they made their appearance. In that volley several of them were killed. The negroes that were not in the immediate vicinity of the door rushed back and waited a moment, and then made another rush out, and all, excepting some who were secreted under the floor, got out. Again there were some of them killed, and some taken prisoners: the prisoners, as fast as they were taken, were taken out near a cottonwood tree, in a cotton field, and put under guard.

That night Nash's mob murdered the prisoners.[12]

Lieutenant Edward L. Godfrey of the Seventh Cavalry later investigated the massacre. No fewer than 108 men died at Colfax, he wrote, 105 blacks and 3 whites. The Colfax massacre was the most violent attack on blacks in the history of Reconstruction. Indeed, it probably ranks as the worst massacre of blacks in the history of the nation.[13]

Three days after the massacre, Twitchell received an anonymous warning at Starlight Plantation that the Colfax mob was planning to attack Coushatta. "I was in the fite at Colfax," the informant claimed. "And if the lord will forgive me for that I wil never be gilty of such a thing agane[.]" A Coushatta lawyer "and one of your depty sherifs" participated in the massacre. "You have men among you who pass for friends but who are Enemys[.] You ar[e] in grate danger they intend to kill all the Yankees and Nigger officers you had better make your escape." Coushatta whites assured Twitchell that if the Colfax mob came, he and his family would be spared; only Negro agitators would be hurt. Instead of running or depending on the friendship of his white neighbors, Twitchell organized a black militia and spread the word that the Colfax mob would meet armed resistance in Red River Parish. The attack never materialized.[14]

Elsewhere, however, the violence continued. One afternoon in May, Governor Kellogg drove to a business office on Magazine Street. There had been rioting in New Orleans the night before, and rumors circu-

12. *House Reports*, 43d Cong., 2d Sess., No. 261, pp. 410–13.
13. *House Executive Documents*, 44th Cong., 2d Sess., No. 30, pp. 436–38.
14. "A true frend" to MHT, 16 April 1873, MHT Papers; *CV*, 134–35.

lated of a conspiracy against the governor's life. As Kellogg returned to his carriage, around which a crowd had gathered, a man named Charles Railey, a McEnery appointee, accosted him and called him a "scoundrel." Sensing danger, the governor leaped into his carriage. "My driver whipped up his team and drove very fast; I had not gone far before I heard a shot, and the bullet passed through my carriage, passing close to my face," he said. Indeed, the ball clipped the hair on the governor's neck. Dozens of people witnessed the incident, and most of them swore that an accomplice of Railey's named Cohen fired the shot; nonetheless, a New Orleans jury acquitted both men.[15]

Kellogg was lucky. Judge Thomas S. Crawford and an associate were less so. A wartime Unionist, Crawford had served in the state constitutional convention with Twitchell and then become twelfth district judge. The twelfth district, east of Red River, had a well-earned reputation for violence. In September, embittered whites ambushed Judge Crawford and District Attorney A. B. Harris en route to court. The shooters then mutilated their victims' bodies by repeatedly firing bullets into them at close range. Governor Kellogg posted a $5,000 reward for the capture and conviction of the killers. No one ever collected the money.[16]

Against this background of politics and violence, another story was unfolding, a story of fading economic hopes and natural perversity. The postwar economic revival peaked in Louisiana in 1871, the year Red River Parish was created, then faded. The hard times hobbled state finances already burdened by war and poverty.

According to legend, Louisiana's corrupt Reconstruction government was to blame for the state's economic woes. Governors Warmoth and Kellogg, it was said, spent money recklessly, running up a huge public debt of $42 million and pushing the state to the edge of bankruptcy. With respect to Kellogg, the charge was wholly untrue. Warmoth, however, had spent money recklessly. Even so, the story of Louisiana's hard times was far more complex than the extravagance of one Reconstruction governor.

15. *New Orleans Republican*, 8 May, 24, 27, 28 June 1873.

16. Fred J. Rushing, "The Assassination of Judge T. S. Crawford, Bitter Fruit of the Tragic Era," *North Louisiana Historical Association Journal* 7 (1976): 131–34; *New Orleans Republican*, 9, 11, 19, 23 September 1873.

To begin with, contingent debt accounted for about 40 percent of the oft-cited $42 million. Contingent debt was what Louisiana owed railroads, canal companies, and other corporations that completed state projects. The operative word here is *completed*. Because the great majority of companies never built anything, never fulfilled their contracts, the state owed them nothing. Thus, Louisiana's *real* debt totaled about $25 million, not $42 million. Moreover, about $10 million of the former figure dated from the antebellum period. The war and Presidential Reconstruction accounted for another $7.5 million. In other words, when the Republicans came to power in 1868 they inherited a pre-existing debt of $17.5 million. Over the next five years, their own spending on levees, schools, roads—plus embezzling officials—added another $7.5 million. Twenty-five million dollars was far more manageable debt than $42 million, but it was still a huge burden. In 1870 and 1871, Warmoth's government respectively paid $1 million and $1.3 million in interest.

Reining in the spiraling debt was nearly impossible under postwar conditions. Before the war, property taxes on land and slaves were the state's main sources of revenue. Emancipation eliminated a whole category of taxable wealth while at the same time undercutting land values all over the state. In truth, land worked by free labor proved less valuable than land worked by slaves. Hence during Reconstruction, public officials, state and local, Republican and Democrat (outside the alluvial *Y*, most parishes were controlled by Democrats), were constantly searching for revenue. Their search led them to double and triple land taxes, angering whites, who were struggling for survival and accustomed before the war to nominal taxes. As if this was not enough, the higher taxes still left governments strapped for money.[17]

Because taxes were assessed and collected locally, parish government was susceptible to public pressure. Taxpayer resistance associations arose all over the state. In May 1873 Thomas Abney, John F. Stephens, and other Red River planters and businessmen held a "Mass Meeting" in Coushatta, which petitioned Homer Twitchell to delay the collection of state taxes until November. Some months later, Red River whites in-

17. Taylor, *Louisiana Reconstructed*, 202–8; J. Mills Thornton, "Fiscal Policy and the Failure of Radical Reconstruction in the Lower South," in *Region, Race, and Reconstruction*, 351, 363, 383.

stitutionalized the protest by forming the Property-holders and Laborers Union. Judging from a newspaper account of the May meeting and the public testimony of men who later joined the group, the tax protest movement in the parish and the later White League had virtually identical memberships. A reading of Shreveport and Natchitoches newspapers suggests an identical pattern in those places.[18]

Debt and taxes helped galvanize white opposition to Republican rule. Unfortunately for the Republicans in that pre–New Deal, pre-Keynesian era, there was little that government could do to affect the business cycle or raise the price of cotton on the international market. The north Louisiana economy was dependent on cotton, and cotton was in decline. Prices and production plummeted simultaneously. In 1870–1871, the peak postwar year, Red River Valley farmers and planters shipped 276,665 bales of cotton to the world markets. Then, year after year, the total fell:

1871–1872	196,104 bales
1872–1873	186,085
1873–1874	170,488
1874–1875	146,435

The causes were many: too much rain and not enough rain, the depredations of the army worm, and overproduction on the world market. The sugar crop in southeastern states underwent a similar decline in these years.[19]

Summer was the season of low water and slack business in the river towns from Shreveport to Alexandria. In most years, trade picked up in late September when the river began its annual rise. But in 1872 the water level in Old Red went right on falling through the autumn months. In early December, from the Arkansas border to Alexandria, the main channel measured barely two feet deep of water. The superstructure of the *Grand Duke*, sunk in the middle of Shreveport's harbor during the war and never before seen, protruded above water. The cost of shipping cotton jumped from one dollar to ten dollars a bale. Traffic

18. *Coushatta Times*, 24 May 1873.

19. Annual statements in *Shreveport Times*, 5 September 1873, 3 September 1874, 8 September 1875; Figures on sugar, ibid., 27 August 1874.

on Main Street slowed to a crawl. "No steamboats, no money and no business," a disgusted Colonel Mason lamented. Merchants in Natchitoches, Coushatta, Shreveport, and other landings slouched despairingly in the doorways of empty stores.[20]

The spring and summer of 1873 brought bad weather and caterpillars. Then hit the double-barreled disaster of a yellow-fever epidemic and the Panic of 1873. In the short run, the yellow fever had the greatest impact. It appeared in mid-August when three men collapsed on Texas Street in Shreveport, fatally ill. Thus began "an eighty-five day siege" of the state's second largest city. Nearly half the town's population caught the fever. Seven hundred fifty-nine died. The newspapers printed the daily roll of the dead like wartime casualty lists. People fled the city, stores closed, the streetcars stood silent in their terminals, the Texas and Pacific trains from Dallas stopped running, and Main Street shut down, the second year in a row. "The epidemic has reached a point that anything like business is out of the question," Colonel Mason wrote. "There is no cotton being received, nobody to buy it if there was, and we might as well discontinue our daily notices until the fever is over." Between 12 September and 21 October not a bale of cotton left the city. Trade resumed in November, but cotton receipts for the month were 50 percent below the slow November of the previous year.[21]

With fearful malignity, the yellow fever spread throughout the valley. It first appeared in Red River Parish at Brownsville, a landing a few miles downriver from Coushatta. A doctor reported twenty-three cases and numerous deaths in the small community. The fever then spread to Springville and Coushatta. Thomas Abney, Julius and Marks Lisso, and other town leaders were stricken. Thomas Abney and Julius Lisso recovered, but Marks Lisso died. The "pen cannot describe the sad havoc this pestilence has made in our neighborhood," a storekeeper wrote. "Coushatta is entirely deserted." Everyone and "everything that could

20. *Shreveport Times*, 3 September, 9, 15, 19, 26, October, 19, 21 November, 7, 11 December 1872.

21. *Shreveport Times*, 6, 13, 14, 16, 17 September, 7, 8 October, 6 November 1873; Perry A. Snyder, "Shreveport, Louisiana, during the Civil War and Reconstruction" (Ph.D. diss., Florida State University, 1979), 207–10; Henry C. Dethloff, "Paddlewheels and Pioneers on Red River, 1815–1915, and the Reminiscences of Captain M. L. Scovell," *Louisiana Studies* 6 (1967): 118–23.

has left. . . . Our store, like the rest, is perfectly destitute of clerks, though we need none at present. Only one more store besides ours . . . pretends to keep open." From south of Coushatta to the outskirts of Shreveport, fifty miles of thickly-settled bottomlands were virtually deserted. The epidemic finally ran its course, but not before visiting Starlight. Marshall's sister Belle Hanna, the wife of George A. King, died in November.[22]

Yellow fever began with body aches, a throbbing head, and raging fever, followed by convulsions and the hideous black vomit caused by internal hemorrhaging. A Shreveport man left a graphic account of his wife's last hours: "Her symptoms proved bad again; black vomit returned—was copious and the case became hopeless. She became unconscious and altho the struggles and groans lasted long I trust her consciousness of pain was not great. I could not well bear the sight. Lay down between my little ones and lost consciousness till . . . all was over. For some seconds I was in suspense feeling that the announcement was made to me in another world."[23]

One day in September, as the yellow fever epidemic mounted to a crescendo, a Shreveport telegraph operator tapped out news from the outside world, news of financial disaster half a continent away in New York City. Jay Cooke, financier of the Civil War, banker of mighty railroads and huge industries, was bankrupt. Two days later, the New York Stock Exchange closed its doors. It was the beginning of the greatest economic collapse the industrial world had ever known. Its waves soon washed the shores of the upper Red River.[24]

The Panic of 1873 was the coup de grace for many a Red River merchant and farmer. About Thanksgiving time, the *Coushatta Citizen* summed up the year's wreckage: "The cotton crop throughout Red River Parish . . . will fall far short of previous calculations. Unfavorable spring and summer, destruction by the caterpillar, the extremely sickly season and the numerous heavy rains since picking commenced, have operated terribly against the people in their efforts to raise and gather the present crop. It really does seem that they have struggled against more disasters, undergone greater hardships, and lived harder and had

22. *Shreveport Times*, 7, 16, 29 October 1873; Twitchell Family Scrapbook.
23. Snyder, "Shreveport," 209.
24. Dethloff, "Paddlewheels and Pioneers," 122.

less credit this year than ever before." The great majority of farmers would run out of supplies that winter, the newspaper predicted; then, having "exhausted their produce, especially their cotton, they will have no means with which to purchase supplies another year."[25]

The litany of woes was unending. The corn crop was generally a failure, and with only a handful of exceptions, farmers had not raised any hogs and had empty smokehouses. Then there was the credit squeeze caused by the panic. According to the *Citizen*, "Our merchants here have already closed down on the credit system; and if they furnish anything on time to the farmer . . . they will not feel safe in doing so until late in the spring, when they can see what will be prospects for another year."[26]

Twitchell, unlike most others in the parish, had made and stored a good corn crop at Starlight. He knew the price would rise after Christmas. Upon learning that Coushatta merchants had cut off credit, he borrowed money and bought every bushel he could find. That winter of 1874 he sold corn on credit, one wagonload per man, accepting only a farmer's word of honor to pay back the debt. He had learned a lot about these hill-country people, who were not all that different from the hill-country people he had grown up with in Vermont. Poor but proud, they put more stock in their word of honor than in legal contracts. The farmer who gave his word would honor it. Whether Twitchell's corn dealings that winter were sound business or profiteering is hard to say.[27]

For Twitchell, the cruelest blow of these times was his wife's slow decline. Judy Coleman had not been bluffing years before when she warned him of Adele's susceptibility to consumption. By 1873 the disease was out of control. Adele wrote her parents, "I suffer terribly at night with *such* a fever I feel almost like one burning up and it is so hard to put me to sleep. I take chloral in great quantities before I can get any rest from coughing & the fever. Sometime the fever would be so high Marshall said I would be crazy. My eyes are so weak I can not [see] and as I write the water runs from them." The doctor "tells me that I may loose a large portion of a lung & yet regain a degree of health and live."

25. *Shreveport Times*, 7 December 1873.
26. Ibid.
27. *CV*, 136.

The doctor warns, however, that "if I give away and loose my courage I will sink right down."[28]

To make matters worse, she was pregnant again: "I am in that condition and the Dr is only waiting to see how I stand it, or whether it is best to bring on an abortion . . . I am for an abortion of course." For reasons unknown, there was no abortion, and she carried the baby to term. That summer she bore a sickly boy who was named Daniel.[29]

In September her condition improved temporarily: "I sit up now some days (nearly all day) but I am very weak and [have] no appetite. I crave beef but cant often get it my throat is still quite sore, and I cough yet." She had a nurse to care for the baby: "I give no milk hardly and he dont like to nurse me because he dont get much and can get it so free out of his bottle."[30]

Twitchell and Isaac Coleman sent train fare to Luella in South Carolina, so that Adele and her twin could spend Christmas together in New Orleans. "I expect you will hardly know me," Adele wrote Luella in anticipation. "I am so pale and poor and my hair has nearly all come out." She was thinking of buying a wig. Although Luella arrived late, the two sisters spent a few days together. It was the last time they would ever meet.[31]

Adele went to New Orleans with her husband for the 1874 senate session. When her condition worsened, she asked to return home but insisted that Twitchell remain at his desk in the senate. The scene at the wharf was funereal. Pale and frail, Adele boarded the steamer. Twitchell escorted her to her cabin, his face wan with despair. Several friends witnessed the parting. The husband's grief was so profoundly moving, one of them wrote, "that we could not in the fullness of heart, utter a word of cheer."[32]

Twitchell, chairman of the finance committee, shepherded Kellogg's debt-reduction package through the senate. The funding act abolished the state's contingent debt and scaled down the debt remaining from $25 million to $15 million. Twitchell was entitled to his share of the

---

28. Adele Coleman Twitchell to "home folks," 12 January 1873, MHT Papers.

29. Ibid.; Twitchell, *Genealogy of the Twitchell Family*, 558.

30. Adele Coleman Twitchell to Judy Coleman, 14 September 1873, MHT Papers; Adele to Luella [October or November 1873], incomplete letter, MHT Papers.

31. Adele to Luella, 23 November 1873, MHT Papers.

32. MHT Scrapbook.

credit. Louisiana's was one of the few Reconstruction governments to grapple seriously with its postwar debt problems. It was sad recompense, though, for the loss of Adele. He never saw her again. She died 14 February 1874, just three months after his sister's death from yellow fever. A few weeks later the baby, Daniel, died. The fates that had hitherto smiled on the carpetbagger and his family now averted their gaze.[33]

33. Twitchell, *Genealogy of the Twitchell Family*, 144; Taylor, *Louisiana Reconstructed*, 260–61; Thornton, "Fiscal Policy and the Failure of Radical Reconstruction," 384–85.

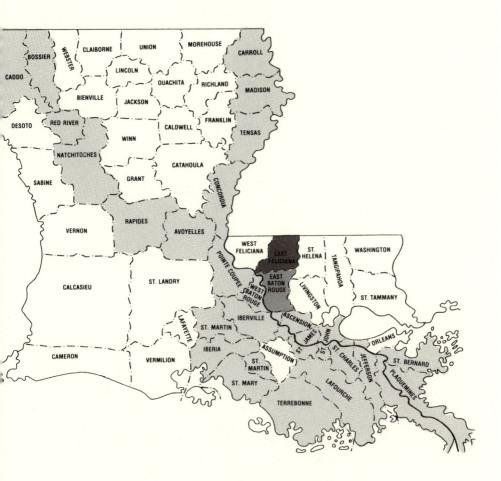

Map 3—Louisiana's Alluvial-Electoral Y

The overwhelming majority of Louisiana's black people lived in the alluvial bottomlands of the Red and Mississippi Rivers. In Reconstruction elections, the bottomland parishes voted Republican, forming a giant electoral Y, conforming to the alluvial Y. In the 1876 governor's election, illustrated here, the shaded parishes voted for Republican Stephen B. Packard, and the clear parishes voted for Democrat Francis T. Nicholls. East Feliciana and East Baton Rouge were disputed.

Letitia Tunnell

 Nicholls received majorities

Packard received majorities

Contested, both candidates claimed majorities

Vote excluded because of fraud, violence, or other irregularities

ELEVEN

THE KNIFE TO THE HILT

W HEN the 1874 senate adjourned, Twitchell headed home to Coushatta. The townspeople met him at the landing and escorted him to the courthouse. A. O. P. Pickens, editor of the *Coushatta Times*, the official Republican organ, introduced him as a solid businessman who always kept his word and never turned his back on a friend. Twitchell reported on the state's fiscal condition and other news from the general assembly. The reception impressed Twitchell. "To all appearances," he recalled, "there was no man in North Louisiana who stood higher in the regards of the people."[1]

If the reception was as warm-hearted as Pickens described it and Twitchell remembered it, appearances were deceiving, because Red River Parish was a troubled place. From the start, Twitchell and his family had aroused feelings of envy and resentment, coupled with grudging respect. Traditionally, economic and political status were an organic whole. Front Street merchants such as Thomas Abney and John F. Stephens and planter-businessmen such as Ben W. Marston and John L. Sandiford, dominated their community's political affairs as well

1. MHT Scrapbook; *CV*, 137.

as its commercial life. Yet currently, a northern outsider and his clique, in combination with a black underclass, dominated the institutions of governance. The ire of local whites mounted as economic depression set in. Courthouse rings were an old southern institution, but ring rule by Yankee carpetbaggers was a different matter. Irate citizens condemned Twitchell as a tyrant and compared him to the Khedive of Egypt.[2]

Corruption in the sheriff's office lent substance to people's discontent. John T. Yates, a Missouri carpetbagger, had been sheriff since the formation of the parish. In December 1873, for reasons that remain obscure, a white man named Newt Gillem shot Yates on the courthouse steps, badly wounding him. Prior to the shooting, complaints against Yates had already aroused Twitchell's mistrust. While the sheriff convalesced in New Orleans, parish attorney William Howell went over Yates's books.[3]

The investigation confirmed Twitchell's suspicions of Yates's dishonesty. The sheriff had repeatedly encouraged black sharecroppers to file legal complaints against the planters on whose land they worked. In investigating a complaint, Yates typically visited the plantation on which the offense had allegedly occurred, served legal papers on the planter, and subpoenaed numerous witnesses. According to Twitchell, Yates then billed the parish "with the full mileage of each paper separately, thereby getting for one journey of perhaps 20 miles, mileage for 200." He then dropped each case, regardless of its merits. Worse than the loss of revenue, this official racketeering left a trail of embittered planters and cynical freedmen. With the proof in hand, Twitchell forced Yates's resignation and named Frank Edgerton sheriff. Edgerton was an outsider, too, and his appointment did little to appease Red River Parish whites.[4]

Underlying the growing political discontent was the region's economic plight. The Mercantile Agency was tracking the fortunes of forty-five Red River merchants, planters, and businessmen. Between 1871 and 1876, nearly three-quarters (73 percent) of the parish's busi-

2. *House Reports*, 44th Cong., 1st Sess., No. 816, p. 679.

3. *New Orleans Republican*, 23 December 1873; *House Reports*, 44th Cong., 1st Sess., No. 816, pp. 705–6; *House Reports*, 43d Cong., 2d Sess., No. 261, p. 390.

4. *CV*, 180–81; *House Reports*, 43d Cong., 2d Sess., No. 261, p. 390.

nesses suffered severe economic difficulties: Merchants saddled with debt retrenched or closed their stores for extended periods. Twenty-three of the forty-five failed altogether. The Mercantile agents recorded the woes of their fellow merchants with laconic panache: "Played out, Busted," "Broke & in Texas," "sold out . . . & moved to Ark," "broke and unworthy of credit," "Dead & insolvent."[5]

The career of W. W. Wordlaw was typical. About 1871, Wordlaw moved from Bienville Parish to Coushatta, where he opened a saloon, a ten-pin alley, and a livery stable. He owned a 2,000-acre plantation a few miles from town. According to the Mercantile reports, in 1872 he was an able man of good character and prospects. A year later he was in trouble and his credit rating was "Doubtful." By June 1874 he had closed all of his businesses and retreated to his plantation. Another saloon keeper, W. H. Snead—who also ran the hotel—started out "likely to succeed." By late 1873 his credit rating was doubtful, too, and six months later he was "Played out and Busted." Eleven miles north of Coushatta, a planter-merchant named John J. Bridges closed his store in the summer of 1873. A year later the Mercantile agent wrote that Bridges owned "one of the few prosperous farms in this country." It was hard to estimate the value of his holdings because of the depreciation of land values. In good times the farm would bring at least ten thousand dollars, but in the present climate no more than three thousand to five thousand dollars.[6]

Furnishing merchants, who supplied farmers, landowners, and sharecroppers with goods and provisions on credit, collecting the debts by taking shares of the farmers' cotton crops, were particularly vulnerable. According to the Mercantile files, Coushatta's chief furnishing merchants were Thomas Abney & Co. and Lisso Bros. The town's two principal merchant houses also represented the two main political blocs. Abney was anti-Twitchell, while the Lissos were pro-Twitchell.

Prior to the panic, with rarely a contrary word, the Mercantile agents' assessments of Abney and his partners were favorable. They were solid, conservative, hardworking merchants, doing a good busi-

5. This sample excludes a very few individuals or firms doing business in Red River Parish but maintaining a main base of operations in another parish. It also excludes firms with no credit evaluations *prior* to 1874 and a few for which there is a single evaluation entry with no follow-up.

6. Louisiana, 19: 6–8, R. G. Dun & Co. Collection.

ness. In December 1873, the tone of the reports changed abruptly. "Short collections, and low prices will strain them dreadfully." Two months later a fire burned down the Abney building. A New Orleans company, a report claimed, had "filed a petition in Bankruptcy ag[ain]st this firm," and other creditors were threatening legal action. The bankruptcy suit proved premature; the partners' insurance and assets enabled them to temporarily weather the crisis. In the summer of 1874—when Abney became president of the Red River Parish White League—they built a new brick store, but did not resume business until fall. The firm, which never fully recovered from these setbacks, broke up the following year.[7]

The same end-of-the-year credit report that told of trouble in Abney's firm found trouble at Lisso Bros. Coinciding with the onset of the panic, Marks Lisso, the senior partner, died of yellow fever. His death plunged the firm into liquidation. Julius Lisso attempted to ride out the tempest, but after years of struggling with debt, finally failed. Next door to Lisso Bros. on Front Street, the nephews Samuel and Paul Lisso also took a fall in the panic, locking up their store in January 1874.[8]

Front Street was a grim place in 1874, and Twitchell made a handy scapegoat. "When it began to be whispered abroad that we were under corrupt radical domination," Abney told a congressional committee, "and that all the offices were filled by corrupt officials, strangers to the people, those who had been accustomed to bring their products to Coushatta for sale or shipment began to cast about for some other point of business, and her former prosperity began to depart." And "in proportion as our people grew poor, those who came there in 1871 with barely a suit of clothes for a change, grew wealthy." Thus, Twitchell and his carpetbagger friends at Starlight, already politically stigmatized by their association with blacks, became the villains in the story of Coushatta's economic woes, too.[9]

Hammered by economic and political blows, the coalition that had buttressed Twitchell's power for three years began to break up. Twitchell's white allies, such as Thomas Paxton, Julius Lisso, and editor Pick-

---

7. Ibid., 6, 17.

8. Ibid., 8.

9. *House Reports*, 43d Cong., 2d Sess., No. 261, pp. 489–90; *House Reports*, 44th Cong., 1st Sess., No. 816, p. 679.

ens, came under increased pressure from their neighbors to abandon the radical party and assert Democratic control over the parish. At the same time, Twitchell grew more dependent on his family, on his friendships with the Deweeses, on blacks such as Andy Bosley and William Peck, on other carpetbaggers such as Edgerton, and on a declining number of native whites such as Judge Penny and parish attorney Howell, who were dependent on public employment. In Red River Parish, as in New Orleans—and across the Deep South—the center could not hold. The stage was set for the White League.[10]

If the years 1873 and 1874 were watershed years in the story of Twitchell and Red River Parish, they were equally critical in the larger history of Radical Reconstruction. Across the South at the beginning of 1873, Republicans dominated—or at least held the upper hand—in seven state governments. Then in late 1873, the Republican regime in Texas collapsed. The following spring, radicalism in Arkansas imploded in the Brooks-Baxter war. In the Deep South, a Democratic "white line" strategy began to emerge in 1873. A year later, emboldened by the panic, the feebleness of southern Republicans, and the northern public's and the Grant administration's growing reluctance to use federal troops in the South, a wave of counter-Reconstruction mobilization and violence swept over the region. Hardest hit were Republicans in Alabama and Louisiana. The Democrats "redeemed" Alabama in the fall of 1874. The Republican regime in Louisiana would survive the year, barely.[11]

The Louisiana White League movement epitomized the "white line" strategy. It began in March 1874 with a manifesto in the *Alexandria Caucasian*. Seven years of Republican rule, the newspaper claimed, had made Louisiana an economic wasteland and yielded a record of "crime, venality, corruption, misrule, and official debasement." If the Republicans remained in power, Africanization and more economic and political chaos lay ahead. The *Caucasian*'s solution to this "*Iliad* of woes" was a "white man's party." The only way to win the November election was a "fair, square fight, Caucasian versus African."[12]

10. Perman, *Road to Redemption*, 135–48.
11. Foner, *Reconstruction*, 539, 547–50; Rable, *But There Was No Peace*, 114–18; Wiggins, *Scalawag in Alabama Politics*, 91–92.
12. *House Reports*, 43d Cong., 2d Sess, No. 261, pp. 906–7.

In ensuing weeks, one Democratic newspaper after another embraced the White League idea—the *Bulletin* and *Picayune* in New Orleans, the *Times* and *Comet* in Shreveport, the *Mansfield Reporter, Opelousas Courier, Natchitoches People's Vindicator, Baton Rouge Advocate,* and a dozen more. On 27 April in Opelousas, Saint Landry Parish citizens formed the first White League club. The Saint Landryites branded the Republicans as a black man's party and blamed the state's woes on Negro government. The issue in the upcoming election, these White Leaguers claimed, "is not between Republicans and Democrats or Liberals, but between the whites and blacks, and that the issue is: Shall the white people of Louisiana govern Louisiana?"[13]

From Opelousas, the White League spread north into the Red River Valley, southeast into the sugar country, and west into Texas. By August there was hardly a corner of Louisiana where it had not appeared. For the White League Democrats, northwest Louisiana was the hinge of redemption. The Red River Valley formed the weaker arm of the alluvial *Y* (See Map 3). Restore white supremacy in the string of parishes lining Old Red and, at the state level, Louisiana Reconstruction would be over. Redeeming the Red River Valley meant taking Red River Parish from Twitchell. As the Vermonter realized, he and his "Yankee colonists" loomed bigger than life in the imaginations of their enemies. They had become Reconstruction symbols. Though the smallest parish in the valley, Red River was "the headquarters," the "fortress," the "Republican Stronghold," of northwest Louisiana. Any conquest of the White League, the carpetbagger wrote, "would be barren and insecure until this fortress fell."[14]

In early June, Charles W. Keeting, the fourth division superintendent of education, informed Twitchell of a recent conversation with Albert Leonard, the editor and proprietor of the *Shreveport Times*. In no uncertain terms, Leonard had charted for Keeting the path of Louisi-

---

13. H. Oscar Lestage Jr., "The White League in Louisiana and Its Participation in Reconstruction Riots," *LHQ* 18 (1935): 637–45; Taylor, *Louisiana Reconstructed,* 281–84.

14. MHT White League document [1875]. This eighteen-page document, in Twitchell's hand, appears to have been written in preparation for his testimony before a House committee in February 1875 (See *House Reports,* 43d Cong., 2d Sess., No. 261, pp. 385–99). In crucial respects, though, this document is more valuable than the congressional testimony. It contains statements and details found nowhere else. It was discovered by the Twitchell family in Burlington, Vermont, after the author had begun work on this book.

ana's redemption in the 1874 elections. Democrats and old Whigs would be united by the White League's call for racial solidarity. White Republicans would be forced into the White League or they would be "driven from the country or killed." With their leaders dead or forced into betrayal, the demoralized blacks would succumb to intimidation.[15]

Ben W. Marston, a prominent Red River planter and member of the Abney faction, visited Shreveport. With Leonard and others, he drafted a White League program for Red River Parish. Upon his return, a rally was organized in Coushatta. In mid-June claiming to represent Red River taxpayers, the "mass meeting" denounced the Kellogg government for poisoning race relations and reducing whites to beggary. One plank pointedly targeted Twitchell: The members of the "white man's party" in Red River, it stated, "have the kindest feelings towards any honest minded Northerner, in or out of office, whose aim is the prosperity and enlightenment of the whole people, [but] we loathe beyond expression the vulture . . . in the shape of man, whose sole aim is to destroy all the wealth, virtue and intelligence in the land."

Surprisingly, the Coushatta platform was endorsed—or so it was claimed—by blacks. After his return from Shreveport, Marston, along with creating a White League, had formed a so-called Black League. The members of this "Colored Man's Party" were his own plantation hands. Through this bogus creation, Marston put anti-Republican words into the mouths of intimidated blacks. "Whereas, we, the colored voters of Red River parish, are getting our eyes open to the great duties devolving upon us, as voters and citizens," the party supposedly resolved, "That we regard the Southern white people, who have been just to us since the war, with great favor, and know the country can never prosper when ruinous taxation and an uncompromising war of races are political watchwords." The document acknowledged that whites "own nearly all the property, pay nearly all the taxes, and control the very roots protecting our families," and encouraged black people to cooperate with their former masters. As a cover, the platform claimed that blacks were entitled to an equitable division of parish offices. The whole business had been transparently orchestrated by whites. After

15. MHT White League document [1875].

only a few weeks, the black auxiliary of the Red River White League vanished from view.[16]

On 4 July the Red River White League held its second Coushatta mass meeting. The same day, Twitchell called a Republican meeting at Black Lake, on the opposite side of the parish. By his own count, the Coushatta meeting attracted ninety white farmers and their families and the Black Lake meeting sixty. The Vermonter deemed the representation at the two meetings a fairly accurate indicator of white sentiment in the parish.[17]

In mid-July, White League momentum accelerated. At a public meeting on the 17th, Abney announced the formation of a "white man's club" in each of the parish's five wards. The storekeeper also told his listeners that a seven-man parish executive committee had been formed, with him as president. White League organizers visited most white households in the parish, urging participation. The Coushatta mass meetings—held every two or three weeks that summer—were important recruitment arenas, too. In that era before radio or television or other forms of mass communications, politics doubled as entertainment, especially in a rural hinterland such as northwest Louisiana. As one historian of southern violence has written, the "festival atmosphere" of these gatherings—enjoyed by the entire family—the "propaganda and hoopla," were instrumental in "turning normally peaceful citizens into angry mobs." White League militia marched and drilled on country roads and in the streets of Coushatta. As reports of White League organizing and intimidation flowed in from the surrounding parishes, local Republicans seemed paralyzed.[18]

Unlike the Knights of the White Camellia and the Ku Klux Klan, the White League was not a secret society. Much of the history of the White League is openly chronicled in the newspapers. The newspapers routinely printed the names of White League members and officers, often prefixing the names with former Confederate military rank; thus,

16. MHT White League document [1875]; *House Reports*, 43d Cong., 2d Sess., No. 261, pp. 385–86; *Shreveport Times*, 16 June 1874.

17. *Shreveport Times*, 12 July 1874; MHT White League document [1875]; *House Reports*, 43d Cong., 2d Sess., No. 261, p. 386.

18. *Natchitoches People's Vindicator*, 8 August 1874; MHT White League document [1875]; *House Reports*, 43d Cong., 2d Sess., No. 261, pp. 386, 493, 497; Rable, *But There Was No Peace*, 132.

it was Captain Thomas W. Abney, Captain Ben W. Marston, and Major John L. Sandiford. The *Shreveport Times,* the leading newspaper in north Louisiana, boldly proclaimed itself "The Organ of the White League." The *Natchitoches People's Vindicator* studded its columns with notices urging whites to attend White League functions.[19]

The White League was less a new organization than a revitalization of the Democratic Party. Major Lewis Merrill of the U.S. Army, an astute observer of north Louisiana, believed the White League was "co-extensive with the white people, and co-extensive with the conservative party." By whatever name, "the conservative, or the democratic, or the White Man's, or the White League," it was the same party with the same leaders. A leader of the De Soto Parish White League later confirmed this view. The White League, he said, "was nothing but a big democratic club, with rifle clubs such as the state national guards. . . . Any white man could join it." He added that the parish executive committee, the "inner circle," was "the life essence" of the league.[20]

The creation of the White League, however, made a significant difference. Its militancy galvanized white opposition to Reconstruction. It politicized men who were only nominally Democrats and put enormous pressure on the small minority of white scalawags who had become Republicans. The *Natchitoches People's Vindicator* advocated a *"Black List,* or book or Remembrance," to make these traitors "as conspicuous for all time to come as the pictures of notorious criminals in the Rogue's Gallery of large cities."[21]

Twitchell initially underestimated power of the White League. In June when it first appeared, he and his friend Julius Lisso agreed that the notion of people closing ranks on "the basis of race and color did not meet with the approval of the better disposed classes of white people." A month later when Lisso went to New Orleans to arrange his marriage to a Crescent City Jewish woman, they talked again. "They are getting to be very hot up there," Twitchell warned his business associate, "and you will have to come out and be a White-Leaguer right straight through or they will drive you out of the country." Lisso re-

19. *Shreveport Times,* 12 July 1874; *Natchitoches People's Vindicator,* 8 August 1874.

20. *House Reports,* 43d Cong., 2d Sess., No. 261, p. 182; Scrapbook, 159: 46, Melrose Collection.

21. *Natchitoches People's Vindicator,* 12 September 1874.

plied: "I am my own man and I intend to be independent." Soon after, Twitchell's doubts that his friend could remain neutral were confirmed. Bowing to personal and business pressures, Lisso joined the White League. His defection snapped Twitchell's anchor in the Coushatta business community. Former allies Thomas Paxton and *Times* editor A. O. P. Pickens also defected. Front Street was now solidly against Twitchell. From Loggy Bayou to Brownsville, virtually every merchant, storekeeper, and planter whose fortunes the Mercantile Agency chronicled belonged to the White League.[22]

The few remaining white Republicans began leaving the parish. Those who remained looked to Twitchell for guidance. He tried to reassure his people, telling them that the national government would not "stand quietly by and see a re-organized confederate army crush out the loyal elements of this country." Such comments probably struck most of his listeners—and perhaps Twitchell himself—as akin to whistling in the graveyard, especially in view of events in neighboring Natchitoches and De Soto Parishes.[23]

Robert Dewees, the De Soto tax collector and supervisor of voter registration, lived in Mansfield. Toward the latter part of July he received a warning to get out of town within forty-eight hours: "We *hate you;* and will have *your life* or your absence. . . . hell is gaping For you, and unless you heed What we have Said; She will Soon Close her Everlasting Jaws upon your Stinking Smoking Carcass." The warning was signed "10 De Soto Tax Payers." Heeding the threat, Dewees took up temporary residence in Coushatta.[24]

Since 1868 the Republicans had controlled Natchitoches, twenty-seven miles downriver from Coushatta, and the Natchitoches Parish government. In May 1874 death threats were posted on city streets against local radicals, including judges D. H. Boult and Henry C. Myers: "Your fate is sealed. Nothing but your blood will appease us." The first week in July, the police jury resigned under the threat of mob violence. Three weeks later, Twitchell attended a Republican nominating convention at the Natchitoches courthouse. White Leaguers min-

22. *House Reports,* 44th Cong., 1st Sess., No. 816, p. 654.
23. *House Reports,* 43d Cong., 2d Sess., No. 261, p. 392.
24. "10 De Soto Taxpayers" to Robert Dewees [July 1874]; W. W. Womack to Robert Dewees, 27 August 1874; Womack to Dewees, 28 August 1874; all in MHT Papers.

gled with the delegates, carrying messages to armed confederates assembled in nearby Fireman's Hall. A White Leaguer named M. J. Cunningham, an attorney, "came in puffing and excited, whittling with his knife." Fearing violence, the Republican delegates renominated Twitchell for the state senate and quickly adjourned. On exiting the courthouse, Twitchell pointedly asked an acquaintance whether Cunningham was the local leader of the White League. Cunningham, overhearing the question, belligerently informed Twitchell that the popular movement needed no leader. When Twitchell rejoined, "What, a movement without a leader?" the exchange heated up, and a crowd gathered. Twitchell accused Cunningham of being a "hot-headed impulsive man" and threatened to expose his devious purposes. Flushed with anger, Cunningham retorted that his party intended to carry the fall election "peaceably if they could, forcibly if they must." Neither Twitchell nor any of the other Republicans dared remain in town for the night.[25]

Two days later on 27 July, hundreds of armed White Leaguers rode into Natchitoches. Forewarned by the *People's Vindicator* and the numerous death threats, Judge Boult and Judge Myers had slipped out of town and made a run for Coushatta. The few remaining officials resigned before the mob. Natchitoches marked the first White League takeover in the state. The ties between the Red River and Natchitoches White Leagues were close. Thomas Abney, Joseph Pierson, and Ben Wolfson were members of the 27 July Natchitoches mob. Before their return home, their neighbors advised them to "clean out" the radical nest in Coushatta or the good people of Natchitoches would come up and "do it for them."[26]

The day the White League seized the Natchitoches Parish government, Twitchell boarded a steamboat in Coushatta. His destination was the annual convention of the state Republican Party in New Orleans. His friend Edward Dewees made the trip, too, but as a precaution took another boat. When the steamer docked at Campti, midway between Coushatta and Natchitoches, the landing was abuzz with the news from

25. *House Reports*, 43d Cong., 2d Sess., No. 101, pt. 2, pp. 106, 143–44; *House Reports*, 43d Cong., 2d Sess., No. 261, p. 215.

26. *House Reports*, 43d Cong., 2d Sess., No. 261, pp. 132–33, 214, 216, 222, 279–83, 386; Lestage, "White League," 249–57; *Natchitoches Peoples's Vindicator*, 25 July 1874.

Natchitoches. Twitchell stood on the deck near the gangplank, his mind racing, trying to digest the Natchitoches story. Should he return to Coushatta, which might be next on the White League agenda, or continue on to New Orleans? In years to come, the agonizing moment would replay itself a thousand times in his mind. As he struggled with indecision, the boatmen pushed the steamer from the bank.[27]

Three days later, Sheriff Frank Edgerton wrote Twitchell of events in Coushatta since his departure: "Pierson & Abney came back from Natchitoches red hot and on the war path." At a meeting the day before, they urged the program adopted in Natchitoches and De Soto. Their words are "too strong for us for us to doubt their meaning any longer," Edgerton reported. "It is simply extermination of the Carpet bag and Scalawag Element. Nothing more nor less. You know how we are situated here. The negroes will support us to a man but it is useless for us to involve them in a conflict which would be simply a massacre unless we had ammunition so that we could hold out until reinforced." If pushed into a corner, he contended, the handful of white Republicans in the parish will probably "form . . . into a band and take [to] the woods and go to bushwhacking." However, he cautioned, "unless we are going to get some aid from U.S. or State forces we would gain nothing as it would be impossible for us to hold out any length of time. My intentions at present are to hold out as long as possible and if necessary make them commit *murder* before they make any man resign. It is barely possible we can keep the crisis off for 10 days and perhaps two weeks. (In the language of Warmoth) if Kellogg is Governor Show it." Red River, the sheriff concluded, was "on the verge of Civil War [and] an accident a drunken man or a crazy fanatic is liable to start it any moment." He added: "It is generally believed here that you have gone after troops [and] it is my firm belief that you can live here only on horseback in the woods if you do not get them." Parish Attorney Howell wrote Twitchell an almost identical warning. A storm is coming, he said and offered his opinion that "just as sure as you return without United States Soldiers the troubles will then commence."[28]

Twitchell replied immediately. He had met with Governor Kellogg

27. *CV*, 140.

28. Frank Edgerton to MHT, 30 July 1874, MHT Papers; William F. Howell to MHT, 17 August 1874, MHT Papers.

and U.S. Marshal Packard, he told his beleaguered sheriff. "As soon as some overt act has been committed, a United States Marshal can be sent up there, and he will doubtless take United States troops with him. I will advise you in case a demand is made for your resignations to be certain first that violence is to be used . . . then to save your life, resign." It is doubtful this advice would have comforted Edgerton. In any event, he never saw it, because the White League intercepted the letter.[29]

On 6 August, Natchitoches leaders, including James H. Cosgrove, editor of the *Natchitoches People's Vindicator*, drove to Coushatta for another White League rally. Cosgrove estimated the crowd at five hundred and pronounced it the largest assembly in Red River Parish's history. "Our sister parish" he claimed, had been reduced to beggary by "the outrageous presence and plunder of the Carpet-bagger Twitchell and the burglar Dewees." Proclaiming the hour of Red River's redemption at hand, Cosgrove promised the crowd every assistance from Natchitoches.[30]

As the hot August days rolled by, the tension in Coushatta mounted. Out-of-town ruffians appear on the streets, Howell wrote Twitchell, bragging "that they had come to kill Republicans."

On the 14th, two hard cases braced Robert Dewees in Gus De Russey's saloon. "Here is one of my Republican friends, now," one of the men announced sarcastically, drawing his pistol. Having seen Dewees wearing a six-shooter earlier that day, he demanded, "Show it to me now." Dewees backed away, claiming he was unarmed.

De Russey came out from behind the bar, saying, "Bob you better go home . . . there is going to be a row."

"Keep them off, Mr. De Russey," said Dewees, escaping through the back door.[31]

The next day a young black man named Frank Commodore was working on a riverboat aground on Coushatta Bar. Learning that he was a prominent Republican, the two strangers accosted him and threatened him with bodily harm. Commodore's friends complained to Sheriff Edgerton, who ordered the arrest of one of the strangers. The

---

29. MHT to Frank Edgerton, in *Natchitoches People's Vindicator*, 19 September 1874.

30. *Natchitoches People's Vindicator*, 15 August 1874.

31. William F. Howell to MHT, 17 August 1874, MHT Papers; Henry Smith [Scott] letter, *New Orleans Republican*, 13 September 1874. The author believes the letter writer was actually Henry Scott.

outsider was drunk, abusive, and fought with Edgerton's deputies, but he was placed in jail.[32]

That night, Abney, Pierson, the younger Lissos, and eight other townsmen, confronted Sheriff Edgerton, his deputy, and Judge Orin S. Penny in the street. With Abney and Pierson probably doing most of the talking, the delegation demanded Commodore's arrest: "You put a white man in jail for getting drunk, you must put this negro in jail, also, for getting drunk." Edgerton replied that Commodore had not been drunk or done anything else to warrant arrest. Did the citizens wish to swear out a complaint? he asked. The residents huddled, then demanded the jailing of Commodore without a charge. When Edgerton still demurred, the townsmen, handguns and shotguns in view, formed a circle around the three Republicans. "War to the knife and the knife to the hilt," someone muttered in the darkness. The gutsy Edgerton still balked at obeying their demand. Convinced they were about to be murdered, Judge Penny urged the sheriff to arrest Commodore. Edgerton reluctantly complied, and Commodore spent the night in jail.[33]

A few days later Edgerton negotiated an agreement, or "treaty," with Abney to keep the peace. For the moment, Red River Republicans thought they could breathe easy. About this agreement, Twitchell would later write: "On this delusive pledge the Republicans reposed in fatal security imagining their personal security to be beyond question."[34]

Brownsville was a small community about ten miles downriver from Coushatta. On the evening of 25 August, the fuse on the Red River powder keg flamed to life. Two black farmers, Thomas Floyd and Daniel Wynn, exchanged angry words with S. R. Jones and Anthony Williams, both white. According to Twitchell, Daniel Wynn had recently declined an invitation to join the Democratic Party, claiming it was wrong "for a colored man to desert the party which had lifted him from slavery." The White League later insisted that the two black men threatened the lives of Jones and Williams, causing the latter to flee his home.[35]

32. Henry Smith [Scott] letter.
33. John H. Carnes to MHT, 17 August 1874, MHT Papers; *New Orleans Republican*, 5, 13 September 1874.
34. MHT White League document [1875].
35. *House Reports*, 43d Cong., 2d Sess., No. 261, pp. 490, 885–86.

About midnight a party of horsemen rode up to the Wynn cabin. Wynn and his wife awoke to the noise of men stomping on their porch and demanding entry. After one of the intruders fired a shot into the house, Wynn triggered a shotgun blast through a crack. "Oh! I am shot," cried one of the intruders, fatally wounded. Wynn, momentarily overcome with fear, hid under the bed, but recovering his wits, escaped by climbing up the chimney. A bullet wounded him in the arm as he dashed to safety in the woods. Thomas Floyd was not to be so lucky.[36]

Minutes later whites rode up to the Floyd place, one-half mile distant. They burst into the house, taking Floyd and his family prisoners. A search produced a pistol. A man named Cobb told Mathilda Floyd to make a light; he punched her with the muzzle of his shotgun when she failed to move with alacrity. Floyd objected to this treatment of his wife. "Damn your wife," Cobb said. The intruders dragged Floyd out of the house into the night.

"After my father was carried off," his daughter later testified, "I heard the report of 5 guns, & heard some of the men say, shoot him in the head God Damn him." The cause of death, the coroner's report read, was "being shot through the head with a load of buck shot." The White League had claimed its first Coushatta victim.[37]

Word of the Brownsville shootings reached Coushatta the next morning. Even though the victims were black, whites talked only of their fears of Negro revolt. Hoping to calm the situation, Sheriff Edgerton, coroner Andy Bosley, Clark Holland, and two other Republicans rode to Brownsville. They found Thomas Floyd's body, took depositions from the Floyd and Wynn families, and questioned others in the area. Finding no evidence of the rumored black rebellion, they returned to Coushatta.[38]

It was Thursday, 27 August. Thomas Abney and his partners had scheduled a dance that evening to christen their new brick store on Front Street. Abney himself had gone to Shreveport earlier in the week and had not yet returned. One suspects that the merchant's chief business in Shreveport was White League business.

As the sun dipped low over the west bluff of the Red River, the party

36. "Inquisition of Thomas Floyd," MHT Papers.
37. Ibid.
38. Ibid.; *House Reports*, 43d Cong., 2d Sess., No. 261, p. 902.

began. About dusk, a teenage boy burst into Abney's store with a report that armed Negroes were marching on Brownsville. In Abney's absence, Thomas Paxton, a former Twitchell ally, was ostensibly in charge. Paxton and other members of the White League executive committee hurriedly conferred with the town's Republican officials. Soon afterward, Sheriff Edgerton and Robert Dewees, accompanied by a few townsmen, set out for Brownsville. For Edgerton, it was his second trip to Brownsville that day. In the meantime, Paxton's executive committee organized armed patrols for Coushatta's defense. Undismayed by the rumored rebellion, the dancers continued to twirl their partners about Abney's store for several more hours.[39]

Sheriff Edgerton's small posse returned after a couple of hours with the news that Brownsville was as quiet as a Sunday morning. The sheriff conferred with Robert Dewees, Homer Twitchell, and other Republicans. They decided to assemble at Homer Twitchell's house on the south edge of town. The word went out. Avoiding the roads, blacks began slipping through the fields and woods to the house. Some of them came because they were sent for; others were simply trying to find out what was going on. They numbered about thirty, many armed with pistols or shotguns.

Like most southern frame houses of that era, Homer Twitchell's house was mounted on small, rectangular brick legs. It was an architectural style that left two feet or more of crawl space between the house and the ground. Homer positioned the blacks under the house. If attacked, they intended to fight.[40]

The dance broke up about ten o'clock. About the same hour Homer Twitchell began to have second thoughts about turning his house into a fort. He and his companions, black and white, were in a classic no-win predicament. If attacked and they failed to defend themselves, they risked extermination. If they fought, they would be accused of instigating a Negro rebellion. Reluctantly, Homer told the blacks to go home. As they slipped off, two mounted White Leaguers stumbled on one or more of them in the dark. One of the horsemen fired a shot, whether

39. Henry Smith [Scott] letter; *House Reports*, 44th Cong., 1st Sess., No. 816, pp. 696–97, 902.

40. John M. Miller letter, *Brattleboro Vermont Phoenix*, 25 September 1874; *House Reports*, 44th Cong., 1st Sess., No. 816, pp. 685–86.

at the blacks or as a signal is unclear. The two White Leaguers rode
back to the center of town, reported in, then returned to the area. They
confronted Homer Twitchell in his yard before riding on. A hundred
yards from his door, two black farmers, Paul Williams and Lewis Johnson, lay concealed in the shrubbery along the street. Williams, for reasons known only to himself, rose and emptied both barrels of his shotgun at the riders. One of the riders, John Dickson, suffered multiple
wounds, the most serious of which was a broken arm. The shots were
heard all over town. The White League had its incident.[41]

In the wee hours of Friday morning, men on lathered horses rode
south to Campti and Natchitoches, west to Mansfield and the Texas
border, north toward Loggy Bayou and Shreveport, east to Winn-
field—spreading the news of Negro rebellion. Homer Twitchell and the
black farmers who came into town that night became the central figures
in a "plot darker than hell," a conspiracy that, according to legend,
"had it not been crushed in the bud, must have caused our blood and
the blood of innocent women to mingle together. Babes, in their inno-
cency, would have been slain to satiate and satisfy the dire thirst of these
incarnate demons." Young Twitchell and his black subalterns, the
White League alleged, had plotted to take over the town while the
whites were diverted by the music-making at Abney's store. This lurid
tale became enshrined in legend, recounted in local histories and passed
down from father to son. Six decades later, during the Great Depression, a special historical edition of the *Coushatta Citizen* featured it as
the lead story.[42]

The picture of Homer Twitchell as a reincarnate John Brown and
the black men under his house as so many Gabriel Prossers and Nat
Turners was pure propaganda, serving the interest of the White
League. Imaginary Negro uprisings were the heavy artillery of redemption. John P. Miller, Homer Twitchell's brother-in-law who lived
through this ordeal, commented on the absurdity of the rebellion story.
Who could believe, he asked, that Homer Twitchell, with thirty black
farmers, would try to seize an entire town under the noses of the Red

41. *House Reports*, 44th Cong., 1st Sess., No. 816, pp. 685–86, 696–97; Miller letter.
The wounded man's name appears as John or Joe Dixon in some records.
42. *Coushatta Citizen*, 17 June 1938.

River White League, "when his family, his friends, his property, and he himself would be sacrificed." It was preposterous.[43]

It worked nonetheless. The next day, newspapers in the region announced the arrival of couriers in Shreveport and Minden bringing reports of Red River blacks rising "against the whites" and threatening their annihilation. The dispatches claimed "that eight hundred armed negroes had assembled below Coushatta and were constantly receiving reinforcement from all quarters." More accurately, the newspapers reported armed whites descending on Coushatta from all parts of the Red River Valley.[44]

To the end of his days, Marshall Twitchell believed that the Red River White League, acting in concert with their counterparts in Natchitoches and Shreveport, orchestrated the insurrection scare and the ensuing news reports. Despite Abney's being in Shreveport, there can be little doubt that Twitchell was right. It strains credibility to believe that men and women, truly afraid of armed insurrectionists, went on dancing and cavorting on Front Street for four hours after being alerted that hundreds of bloodthirsty blacks were only a few miles away.[45]

The day after the dance, a Friday, scores of gun-toting, hard-faced strangers began riding into Coushatta. The influx continued into Saturday. Estimates of their numbers vary from several hundred to more than a thousand. They had come from Shreveport, Minden, Natchitoches, Mansfield, east Texas, and a dozen other places. They had come to root out radicalism in Coushatta.[46]

The angry visitors clustered in bunches near the offices and homes of Republican officials, shouting insults and threats. Fearful that if they failed to act, the mob would start lynching Republicans right there in the streets, at about four-thirty on Friday, the White League executive committee swung into action. With two or three dozen men at his back, Joe Pierson arrested Homer Twitchell and Henry Scott at their homes. He also arrested Clark Holland, who happened to be at Scott's house. Pierson accused Homer Twitchell of shooting John Dickson the night

43. Miller letter.
44. *New Orleans Times*, 30 August 1874; *Shreveport Times*, 30 August 1874.
45. *CV*, 143–44.
46. *House Reports*, 43d Cong., 2d Sess., No. 261, p. 493.

before. Another posse rounded up Sheriff Edgerton, Deputy Sheriff Gilbert Cone, Robert Dewees, and William Howell, accusing them of complicity in the shooting. At roughly the same time, twenty prominent black Republicans were taken into custody. The twenty-seven prisoners, both black and white, spent the night in the basement of Abney and Love's store.[47]

Saturday saw Abney returned from Shreveport. That morning, Kate Holland wrote her "Darling [Husband]" of the terrible night she and the other wives had passed at Starlight Plantation. "Where *Can* I see you?" she asked. Clark Holland replied: "Katie you can not come up here and dont think of coming for one moment. We are all right and perfectly safe. . . . Everything will turn out right." Abney, the husband claimed, "will see that we are not harmed." Henry Scott tried to reassure his wife, too: "I think they mean to give us a fair show and I think we can convince them that we are not to blame for what has happened. Keep up good cheer and trust in God for support and comfort in this time of trial for he will deal justly with us." No doubt the black men's families tried to get messages past the guards, too. If they were successful, no record of it has survived.[48]

Saturday's street mob was even bigger than Friday's. "Where in the name of God did all these people come from?" William Howell asked. In the August heat, the crowd scratched and paced about the temporary prison like a hungry predator circling a piece of raw meat. It was all the town leaders could do to keep the mob at bay.

Inside the brick store, Abney's executive committee brought the white prisoners up from the basement and began grilling them. This White League star-chamber continued into the afternoon. The defenseless captives endured the verbal hammering as best they could, their emotions whipsawed between their interrogators inside the store and the brutal mob on the street.[49]

Late that afternoon, the mock trial ended. The Republican officeholders' former friends and neighbors demanded their resignations and gave them a statement to sign: "We the undersigned officers of Red

47. Miller letter; MHT White League document [1875].
48. Clark Holland letters [August 1874], in the possession of Clark Holland, the great-grandson of Twitchell's brother-in-law, Medfield, Massachusetts.
49. Miller letter.

River and De Soto Parishes . . . propose on our part to leave the State of La., and surrender to the people the offices we hold and here request an escort of citizens to protect us out of the State. We further testify that the leading citizens of the political organization of the white people here, used all their efforts to protect our lives and discountenanced and opposed the efforts of any violence towards us in any way." Edgerton, Homer Twitchell, Robert Dewees, Clark Holland, and William Howell signed. Henry Scott, who held no local office, did not sign, nor did Gilbert Cone. Cone, in fact, was released that evening, evidently for betraying the others. At Starlight, George King, John P. Miller, and the women remained in seclusion. The black prisoners were not included; they must wait their turn.[50]

The Coushatta White League drafted a companion proclamation over the signatures of Abney, Thomas E. Paxton, Joseph Pierson, Julius Lisso, John F. Stephens, Leander E. Love, and more than a dozen other local leaders. It depicted the fallen Republican officials as bad men—scalawags and carpetbaggers—who were guilty of "inculcating vicious ideas into the minds of the colored people of Red River, and arraying them against the true interest of the country." The only specific charge made against the five radicals, however, was complicity in the attack on John Dickson two nights before.[51]

Although a formal announcement was not made until the next day, word of the resignations was on the streets within the hour. A rumor spread that the Republicans would try to leave for Shreveport that night. Anticipating the event, a large body of men rode north of town and lay in wait on the east river road. Many of the riders waiting in ambush were doubtless "Captain Jack's" men from De Soto Parish. Captain Jack's real name was Richard Coleman. His nickname was probably taken from a Modoc Indian. On Good Friday 1873, in the lava beds along the California-Oregon border, the Modoc chief known as Captain Jack treacherously murdered General E. R. S. Canby during a peace conference. Southern Republicans often used Modoc savagery as a yardstick for measuring the violence of the White League and its kin. It was a comparison that Richard Coleman did not shrink from. By calling himself Captain Jack, he boldly announced that he intended to do to

50. *Natchitoches People's Vindicator*, 5 September 1874.
51. Ibid.

the Twitchells what the Modocs had done to General Canby. (Canby, incidentally, had accepted the surrender of Louisiana's General Richard Taylor in 1865). Virtually nothing is known of Coleman. He was not related to Twitchell's inlaws in Bienville Parish. He reportedly lived in De Soto Parish, but there is no record of him in the parish courthouse, nor can he be found in Confederate military records.[52]

The prisoners planned to go on horseback to Shreveport to catch the Texas and Pacific train to Marshall, Texas. From there, they could swing south to Galveston or northeast toward Saint Louis. A big question concerned the time of departure. The White League, then and later, depicted the Republican prisoners as doing everything by choice: the prisoners *chose* to resign; they *chose* to leave the state; they *chose* their own guards; they *chose* to leave Sunday morning. This was self-serving propaganda. By definition, prisoners—like slaves—are not masters of their fate. The captives' time of departure, however, was a matter about which there was some discretion.

The Coushatta White League was united in its conviction that the Twitchell ring must be dismantled and its leaders exiled. But Abney, Julius Lisso, and Paxton, among others, clearly hoped to accomplish this without bloodshed. Late Saturday evening, fearing for their safety, Abney moved the white prisoners to the second floor of the Coushatta Hotel. He warned Howell, his personal attorney, and Clark Holland against leaving in the morning. Abney assured them that the townspeople could handle the mob and suggested that they remain in town a day or two longer, allow the mob to disperse, and then leave. Understandably, the two Republicans and their fellow captives were a good deal less confident about the mob letting them escape so easily. For two days they had been lashed by its fury. As long as they were in Coushatta, they were in danger. "I think we had better go," Howell told Abney. With the exception of Henry Scott, the other prisoners agreed. In private, Scott told Abney—both men were master masons—that he did not want leave in the morning. Late that night, the storekeeper took Scott out of the hotel, hiding him in his barn.[53]

Clark Holland's last notes to Katie were full of pathos. Neither he nor any of the others could come home, he stated. The danger was too great. "We are agoing to leave the state under a g[u]ard of our own

---

52. Miller letter.
53. *House Reports*, 43d Cong., 2d Sess., No. 261, pp. 491–93, 505; Miller letter.

selection," he wrote. "Paxton will attend to all of your wants. We depart by our own choice. Send us the saddle bags the navy sox and Pocket Pistol and 2 or 3 of Handkfs, Shirts & Collars. Paxton will see to the Plantation. Send me all the money that I sent you by Lisso." Later, he wrote that he had received everything and would be leaving in the morning: "Dont worry for it is all for the best. Kiss little Bertie for me." After a fitful night, he wrote his last note Sunday morning: "I think that we will get through without any trouble. I am glad that I have not got another night to spend in Coushatta. . . . Good Bye and may God Bless you and I hope it will not be long before you can be with us."[54]

Early Sunday morning, the Republicans completed their final preparations. Contrary to legend, they were not allowed to choose their guards. Abney selected the escorts, about twenty-five in number, giving the captives a chance to object to his choices. They turned down only one man, Cobb, the same Cobb who had jabbed Thomas Floyd's wife with a shotgun four days and a lifetime before. At the last moment, fate rolled the dice. Monroe Willis, the husband of Marshall Twitchell's sister Helen, had been arrested earlier but released. Some of the townsmen now ordered him to join the prisoners. Once again the prisoners numbered six. About nine-thirty that morning, they mounted up. The exiles carried a small fortune in jewels and cash for the trip.[55]

The sun beamed brightly, and the smell of wet grass and dust kicked up by the horses mingled in the air as the procession headed out of town. They rode north for some miles and then forded the river to the west bank. In early afternoon, near the Caddo Parish line, they stopped at the Robinson farm for dinner. Their route was widely known; the Robinsons, for example, obviously were forewarned that thirty-odd men would be coming to dinner. After dinner, they resumed their journey and in midafternoon crossed into Caddo Parish near Ward's Store, twenty miles below Shreveport. The prisoners rode near the front. Some of the horses were tiring, and the line had become strung out.

About four o'clock, people at the rear of the column saw forty or fifty riders closing fast. Leading the pursuers was a heavy-bearded man "literally covered with dust." He must have seemed like an apparition from hell, because in the steamy heat, the dust would have been soaked

54. Holland letters.
55. Miller letter.

with sweat, running in muddy streams down his body. In a matter of minutes, the riders burst past the rear guards, heading straight down the line toward the prisoners. They bellowed for the escorts to "clear the track" or die with the prisoners. The guards moved out of the way.[56]

At the head of the column, the prisoners and lead guards had stopped to allow the stragglers to catch up. It appears they had no warning from the rear guard. Robert Dewees spied the danger first. "Mount and ride for your lives," he cried. The captain of the guard shouted that they were on their own. The Republicans bolted for their horses, but too late. A hail of bullets blasted Dewees from his horse as he tried to mount. "Give me a gun, I don't want to die like a dog!" shouted Homer Twitchell a moment before a bullet shattered his face. Edgerton, according to a guard's account, flung himself "flat on his horse, escaped the first volley, and made considerable distance before he was finally shot from his horse, answering back to their calls of surrender that he would die first." Holland, Willis, and Howell surrendered. At no point did the guards offer them any protection.[57]

Captain Jack and his toughs escorted the three survivors to Ward's Store and passed several hours debating their fate. One of the original guards, a planter named H. C. Stringfellow, clearly had not anticipated this outcome. He reportedly offered a thousand dollars for the life of each captive. Unfortunately, he did not have the money in hand, and the cutthroats decided to rob and murder them instead. They formed a makeshift firing squad and executed Howell and Willis. Desiring sport, they offered Holland the chance to make a run for it. "No," he said, "you have murdered my friends, now you may kill me." He stepped forward to the bodies of Willis and Howell and died. Stringfellow and some of the other guards who had witnessed the day's gruesome events buried the six bodies in two graves about two miles apart. Stringfellow put up little fences around each of the sites so that the bodies could be found again. The next morning, the escorts drifted back into Coushatta in bunches, reporting that "Texans" had ambushed and murdered the prisoners. Some members of the lynch mob rode past Starlight, where one of the Twitchell sisters was on the piazza with the children. One of

56. *House Reports*, 43d Cong., 2d Sess., No. 261, pp. 494, 502; Bryan, *Wild Work*, 310–20.

57. Bryan, *Wild Work*, 313–15; *CV*, 146.

the horsemen shouted out that the next time he and his mates visited Coushatta, they would not leave a "woman or child of northern stock" alive.[58]

There was another murder that weekend: a black leader named Levin Allen, who lived south of Coushatta. Two years before in the time of the disputed election, a white man on horseback had attempted to ride over Allen in the street. The powerfully built Allen grabbed the horse's bridle and shoved the animal back, causing the rider to fall and break his leg. "Mr. Allen," Marshall Twitchell said, "was a republican, under any and all circumstances, and it requires a brave colored man to say that in North Louisiana." Sunday evening a few hours after the murders upriver, a party of whites took Allen from his home into the woods. They shot him, broke his arms and legs, and tortured him to death over a fire.

Sunday afternoon following the departure of the six white Republicans, Abney's executive committee moved the black captives from the store basement to the jail. On Monday a second vigilante trial began, continuing through Wednesday. In the meantime, Captain Jack's men returned from their bloody work upriver. They told Abney's people to dispense with this trial business and just hand over the prisoners. For the moment, the Coushatta leaders resisted. The black Republicans confessed that they had gone to Homer Twitchell's house with weapons the night of the dance; they also identified either Louis Johnson or Paul Williams as the man who had fired on Dickson. Williams himself freely admitted the shooting. No one, however, confessed to a Negro-carpetbagger plot to massacre Coushatta whites. On Wednesday night, a mob hanged Johnson and Williams in the forest bordering the town. Ironically, only a few feet away, Twitchell's chief black lieutenant Andy Bosley lay concealed in an old well. The other black prisoners were released.[59]

A congressional committee later looked into Johnson and Williams's deaths and, indeed, the whole Coushatta affair. Thomas Abney had been a member of the twenty-five-man trial board. The lawmakers lis-

58. Bryan, *Wild Work*, 313–14; *CV*, 146–48; *House Reports*, 43d Cong., 2d Sess., No. 261, p. 388.

59. MHT White League document [1875]; *House Reports*, 43d Cong., 2d Sess., No. 261, pp. 388–89, 395.

tened, scarcely believing their ears, as he struggled to explain how
Coushatta whites illegally arrested and tried Johnson and Williams, yet
paradoxically, disclaimed any responsibility for their deaths. Abney said
the trial panel voted, not to execute Johnson and Williams, but to return them to jail, which naturally led the visiting congressmen to ask
how it was they came to be hanged. "If you will allow me to state," he
testified, the jury, or "investigation," "did not feel at liberty to discharge" Johnson and Williams because they admitted shooting Dickson. The mob—the outsiders—grabbed them as they were being returned to jail.[60]

Meanwhile in New Orleans, Twitchell and Edward Dewees waited
out the end of August with mounting anxiety. Their last letter from
Coushatta was more than a week old, almost ancient history. They had
conferred repeatedly with Governor Kellogg about federal troops for
Coushatta, but far away in Washington, President Grant remained
deaf to Kellogg's appeals. On the Saturday their brothers were put on
trial in Abney's store, they took the train to Pass Christian, a resort on
the Mississippi coast where Dewees had a house. Early Monday morning, Twitchell's lawyer in Minden wired the bad news to Pass Christian.[61]

One can imagine the telegraph operator walking briskly through the
near-empty streets, catching whiffs of coffee and bacon, grim message
clutched in hand; knocking on the door of the quiet house; then Dewees coming to the door, Twitchell rising from the breakfast table; the
two men reading the cable, then reading again, still again, agony washing over their faces, their minds struggling in denial. All could not be
dead. Surely some were only wounded. Twitchell perhaps recalled the
time the *New Orleans Republican* had published his obituary, the false
report of his death that circulated Townshend after the Battle of Wilderness. Surely, not all were dead.

The two friends took the first train into New Orleans and went immediately to the governor's office. The telegram from Twitchell's lawyer only confirmed what Kellogg had already heard. There was no mistake. The governor wired Washington, D.C., that the news from Red
River Parish was true. The White League had murdered six Republican

60. *House Reports*, 43d Cong., 2d Sess., No. 261, pp. 497–98.
61. *CV*, 141.

officials. Twitchell and Dewees telegraphed Washington, too, imploring the government to send troops to Coushatta. Kellogg posted a five thousand dollar reward for information leading to the arrest and conviction of the killers.[62]

The bloody upheaval in Red River Parish rocked Republican Louisiana and emboldened White Leaguers all over the state—and beyond. Indeed, Coushatta was now news in New York and Chicago. Historians have generally recognized Coushatta's significance in the story of "white line" violence in the Deep South. What happened beyond the killings and the toppling of the Twitchell organization, however, remains largely unexplored in the historical literature. Excepting a postscript about Twitchell's subsequent career, most accounts of Coushatta conclude with the events of August 1874. It was otherwise for Marshall Twitchell. The murders of his family and seven other Republicans were more than a horrific instance of "white liner" violence. The world he had known was torn asunder, never to be restored. For him, the story of the Coushatta massacre was just beginning. The day he learned of the killings, after seeing the governor, he headed for the U.S. Fifth Circuit Court where he obtained an appointment as U.S. commissioner. The office clothed him with the authority to investigate the murders of his family, issue arrest warrants, organize posses, and obtain the army's help in carrying out these tasks. He was determined to bring the murderers of his family to justice.[63]

In some respects, the Twitchell story resembles the story of Wyatt Earp's family in Tombstone, Arizona, a few years hence. The Earp brothers were good Republicans, and their enemies, the Cowboys, were renegade Democrats from Texas. The famous Gunfight at the OK Corral, like the violence in Coushatta, was both an end and a beginning.

62. Ibid.; *Senate Executive Documents*, 43d Cong., 2d Sess., No. 17, pp. 11–12; *New Orleans Republican*, 6 September 1874.

63. MHT Papers. The powers of U.S. commissioners were expanded in the 1870 Enforcement Act. Fleming, *Documentary History of Reconstruction*, 2: 105–7. Brief, accurate accounts of the Coushatta massacre appear in Taylor, *Louisiana Reconstructed*, 287–91; Foner, *Reconstruction*, 551; Rable, *But There Was No Peace*, 133–35; Joseph G. Dawson, *Army Generals and Reconstruction: Louisiana, 1862–1877* (Baton Rouge, 1982), 162–63. Longer accounts (Tunnell, *Crucible of Reconstruction*, 175–209; Shoalmire, "Carpetbagger Extraordinary," 185–93), still telescope postmassacre events.

After the murder of one brother and the maiming of another, Wyatt Earp set forth on his Vendetta Ride to bring the Cowboys to justice. Marshall Twitchell would act out his own vendetta. He was not as ruthless as Wyatt Earp, and unfortunately for him, the White League was an even more dangerous foe than the Cowboys.[64]

64. Allen Barra, *Inventing Wyatt Earp: His Life and Many Legends* (New York, 1998).

TWELVE

TWITCHELL UNDER SIEGE

I N the days and weeks after the massacre, Marshall Twitchell's remaining kinsmen and allies were in hiding. His black subaltern Andy
Bosley and George A. King, his surviving brother-in-law, took to the
woods. Thomas Abney advised Henry Scott, who was hiding in his
barn, to make a run for it. Scott, posing as Abney's messenger, reached
the army post at Colfax. A few days later in New Orleans, Scott wrote
a narrative of the massacre for the *New Orleans Republican*. John M.
Miller and his sister Lottie, Homer Twitchell's widow, remained at
Starlight after the killings in "murderous suspense." Miller and the
family contrived to keep Homer's death from Lottie. (They had only
been married since January.) Advised by whites on 9 September to
"scratch gravel," Miller and his sister caught the next steamboat to
Shreveport, then traveled by rail to Vermont. Lottie was told of Homer's death only after she and her brother reached Fayetteville, Vermont,
whereupon, she collapsed in mournful bereavement. Miller published
an account of the massacre in the *Brattleboro Vermont Phoenix*. Twitchell's mother and sisters remained in seclusion at Starlight.[1]

1. Miller letter, *Brattleboro Vermont Phoenix*, 25 September 1874.

Although A. O. P. Pickens, editor of the *Coushatta Times*, had recently sided with the White League, he feared that his earlier association with Twitchell could bring sudden retribution. At the first opportunity, Pickens fled to Texas. In his absence, Abney's citizens' committee took over the newspaper. In early September, the *Coushatta Times*, masquerading as a Republican organ, published the "Red River Riot," purporting to tell the true story of the massacre. The story was mostly written in the passive voice: "couriers were sent," men "were confined," "guards were doubled," "negroes were arrested," etc. Things happen, in other words, but the people who made them happen, beyond a vague reference to a "committee of old and reliable citizens," remained anonymous. In this account, when a gang of "supposed Texans" overtook and murdered the six Republican prisoners, the guards did "everything in their power . . . to avert the doom of these unfortunate and erring men." One statement alludes to the former amicable relationship between the murdered officials and Coushatta's business elite: "We acknowledge that the republican party has favored us when most needed; we acknowledge that these identical men were once counted our friends, and some of them have lent us helping hands on different occasions. . . . Some of these very men, in 1872, rendered us a lifetime favor—assisted in a most exemplary manner in the burial of our aged grandparent."[2]

Twitchell, still in New Orleans, could scarcely believe the world he had left just five weeks before could have altered so dramatically. To him, the killing of his family and friends after promising them safe conduct was monstrous treachery, surpassing the savagery of the Modocs who had murdered General Canby. He experienced a profound sense of personal betrayal but professed to reserve final judgment until all the facts were in. As he wrote in the *Republican:* "I am not yet prepared to believe in the depths of depravity to which my personal friends and friends of the victims in the Democratic party must have sunk to enter such an unnatural plot to end with such a cowardly massacre."[3]

For President Grant, far away on the Potomac, the Coushatta murders were ill-timed. Nine years after the war in the midst of the first great

---

2. Given the confusing authorship, it is unclear exactly whose "aged grandparent" is referred to. *House Reports*, 43d Cong., 2d Sess., No. 261, p. 905.

3. MHT letter in *New Orleans Republican*, 5 September 1874.

depression of America's industrial age, the northern public was tired of the expense and frustration of Reconstruction, with its disputed elections, race riots, and seemingly endless federal intrusions. Louisiana, moreover, was only one state. In the summer and fall of 1874, Republicans in Mississippi, Alabama, Tennessee, Georgia, and South Carolina pleaded for federal protection.[4]

Coushatta caught the U.S. Army unprepared, too. The Nineteenth Infantry, a veteran Reconstruction regiment, had left Louisiana for the Indian frontier in June. Fearing yellow fever more than the White League, General William H. Emory, the commander of the Gulf, had ordered most of the remaining troops in Louisiana to Holly Springs, Mississippi. The day Twitchell and Dewees learned of their brothers' murders, there were only 130 federal soldiers in the entire state.[5]

Events in New Orleans soon eclipsed those in Coushatta. The Crescent City White League, inspired by the uprisings in Natchitoches and Red River Parish, was organized in militia battalions and eager for a fight. "I had become acquainted with many of the gang leaders of roughs, which infest the city and are always for sale to the highest bidder," Twitchell wrote of this so-called militia. From private sources he learned that an attempt to overthrow the state government was imminent. He may even have gotten wind of a bizarre plot to kidnap Governor Kellogg and other officials and ship them to a foreign country. Twitchell warned party leaders of the danger; however, he said he "could not, either with honor or safety, give the source of the information or impress others with the full gravity of the situation." Dismayed and frustrated by his colleagues' underestimation of the White League, Twitchell returned to Pass Christian with Dewees to, as he phrased it, "await the appearance of a danger sufficiently vivid for our friends to see it."[6]

On Saturday, 12 September, at about the time Twitchell and Dewees left for Pass Christian, the steamer *Mississippi* docked in the Crescent City with a cargo of weapons. Governor Kellogg and General James Longstreet mobilized the state militia and the Metropolitan Police to keep the ship's cargo out of the hands of the White League. At the same

4. Foner, *Reconstruction*, 512; AGO file 3579, RG 94, M-666, reel 170, NA.

5. Dawson, *Army Generals and Reconstruction*, 156–58, app. 3.

6. *CV*, 148; Taylor, *Louisiana Reconstructed*, 292.

time, the White League was determined to unload the guns. "Danger of Conflict imminent," U.S. Marshal Packard wired Washington on Sunday. "No troops here at present but Gen Emory telegraphs me that he will send detachments from Jackson tonight."[7]

On Monday morning, several thousand angry whites assembled on Canal Street. The speakers condemned Kellogg as a usurper and appointed a committee to press the governor for his "immediate resignation." About noon, the governor refused to receive any communication from men he termed armed insurgents. At three o'clock Marshal Packard wired Washington that the White League had taken over city hall and cut the police and fire department telegraph wires. Kellogg sent a frantic cable to the U.S. attorney general, pleading for federal intervention, urging, "Important. Please answer immediately."[8]

In late afternoon at the foot of Canal Street, six hundred police and three thousand black militia clashed with a White League force numbering in the thousands. A fight on this scale had not been seen since Appomattox, even in the Indian wars. The police bore the brunt of the attack and after a brief fight, broke and ran, along with the militia. As so often happened in Reconstruction, the army was late. When the troop train from Holly Springs pulled in at five o'clock, the battle was over. For the next three days, Kellogg's government cowered in the customhouse while the White League ruled the city. In the story of Louisiana's redemption, the battle of 14 September would become legendary as the "Battle of Liberty Place." To this day, at the foot of Iberville Street, a controversial white obelisk commemorates the White League victory.[9]

Learning of the battle, the next day Twitchell took the New Orleans train from Pass Christian on a private mission. The train station stood at the foot of Canal Street overlooking the river, only a few hundred

7. Taylor, *Louisiana Reconstructed*, 292–93; Stephen B. Packard to George H. Williams, 13 September 1874, JDR, RG 60, M-940, reel 2.

8. Taylor, *Louisiana Reconstructed*, 292–93; Stephen B. Packard to George H. Williams, 14 September 1874, and William Pitt Kellogg to George H. Williams, 14 September 1874, JDR.

9. Taylor, *Louisiana Reconstructed*, 292–94; Stephen B. Packard to George H. Williams, 14, 15 September 1874, JDR; William Pitt Kellogg to George H. Williams, 14 September 1874, JDR; James W. Loewen, *Lies across America: What Our Historic Sites Get Wrong* (New York, 1999), 214–19.

yards from the customhouse. The scene he beheld was reminiscent of Mexico City or Paris in revolution: the streets barricaded and armed men everywhere. Ignoring the menacing presence of patrolling White Leaguers, he walked quickly to the Louisiana Savings Bank and Safe Deposit Company on Camp Street in the financial district, a few blocks south of the French Quarter. The building was bolted tight. Twitchell shouted and banged on the doors and finally gained entry. Removing valuable securities from his safe-deposit box, he carried them a few blocks to the customhouse, where he deposited them in the safe. Timing his moves, he walked hurriedly from the customhouse, and with only moments to spare, caught the train back to Pass Christian.[10]

Twitchell had come under surveillance as soon as he left the train station. "I do not know who was the most surprised," he later wrote, "my enemies on the street as I passed them at a rapid walk, or my friends in the Custom House at my appearance there." However valuable the papers in his safe-deposit box, the suspicion arises that Twitchell's daring journey through the heart of New Orleans had a deeper motivation, not even consciously realized. It was an act of absolution. His kinsmen were dead, while he was alive. If the White League had shot him down, his guilt might have been assuaged.[11]

In New Orleans, the White League battalions paraded in victory through the city. "So ends the Kellogg regime," the *Picayune* announced. "Big, inflated, insolent, overbearing, it collapsed at one touch of honest indignation and gallant onslaught." Around the state, Democratic newspapers trumpeted victory. "The war is over," newspapers in Shreveport and Natchitoches reported. The radicals, the papers claimed, "have just made a complete surrender—everything in our hands." Inspired by the New Orleans uprising, the White League had toppled parish governments all over the state.[12]

However much President Grant wanted the national government and the army out of the South, however tenuous the Kellogg government's claim to legitimacy, no president could allow armed insurrectionists to overthrow a state government. By the end of September, the president had put more than eleven hundred troops back into Louisi-

10. *CV*, 148–49.

11. Ibid.

12. Lonn, *Reconstruction in Louisiana*, 272–73; *Natchitoches People's Vindicator*, 19 September 1874.

ana. The army occupied New Orleans and resurrected the Kellogg government. Grant ordered the White League to disperse and yield to Kellogg's lawful authority.[13]

When Governor Kellogg and his officials returned to their duties in the state house, for the most part they found their offices and files as they had left them. The symbols and accouterments of power, however, mattered less than the substance of power. Already weak, the Republican regime was now even further enfeebled. Without some degree of cooperation from conservative whites, it could not govern.[14]

The immediate problem was the looming November election. Unless Republicans and Democrats/White Leaguers agreed to some sort of armistice, there would be chaos on election day. In late September the two sides compromised, creating a bipartisan five-man advisory board to oversee the election. In return for this and the appointment of two Democrats to the state Returning Board, which decided disputed elections, the Democrats promised to abandon their violent campaign tactics. It was not the first or the last such compromise, and it boded ill for the Republican regime. As General Emory—who had followed the negotiations—informed the War Department: "It may ease matters for the time being but it looks like a recognition of the legal rights of insurgent parties." The peace, moreover, would last only if the Democrats won control of the legislature. In the event of Republican victory, the violence would resume.[15]

In the meantime, Twitchell and other exiled Republicans waited in New Orleans for the army's help in reclaiming the countryside. Republican officials—sheriffs, judges, tax collectors, coroners, justices of the peace—had been arrested, killed, forced to resign, or simply run out of fifteen parishes, eight of them in the Red River Valley. Most of the takeovers followed the same well-thumbed and tattered script as in Coushatta, but without the massacre. After the fall of Bayou Sara in West Feliciana Parish in mid-September, the *New Orleans Republican* reported sardonically: "This makes the five hundredth dreadful negro riot which has been reported since the last election, and we have yet to hear

13. *New Orleans Republican*, 16 September 1874; Dawson, *Army Generals and Reconstruction*, 174–80.

14. *New Orleans Republican*, 20 September 1874.

15. Ibid., 22, 30 September 1874; Emory to Townshend, 30 September 1874, JDR; Emory to Townshend, 1 October 1874, AGO file 3579.

of the loss of any whites." How is it, the editor asked, that "the negroes always are beaten when they go into the riot business."[16]

The last Sunday in September, Twitchell left New Orleans on the *Belle Rowland* with E Company of the Third U.S. Infantry, bound for Coushatta. Other companies of bluecoats steamed toward Monroe, Saint Martinsville, and the Red River Valley towns of Shreveport, Belleview (in Bossier Parish), and Alexandria. The Democratic newspapers tracked the *Belle Rowland*'s progress upriver. At each landing, angry whites scowled at Twitchell, muttering oaths. Many blacks, however, cheered and waved hats and scarves, "showing every possible evidence of joy." On 4 October, the forty-five men of E Company disembarked and established Camp Coushatta at nearby Springville.[17]

"At last the man, [M.] H. Twitchell . . . has returned to Coushatta," reported the *Natchitoches People's Vindicator*. The paper's prose was vintage Reconstruction invective: It was "an insult to humanity to call *such a person* as Twitchell, a man"; he and his pal Dewees had first come into the region "with burglars tools"; Twitchell was "the *foul thief of a thieving Senate*," etc. If Twitchell read the paper, and there is a good chance he did, one line of the *Vindicator* column would have made the carpetbagger wince: "His hands [are] red with the blood of his own kindred, for he, and he alone, is responsible for their death[s]."[18]

A month after the massacre, Abney's executive committee was still running Coushatta, and Captain Jack was reported to be watching the town. As U.S. commissioner, Twitchell, with an armed guard, set up headquarters at the courthouse. He was afraid for his own safety and that of other Republicans and the surviving members of his family. The day after his arrival, he met with a citizens' conference committee headed by Abney and Julius Lisso, Twitchell's former friend. The tension-packed meeting produced a written agreement, signed on 6 October by Twitchell, Abney, Lisso, and nine other town leaders. This Coushatta compromise emulated the pact between the Kellogg government and the New Orleans White League. The main tenets of the accord were: 1) Officers appointed to replace the murdered officials

16. *New Orleans Republican*, 19 September 1874.

17. *CV*, 149; *Shreveport Times*, 3 October 1874; U.S. Military Posts, 1800–1916, RG 94, M-617, reel 258.

18. *Natchitoches People's Vindicator*, 10 October 1874.

would be parish residents; 2) a bipartisan committee would oversee the November election; 3) Commissioner Twitchell would arrest only actual participants in the recent massacre; 4) and those arrested would be entitled to immediate hearings. In return, the "Conservative People's party" promised to end the tactics of intimidation and violence. An unstated sine qua non of the agreement was that the White League would choose the next sheriff. Ratification by a town meeting followed two days later.[19]

Neither party to this truce had any intention of keeping it. Twitchell believed that Abney and the town leaders were responsible for the murders of his family. He signed the document to expedite gathering evidence that would bring the perpetrators to justice. For their part, even as the ink on the paper dried, Abney and the other signers plotted Twitchell's assassination.

For the next few days, Twitchell stayed close to the soldiers. The absence of cavalry hampered his investigation. Without horses, there was no way to recover the bodies in Caddo Parish, hence no prima facie evidence that the murders had even occurred. The people in Red River Parish, white and black, were so terrified of the White League and Captain Jack that only a handful would talk about the massacre. These few slipped into town after dark, and even these brave souls would not speak for the record. They told their stories only on condition that they would never have to testify in court. When a congressman later pressed Twitchell to reveal the names of individuals who had witnessed the massacre, he replied, "If I were to answer that question, I would expose the witnesses—the only ones living—to certain death."[20]

On 8 October, after the ratification of the compromise, Abney's citizen's committee pressed Twitchell to appoint new parish officials. He refused to be rushed, however. As the people leaving the courthouse milled about on Front Street, Twitchell became separated from his military guard. A pair of old friends, their voices trembling with emotion, warned him that he was to be the target of an assassination. The carpetbagger may have been once again deliberately flirting with death. A steamer from Shreveport had just docked. The detachment of soldiers on board was heading down river. "I walked onto the boat through the

19. *CV*, 149–51; *House Reports*, 43d Cong., 2d Sess., No. 261, p. 396.
20. *House Reports*, 43d Cong., 2d Sess., No. 261, pp. 388, 396.

mob, who were only waiting for it to shove off before they seized me," Twitchell related. Safely on board, he turned and told Abney's committee that he was going back to New Orleans. If they wanted an election in the parish, "they must learn to control the mob." If they had "known what my decision was to have been before I reached the boat," Twitchell claimed, "I should never have reached it." The crowd rustled and stirred threateningly, but quieted when the bluecoats prepared to repel an attack.[21]

Within days of Twitchell's departure, Coushatta claimed another victim, Thomas Paxton, the former parish attorney. Although he eventually joined the White League, indeed, became chairman of the executive committee in Abney's absence, Paxton had remained loyal to Twitchell longer than most Red River scalawags. He was probably one of those who visited the courthouse after dark and warned Twitchell of the plot to assassinate him. Paxton went fishing after Twitchell left, carrying bait, fishing pole, and a bottle of whiskey given to him by his "friends." He was found dead. The whiskey, Twitchell was later informed, had been fatally doctored.[22]

Reaching New Orleans, Twitchell took his findings to U.S. Attorney James Beckwith, the federal prosecutor for the District of Louisiana. Earlier in the year, under the 1870 Enforcement Act, Beckwith had obtained convictions against William Cruikshank and two other defendants in the Colfax massacre. Unfortunately, on appeal at the circuit level, Supreme Court Justice Joseph Bradley overturned the convictions. Bradley ruled that the government failed to allege that the Colfax killings were racially motivated. Moreover, the Fourteenth Amendment, he said, protected blacks and other citizens against state actions, not the actions of private citizens. Cruikshank and mob were private citizens. The government appealed the case to the U.S. Supreme Court. Because Bradley was a sitting member of the court, however, his opinion cast an ominous shadow over the convictions—and future trials.[23]

During his brief stay in Coushatta—the timidity of witnesses notwithstanding—Twitchell had learned the basic facts of the massacre and

21. *CV*, 152; *House Reports*, 43d Cong., 2d Sess., No. 261, pp. 389, 396.

22. *CV*, 173; *Senate Reports*, 46th Cong., 2d Sess., No. 388, p. 1099.

23. Lou Falkner Williams, *The Great South Carolina Ku Klux Klan Trials, 1871–1872* (Athens, Ga., 1996), 136–37; A. Leon Higginbotham Jr., *Shades of Freedom: Racial Politics and Presumptions of the American Legal Process* (New York, 1966), 88–89.

compiled an impressive list of suspects. While Beckwith was satisfied with the accuracy of Twitchell's findings, the prosecutor was skeptical of being able to obtain jury convictions against Abney and the other ringleaders. "A large portion of the Whites in the state," he wrote the U.S. attorney general, "will consider any attempt to punish the crime is remorseless persecution and quote Justice Bradley on the enforcement act as conclusive against the jurisdiction of the federal courts." Overruling his own reservations, Beckwith issued arrest warrants against Abney, Julius Lisso, John F. Stephens, Richard Coleman (Captain Jack), Joe Pierson, *Vindicator* editor James B. Cosgrove, and sixty-two other prominent whites from Red River, De Soto, and Natchitoches Parishes. The charges were "conspiracy and murder" under the 1870 Enforcement Act. Thus began the proceedings in *U.S. v. T.W. Abney et al.*[24]

The warrants could not be served without federal soldiers. Governor Kellogg appealed to General Emory for help. Twitchell's report, in conjunction with other intelligence, was overwhelming: northwest Louisiana was in a virtual state of insurrection. In response, General Emory created the District of the Upper Red River, under the command of the Seventh Cavalry's Major Lewis Merrill. Before coming to Louisiana, Merrill, a Republican, had fought the Ku Klux Klan in the Carolinas and Georgia. Democratic newspapers in South Carolina had nicknamed him "Dog Merrill." North Louisiana newspapers would prove equally inventive. After his appointment Merrill talked with Twitchell about the Red River situation and Twitchell's investigation.[25]

A few days later, Merrill reached Shreveport. Northwest Louisiana, he shortly informed Emory, bordered on anarchy: "The Kellogg representatives of the civil authority were violently ousted from their offices at the same time that the State government was overthrown in New Orleans, and the McEnery officers were and are now in the possession of

24. James R. Beckwith to George H. Williams, 17 October 1874, JDR; "U.S. v. Abney" documents, MHT Papers; List of names on the arrest list in *Natchitoches People's Vindicator*, 12 December 1874.

25. Major Lewis Merrill to AAG, Gulf, 24 August 1875, U.S. Army Continental Commands, District of the Upper Red River, RG 393, NA (hereinafter cited as District Upper Red River); E. R. Platt to Merrill, 15 October 1874, District Upper Red River; *Shreveport Times*, 27 October, 15 November 1874.

the offices. . . . No civil process of any kind emanating from State authority can be issued or enforced for want of the legal officers to issue it. . . . The peace and good order of this whole section is at the mercy of any one who can get followers enough to begin a riot." The town leaders, Merrill claimed, "are some half-dozen reckless, passionate men, of broken fortune who miss no chance to foment trouble, and whose whole time is occupied in setting afloat disturbing rumors, and blowing into a flame every ember of sensation and excitement which they find." In Merrill's estimation, the most important of these leaders was Albert Leonard, general of the White League militia and owner of the *Shreveport Times.* "He is a reckless but shrewd man . . . with only one hope—that in a storm he may come to the surface," said the major.[26]

Merrill feared the upcoming election would turn into a bloody riot unless he restored respect for federal law. Pretexts for action were numerous, but one particularly egregious example of intimidation had occurred shortly before Merrill's arrival. On 14 October, Shreveport's leading merchants signed a pledge to require their "employees to vote the people's ticket at the ensuing election." Workers who refused would be dismissed. The merchants further pledged to deny credit to planters who hired or rented lands to Republicans. Believing such economic coercion violated the 1870 Enforcement Act, Merrill filed charges with the U.S. commissioner, who issued arrest warrants against five leading merchants. A federal marshal quietly served the warrants. Despite inflammatory rhetoric in the newspapers, the arrests did have the effect, at least temporarily, of lowering the temperature in the state's second-largest city.[27]

The Shreveport arrests reflected a broader strategy. In October and November, eight federal posses, traversed the District of the Upper Red River making arrests under the Enforcement Act. In the main, the purpose of these arrests was to curtail open defiance of the government

26. *House Reports*, 43d Cong., 2 Sess., No. 101, pt. 2, pp. 66–68; Gilles Vandal, "Albert H. Leonard's Road from the White League to the Republican Party: A Political Enigma," *LH* 36 (1995): 67–69.

27. *House Reports*, 43d Cong., 2d Sess., No. 101, pt. 2, pp. 66–70; *New Orleans Republican*, 21 October 1874.

and stop White League violence. Prosecution was secondary—except in Coushatta.[28]

The U.S. marshal's office in New Orleans handed the Coushatta assignment to U.S. Deputy Marshal J. B. Stockton. Stockton's movements in New Orleans, prior to his departure, are unknown, but clearly he talked with Twitchell and the Vermonter's kinsmen Henry Scott, now a federal deputy marshal, because the three men arranged a rendezvous at Coushatta.

Stockton left New Orleans carrying secret orders for the military commanders at Shreveport and Coushatta. (Nothing could be trusted to wire because the Shreveport telegraph office was a White League listening post.) On Friday 16 October, Stockton rode south from Shreveport. With him were Lieutenant Donald McIntosh and G Company of the Seventh Cavalry. At midmorning on Sunday, the Stockton-McIntosh posse rendezvoused with Henry Scott at Coushatta. The town was quiet. Many people were in church. The troopers picketed the roads, blocking the exits. Scott guided the posse into town. Stockton arrested men on the street and in their homes. When the posse stopped a townsman and learned his identity, Stockton would ruffle his paper and run his eyes down the long column of names to see whether the man was on the list. One man walked up to him and asked, "Have you a warrant for me." Without incident, Stockton arrested Thomas Abney, John F. Stephens, George Cawthorn, and ten other stunned townsmen. (Julius Lisso, among others, was out of town.) It was a day Coushatta would never forget. Thomas Abney later testified about it before a congressional committee: "The cavalry came and picked up indiscriminately everybody, it produced the greatest consternation among the people that I ever saw." A congressman asked him how many warrants Deputy Marshal Stockton had. People "said there were about seventy-five. Mr. Stockton had a sheet of paper about as long as . . . three of these sheets," Abney said, holding up a full-size piece of paper for the committee and spectators in the room to see. On Monday, Stockton's posse headed for Natchi-

28. "List of U.S. Detachments of U.S. Troops furnished to U.S. Deputy Marshals in performing their duties," 20 October to 30 November 1874, District Upper Red River; *New Orleans Republican*, 21 October 1874.

toches, leaving the prisoners in the courthouse jail with a military guard from Camp Coushatta.[29]

A day or two later, Twitchell's steamer docked at Coushatta. Exasperated by the want of cavalry, now in Natchitoches, the carpetbagger rented six horses and made them available to the foot soldiers at Camp Coushatta. Led by Twitchell's informants, Deputy Scott and a posse of mounted infantry arrested four more suspects in the surrounding countryside. The only additional Coushatta arrest occurred because Ben Wolfson verbally abused Scott. When Wolfson's sister complained, Twitchell told her that her brother "talked too much."[30]

In the meantime, Deputy Stockton and Lieutenant McIntosh arrested seven Natchitoches residents for complicity in the Coushatta murders. *Vindicator* editor James H. Cosgrove did not submit quietly. The editor and another man entered town by carriage on the Grand Ecore Road. At the juncture of Front and Washington Streets, after an informant pointed them out, a U.S. trooper, pistol in hand, ordered them to stop. In the *Vindicator's* rendition of the event, Cosgrove demanded indignantly: "And who are you, who dares arrest a gentleman on the public highway. . . . Where is your authority for this outrage?" The *Vindicator* neglected to print a few colorful details of the affair contained in Lieutenant McIntosh's report: namely, that Cosgrove erupted in a drunken rage. The editor "grossly insulted" Deputy Stockton and "threw a chew of tobacco in his face." Cosgrove then turned his wrath on McIntosh. He "made threats against me," the lieutenant wrote, "and in a violent and defiant manner used indecent and insulting language in the full hearing of the guard and enlisted men of my command."[31]

Two days after Cosgrove's arrest, Stockton wired Marshal Packard in New Orleans. "You cannot imagine the state of affairs here," he

29. E. R. Platt to commanding officer, Shreveport, 12 October 1874, and Platt to commanding officer, Coushatta, 12 October 1874, District Upper Red River; J. B. Stockton letter in Stephen B. Packard to George H. Williams, 23 October 1874, JDR; Stockton letter in Packard to Williams, 1 November 1874, JDR; Lieutenant Donald McIntosh report to AAG, Gulf, in Major Lewis Merrill to AAG, Gulf, 18 November 1874, Letters received, AGO, RG 94, M-666, reel 172, NA (hereinafter cited as McIntosh Report).

30. McIntosh Report; *House Reports*, 44th Cong., 1st Sess., No. 816, pp. 654.

31. McIntosh Report; *Natchitoches People's Vindicator*, 24 October 1874.

wrote. The white citizens publicly avow, Stockton claimed, that "as soon as I go away with the cavalry they intend to kill all the prominent white and black republicans in the parish." While the arrests had temporarily restored order, Stockton feared that his posse's actions would, in his words, "only add increased revenge when we retire."[32]

The Stockton-McIntosh posse remained in Natchitoches until election eve, then on 3 November headed back to Coushatta. In all, the posse and Twitchell's mounted infantry made twenty-five arrests. Most of the men for whom warrants had been issued, Lieutenant McIntosh wrote, "have either fled the State or gone to parts of it where they are not so well known." Other suspects were hiding out in the swamps and woods. The lieutenant blamed Deputy Marshal's Stockton's lax pursuit for the escape of the chief culprits: presumably Captain Jack and associates.

Major Merrill appended a letter to McIntosh's report explaining Stockton's "apparent apathy in certain cases." Based on a personal interview with the deputy marshal, "I learn many facts," Merrill wrote, "which if known to Lieut. McIntosh would have materially modified his views of Mr. Stockton's discharge of his duty." In addition to making arrests, Merrill said, the deputy marshal "was charged with certain investigations in connection with the savage and brutal murders to which Lieut. McIntosh refers." Merrill did not elaborate, but the nature of Stockton's orders can reasonably be deduced. The U.S. marshal's office and prosecutor Beckwith needed Stockton to build a trial case, and therein lay the dilemma. The deputy marshal was no more successful than Twitchell in finding witnesses willing to testify in court. Without such witnesses, it probably made little sense to Stockton to track down every name on the warrant list. The more so because the likes of Captain Jack were apt to shoot if cornered.

On the return trip to Shreveport, the posse located the graves of the six massacre victims and disinterred them. They lay "where they were killed, in two graves—three in each." Lieutenant McIntosh found a note indicating that Homer Twitchell had received eight hundred dollars from Julius Lisso, but not the money itself. The dead men had been "robbed of all valuables by the murderers." One of the corpses, "(name unknown)" McIntosh reported, "was so perforated and gashed with

32. Stephen B. Packard to George H. Williams, 1 November 1874, JDR.

bullets that it was only with great care that it could be moved without falling to pieces; while the private parts of another (name also unknown) were mutilated—shot off."[33]

The evidence found at the scene, incriminated several individuals as "principals and accessories" McIntosh said, "not heretofore known to have been connected with the occurrence, and corroborates as to others the evidence already in possession of the proper authorities." The evidence McIntosh found so compelling was less so to Beckwith. Two months later the prosecutor dropped the charges against Cosgrove and the Natchitoches defendants. No record of the dismissal of charges against Abney and the others arrested at Coushatta has been found, but *U.S. v. Abney* never went to trial. Even so, the threat of prosecution lingered like an ominous cloud over the Red River Valley.[34]

The Coushatta manhunt made for a tense November election. Abney, John F. Stephens, and a dozen others were prisoners in the Coushatta courthouse on election day. Acting as spokesman, lawyer Stephens said the prisoners wanted to vote, claiming they retained their rights as citizens until convicted in a court of law. After some wrangling, Deputy Scott allowed them to go under guard to the polls in groups. After the election, most of the defendants posted $5,000 bonds and were released.[35]

The *Shreveport Times*, the *People's Vindicator*, and other Democratic newspapers made the most of the situation. Their headlines cried, "Cavalry Raid on Coushatta," "Intimidation," "Wholesale Arrests," "Federal Tyranny," and so on. The arrests in Shreveport, Coushatta, Natchitoches, and other towns, the press charged, were flagrant attempts to scare north Louisiana whites from the polls. To be sure, Twitchell, Deputy Stockton, Lieutenant McIntosh, and Major Merrill were not primarily concerned with the election. Still, there was an element of truth in these claims. The Democratic vote in Red River Parish fell from 362 in 1872 to 265 in 1874, a 27 percent decline. The word

33. McIntosh Report.

34. McIntosh Report (Although McIntosh attributed the note concerning the eight hundred dollars to Robert Dewees and his wife, it was actually a note from Clark Holland to his wife, Katie, with a postscript concerning Julius Lisso getting the money for Homer Twitchell.); *U.S. v. T. W. Abney et al.*, U.S. Circuit Court, New Orleans, CR 27, Fort Worth Depository, NA.

35. *House Reports*, 44th Cong., 1st Sess., No. 816, p. 699.

was out that anyone wanted for the Coushatta murders would be arrested when they came to vote. And because there was no way of knowing precisely who was on Deputy Stockton's list, individuals who had been involved in the massacre, even peripherally, stayed home on election day.[36]

The most important event of the campaign was the Coushatta massacre itself. Asked whether the murder of the six white officials did not have more impact than the killing of a comparable number of blacks, Twitchell replied, "It affects them a thousand times more." Lacking "the ability and education of their leaders," the Negroes were "in a measure powerless," and knew it, he said. "They look to the white man for protection; they had been protected under our influence and under our government in the parish. . . . and they felt that, if the White League was strong enough to take their leaders from them, and murder them in cold blood, they were strong enough to reduce them to slavery, or anything else they chose." Major Merrill voiced a similar opinion before a congressional committee. "I have very carefully investigated the result of the Coushatta massacre in its effects upon the negroes," he said, "and for miles many miles' distant from the locality . . . for weeks and weeks after, scarcely a negro, and in no instance a negro who was at all prominent in politics, dared to sleep in his house at all."[37]

Blacks had voted safely in Coushatta, where federal troops guarded the polls, but in the hills they ran a gauntlet of mounted and armed whites patrolling the roads and taking names. The Republicans carried the parish, but their vote was down more than 18 percent, from 913 in 1872 to 745 in 1874. In his bid for senate reelection, Twitchell was defeated. He carried Red River but lost the other three parishes of the Twenty-second District, De Soto, Natchitoches, and Sabine. In Mansfield, the White League greeted black voters election morning with warning blasts from cannons and shotguns. The De Soto election was so one-sided that the Republican supervisor of registration refused to

36. *Natchitoches People's Vindicator*, 24 October, 28 November 28, 1874; *Shreveport Times*, 22, 23, 27 October, 11 December 1874; *House Reports*, 43d Cong., 2d Sess., No. 261, pp. 389, 720; *House Reports*, 44th Cong., 1st Sess., No. 816, p. 727; "Statistics of Population, Registration and Election in Louisiana, 1867 to 1876," insert in *House Miscellaneous Documents*, 45th Cong., 2d Sess., No. 31 (hereinafter referred to as the Potter Commission).

37. *House Reports*, 43d Cong., 2d Sess., No. 261, pp. 176, 389.

send the returns to New Orleans; thus, no vote from De Soto Parish was ever counted, negating the Democratic triumph. In Bienville, Twitchell's former home, nary a Republican voted. The Coushatta killings "has had a very bad effect on the republicans of this parish," one radical wrote. Never before, he said, had the radical party been "so completely run off the track as the White Leaguers has them now." As he had done in 1868, Twitchell advised Bienville blacks not to vote. Throughout the Red River Valley, the White League and the legacy of Colfax and Coushatta made the election a sham.[38]

Statewide, the Democrats claimed victory and on the basis of the reported returns were indeed the winners. It was for just such elections, however, that the Republicans had created the state Returning Board. On 11 November, ex-governor James Madison Wells called the Returning Board to order in New Orleans' Saint Louis Hotel, which served as the state house from 1873 to 1877. After a flurry of legal motions, protests, and unsolicited instructions in the opening sessions, the five-man board settled down to the tedious business of scrutinizing the election returns, ward by ward, for nearly half the parishes in Louisiana. Republicans from every corner of the state planned to testify.[39]

Friend and foe alike anticipated Twitchell's appearance, scheduled for early December. The arrests of eighteen Red River planters and business leaders, as well as the continued presence of an infantry company at Camp Coushatta, had temporarily quieted the countryside and permitted him to return home to Starlight. However, as the date of his appearance before the Returning Board approached, White League activity revived, and he learned that his enemies intended to prevent him from testifying. The first Saturday in December, he called on a local doctor known to be active in the Democratic Party, complaining of illness and asking for medicine ("which I took care not to take"). He then rode back to Starlight and pulled the blinds shut in his bedroom. After dark he saddled his fastest horse and, with a trusted guide, mounted the bluff overlooking Starlight, then galloped west into the hills toward Texas. Fifteen miles out, he and his companion reached a plantation where Twitchell had arranged for a change of horses. Within minutes

38. *House Executive Documents*, 44th Cong., 2d Sess., No. 30, p. 366; *House Reports*, 43d Cong., 2d Sess., No. 101, pt. 2, p. 106; *New Orleans Republican*, 6 December 1874.
39. *New Orleans Republican*, 12, 14 November, 12, 22 December 1874.

they rode on, now heading north along Bayou Pierre Lake, then doubling back north-northeast, crossing the Red River, riding the long, lonely roads through the broken hill-country of upper Red River Parish. "About midnight we heard someone cross a bridge behind us; instantly our horses were checked and our revolvers made ready. I proposed that we ride into the woods a few paces and let them pass." Twitchell's guide, relaxing in the saddle, said the precaution was unnecessary. Only one rider "crossed the bridge, and no one or two men are going to follow us."[40]

Shortly before dawn, they swam their horses across Black Lake Bayou into Bienville Parish. In midmorning they reached Brush Valley, where they stopped at the cabin of one of Isaac Coleman's former slaves. After resting and feeding their horses, they pushed on, passing after sunset through Vienna, "a small town run by whisky and the White League" in Lincoln Parish, a few miles north of modern-day Grambling and Louisiana Tech Universities. Fearing that he would be recognized at a hotel, Twitchell and his guide sought food and shelter at a farmhouse. Twitchell was at his charming best with his host: "I never exerted myself more to please, or guarded my Northern peculiarities of speech closer than I did that evening. We went to bed with the satisfaction of having kept the people so thoroughly amused that they had forgotten to ask any questions concerning their guests."

The next morning after the stableman saddled their horses, Twitchell's host asked his name. "I immediately gave my name and address at Coushatta so that the old gentleman might not have the least doubt who I was." Relishing the moment, the carpetbagger recalled: "I had seen many surprises in my life but none which exceeded that of old Mr. Kidd and his family. He politely declined pay for our entertainment and with much civility bade us good morning as we walked to our horses." That afternoon Twitchell rode into Monroe, the railhead of the Vicksburg, Shreveport, and Pacific Railroad. The next day he was in New Orleans, ready to appear before the Returning Board. Back in Red River, the White League was still waiting for him to emerge from his sickroom.[41]

Claiming massive intimidation, Twitchell and other Republican wit-

40. *CV*, 156.
41. *CV*, 156–57; *House Reports*, 43d Cong., 2d Sess., No. 261, pp. 389–90.

nesses contested the election returns in eight northwest Louisiana parishes covering the entire watershed of the Louisiana Red River Valley. On Christmas Eve the Returning Board awarded the radical party control of the senate. In the twenty-second district, the board reversed J. B. Elam's victory over Twitchell. Elam had filed suit in the Orleans Parish Superior District Court to force a count of the returns from De Soto Parish, but the court dismissed the case. The board's most important, and most controversial, decisions concerned the house of representatives. Out of 111 seats, it gave the Republicans 54 seats and the conservative Democrats 52, with 5 to be decided by the house itself.[42]

After his appearance before the Returning Board, Twitchell remained in New Orleans for the January opening of what promised to be a turbulent session of the legislature. In the meantime, after months of watching the lightning flashes along the lower Mississippi, President Grant finally ordered General Sheridan to the Crescent City to put more backbone into General Emory and take command if necessary.[43]

On 4 January when the lawmakers assembled, the old Saint Louis Hotel was a circus. Twitchell entered the building through a cordon of federal troops, commanded by General Régis de Trobriand. Rumors circulated that Governor Kellogg was to be assassinated. Reporters and spectators milled about, and an unusual number of men claiming to be sergeants-at-arms tried to get past the doorkeeper. In the house fifty-two Republicans and fifty Democrats answered the roll. In an extraordinary move, the Democrats seized the speaker's chair and tried to organize the house. A melee ensued, and both Republicans and Democrats appealed to de Trobriand for help. An hour or so later, after conferring with Governor Kellogg and General Emory, de Trobriand led a squad of soldiers into the house, bayonets gleaming, and expelled eight Democratic members unrecognized by the Returning Board. The entire Democratic membership of the house then exited the chamber.[44]

That night, General Sheridan assumed command of the Gulf Department. "I think the terrorism now existing in Louisiana, Mississippi,

42. *New Orleans Republican*, 25 December 1874; *Appleton's American Annual Cyclopaedia and Register of Important Events, 1874*, 491–92.

43. *Appleton's Annual Cyclopaedia, 1874*, 493.

44. Marie Caroline Post, ed., *The Life and Memoirs of Comte Régis de Trobriand . . . by His Daughter* (New York, 1910), 445–52; Dawson, *Army Generals and Reconstruction*, 202–9.

and Arkansas," he wired the War Department, "could be entirely removed . . . by the arrest and trial of the ringleaders of the armed White
Leagues." Sheridan proposed that Congress or the president brand
them as "banditti" and let the army try them under martial law. Sheridan's banditti dispatch ignited a firestorm of controversy and became
one of the defining moments of Reconstruction. The northern Democratic press screamed "Tyranny!" and even many northern Republicans
denounced de Trobriand's and Sheridan's actions. While Louisiana
Democrats were clearly up to no good, the idea of military trials of ci-
vilians and the image of federal soldiers evicting lawmakers from a legislative hall had a visceral impact on northern public opinion. Like no
other event, the "banditti affair" cemented Republican Louisiana's "Albatross" status.[45]

The army had aborted a Democratic coup, but its intervention failed
to break the impasse over the Kellogg government's right to rule. This
problem soon became the province of the U.S. House of Representatives. Two House subcommittees investigated Louisiana affairs that
winter. The first week of January, during the banditti crisis, Twitchell
and other witnesses testified before the first of these subcommittees
meeting in New Orleans. This body had no sooner adjourned and its
members departed than the second House delegation arrived, headed
by Republican William A. Wheeler of New York. At its headquarters in
the Saint Charles Hotel, in late January and early February, Wheeler's
subcommittee examined Twitchell, Thomas Abney, Major Merrill,
Governor Kellogg, James Madison Wells, and seventy-five other witnesses about Louisiana's troubles.[46]

Several days into the hearing, Louisiana Democrats asked Wheeler's
subcommittee to supersede the radical Returning Board and arbitrate
the 1874 election. Out of this request, after two months of deliberation
between factions in New Orleans and Washington, grew the "Wheeler
compromise." In this attempt at compromise, the Republicans acqui-
esced in a Democratic takeover of the Louisiana house. In return, the
Democrats promised not to impeach Governor Kellogg and to assist
him in maintaining the rule of law in the state. Because important seg-

45. *Appleton's Annual Cyclopaedia, 1874*, 498–99; Gillette, *Retreat from Reconstruction*,
123–28; Rable, "Republican Albatross," 109–30.
46. *House Reports*, 43d Cong., 2d Sess., No. 261.

ments of both parties opposed the Wheeler compromise, like earlier compromises, it was fated to fail.[47]

Asked by the visiting congressman about the condition of governance in the state, Major Merrill answered perceptively: "There is not in Louisiana to-day any such thing as a government at all—nothing which has the attributes of a government. When I say that, I mean that a government has among its attributes power to enforce at least some show of obedience to law, and that does not exist to-day in Louisiana. The State government has no power outside of the United States Army, which is here to sustain it—no power at all. The White League is the only power in the state."

Congressman Wheeler asked Merrill what would happen if Merrill quit the army, took off his uniform, and tried to stay in Louisiana. Merrill said, "I should want to borrow a Gatlin gun, at least."[48]

47. *Appleton's Annual Cyclopaedia, 1875*, 457–58.
48. *House Reports*, 43d Cong., 2d Sess., No. 261, pp. 179, 181.

THIRTEEN

THE STRANGER IN THE GREEN EYE GOGGLES

I N the summer of 1875 Twitchell visited Vermont. In Newfane, a village three miles below Townshend on the West River, he paid six thousand dollars for the Kimbell House, and soon his mother, Elizabeth, his young son, Marshall, and his orphan nephews, Bert Holland and Homer King, occupied its spacious rooms. Neither his mother nor the three children would ever see Louisiana again. Twitchell took seriously the White League threats against the boys' lives.[1]

While in Newfane, the widower renewed an acquaintance with his school-days sweetheart Henrietta Day. He had first met Henrietta in 1859 when her guardian, the Reverend Chester L. Cushman, had become the minister of Townshend's First Congregational Church. After finishing her studies at Leland Seminary, Henrietta went on to Mount Holyoke College and then taught at academies in Brimfield and Wilbraham, Massachusetts. She never married, and that summer of 1875 she and Twitchell fell in love again. He proposed to her and she accepted.[2]

1. General Pardon T. Kimbell was a recently deceased War of 1812 military hero. *CV*, 161; Property sales and releases, MHT Papers.
2. Obituaries in MHT Scrapbook; Marshall Twitchell to Henrietta Day, 12 October 1875, MHT Papers.

Twitchell returned to Louisiana by rail, through Indianapolis, Saint Louis, Little Rock, and Marshall, Texas. At Shreveport he caught a steamer to Coushatta. Realizing the danger, he stayed only a brief time at Starlight before traveling on to New Orleans. The shadow of violence pursued him to the Crescent City. The story is told in a remarkable letter he wrote Henrietta in mid-October, one of the few letters in his own hand that have survived the Reconstruction years. Among other things, the letter reveals that his decision to remarry was not mere convenience. He referred to "those anticipated pleasures of which I have thought and dreamed with you my darling." The letter's general tone was, however, dark, foreboding, and anxious. "I am just in from the streets where I have been looking for a danger of which I was warned last night. . . . I received a telegram in cypher from Coushatta telling me to 'load my pistol, refuse all company and stay in my room.' I armed myself and went all over town last night and again this morning looking for the danger of which I was warned, cant find it, but I fear this continual harrassing will make a demon of me."

Reports had reached him of legal schemes to seize Starlight Plantation and other lands. It almost made him regret that he and Henrietta had revived "that old passion." If his enemies took his property, he wrote, "I should feel honor bound to release you whatever it might cost my feelings." Perhaps from his own guilt, he believed his sisters blamed him for the deaths of their husbands. He yearned to set "aside as my enemies do, the laws of God and man, and for their country become an avenger." Dwelling on these things, he had fallen asleep the previous night, "and strange for me, commenced dreaming." In the dream, he stood in a room before his weeping mother and sisters and frightened son. He was set to avenge the murders of his family: "I turned to go and you stood before me attempting to put your arms around my neck. I attempted to avoid you, but at every turn you were in front of me. I felt if you once had your arms around my neck my resolution would fail." No matter which way he turned, Henrietta blocked the door. "I awoke and was thankful it was only a dream."[3]

Yellow fever again that fall visited Coushatta, where his sisters Kate and Helen still resided. Like her sister Belle the year before, Kate succumbed to the disease. In mid-November, Marshall received a telegram

---

3. Marshall Twitchell to Henrietta Day.

informing him of still another family member's death. It was almost too much for him to bear.[4]

The fever also swept through E Company, billeted near the Coushatta courthouse. By November, four soldiers and a laundress were dead. The company commander moved the troops back to Springville. In early December, with only twenty-one men fit for duty, E Company abandoned Camp Coushatta and headed for Mississippi.[5]

In all probability, Twitchell dared not go home for Kate's funeral, but remained in New Orleans, awaiting the January meeting of the legislature. The 1876 session, his sixth, was the climax of his senatorial career. When he first entered the senate, only seven members of the body were black. Now fifteen African Americans composed a majority of the twenty-five Republican senators. In 1872 the black lieutenant governor Oscar J. Dunn had presided over the chamber; now black lieutenant governor Caesar C. Antoine performed that duty.

The Republicans, expecting another stormy session, chose Twitchell as Republican manager, or majority leader, in the senate and as chairman of the party's joint house-senate caucus. Exercising leadership in the hostile climate of 1876 demanded courage and endurance as well as skill. One by one, the former Confederate states had been redeemed from Republican control. Reconstruction now survived only in Louisiana, South Carolina, and Florida.[6]

Meanwhile, public support in the North for southern Republicans had diminished. In the "war of words" over Reconstruction, southern Democrats and their northern allies were clearly winning. Northern press coverage of Coushatta was a case in point. In New York, Chicago, and Philadelphia, even Republican newspapers printed the racist disinformation of the Louisiana White League: "800 armed Negroes" marching on Coushatta, whites mobilizing for defense, radical ringleaders jailed, bloody race war averted, and so on. Even as the grisly details became known, most northern newspapers printed White League justifications of the violence side by side with Republican condemnations. Readers were left with the suspicion that the massacre victims had been done in by their own wicked deeds.

4. *CV*, 161.

5. U.S. Army Continental Commands, Coushatta Post Records, RG 393, letterbook, NA; U.S. Military Posts, 1800–1916.

6. *CV*, 162; *New Orleans Republican*, 5 March 1876.

The North's moral conscience had been numbed by nine years of Reconstruction violence. There had been so many bloody outrages in the South that not even well-informed people could keep them straight. Such attitudes prevailed in Washington, too. As early as 1871, Secretary of State Hamilton Fish had grown weary of recitations of Ku Klux Klan atrocities in cabinet meetings. Attorney General Amos T. Akerman has the Klan "on the brain," Fish wrote. In one cabinet meeting, Akerman related the latest instances of Klan violence—"one of a fellow being castrated—with terrible minute & tedious details of each case—It has got to be a bore, to listen twice a week to this same thing." Echoing Fish's sentiments, the *Louisville Ledger* opined in 1876 that "Louisiana is becoming a bore. Its perpetual squabbles and uprisings are getting to be drearily monotonous." The most visible sign of northern disenchantment with Reconstruction was President Grant's ever-increasing reluctance to use troops in the South.[7]

When Twitchell entered the Republican caucus that last year of Reconstruction, he found his colleagues, black and white, disheartened by the realization that, from the perspective of their northern allies, they had become expendable. It was as if he and his colleagues had become an embarrassment to the national party, like down-at-heel relatives who must be excluded from public view.[8]

Nearly three weeks of the session slipped by before the lawmakers settled down to work. Ostensibly the Wheeler compromise was still in place, but the agreement inspired little confidence. Democratic house and Republican senate wrangled over issues large and small. In the latter category, an article in the *New York Herald* dredged up the five-year-old election of J. Rodman West to the U.S. Senate. Back in 1871, Twitchell's first year in the state senate, the *Herald* charged that Twitchell and other Republicans had accepted bribes to vote for West. A joint senate-house committee, chaired by a Democrat, investigated the charges and unearthed no corroborative evidence. Twitchell pressed the matter. In a letter to the committee chairman, he asked straight-out whether any witness, "either directly or by implication," had supported the allegation of bribery against him. The chair replied "most emphatically" that not a single utterance had been heard to support the charge.[9]

7. Hamilton Fish, Diary, 24 November 1871, Library of Congress, Washington, D.C.; *Ledger* quoted in *New Orleans Republican*, 7 March 1876.
8. *CV*, 162.
9. Lonn, *Reconstruction in Louisiana*, 388–91; *New Orleans Republican*, 7 March 1876.

Whether this was the whole story is impossible to say. Money frequently bought lawmakers' votes in the Louisiana legislature, as it did in New York and Pennsylvania and the rest of the country. Mark Twain did not call this era the "Gilded Age" for nothing. Still, charges of corruption in the Reconstruction South, with or without substance, were as common as fireworks on the Fourth of July. In 1874, for example, a congressman asked Major Lewis Merrill if the Louisiana situation would be improved by the election of a new government composed of honest Republicans. The new officials would need to be nonresidents, the major replied. Realizing his questioner did not understand, Merrill explained: "I don't intend to say that . . . there are no honest Republicans in Louisiana. I do not think that. . . . What I do think is that no Republican, whatever his actual character may be, if he were once in office, could have the reputation of being honest in this State."[10]

The most divisive bill of the 1876 session was a Democratic election measure that eliminated the five-man state Returning Board. The bill passed the house but hit a wall of resistance in the senate. The Democrats grumbled darkly about riots and bloodshed if they did not get their way. Senator Edward D. White—in later years associate justice of the U.S. Supreme Court—predicted the doom of thousands of Negroes unless the senate capitulated. The Republicans, on the other hand, viewed the Returning Board as their only trump card in an otherwise crooked game. Twitchell chaired the conference committee; neither side would budge, and the effort to pass an election law collapsed. The remnants of the Wheeler compromise tumbled with it.[11]

The heart of the Wheeler compromise was the Democrats' promise not to impeach Governor Kellogg, a promise they now reneged on. On 25 February the house created an impeachment committee, which two days later reported that Kellogg had been "guilty of many and divers high crimes and misdemeanors in office." In particular, the committee alleged that in 1874 the governor had used treasury funds designated for interest payments on the debt to pay other state expenses, mainly those of the Metropolitan Police. Kellogg had restored the money from other revenues, and his personal honesty was never in question. More-

10. *House Reports*, 43d Cong., 2d Sess., No. 261, p. 180.
11. *Appleton's Annual Cyclopaedia, 1876*, 481; *New Orleans Republican*, 4, 5, 17 February 1876.

over, the transfer of funds had occurred before the Wheeler compromise, the terms of which clearly shielded him from removal for prior acts. Nonetheless, along strict party lines, the house voted sixty-one to forty-five for impeachment. The speaker appointed a committee to draft articles of impeachment and to notify the senate to prepare for trial. The house then adjourned for a day.

The occasion of the one-day adjournment was Mardi Gras. The impeachment vote was on a Monday; the next day was Fat Tuesday, the climax of Mardi Gras when Rex reigned as the King of Carnival and schools, businesses, and government offices were closed. When the house reconvened on Ash Wednesday, the first day of March and the beginning of Lent, there would only be two days left in the session.

The impeachment proceedings should have required two or three weeks. The house committee had conducted no real investigation, and Kellogg had been given no opportunity to explain his actions. Moreover, with only two days left in the session after the one-day adjournment, there was no time to investigate the charges or to conduct a proper trial. And even if there had been, the trial would have been in the Republican-dominated senate, where Kellogg's acquittal was a foregone conclusion. So what were the Democrats planning? Because the Louisiana constitution suspended a governor under impeachment, the Democrats deliberately moved to impeach Kellogg so late in the session there would be no time for a trial. Thus the legislature would adjourn with the governor under suspension. The tactic was calculated to throw the wobbly Republican regime further off balance in an election year. That Lieutenant Governor Caesar C. Antoine would become acting governor only sweetened the plan. An African American in the governor's chair would further diminish the regime's legitimacy, even in the North.

It was a clever plan, but the Democrats had overlooked important details. First, in voting for impeachment, the Democratic lawmakers merely endorsed the majority report of the special impeachment committee, without formally specifying the charges against Kellogg. Second, the Democrat-controlled house adjourned to celebrate Mardi Gras, leaving the Republican senate still in session.[12]

When the house, at about five o'clock in the afternoon, voted for

12. *New Orleans Republican*, 24, 29 February, 1 March 1876.

impeachment, Twitchell and the senate were debating state aid for the Texas Pacific Railroad. Shortly thereafter, the senate went into executive session and received a delegation from the now-adjourned house, which officially announced the impeachment. A hurriedly summoned council of war met in Lieutenant Governor Antoine's private chamber. Twitchell, Kellogg, a three-man defense team of Republican lawyers, former governor Warmoth, the chief justice of the state supreme court, and a dozen other party leaders were present. Initially, Chief Justice John T. Ludeling seemed to express the consensus of the meeting. The law, he said, required the senate to proceed with caution and judicial restraint. Warmoth and Twitchell disagreed. If the assembly adjourned with the governor under suspension, Twitchell warned, it would be the death knell of Republican government in the state. He urged that the impeachment trial be held immediately—that very night.[13]

Someone voiced the opinion that a hasty trial would be irregular. Undeterred, Twitchell replied "that if assassination and revolution could be checked and right prevail with a slight judicial irregularity, I thought we had better have the irregularity." Within minutes Kellogg made his decision: The trial would begin immediately. Twitchell returned to the senate, leaving Kellogg conferring with his lawyers.[14]

Taking his seat, Twitchell moved, "the Senate do now organize itself into a High Court of Impeachment." The resolution carried, and Chief Justice Ludeling, on cue, seated himself as presiding judge. The governor and his lawyers took their places. The secretary called the roll. After administering an oath to the thirty-four senators present, Ludeling announced the senate ready for trial. The voice of the sergeant-at-arms rang out: "Hear ye! hear ye! hear ye! All persons are commanded to keep silent on pain of imprisonment while the Senate of the State of Louisiana is sitting for the trial of the articles of impeachment of William Pitt Kellogg, Governor of Louisiana."[15]

Kellogg's lead counsel said the governor was ready for trial and asked the court to set a time limit for the house to present its articles of impeachment. Twitchell then moved to notify the house of the senate's readiness for trial and that the time affixed for the house to file "specific

13. *CV*, 163–64; *New Orleans Republican*, 29 February, 8 March 1876.
14. *CV*, 163–64; *New Orleans Republican*, 8 March 1876.
15. *Louisiana Senate Journal, 1876*, 289–90.

charges" against the governor was "7 P.M. of this day." In other words, the now empty lower chamber had forty-five minutes in which to comply. Senate Democrats tried to amend Twitchell's motion, to no avail; it carried. The senate adjourned for thirty minutes to await the house's response. The senate secretary carried the notification to the house and found its doors locked. When after thirty minutes no one representing the house appeared, the governor's lawyers moved to terminate the trial. To seal the outcome, Twitchell introduced resolutions dismissing the impeachment and exonerating Kellogg. Before the vote could be taken, five house Democrats burst into the senate, claiming to be the house trial managers. Senate Republicans quickly determined, however, that the group was an ad hoc delegation without formal authority. Rejecting the self-appointed group, the senate approved Twitchell's resolutions acquitting the governor. In less than two and a half hours, the Kellogg impeachment trial was over.[16]

Furious Democrats attacked the unfairness of the trial and in the brief time remaining in the session, actually drafted the specific articles of impeachment that had been missing Monday night. Kellogg answered the charges, and Twitchell obtained passage of a senate resolution labeling the impeachment a "political conspiracy." The *Republican* denounced house Democrats as "Coushatta Guards" and labeled the impeachment "Coushatta tactics." If possible, the political climate grew even more bitter, but the effort to revive the impeachment failed. The governor had had his night in court.[17]

Across the state, Democrats fumed over the event. In north Louisiana not far from Twitchell's home, the *Mansfield Reporter* placed the blame squarely on Twitchell. "It must have been apparent," said the *Reporter*, that the senate majority, dominated "as it was by that shrewd, silent, unscrupulous, untiring Machievelli [*sic*] . . . H. M. Twitchell, would never yield to the demands of the House." It was predictable "that he of the sinister eye, who furnishes most of the backbone to his party, and is the impersonation of the devil himself to his political enemies," would watch over the senate with such "sleepless vigilance" as to prevent the impeachment of the governor.[18]

16. Ibid., 289–90, 292–95; *New Orleans Republican*, 29 February, 2 March 1876.
17. *New Orleans Republican*, 1, 3, 7, 8 March 1876.
18. MHT Scrapbook.

The 1876 session's tug-of-war with the Democratic house had been the most stressful moment of Twitchell's senate career. The protracted struggle for legislative supremacy wore the Republicans down. With money and other inducements, the Democrats chipped away at the radicals' senate majority. Day after day, Twitchell struggled to maintain party cohesion, even arranging for Republican senators to take their meals in pairs, "taking good care that no two weak ones should go by themselves." Twitchell became so caught up in the turmoil that he sometimes ignored his own needs. He customarily dined at a French Quarter restaurant near the state house. One morning at table, following a session that had gone on past midnight, he told his waiter he was feeling poorly. When the man remarked that the senator had not come to dinner the day before, it suddenly dawned on Twitchell that he had not eaten for twenty-four hours.[19]

With spring, a company of U.S. infantry returned to Coushatta. Captain J. Ford Kent, the company commander, concerned about the health of his men, set up camp at Springville, assuring headquarters that Springville was only a twenty-minute march from the courthouse. Twenty minutes was to prove a very long time.[20]

After the general assembly's adjournment and at the last Republican caucus of the winter, Twitchell reminded his fellow lawmakers that it was an election year and that assassination was an ever-present danger. He returned to Starlight Plantation in late April, planning to spend a few days attending to business and civic affairs before heading North to Vermont.[21]

He found two new faces at Starlight, John W. Harrison and William S. Mudgett, both of whom had settled in the parish since the massacre eight months before. The Irish-born Harrison was helping Marshall's sister Helen run Starlight. During the war he had served in the Seventh Vermont Infantry; then, like Twitchell, he had won promotion in the USCT. Before moving to Starlight, he had been a Republican official in Lincoln Parish. Sometime that past winter, a warning had been left at Starlight, signed by a mysterious "gogle ied man" and addressed to

19. *CV*, 162–63.
20. J. Ford Kent to AAG, Gulf, 8 March 1876, Coushatta Post Records, RG 393, NA.
21. *CV*, 169–70.

"Twitchel Ring Harrison & others of the Court House ring." The goggle-eyed man, probably Captain Jack, was bitter: "I have Bin maid to leave my home & friends & family on the account of you & your crowd." The message advised Twitchell and Harrison to head for the "wilds of Califeony" because "this part of the country has Become [?] unhealthey that you cant stay here." Time was running out. Heed this warning, the message said, and leave, "for I will come again at the proper time."[22]

Mudgett had been a captain in the Second Maine Regiment, then colonel of the Eightieth USCT. Years before, Mudgett had considered court-martialing Twitchell over the killing of Private Wallace Harris. Since leaving the army, Mudgett had been a customhouse official and a cotton planter. Twitchell had recently arranged the Maine native's appointment to the Red River Parish Police Jury. He was staying at Starlight, planning to attend, as was Twitchell, a police jury meeting in Coushatta on 2 May.

On May Day, Twitchell crossed the river into Coushatta and stayed longer than usual. To his surprise, there appeared to be some kind of Democratic powwow in progress. In late afternoon, he asked a prominent Democrat "if he was not a long distance from home for so late an hour." The man replied that a matter of great moment was being decided. Only in hindsight did the meaning of the reply become apparent. At Starlight that night after supper, Harrison, Mudgett, and George King, Twitchell's surviving brother-in-law who was now the sheriff, fired off a number of rounds from their pistols, probably more out of boredom than anything else. King had remarried after Belle Twitchell's death. Alas, his new wife, Ida Bosley King, a young woman about twenty, died within a year, probably in childbirth. Ida's mother, Carolyn Bosley, lived in Coushatta.[23]

Shortly after sunrise the next morning, Starlight Plantation stirred to life. Smoke drifted up from the chimneys; black women fried bacon

22. The name of Richard Coleman (Captain Jack) was on deputy Stockton's 1874 warrant list. Captain Jack was the author of a previous warning sent to Starlight. MHT Papers.

23. *CV*, 170; *House Reports*, 44th Cong., 1st Sess., No. 816, p. 655; It is very possible that George King's second wife and new in-laws were light-skinned mulattos, related to Andy Bosley. While the 1870 census lists Ida and her mother and sister as white (of Irish descent), the census-taker may have been in error, or Ida's family may have been passing

and baked biscuits while their men milked cows and carried feed to horses and mules. There was a rustling of animals, leather, and harness in barns and sheds. Twitchell, Helen, and their guests ate breakfast and then made ready for the trip to the Coushatta courthouse. Twitchell and King drove off in a rig sometime before nine. Mudgett followed about ten minutes later. Thus began a day that none of them would ever forget and one of them would not survive.

Just after sunrise, a stranger rode into Coushatta on a small mouse-gray horse. He entered Patrick Delaney's blacksmith shop overlooking the river and told Delaney he wanted his horse shod, but he was uncertain whether heavy or light shoes should be applied. There was no hurry, the stranger said; he would let Delaney know his wishes when his brother showed up in an hour or two. Delaney trimmed the horse's feet and went to work on other tasks. While he worked, the stranger patiently watched the river, saying little. His garb was strange: black slouch hat, the brim pulled low over his face; a false beard (thick and black); green eye goggles; and a long oilcloth coat. Near nine o'clock, spying three men board a skiff on the far side of the river, he mounted his horse and pulled a sixteen-shot Winchester repeater from a saddle holster.

The stranger rode down the row of stores on Front Street. He stopped in front of the doctor's office, dismounted, and hitched his horse. Rifle in hand, he passed between the buildings and walked along the river, carrying the rifle low, close to his body, and parallel with his right leg, so that it could not be seen by the men in the approaching boat. He stopped at a woodpile above the landing just behind the stores of Julius Lisso and Sam Lisso.[24]

When Twitchell and King boarded the skiff, Dennis Sams, the black ferryman, warned them not to cross the river. "I was so accustomed to

for white. The same census-taker, after all, listed Andy Bosley and his wife Martha as white, too. The tip-off is the child, George King Jr., who resulted from the union of George King and Ida Bosley. The child remained in Coushatta after Reconstruction. In 1880, he lived in the household of William and Eliza Bosley. According to the census-taker, William was white and Eliza, his wife, was mulatto. More important, the census-taker recorded the six-year-old George King as mulatto. The boy died in the early 1880s. Federal manuscript census, population, 1870 and 1880; Joseph Shaughnessy to Emmus George Twitchell, 23 November and 10 December 1938, MHT Papers. Joseph Shaughnessy was a soldier stationed at Camp Coushatta in 1876. He married the sister of Ida Bosley King.

24. *House Reports,* 44th Cong., 1st Sess., No. 816, pp. 659–70; Julius Lisso to Michael Lisso, 5 May 1876, Melrose Collection; *Brattleboro Vermont Phoenix,* 19 May 1876.

negro timidity," Twitchell recalled, "that I disregarded his advice and ordered him to pull for the Coushatta shore." Over the years, Twitchell had received many death threats. He had avoided ambushes by a combination of guile, audacity, and luck. On this day, neither stratagem nor luck was with him.[25]

He sat in the boat reading a newspaper. A few yards from shore, he looked up and saw the stranger standing on the bank above, aiming his rifle at him. "Down in the boat!" Twitchell yelled. A moment later, a bullet slammed into his left thigh. "I immediately went over into the water," Twitchell recalled, "passing under the skiff, and caught hold of the lower edge with my hand, keeping the skiff much of the time between myself and the assassin, while all the while I was partially concealed under the boat and in the water." King fired off two or three pistol shots before the assassin swung his rifle on him and shot him in the head. King pitched back dead in the boat. Despite the poor target that Twitchell presented, the goggle-eyed man put two bullets in his right arm, breaking the bone. Desperately, Twitchell grabbed hold of the skiff's gunwale with his left arm. The boat was drifting with the current, the distance from shore increasing; still the assassin worked his weapon until he shattered Twitchell's left arm.[26]

When the shooting started, there was a small crowd gathered at the courthouse mailroom, about two hundred yards distant, to meet the eastern mail rider who arrived on Tuesday mornings. The people at the courthouse heard the shots, but as Julius Lisso wrote and as events at Starlight the night before demonstrated, "Shooting is a common occurrence and . . . no one paid any attention to it." Lisso's words may have been disingenuous. Some of the people, possibly even Lisso, must have surmised what was occurring.[27]

The assassin performed his grisly work in full view of ten or twelve black men. Duke Hayes and E. W. Rawles watched the shooting from the gallery of Rawles's warehouse. A former soldier, Rawles observed with admiration that the marksman "shot left-handed and right-handed." Gus De Russy, owner of a riverfront saloon and grocery, also witnessed the ambush. One merchant, thinking the stranger was shooting an alligator, ran out of his store and approached within a few feet

25. *CV*, 170–71.

26. Ibid.; Julius Lisso to Michael Lisso; *House Reports*, 44th Cong., 1st Sess., No. 816, pp. 659–70.

27. Julius Lisso to Michael Lisso; *House Reports*, 44th Cong., 1st Sess., No. 816, p. 689.

of the gunman. The shooter whirled, pointed back to the store, and barked, "MARCH." The storekeeper retreated in "double quick time." Ben Wolfson galloped up on a horse to investigate. Again the rifleman pivoted, bringing the barrel to bear on Wolfson, and snarled, "God damn you, go back." Wolfson beat a hasty retreat as well. Of all the witnesses, only Mrs. E. J. Merrill, a newcomer in town, interfered with the attack.[28]

Mrs. Merrill was sewing when, looking out her window, she saw the stranger walk up to the woodpile and open fire with his rifle. Her children screamed, "It is an alligator. Let us go and see the alligator." Mrs. Merrill hurried outside, ordering her children to stay inside. She met her neighbor Mrs. Lee and said to her, "My children say it is an alligator, but I am afraid it is worse than an alligator." Panicking, Mrs. Lee began to scream that the stranger was killing her husband. Mrs. Merrill assured her neighbor that her husband was safe, calmly observing that he wore a white hat and the men in the boat wore dark hats. When the assassin emptied his rifle, he walked back between the stores to his horse.

He soon returned on horseback, brandishing a heavy pistol. Mrs. Merrill described the scene vividly: "Captain Twitchell was in the water endeavoring to save himself by holding on to the boat. . . . I saw a man who looked to be dead lying in the skiff. I said to the ferryman, 'For God's sake save that drowning man.' Then I pleaded with the man to forbear shooting, and begged for mercy, but he still continued to fire, in spite of all my entreaty, until he had fired four shots from his pistol." Mrs. Merrill said she then "saw the negro reach down from the skiff that he might . . . get Captain Twitchell out of the water, and he succeeded. The man then shot at the ferryman." The expertly aimed bullet hit Dennis Sams in the hand and "broke his hold on Captain Twitchell."[29]

By this time, Mudgett had ridden up on the far side of the river. He drew his revolver and fired several shots at the gunman, but the range was too great. Mrs. Merrill cried out to Dennis Sams, asking if Twitchell was dead. Struggling to stay afloat, Twitchell gasped an instruction to the ferryman, and Dennis Sams shouted back that, yes, the captain was dead. Twitchell drifted face down in the cold current, his dark blood staining the water, playing dead most convincingly. The stranger turned his horse toward Front Street and quietly rode off, muttering to

28. *House Reports*, 44th Cong., 1st Sess., No. 816, pp. 657, 659–62, 670–71; Julius Lisso to Michael Lisso.

29. *House Reports*, 44th Cong., 1st Sess., No. 816, pp. 660–61.

himself, rifle in one hand, cocked pistol in the other. The only words he spoke to anyone were to Mrs. Merrill's black servant woman. She looked up as he rode by and said, "It is not no alligator." He replied, "Yes; it is a damned black alligator."

As soon as the assassin was out of sight, Dennis Sams, despite his wound, pulled the boat alongside Twitchell. "I threw my only uninjured limb on the edge of the boat, and the ferryman with his uninjured arm, rolled me over into the skiff upon the body of King."[30]

Mudgett and others carried Twitchell to a cabin on the edge of town. He had been hit six times, twice in each arm, once in the thigh, and a minor flesh wound in the back of the neck. He was weak from cold and loss of blood, and his attendants—except for Mudgett, their identities are unknown—put hot bricks in his bed to warm him. In their haste and excitement, they severely burned his right foot. An hour or so later, they moved him by wagon to the home of King's mother-in-law, Carolyn Bosley, in Springville near Camp Coushatta.

Dr. William C. Carson, the army surgeon, took over Twitchell's care. The next morning Carson amputated Twitchell's left arm near the shoulder. On 4 May, Lieutenant Governor Antoine, acting governor in Kellogg's absence, posted a five-thousand-dollar reward for the apprehension of the assassin.[31]

Nursed by his sister Helen, John W. Harrison, and Mudgett, Twitchell fought to live. For weeks the struggle was touch and go. Twitchell recalled with Puritan conviction: "So severe was the struggle that had I been addicted . . . to whisky, tobacco, or anything weakening to my system, the result would not have been long in doubt." Fearing the assassin would attempt to finish his work, Harrison and Mudgett took turns guarding the house. Even Dr. Carson sometimes sat outside the sickroom with a rifle across his lap.[32]

It was later reported that Twitchell's survival had caused a falling-out between the gunman and his anonymous employers: The goggle-eyed hired gun wanted his money, but his employers claimed he had not finished the job. One story has the killer lamenting his failure to

30. Ibid., 659–61; *CV*, 171–72.

31. *New Orleans Republican*, 6 May, 23 June 1876; *CV*, 172. In his autobiography, Twitchell mistakenly has Colonel Galusha Pennypacker commanding Camp Coushatta. The military records make clear that Captain J. Ford Kent was in command. Twitchell probably saw Pennypacker later in New Orleans.

32. *CV*, 172; MHT Scrapbook.

shoot the ferryman: "If I had shot the damn nigger," the assassin supposedly says, Twitchell would have drowned "before anyone could have reached him from the shore."[33]

For four long weeks, Twitchell lay in bed, keeping his shattered right arm still, hoping to save it. Rumors of his impending demise had been widespread ever since the shooting. Only a miracle, it seemed, could keep him alive. On 29 May a small delegation of townsmen called on him. Under the scrutiny of Twitchell's friends, they seated themselves and made "commonplace conversation." Listening to them, Twitchell soon deduced the purpose of their visit: they had come to gauge for themselves his prospects for survival. Beneath the arm bandages, maggots crawled in the wounds. Gangrene had set in. "They could not have made their call at a better time," Twitchell said later, "the decaying arm, impregnating the room with its disagreeable odour, must have convinced them that in a short time the job would be finished."[34]

Late that afternoon, Dr. Carson entered the sickroom. The surgeon was ill at ease and reluctant to come to the point. Finally, he spoke plainly. To save Marshall's life he must take off the right arm, too. "I said very well," Twitchell recalled, "and turned my face to the window, watching the sun as it disappeared behind the trees, reviewing my past life, and trying to imagine what would be my future in the world, without arms and all my near relatives in the grave, except one sister [and] a mother." Carson left, and Helen, guessing the truth, moved to her brother's bed. In a subdued voice, he told her the news and said he did not know if he wanted to live. She reminded him that he had always made a living with his head instead of his hands: "There are plenty of hands in the world to do the work of heads which have the ability to direct." The next morning Carson amputated Twitchell's right arm.[35]

As Twitchell struggled to recover from this second amputation, the African American churches in the region coincidentally staged revival meetings in the groves of tall trees bordering Camp Coushatta. (To this day, Red River and Bienville Parishes are dotted with African Methodist Episcopal and Baptist churches founded in the early days of Reconstruction.) Twitchell knew most of the black families in the parish and

33. *CV*, 172.
34. Ibid., 172–74.
35. Ibid.

had a wide acquaintance with black ministers. Since his days in the Freedmen's Bureau, he had become the chief symbol of Reconstruction in the region and of the rights guaranteed by the Fourteenth and Fifteenth Amendments. He had personally registered most of the black men in the region as voters and had helped organize the local Reconstruction governments. "I was the first to break the prejudice of the white people by selling them [the freedmen] lands and encouraging them to make homes for themselves." He "had established and protected their schools." If this rendition of events is overly paternalistic, allowing too little credit for what African Americans did for themselves, it nonetheless explains why a chorus of prayers for Twitchell's recovery rose from the Springville church meetings.[36]

Two or three days after the surgery, a delegation of African American ministers called on Twitchell. Dr. Carson let them in to see his patient but warned them not to excite him. As Twitchell recalled the scene, "They filed into my room, ranged themselves by my bedside, and stood there with the tears rolling down their cheeks." Their grief was genuine, but there was more behind their tears than his personal tragedy. The stricken carpetbagger who lay before them was symbolic of their own fading hopes, his crippled, armless body a metaphor for Reconstruction's dying promises. The churchmen made an effort to follow Dr. Carson's instructions, but after several questions from Twitchell, confessed their real concern. A rumor had reached them that an ardent foe of black schools, a "drunken gambler," was to take over the school board after Twitchell's death, which was expected daily. Marshall vowed to recover, but in his heart-of-hearts he must have known, as did his visitors, that the fate of local schools, like so much else, had slipped beyond his grasp.[37]

News of another sad event soon reached the sickroom. On 4 June the *New Orleans Republican* reported that Edward Dewees had died the previous day at Pass Christian. The story was vague concerning the illness that led to his death. Comparing it with Twitchell's perilous condition upriver, the column simply stated that of all the victims of Coushatta, "Dewees alone has escaped the hand of the assassin and passed over the river by natural death."[38]

36. Ibid., 175.
37. Ibid.
38. *New Orleans Republican,* 4 June 1876.

Marshall H. Twitchell (with prosthetic arms), American consul in
Kingston, Canada, circa 1880.
Courtesy of Mary Twitchell

Clockwise from lower right: Marshall Harvey Twitchell; his second wife,
Henrietta Day Twitchell; and their sons, Emmus George and
Marshall Coleman; circa 1900.
The University of Vermont Library

Marshall H. Twitchell in his tailored Civil War uniform, circa 1900.
Courtesy of Mary Twitchell

FOURTEEN

CONDEMNING THE VICTIM

THE assassination attempt on Twitchell triggered a flurry of denunciations in the northern press, which initially assumed that both men were dead: "More political Murders in Coushatta," "Twitchell and King Foully Killed," "The Bloody Shirt Again Unfurled," "Louisiana Lawlessness," "White Liners Drenched With Gore," 1876 campaign "inaugurated with assassination and murder," and so on. In a speech to Union veterans, Ben Butler asked, "Is this the liberty we were promised at Appomattox? Has the country carried on this long and bloody war for no other better and greater result than this?"[1]

At the time of the attack, a committee of the U.S. House of Representatives chaired by Randall Lee Gibson, a Louisiana Democrat elected in 1874, was already scheduled to investigate allegations of corruption in the New Orleans Customhouse. The House added the Twitchell shooting to the Gibson committee's agenda, instructing Gibson to conduct a full investigation of the latest Coushatta "murder or murders."

1. *Chicago Tribune*, 3 May 1876; *Washington National Republican*, 3 May 1876; *New York Times*, 3, 8 May 1876; Butler quote in *New Orleans Republican*, 6 June 1876.

Specifically, the House wanted to know whether the Twitchell-King shooting was politically inspired.[2]

Gibson appointed William Woodburn of Nevada, a Republican, and John Luther Vance of Ohio, a Democrat, as a two-man Coushatta subcommittee. Vance and Woodburn left the Crescent City, landing at Coushatta on 6 June 1874. The next morning, the two congressmen rode to the Bosley house to interview Twitchell in his sickroom. It was barely a week after his second amputation. A bullet was still in his leg, and he was too weak to rise, but his mind was alert. For more than an hour he answered politely phrased but loaded questions about his career, about alleged corruption of the Republican parish government, about Deputy Stockton's arrests, and about personal enemies who might have tried to kill him. Was he under indictment for embezzlement of parish funds? Had he ever sworn to reduce "the people of this parish to beggary?" With grim humor, Twitchell asked the two congressmen if their mission was to indict him "for being shot."[3]

For two days, the two congressmen held open hearings in the Coushatta courthouse. They examined thirty-four witnesses, six of whom had previously been arrested on suspicion of participation in the 1874 massacre. A seventh witness had been on the warrant list but avoided arrest, and an eighth had two close relatives on the list. The panel permitted Twitchell's friend William S. Mudgett to ask questions on Twitchell's behalf. Republicans who attended the hearings said that Woodburn, the "so-called Republican," outdid Vance in attacking Twitchell's record. During his brief stay in Coushatta, Woodburn reportedly won large sums of money playing poker. Twitchell believed his poker winnings were a discreet bribe.[4]

The testimony describing the shooting was generally consistent. No one recognized the goggle-eyed assassin—or so they said. Twitchell's record in the parish came under scrutiny. Z. T. Wester, the Republican clerk of court, said he thought Twitchell's governance had been economically sound. He conceded, though, that local people had reason to be resentful: "The greatest complaint I hear against Mr. Twitchell is

2. *House Reports*, 44th Cong., 1st Sess., No. 816, p. 645.

3. Ibid., 645, 649–57; MHT to editor of Vermont *Record and Farmer*, 15 September 1876, MHT Scrapbook.

4. MHT to editor Vermont *Record and Farmer*, 15 September 1876, MHT Scrapbook.

that he came down here with a pretty large family, and he always brought a man here to fill every office pretty near." Men less kindly disposed to Twitchell put the case with more feeling. "Mr. Twitchell has been controlling and conducting the parochial affairs almost exclusively," affirmed James F. Pierson. "It has been charged for years, and I think with good reason, that it was almost impossible for a man to hold office in that parish without the friendship or concurrence of Mr. Twitchell."[5]

Two of the town's leading merchants vouched for Twitchell's business integrity. Asked about his reputation "for probity and honor," Leander E. Love, Thomas Abney's former partner, said, "he is upright." In business matters, Woodburn asked, was Twitchell a man of his word? He "always has been so with me," Love responded. Where business and finance were involved, Julius Lisso said, "I have the utmost" faith in Twitchell. However, Lisso admitted that in political affairs he had no trust in Twitchell at all. Neither merchant accepted the notion that Twitchell was shot for political reasons. Nor did most of the other witnesses.[6]

Asked if a northern Republican who settled in Red River Parish would be "in any danger of personal violence," John H. Scheen—who had first nominated Twitchell for public office ten years before—said, "No, sir." Asked if he knew of any Republicans who had been harmed because of their politics, Scheen said, "I do not." Nor did Scheen or most other witnesses admit knowing anything about the White League. "There never has been any organization in the parish of Red River known as the White League," said Ben W. Marston, one of those arrested in 1874.[7]

A tiny minority of the witnesses addressed the political question honestly. "Since the massacre of 1874," said Wester, "I do not honestly believe a man could live here and advocate republican principles, and go ahead with them without being molested." Andrew Bosley, who had barely escaped with his life two years before, was downright defiant. He

---

5. *House Reports*, 44th Cong., 1st Sess., No. 816, pp. 673–74, 725.

6. Ibid., 694, 721.

7. Ibid., 676, 695, 725, 732. Marston qualified his statement somewhat, adding, "since the year of the first presidential election of General Grant, . . . that was 1868. At that time there was an organization here somewhat on the order of the White League." Ibid., 676.

said whites had repeatedly threatened him, but he had learned to ignore the threats: They "scared all the scare out of me in 1874. . . . I have got no other home to go to. My property is here. I have made it here, and I have made up my mind to die here. Let them kill me. I have got to die any way." Responding to questions from Mudgett, Bosley said there was no way to organize Republican clubs in the coming campaign without federal protection: "I consider the parish government powerless. I also, under the present circumstances, consider the General Government powerless. It has . . . under the Constitution, guaranteed to protect the citizens in their political rights anywhere, but it does not do so in this part of the country." Black people were disheartened, he said, and he stated matter-of-factly that black witnesses called before this committee had been threatened.

Congressman Vance pressed him on his relationship with Twitchell. Was he not, Vance asked, generally known as Twitchell's "political agent, or striker, as it is called here?" Bosley rejected the characterization: "Not for Twitchell—no sir. I am a political man for the good, I think, of the colored people, and for all Republicans, not for any man in particular." He had worked with Twitchell, he said, "because he was a Republican and acted with other Republicans, as any man would do with his party."[8]

Some of the most revealing testimony about the shooting concerned Republican sheriff John H. Carnes, who had replaced the murdered Frank Edgerton. The day of the shooting, Sheriff Carnes organized a posse that pursued the assassin, but Carnes did not lead it. Instead, he sent his Democratic deputy. The posse soon lost the gunman's trail and returned empty-handed. According to Twitchell, Carnes explained his action thus: "If I had gone to arrest him, or attempted to with a posse of these people here, I expect they would hang me to a limb." Called before the subcommittee, Carnes conceded that he had indeed been afraid to lead the posse. "I reckon I saw a little too much in 1874," he admitted.[9]

With the nation mired in economic depression, the national Democratic Party had swept the 1874 congressional elections. With the Democrats in control of the House, the outcome of the Coushatta in-

8. Ibid., 690, 709–11.
9. Ibid., 651, 667–69.

vestigation was a foregone conclusion. In that era, as in our own, congressional investigating committees invariably issued majority reports that served the interests of the majority party. Gibson doubtless knew he could count on the pliable Woodburn when he appointed him to the subcommittee.

The subcommittee's report thus became, as Twitchell had predicted, an indictment of the victim. The assassination attempt was, the report concluded, "not of a political character." According to its findings, Twitchell had badly mismanaged parish affairs and made many personal enemies. Parish taxes bordered on confiscation; the school funds had been misappropriated; and "gross frauds were perpetuated" in building levees and the courthouse. Space, wrote Vance and Woodward, did not permit a full recitation of the "irregularities and malpractices of Mr. Twitchell and his associates," which were equally condemned by the best citizens of both parties. The report concluded "that the people of Red River Parish, irrespective of party, are desirous of political quiet, and are prepared to welcome . . . men of all parties who are disposed to conduct themselves as law-abiding, peaceable citizens."[10]

The litany of corruption was mostly a smoke screen for political murder. Twitchell had played the political game by the standard rules, rewarding his friends, punishing his enemies by denying them offices and other emoluments. He and his family had tightly controlled the school moneys for both Red River and Bienville Parishes. Twitchell was president of the Red River school board, and his brother Homer had been school treasurer. (Isaac Coleman and his son Gus held the same positions, respectively, in Bienville Parish.) Twitchell often paid teachers' salaries from his personal bank account in New Orleans. While this practice seemed highly questionable to congressmen Vance and Woodburn, not only were there no banks in Coushatta, there was no one the Twitchells could trust with large sums of money, especially school money designated for educating blacks.

At the time of his death, Homer Twitchell was tax collector as well as school treasurer. Marshall was his bondsman for both offices. Twelve thousand dollars in school money was said to be unaccounted for *after* Homer's murder. Whether Homer's accounts were in order at the time of his death is impossible to know because the White League took pos-

10. Ibid., 647–48.

session of his records. Was the money actually missing, or were the exonerating records destroyed? If the money was stolen, was the thief Homer or the mob that ransacked his offices? The governor appointed, successively, two replacements as Coushatta tax collectors, both of whom were prevented by the White League from carrying out their duties. As to Marshall Twitchell, during the brief times he visited Coushatta after his brother's murder, he was preoccupied with finding Homer's killers, not auditing his books. Ironically, George King had become school-board treasurer shortly before his murder. Marshall Twitchell later transmitted what remained of the parish school-board records to New Orleans for examination by the redeemer legislature. On the basis of vouchers showing moneys paid out, the legislative report, signed by H. N. Ogden (former leader of the New Orleans White League), absolved him of all responsibility for the twelve thousand dollars.[11]

With respect to the tax collector's office, according to Twitchell, Mudgett and other Republicans urged the subcommittee to examine the courthouse records themselves. A Republican justice of the peace, in fact, told the committee that the tax collector's office had recently been audited by a committee of local citizens: "It has not been over two months ago, if I don't mistake. The tax-payers of the parish investigated it, and recognized the report of the tax collector being true."[12]

Later that summer after the hearings, the governor proposed making Julius Lisso tax collector, but Lisso wanted no part of the job. "The people of Red River parish have been hard to please in the matter of the tax collector," averred the *New Orleans Republican*. "Two, Twitchell and King, were killed at Coushatta; two others have not been allowed to perform their duties." The people in the region, the journal concluded with only modest exaggeration, "look upon the tax collector as the natural enemy of mankind, and when one appears there they hold a mass meeting to decide upon the manner of his death."[13]

Of all the allegations leveled at Twitchell, the most persistent concerned the cost of the courthouse. In 1872 the state legislature empowered the Red River Police Jury to issue $20,000 in bonds to finance construction of a courthouse in Coushatta. The building contract was let

11. *CV*, 186–87.
12. *House Reports*, 44th Cong., 1st Sess., No. 816, p. 720.
13. *New Orleans Republican*, 27 July 1876.

for $16,500 to Sheriff John T. Yates, who borrowed the construction costs from Lisso Bros. Unable to complete the job, Yates sold out to Twitchell, who finished the construction. The courthouse ran over cost. The final price tag was about $20,000, not counting the jail, which was added later at a cost of several thousand dollars. Both Twitchell and Lisso attributed the cost overrun to Yates's poor business judgment. The extent to which Twitchell profited from the deal is unknown, but presumably he did make money.[14]

When the courthouse was first built in 1872, the only controversy it provoked was the claim that it could have put up for less than $16,500. Beyond this, the cost of the courthouse was not an issue until *after* the Coushatta massacre. In his 1875 congressional testimony, Thomas Abney said the courthouse had cost $20,000 plus another $7,000 to add a jail. His chief attack on the Twitchells was for running up an overall parish debt of $40,000, the latter figure a matter of public record. Only with the shooting of Twitchell and King, the second "Coushatta affair," did the cost of the courthouse begin to assume epic proportions. Looking down at Twitchell in his sickbed, Congressman Woodburn asked him if the building had cost $60,000. "That is impossible," Twitchell snapped. Nonetheless, the parish judge told the congressional visitors that the cost was $65,000. The subcommittee's report put the figure at "upward of $40,000." Over the years, the figure of $60,000 became ensconced in local legend. In 1938, a special historical edition of the *Coushatta Citizen* displayed a photo of the "old courthouse," built, it claimed, "during the reign of carpet baggers" at a cost of "approximately $60,000."[15]

Marshall Twitchell was no saint. Politics in nineteenth-century America was a rough business, even rougher in Reconstruction Louisiana, where bullets often decided elections. In view of his state and parish contracts, including perhaps the courthouse, and his land investments, Twitchell understood the principle of "honest graft" (the words of a later New York City political boss). Relying on insider knowledge gained from political and business connections, Twitchell made

14. *New Orleans Republican*, 16 March 1872; *House Reports*, 44th Cong., 1st Sess., No. 816, pp. 653, 722.

15. *House Reports*, 43d Cong., 2d Sess., No. 261, p. 496; *House Reports*, 44th Cong., 1st Sess., No. 816, pp. 653, 718; *Coushatta Citizen*, 17 June 1938.

shrewder investments than he could otherwise have done. The ethics of that age, however, were not ours, and not even his enemies considered "honest graft" to be criminal. No evidence has ever come to light proving, or even establishing the probability, that he looted the public treasury of Red River Parish. Considering that from 1874 on, his bitter enemies controlled the parish records and the courts, if evidence against Twitchell existed, he would have been prosecuted. Like so much else from that bygone time, the story of carpetbag corruption in Red River Parish is just another Reconstruction legend.

The Coushatta subcommittee's report notwithstanding, Louisiana Republicans never doubted that the motive behind the Twitchell shooting was political. In New Orleans, Governor Kellogg offered what became the conventional interpretation of the attack: It was part of a plot to gain control of the state senate. Under the state constitution, Louisiana senators served four-year terms; half were elected every two years. Twitchell had been reelected with the 1874 division; the second division was elected in November 1876. An essential step in the organization of the next senate in January 1877 would be the certification and swearing in of new members by the holdover senators from 1874. Because there were nine holdover Republicans and nine holdover Democrats, the Republican lieutenant governor was positioned, in the event of disputes, to break tie votes in favor of seating members of the radical party. The absence of a single Republican senator, however, would give the Democratic holdovers a majority and the opportunity to engage in dirty tricks. A Democratic majority might delay the certification of new Republican senators, effectively giving the conservative party control of both legislative houses, regardless of the election outcome. It was Kellogg's belief that a Democratic plot had targeted Twitchell for assassination to achieve this goal. In congressional testimony and in his autobiography, Twitchell gave credence to this theory as well.[16]

To Kellogg and Twitchell, both eager to promote federal intervention in the state, the notion of a high-level Democratic conspiracy gave the shooting a desirable political spin. Surely the national government would not stand idly by and let Louisiana Democrats employ such foul means to overthrow a Reconstruction government. For Twitchell per-

16. *Chicago Inter-Ocean*, 4 May 1876; *House Reports*, 44th Cong., 1st Sess., No. 816, p. 656; *CV*, 169–70.

sonally, it must have been flattering—to the extent that such a thing could be flattering—to believe that the attempt on his life was an act of high (or low) statecraft, the fate of the government hanging on the outcome. And he may have been right. There are reasons, however, for suspecting otherwise.

For one thing, if top Democratic leaders had set out to kill a senator, they would likely have picked a less high-profile target than Twitchell. Any dead senator would have sufficed. With three members of his family already murdered, another Twitchell murder was certain to draw maximum press coverage in the North and provoke more calls for federal intervention, exactly what Democratic leaders wanted to avoid. For another thing, a senate conspiracy plot demanded an unlikely degree of cooperation between New Orleans Democrats and the goggle-eyed assassin. The timing was wrong, too. The high-level Democratic meeting in Coushatta—where was decided that question of long standing—occurred late on the afternoon of 1 May. The goggle-eyed man rode into Coushatta at daybreak the next morning. There was hardly time for Democratic leaders in New Orleans to have had a say in the matter.

Surely, there was a conspiracy, but it has all the earmarks of a conspiracy hatched in Coushatta where Twitchell was most passionately hated. Because of this carpetbagger, a federal marshal had arrested and jailed Coushatta's most distinguished citizens. The first citizen of the town, in fact, had been forced out of the state. The case of *U.S. v. Abney*, while it never came to trial, excepting the charges against the Natchitoches defendants, was never dismissed either. When Abney testified before a congressional committee in early 1875, he was still under bond. Within weeks of his appearance before the committee, he sold his interest in Thomas Abney & Co. and left Louisiana, a move the Mercantile files attribute directly to his legal problems with federal authorities. And, if we may believe the goggle-eyed man, he too was on the run because of Twitchell. "The White League believe, and perhaps rightly," Twitchell said in congressional testimony, "that I shall attempt to ferret out the murderers of those men, and my presence there is looked upon as being filled with absolute danger to all those parties."[17]

17. Abney was last reported living in New York. *Natchitoches People's Vindicator*, 21 August 1875; *House Reports*, 43d Cong., 2d Sess., No. 261, p. 390.

In late March 1876, five weeks before the attack on Twitchell, the U.S. Supreme Court handed down its decision in *United States v. Cruikshank*. Observing that the prosecution neglected to specify race as the cause of the Colfax massacre, the court upheld Justice Bradley's circuit-court ruling, reversing the convictions of William Cruikshank and two other defendants. The Fourteenth Amendment, said Chief Justice Morrison R. Waite, writing for the Court, "prohibits a State from depriving any person of life, liberty, or property without due process of law; but this adds nothing to the rights of one citizen as against another." In other words, because the members of the Colfax mob acted as private citizens, not as agents of the state of Louisiana, when they shot and burned to death more than one hundred black men, they could not be prosecuted under federal law. For all practical purposes, the decision gutted the 1870 Enforcement Act, the basis of *U.S. v. Abney* as well as *Cruikshank*. Louisiana Democrats applauded the ruling; Republicans bemoaned it. The *Alexandria Louisiana Democrat* congratulated Cruikshank, a resident of the town, and claimed that "our rights, so long crushed by Federal bayonets . . . have finally been accorded us by the highest judicial tribunal in the land."[18]

The Cruikshank decision lightened but did not dispel the prosecutorial shadows on Front Street. Twitchell had long since ceased relying on the federal courts. A year earlier, in February 1875, the Vermonter had introduced a senate bill "authorizing and requiring a criminal prosecution" of "all persons implicated" in the August 1874 Coushatta murders. If the Red River Parish courts were interfered with in any way, the measure stipulated that the cases would be transferred to Jefferson Parish in southeast Louisiana. In March 1875, citing the nearness of adjournment, the senate judiciary committee declined to take action on the measure.[19]

In the 1876 senate, just three months before his shooting, Twitchell introduced a revised version of his Coushatta prosecution bill, which also failed to pass. Hindsight, of course, tells us that the bill had no chance of passage, that Twitchell's best efforts notwithstanding, the

18. Higginbotham, *Shades of Freedom*, 88–89; *U.S. v. Cruikshank et al.*, *United States Reports, Supreme Court*, 92: 554; *Alexandria Louisiana Democrat*, 5 April 1876; *Natchitoches People's Vindicator*, 1 April 1876.

19. *Senate Journal*, *1875*, 145; *New Orleans Republican*, 3 March 1875.

murderers of his family would never be punished. But the men arrested in 1874—like Twitchell himself—lacked hindsight's certitude. They could not know that Rutherford B. Hayes would be the next president nor be certain that the next president would end Reconstruction. God forbid, what if some old radical became president? Unlikely, to be sure, but no more unlikely than Lincoln in 1860 or Andrew Johnson in 1865. What if the Republicans remained in power in New Orleans another four years? Fear of Reconstruction would haunt white southerners for more than a decade after it actually ended. In early 1876 it seemed far from over on the upper Red River. While the culprits probably discounted the danger of state prosecution, there was always the nagging doubt: What if the carpetbagger did succeed? What if the damned Yankee did get the cases to trial? Even if acquitted, in these hard times, the lawyers' fees, the appeals, the time away from work, would destroy them.[20]

Last, but not least, was the Kellogg impeachment; and if we may judge by the *Mansfield Reporter*, in northwest Louisiana, Twitchell, not the governor, was the story's chief villain. It was Twitchell, the carpetbag Machiavelli, that "impersonation of the devil himself," whose iron-willed "backbone" and "sleepless vigilance" had thwarted the impeachment. Was it merely coincidence that Twitchell's first scheduled public appearance in Coushatta after the impeachment found the goggle-eyed man waiting on the Red River bluff?[21]

Twitchell had become legend, the demon-radical boss of Red River Parish, a potent Reconstruction symbol. His vendetta against Front Street—indeed, his very existence—besmirched the honor and threatened the public peace of northwest Louisiana. Twitchell—and Twitchell alone—had made Coushatta, like Colfax, a byword for murder and mayhem across America. In the Kellogg impeachment, Twitchell— chiefly Twitchell—had made fools of Democratic leaders. He was the worst kind of carpetbagger—manly and brave, his word was his bond—a skilled politico, a successful modernizer, a protector of the freedmen. The upper Red River Valley would not be fully redeemed, white supremacy and honor fully restored, until his presence was removed. Because his term of office lasted through 1878, the only way to

20. *New Orleans Republican*, 21 January 1876.
21. MHT Scrapbook.

be rid of him quickly was to kill him. No matter which of these explanations one favors, the motive behind the Twitchell assassination plot was political.[22]

On 19 June 1876, with Helen Twitchell (the widow of Monroe C. Willis), Dr. Carson, and a military guard, John W. Harrison and Mudgett carried Twitchell on board the steamer *Durfee*. A large crowd had gathered at the landing to witness his departure, but there was no trouble. For the last time, Twitchell looked upon Coushatta and the broad cotton fields of Starlight Plantation. What thoughts passed through his mind, we can only imagine. Two days later he was in New Orleans. People milled about his hotel as his litter was carried in. He heard someone in the crowd remark: "What a pity they did not finish him up the river."[23]

He granted an interview to a reporter from the *Republican*. He talked about the shooting and subsequent investigation. He credited Dr. Carson with saving his life. Although the bullet lodged in his thigh was painful, "Mr. Twitchell," the reporter wrote, was "uncommonly cheerful for a man who can not feed himself or even walk without assistance. . . . He says that although he can not shake hands with friend or foe, and that the doctors have to feel in odd places for his pulse, he will hereafter give more attention to his brain, his only source to earn a livelihood."[24] Twitchell and his sister, accompanied by Harrison, were headed home to Vermont. Helen had lost as much as her brother. Not a woman of strong constitution, she had been under a terrible strain. Her husband and younger brother and two kinsmen had been brutally murdered; her sisters had died of yellow fever, and now Marshall was horribly maimed. Moreover, because Marshall Twitchell had rarely been at Starlight during the last two years, the burden of running the plantation had fallen on her.

The party left New Orleans by train, reaching Indianapolis in early July, where they planned a brief stopover with Charles W. Smith, Twitchell's old friend from the 109th USCT. Twitchell was news, and

22. Bertram Wyatt-Brown, *Southern Honor: Ethics and Behavior in the Old South* (New York, 1982).

23. *New Orleans Republican*, 21, 23 June 1876; *CV*, 189.

24. *New Orleans Republican*, 23 June 1876.

a reporter from the Republican *Indianapolis Journal* came to interview him. The reporter found him remarkably upbeat and related this account: Mr. Twitchell "spent eleven of the best years of his life" in Red River Parish and has done much to modernize that part of Louisiana. "He introduced the first new machinery into the parish after the war, has erected several mills and inaugurated other improvements." He is proud of his record as president of the school board, claiming credit for Red River's ten public schools. "In deference to Southern prejudice the white and black schools are separate, though both are run on the same basis." By law, "the whole poll tax goes to the school fund, and as every colored man pays a poll tax and many of them property tax, they contribute their full proportion to the schools. And Senator Twitchell says they pay their taxes not only cheerfully, but promptly, regarding it as an honorable badge of citizenship."

If the Democrats carry Louisiana in the upcoming election, Twitchell predicts that white Republicans will be run out of the state and the black people "reduced to a condition of serfdom not differing materially from slavery," the reporter continued. The Negroes "are easily intimidated, and are but just beginning to outgrow the demoralizing and dehumanizing effects of slavery on their race." Without government protection, they will "quickly succumb to the forces brought to bear on them and sink back into a condition little if any better than the one from which they recently emerged." If the Democrats win, in Twitchell's estimation, "every colored school in the State will be wiped out instantly."

The column contains an interesting, if overly flattering, description of its subject: "Senator Twitchell is a very gentlemanly appearing person, pleasant in conversation, and though not yet recovered from his wounds, gives evidence of great vitality. He has a genuine New England face; sharp, clean cut features, a clear, honest eye, and an intellectual head. His thin lips and square jaws indicate bravery and force of character, while his modest manner and quiet expression fascinate and fix attention." The account mentions his war record, but not the prominent scar on his right cheek.[25]

On the day of their planned departure, Helen was too ill to travel. Her condition worsened day by day, and on Sunday 9 July she died in

25. MHT Scrapbook.

the Smith home. The last two days of her life, fever and convulsions racked her frail body. In her delirium, she kept returning to the Bosley house where Marshall had been guarded night and day. She would scream in terror, "Is the guard here? Is the guard here?" At other times, her eyes would blaze, and she would lift her head, staring wildly at the people in the room. Recognizing them, she would say softly, "Yes, I know you; I am not afraid of you; you are Marshall's friends." Then her head would recline, and she would sleep again.[26]

The exact cause of her death went unrecorded, but whatever it was, it was secondary to deeper afflictions. Only her brother truly understood. Though her body was frail, a strong will and sense of responsibility had kept her going for two years. Since the last terrible shooting, her life had become a nightmare from which there was no awakening. Day and night she had fretted over Marshall, fearing that every step on the porch, every banging window shutter, every neighing horse, signaled the return of the goggle-eyed assassin, come to finish his work. Now in Indianapolis, they were finally safe, among friends. As her brother put it, "her system relaxed, and she had not the strength to recover." The man in the green goggles had killed her as surely as he had killed George King.

Marshall Twitchell had endured Homer's murder and the murders of his other kinsmen; he had endured Belle's and Kate's deaths; he had endured the terrible pain and humiliation of losing his arms; but with Helen's death, the deep spring of courage that had sustained him through four years of war and the ordeal of Reconstruction was finally exhausted. "I do not think I am lacking in affection for my friends and relatives," he wrote in his autobiography,

> but the manner in which they were taken away, the venom of the Southern press, and the fact that so many people of both races were looking to me for protection, support, and encouragement dried up the fountain of my tears; and every fresh outrage but stimulated me to greater exertions for the acquisition of wealth and power for the punishment of the wrongdoers. Until I was rendered so helpless by their last attack, I firmly believed that

26. *CV*, 189–90; *Indianapolis Journal*, 10 July 1876; *New Orleans Republican*, 16 July 1876.

right would finally prevail and that I would see the murderers legally punished for their crimes in the judicial district where those crimes were committed. When informed that Helen was dead, that the last of my family was gone, the only hands which I could trust to do my bidding powerless in death, I fully recognized that justice for the murders of my family would never be done, and for the first time tears came to my relief.[27]

In late June 1876, the Sioux had wiped out General Custer's Seventh Cavalry. Custer and the Twitchells were strangely coincidental stories. Deputy Stockton's posse had been composed of Seventh Cavalry. Lieutenant Edward L. Godfrey, who had investigated Colfax in 1873, supervised the burial of 212 troopers at the Little Big Horn.

In mid-July, the nation's press was still sorting out the Custer disaster. For a brief moment in some of the nation's leading newspapers, the story of Helen Twitchell's trials and death vied for prominence with accounts of the Little Big Horn. The *Indianapolis Journal* and the Reverend Dr. Jeremiah Bayliss of Trinity Methodist Episcopal Church shared the credit. Twitchell buried his sister the day after her death in Indianapolis. "We are sometimes accused of flaunting the bloody shirt," said Dr. Bayliss in his funeral oration, "of reviving memories which ought to sleep in forgetfulness; of dragging before the startled and unwilling eyes of this age the ghastly skeletons of horrors." These remarks set the tone of his entire oration. He reviewed the history of the Coushatta massacre, the shooting of King and Marshall, and of Helen's travails, "the faithful sister, smitten by shock after shock." The events in Coushatta, he said, are "almost too diabolical to be believed. Even after all we have heard of Fort Pillow, and Andersonville and Belle Isle," they astonish good people. Is it any wonder, he asked, that this woman "died without dread. She was too weary of human cruelty and wrong to desire to remain longer here." The southern people, he asserted, killed this woman as surely as if they shot her through the heart. "Indianapolis is called to-day to the task of burying one of the victims of Southern hate, and the victim is a woman. . . . And this is America, 'the land of the free and the home of the brave.'" The following Sunday in his evening sermon, Dr. Bayliss reviewed the tragedy again, at greater length. The *Journal* printed the complete texts of both addresses.[28]

27. *CV*, 189–91.
28. MHT Scrapbook.

The *Journal*'s coverage of Helen's death, occurring in Indianapolis, might have been expected. But when the *Chicago Tribune*, the *New York Times*, the *Washington National Republican*, and other northern newspapers—not to mention the *New Orleans Republican* and the *Brattleboro Vermont Phoenix*—picked up the story and reprinted it, including the text of Bayliss's two-thousand-word oration, it clearly demonstrated intense national interest. The headlines were flamboyant: "A Victim of Demons," "Victim of Southern Outrages," "Another Result of Louisiana Outrages," "Tale of Southern Diabolism," "Whole Family Were Sacrificed," "Recital of Infernal Atrocities," and so on. Two months before, coverage of the Twitchell-King shooting had been short-lived; now the Twitchell saga was reborn, larger than ever.[29]

While Dr. Bayliss's solicitude for the Twitchells was no doubt genuine, his actions had political ramifications. The Hayes-Tilden presidential campaign was heading into its final months. It looked to be a close election, and Indiana was a pivotal state. In a period in which most men still "voted as they shot" in the Civil War, the tale of an upright northern family destroyed by the Louisiana White League was tailored to reflect maximum discredit on the Democratic Party.

The *Atlanta Constitution* refuted the "pretended horrors of the Twitchell case" and accused Bayliss of abusing "the sacred character of his office." The *New Orleans Bulletin* put Helen in the same character of martyrdom with Charles Dickens's Nancy Sykes from *Oliver Twist*. The journalistic skirmishing was bitterest in Indianapolis, where the *Journal* jousted with the Democratic *Sentinel*. "The Republican party of this state," the *Sentinel* wrote, "have imported the notorious Twitchell from the South to make a martyr of him during the canvass." Making a hero of Twitchell was "like an effort to canonize the devil," the paper claimed. Citing a story from the *Natchitoches People's Vindicator*, the *Sentinel* charged that "Twitchell seduced a young lady under the pretext of marriage . . . and he was shot by her brother." As to the "politico-funeral sermon" of Bayliss, the paper stated that it was a known fact that his true church was the Republican Party. The *Sentinel* touched bottom, though, with this stroke: "As soon as one of the old broken down street-

29. *Chicago Tribune*, 10, 16 July 1876; *New York Times*, 13, 14 July 1876; *Washington National Republican*, 25 July 1876; *New Orleans Republican*, 16 July 1876; *Brattleboro Vermont Phoenix*, 21 July 1876.

car horses sent here . . . to recuperate, dies, from outrages committed upon it in the South, Brother Bayliss will be engaged for a funeral harangue [which] the *Journal* will report verbatim."[30]

After the funeral, Twitchell and Harrison traveled to Newfane, Vermont, for a sad reunion with his mother, Elizabeth; his six-year-old son, Marshall Coleman; and his orphan nephews. Of the nine members of the Twitchell clan who had settled in Louisiana years before, only Marshall and his mother remained alive.

The controversy ignited in Indianapolis followed Twitchell home to Vermont. Democratic newspapers claimed that he had joined the USCT during the war to avoid combat, that he and his family socialized exclusively with Negroes in Louisiana, and that his whole purpose for settling in Louisiana was to bring on a "war of races." The attacks on his war record caused his former commander from the 109th USCT, Colonel Bartholomew, to publish a rejoinder assuring the public that Twitchell was a true gentleman, a brave soldier, and a veteran of "twenty hard fought battles." In late July when the government published the Vance-Woodburn report, the Democrats had new ammunition. The *New York Herald* and other Democratic papers treated the report's findings as unimpeachable proof of Twitchell's villainy. The Democratic Party was especially grateful for the fresh dirt, because reports of the massacre of six black men in Hamburg, South Carolina, had hit the newspapers. In fact, the 1876 campaign, before it was over, offered the northern public a gruesome panoply of southern atrocities from the Carolinas to Texas.[31]

In broad perspective, the tempest over the Twitchells was only a brief, poignant incident in a sectional dispute over the legend of Reconstruction that would go on for the next hundred years. Echoes of it still resound in the South in the early twenty-first century.

Twitchell's movements in the late summer and fall of 1876 are sketchy. A few facts stand out. At home in Newfane, the bullet in his leg shifted position one day, and he fell. A doctor came from Brattleboro and cut it out, but Twitchell never regained full use of the leg. Gradually his bodily strength returned. Sometime late that summer or

---

30. *Atlanta Constitution*, 30 July 1876; *Bulletin* quoted in *New Orleans Republican*, 16 July 1876; *Indianapolis Sentinel*, 12, 15 July 1876; MHT Scrapbook.

31. Quoted in *Indianapolis Journal*, 17 July 1876, and in MHT Scrapbook.

in early fall, he and Harrison visited the Philadelphia Centennial. He purchased artificial arms, which he wore for the rest of his life. Then on 26 October, he married Henrietta in South Wilbraham, Massachusetts, her uncle performing the ceremony. How she responded to the amputation of his arms, what transpired between them before and after the marriage, is unknown.[32]

In mid-December Marshall and Henrietta boarded the train for New Orleans. He was still officially a state senator, and Louisiana was in the midst of another disputed election. This time the entire country was affected. Louisiana Democrats in 1876 had run General Francis R. Tillou Nicholls for governor. The Republican candidate was U.S. Marshal Stephen B. Packard, a man well known to Twitchell. On the face of the returns, Nicholls and the Democrats had won control of the state government and given Louisiana's 8 electoral votes to Tilden. The state Returning Board reversed the decision on 6 December, awarding the state elections to Packard and the Republicans and Louisiana's electoral votes to Hayes. In early January the Republicans barricaded themselves in the Saint Louis Hotel—which soon acquired the nickname "Fort Packard"—admitting only those lawmakers sanctioned by the Returning Board. The Republicans inaugurated Packard as governor, and the Democrats swore in Nicholls. Once again, as in 1873, the state had two governments.

Two other southern states had Republican returning boards, South Carolina and Florida. The South Carolina and Florida boards were not as freewheeling as their Louisiana counterpart, but each awarded their state's electoral votes to Hayes. In all, southern returning boards awarded Hayes 19 electoral votes (while Democrats north and south cried foul and contested the votes). There was also a contested electoral vote in Oregon, making a total of 20.

It was one of the closest presidential elections in American history. Tilden had 184 electoral votes and Hayes had 165. Because of the 20 disputed votes, however, neither candidate had the 185-vote majority required for election. Tilden, of course, needed only 1 of the disputed votes to win, while Hayes needed all 20. Emotion and rhetoric ran high that winter of 1876–1877. Only twice before, in 1800 and 1824, had a

32. *CV*, 193–94; MHT Scrapbook, *Brattleboro Vermont Phoenix*, 15 December 1876.

presidential election created such controversy and uncertainty as to its outcome.

The stalemated elections—both state and national—suspended Twitchell in a political twilight zone. In the first days of 1877, the Republican senate in the Saint Louis Hotel counted only twenty heads; the absence of a single member would break the quorum. The session was barely a week old when the Democrats, employing bribery, induced four Republican senators to desert Fort Packard and break the quorum. Desperate to restore the quorum, Twitchell fought fire with fire. He offered Emile Weber, one of the wayward Republicans, ten thousand dollars in negotiable state warrants as an inducement to return, preferably bringing one or more of the other defectors back with him. Webber took the warrants but continued to boycott the radical senate. For the rest of the winter, Twitchell and his fellow Republicans met each day only to disband for want of a quorum. The ten thousand dollars in warrants, moreover, would return to bedevil the senate leader after Reconstruction.[33]

To the *New York Graphic*, this latest Louisiana crisis was a subject of comic relief. The Packard and Nicholls lawmakers, it reported tongue-in-cheek, were importing weapons from abroad—notably a "monster gun from England"—killing one another right and left and holding their meetings in bomb-proof bunkers. Governor Packard had papers awaiting his signature "shot from his hand while taking his morning drink." The Democratic speaker of the house "yesterday had his head carried off by a cannon ball, but the trunk remained seated firmly in the chair and answered every purpose until the close of debate." According to reliable sources, the paper claimed, the rival state houses were digging vast tunnels beneath one another's chambers: "Last evening the opposite parties met and a terrible conflict ensued under ground. The slain of both sides were so numerous that the sergeant-at-arms of both legislative bodies made a requisition on the two legislatures for recruits to fill the gap in the ranks but a quorum could not be collected."[34]

In mid-February reality eclipsed parody. A distraught young man claiming to be a reporter entered Packard's crowded office in the Saint

---

33. MHT Scrapbook; *House Miscellaneous Documents*, 45th Cong., 3d Sess., No. 32, pt. 3, pp. 224–25, 231–37.

34. *New Orleans Republican*, 21 January 1877.

Louis Hotel and thrust a pistol in the Republican governor's face. The alert Packard batted down the assassin's hand. The weapon's discharge struck the governor a glancing blow in the knee. Instantly pistols appeared from beneath coats all over the room. A bullet shattered the assassin's arm. Had not Packard at that moment stepped in front of the youth, shielding him, his colleagues would have perforated the boy with bullets. And so it went in the waning days of Reconstruction.[35]

The story of how the federal Electoral Commission and the Compromise of 1877—whatever its exact arrangements—resolved the crisis has often been told and need not be repeated here. Suffice it to say that the Republican majority on the election commission awarded all 20 disputed votes and the presidency to Hayes, who, although a Republican, entered the White House determined to restore "Home Rule" to the South and end Reconstruction.

Once in office, the dilemma for Hayes was how to withdraw federal protection from Louisiana and South Carolina Republicans without throwing them to vengeful Democratic wolves. Near the end of March, Hayes appointed Wayne MacVeagh, a Pennsylvania Republican, to head a special five-man presidential commission. The commission arrived in New Orleans in early April to broker a deal with Democratic Governor Nicholls. Amenable to compromise, Nicholls promised to permit Republicans whose elections were recognized by both parties, as well as some whose seats were contested, to take their places in the redeemer legislature. In return, Nicholls promised, Louisiana Democrats would restore public peace, refrain from persecuting their Republican foes, maintain public schools for both blacks and whites, and enforce the Reconstruction constitutional amendments.[36]

Like most southern Republicans, Twitchell ticked off the final days of Reconstruction with a mounting sense of dismay and betrayal. He was angry that Hayes used Louisiana's electoral votes to enter the White House, but now, seemingly without a thought for the lives of Louisiana Republicans, intended to allow Nicholls and the Democrats to claim control of the state. On 21 April 1877, the Republican legislature disbanded. A number of Republicans, Twitchell among them, entered the Nicholls legislature. Three days later, the federal troops

35. Ibid., 17 February 1877.
36. *DAB*; *Appleton's Annual Cyclopaedia, 1877*, 460–62.

guarding the state house withdrew to their barracks. Twitchell and two of his colleagues wrote Governor Packard, observing that with the president against him, Packard's situation was hopeless. Packard renounced his pretensions to office.[37]

A day or so later, a telegram from Coushatta appeared in the New Orleans newspapers: "Just fired one hundred guns; will fire one hundred more on the second day of May." After a moment's reflection, most readers doubtless recognized the date as the anniversary of the Twitchell-King shooting. The *Coushatta Times* later reported that on 2 May 1877, a carpenter "built a pair of wooden goggles and a gun and suspended the two on a pole on the river front of Coushatta." It was a fitting symbol of the way in which Louisiana whites, having lost the Civil War, had triumphed over Reconstruction.[38]

In the lore of the upper Red River, the goggle-eyed man was Captain Jack, who in time became a heroic figure. The story goes that when the gunman was an old man in his seventies, he returned to Coushatta from Arkansas, where he had fled years before. His wife warned him against entering Louisiana, to which he reportedly replied: "Why those folks down there are my friends—we fought for what we knew to be right and proper. They'll be powerful pleased to see me, I'm figuring, and me them."[39]

37. MHT Scrapbook; *Appleton's Annual Cyclopaedia, 1877*, 462–65.
38. *New Orleans Republican*, 19 May 1877.
39. *Coushatta Citizen*, 17 June 1938.

FIFTEEN

THE LAST BATTLES OF COUSHATTA

T HE MacVeagh Commission-Governor Nicholls compromise was to influence the rest of Twitchell's life. The dust of Reconstruction was still settling when he began looking for a federal appointment. "I intend to go to Washington," he wrote John W. Harrison at Starlight, and "bother the officials there until to get rid of me they will give me something." Ex-governor Kellogg, now in the U.S. Senate, wrote President Hayes on his behalf, as did James Madison Wells and Thomas C. Anderson, members of the Louisiana Returning Board whose legerdemain helped make Hayes president. Anderson and Wells described Twitchell as "a living monument" to Reconstruction. Congressman Chester B. Darrall attested to his "honesty and integrity," adding, "You know that all of his family have fallen victims of cruel persecution and that Mr. Twitchell himself is maimed and helpless."[1]

As luck would have it, President Hayes had an uncle living in Newfane, Vermont. In August 1877 while visiting his kinsman, he met Twitch-

1. MHT to [John W. Harrison] 23 August 1877, MHT Letterbook, MHT Papers; William Pitt Kellogg to MHT, 3 May 1877, James Madison Wells and Thomas C. Anderson to Rutherford B. Hayes, 10 May 1877, and Chester B. Darrall to Hayes, 24 October 1877, all in MHT Papers.

ell at a reception on the town commons. The minister who introduced the president to the crowd spoke of his southern policy and of "several sons of Newfane" who have "suffered martyrdom in the South." After the speechmaking, Twitchell conversed with the president, asking him about the status of southern blacks. "I believe the condition of the colored people is better to-day than it has ever been," Hayes replied. The repeated failures of Reconstruction, he said, "rendered a change necessary, and no change, as you can testify from your own experience, can be for the worse." It was time to let "bygones be bygones." Oberlin College teachers working in the South, the president said, assured him that social conditions had undergone a marked improvement in recent months. Although he knew better, Twitchell tactfully let the subject drop.[2]

Afterward, Twitchell wrote Harrison that the president "talked to me until I was tired of his talking." Even so, he had some empathy with Hayes's position. Hayes, indeed any president, he acknowledged, had only limited power to influence people's lives. If the majority of people in a given locality resolved "to burn people at the stake" over religion or politics, there was, Twitchell had to admit, little the government could do about it.[3]

The president took the MacVeigh Commission-Nicholls agreement seriously: He genuinely wanted to protect Louisiana Republicans from Democratic reprisals. Because he could not use troops, he needed the help of radical lawmakers, such as Twitchell, who were still members of the post-Reconstruction general assembly. Twitchell, who had been elected to a four-year term in 1874, legally was still a Louisiana resident. A solid core of Republican lawmakers would make it more difficult for redeemer Democrats to use the state government as an instrument of reprisal against the minority party. Although exactly how and when is unclear, the evidence suggests that Twitchell and President Hayes came to a personal understanding. Twitchell needed a federal appointment; Hayes would let him earn it by returning to Louisiana and finishing out his term in the senate.

One last time, Twitchell made the long train trip from Vermont to New Orleans. From January to March 1878, he served his last term

2. *Brattleboro Vermont Phoenix*, 24 August 1877.
3. MHT to [John W. Harrison] 23 August 1877.

in the Louisiana senate. After adjournment, he went to Washington. Hayes upheld his end of the bargain and in early April appointed Twitchell the American consul in Kingston, Canada. Kingston was a small city located on the east end of Lake Ontario at the head of the Saint Lawrence River. Hayes and his advisers chose Kingston, Twitchell said, "because there was little to do; it was near my former home and in all respects was thought to be a comfortable place for me to stay during the short time which they considered I had to live." He took up his duties in Kingston in early May 1878. He would still be serving in the Canadian city when Rutherford B. Hayes was in his grave.[4]

An old hand in the consular service came from Toronto to show Twitchell the ropes. With his quick mind, Twitchell soon mastered the consulate's administrative routine. The most difficult aspect of his job, in fact, was its very normality. After Louisiana, the quiet of Kingston was unnerving. For most of his adult life, he had been inured to action and danger, first in the war, then in Reconstruction. For years he had worn a pistol under his coat and slept with a weapon by his bed; each night, he had carefully closed the shutters before lighting the lamps; secrecy and stealth had become second nature to him. He had become virtually addicted to life on the edge. Thus, the most difficult part of his new life was learning to live without the tension, without the danger, without the surges of adrenaline. The struggle was all the more difficult because of his disability. He was totally dependent on others. He could not feed, dress, bathe, nor perform bodily functions by himself. Someone else must lift the fork to his mouth, the glass to his lips.[5]

Below the border in the United States, controversy still swirled about his name. Reconstruction was over, but emotionally, for combatants like Twitchell, it would never really be over. Twitchell had been in Kingston less than a month when the Potter Commission, a congressional committee chaired by New York Democrat Clarkson D. Potter, opened its inquiries into the 1876 presidential election. Much of the testimony before Potter's committee concerned events in Louisiana's East and West Feliciana Parishes, a carpetbagger named James E. Anderson, and two white Unionists, Don and Emile Weber. A native of Pennsylvania, James E. Anderson was the Potter Commission's keynote

4. Ibid.; *CV*, 198; SDR, M-T472, RG 59, NA.
5. *CV*, 201.

witness. He testified that he and his friend Don Weber, as election supervisors, had manipulated the returns in their respective parishes so as to give Hayes majorities over Tilden. The state Returning Board then legitimized their fraud.

In the weeks after the election, as the ballots were being counted and recounted, "visiting statesmen" from the North flocked to the Crescent City to watch the Returning Board's every move. According to supervisor Anderson, one of these visitors, Senator John Sherman of Ohio—brother of General Sherman and confidant of Hayes—had encouraged his and Weber's vote fraud. When the two supervisors expressed concerns about their safety, Sherman assured them in writing that they would be protected and taken care of: "Gentlemen. . . . Neither Mr. Hayes, myself, the gentlemen who accompany me, or the country at large can ever forget the obligation under which you have placed us . . ." etc.[6]

The two supervisors were right to be afraid. After the election, Don Weber remained closeted in New Orleans for months, afraid to appear on the streets. In early March 1877, he returned to his home in Saint Francisville, in West Feliciana Parish. A day or two later, unknown assassins shot him dead.[7]

Don Weber obviously could not testify before the Potter Commission. His older brother, however, a former sheriff and member of the state senate, claimed to be privy to the Feliciana vote fraud and to the negotiations with Senator Sherman. Appearing before Potter's committee, Emile Weber vouched for Anderson's election-fraud story and the authenticity of the Sherman letter: "I read the letter several times. It was in the handwriting of Mr. Sherman. I am familiar with Mr. Sherman's writing."[8]

Emile Weber's testimony strayed into statements about Twitchell and alleged corruption in the Louisiana senate. During the crisis winter of 1877, when not only the presidential election was in dispute, but both the Nicholls Democrats and the Packard Republicans claimed to be the true state government, Emile Weber had initially taken his sen-

6. Frank P. Vazzano, "The Louisiana Question Resurrected: The Potter Commission and the Election of 1876," *LH* 16 (1975): 39–43; Potter Commission, pt. 1, 1–17.

7. Potter Commission, pt. 1, 596–98.

8. Ibid., 591.

ate seat in the Republican statehouse. After a few days, however, he and three others jumped ship and went over to the Democrats, leaving the Republican senate without a quorum. By his own admission, Weber received $1,000 from the Democrats to break the Republican quorum. A few days later, Twitchell made him a counteroffer, $10,000 in state warrants as an inducement to return to Fort Packard. The warrants probably were negotiable only if only if Hayes became president and recognized the Packard government. Without a senate quorum, the Republican legislature was paralyzed. It could not even appropriate funds to run the government. As Weber told the story, Twitchell wanted a big appropriation—a $500,000 bill was pending—so that he and his associates could loot the state treasury. The more likely explanation is that Twitchell desperately was trying to maintain the legitimacy of the Packard government. By definition, a government whose senate cannot muster a quorum to transact public business lacks legitimacy.[9]

Over the course of the Potter Commission inquiry, both James E. Anderson and Emile Weber lost most of their credibility. The Sherman letter turned out to be a fraud, and Weber was caught in a further series of lies and contradictions. One witness testified that Weber—only a few hours earlier—had offered him $500 to back up his false statements to the commission. Most embarrassing was Weber's remarkable reversal of views on Louisiana violence. In previous testimony before a congressional committee and in numerous public statements, he had depicted a condition of society in West Feliciana akin to Twitchell's Red River Parish: Republicans, white and black, intimidated, murdered, or run out of the country. Grilled by Republican members of the Potter Commission, Weber admitted that he had posted guards around his house during the presidential election, that he had abandoned his home after the election, and had not dared return during the past two years. Then there was the undeniable fact that five months after the election, his brother had been shot down in broad daylight in the center of Saint Francisville. Committee members produced a letter that Weber had written for publication just two weeks after his brother's murder. In it he charged that Louisiana's redeemer government was "founded on blood" and that the murderers of his brother were well-known ap-

9. Ibid., pt. 3, 225–26, 238–43, 405–6.

pointees of Democratic governor Nicholls. To avoid the fate of his brother, he and his brother's widow, he said, "abandoned all our property" in Saint Francisville "and left it at the mercy of the brutes."[10]

Before Potter's committee, however, Weber claimed he had been misinformed or had exaggerated the extent of Democratic violence: "I must have been mistaken"; "the testimony . . . I gave at that time was hearsay testimony"; "I have learned since that these reports were incorrect"; "if I made that statement it must have been exaggerated"; "I had no knowledge whatever of what I spoke." Obviously uncomfortable and sounding like the witnesses before Vance and Woodward's Coushatta subcommittee, he told his skeptical listeners that he no longer believed his brother was killed for political reasons. Weber's dramatic change of mind was most likely motivated by concern for his 2,500 acres near Saint Francisville and the hope that, in betraying the Republicans, his white neighbors would permit him to return home.[11]

Twitchell did not testify before Potter's committee. Angered by the hearings, however, he wrote a newspaper rebuttal. He branded Weber a "subservient tool" of Louisiana Democrats and said the man was "ever ready to perjure himself for the benefit of his brother's murderers." He vociferously denied Weber's charge of senate corruption: "During the years . . . I was chairman of the Republican caucus of the Senate, I never knew or heard before that the caucus was used for any purpose which could be termed corrupt." Twitchell was splitting hairs. If by corruption, he meant stealing public money, a criminal offense, he was doubtless correct. On the other hand, he admitted giving Weber the $10,000 in warrants.[12] Neither man used the word bribe. Twitchell said that the warrants were to enable Weber to protect himself from his enemies. Weber testified about the matter: "I did not intend to say that I was bribed . . . to make a quorum. I considered this a personal favor." In general usage, however, such "personal favors," then and since, are bribes.[13]

Contrary to his vacillating accounts of Democratic violence, We-

10. Vazzano, "Louisiana Question Resurrected," 45–52; Potter Commission, pt. 1, 596; Potter Commission, pt. 3, 198–203, 222–23.

11. Potter Commission, pt. 3, 198–203.

12. The $10,000 figure was invariably used in the hearings by all the witnesses, including Twitchell, but an audit revealed $7,269.70 in warrants.

13. MHT Scrapbook; Potter Commission, pt. 3, 231–34.

ber's allegations of senate corruption antedated the presidential election crisis. In February 1874, four years before his Potter Commission testimony, he alleged that twenty-three senators had taken money for their votes on a Crescent City marketing bill. Then before Potter's committee, he claimed that nineteen senators, including himself and Twitchell, had received $1,000 each for their votes on a recent levee act. In fact, according to Weber, Twitchell was one of the leaders of a senate bribery ring. Given Weber's dubious credibility, none of this would have stood up in court. Indeed, bribery was not even a crime in Reconstruction Louisiana, just another form of "honest graft." Still, there was probably substance in Weber's allegations. Twitchell did give him the warrants, and more than $4,000 of the warrants had been signed over to Twitchell personally. In Reconstruction New Orleans, corruption was part of the environment, a means of personal advancement and a tool of the political trade, used by both Democrats and Republicans. It was also standard operating procedure for business interests seeking charters or concessions from the state. Twitchell probably could not have functioned as caucus leader had he disdained its use. He no doubt profited personally as well. It helps explain his ability to buy land and corn even during the worst days of the depression.[14]

To put all this in perspective, corruption was generic to the Gilded Age. This was the era of Boss Tweed, Credit Mobilier, and the Erie Ring. This was a time in which railroad executives routinely calculated the cost of bribing lawmakers and judges into the costs of doing business. This was, moreover, Louisiana, with a well-earned reputation, then and since, as one of the most corrupt states in the nation. Governor Warmoth, after whom Twitchell originally wanted to name Red River Parish, summed it up best: "Why, damn it, everybody is demoralizing down here. Corruption is the fashion." Nor did the end of Reconstruction alter the situation. In fact, Louisiana's Democratic redeemers compiled a record of graft and embezzlement that surpassed anything from the carpetbagger era. As regards Twitchell, he acquired Starlight Plantation and most of his wealth *before* he entered the state senate, and his administration of parish affairs generally was honest. To the extent that he was corrupt, "it would be nearer the truth," as Richard N. Current writes of Warmoth, "to say that Louisiana corrupted *him* than to

14. *New Orleans Republican*, 20, 24 February 1874; Potter Commission, pt. 3, 232–35.

say that *he* corrupted Louisiana." Finally, violence, not bribery, was the worst corruption of Reconstruction. The *white line* violence that swept the Deep South in the 1870s did far more to crush honest government in the region than grafting politicians. The American political system can, and has, survived any number of Teapot Domes; it fares much worse against terrorists.[15]

The Potter Commission kept Twitchell's name in the public eye, especially in his native Vermont where one of his bitterest critics was the Democratic *Windham County Reformer*. Decrying the local people's foolish sentimentality about Twitchell, this Brattleboro newspaper reported every allegation against him as if it were gospel. The Vance-Woodward subcommittee, the paper claimed, "agreed unanimously that Twitchell had been guilty of the most inexcusable corruptions." Ergo, opined the *Reformer*, the man was "a scoundrel," an "ex-thief"; his appointment to a "fat sinecure" in Canada was a disgrace. None of the Twitchell "crowd in the South ever had a decent character at home," it said. The *Reformer* depicted the discrepancies between Weber and Twitchell's testimony as so much name-calling by "southern carpet-baggers," which well-informed people should not take seriously. Another Democratic journal, the *Montpelier Argus and Patriot*, also catalogued Twitchell's "carpet bag dishonesty." Probably taking its cue from the *Natchitoches People's Vindicator*, the *Patriot* charged that the real motive behind the Coushatta bloodletting was Twitchell's "betrayal and seduction of a young lady of good family."[16]

Papers such as the *Reformer* and the *Patriot* often got as good as they gave. One indignant ex-editor complained to the *Reformer* that he thought it most unlikely that President Hayes made a habit of appointing criminals to office: "Will you please state definitively what are the crimes which Mr. Twitchell has committed. . . . What did he do? Did he shoot his arms off? Did he commit murder? Did he steal anything of the rebels, their farms or even their spoons?" During the 1880 presidential campaign, a Twitchell kinsman reviewed the story of the "Coushatta Outrage" in the *Vermont Phoenix*. Referring to the *Reformer* as the *Defamer*, the author pretended to recommend that the North adopt the

---

15. *House Reports*, 43d Cong., 2d Sess., No. 261, p. 973; Richard N. Current, *Three Carpetbag Governors* (Baton Rouge, 1967), 63; William Ivy Hair, *Bourbonism and Agrarian Protest: Louisiana Politics, 1877–1900*, (Baton Rouge, 1969), 27–31, 141.

16. MHT Scrapbook.

political mores of the South. He singled out the Democratic candidate for vice-president of the United States, the Honorable William H. English of Indiana, who had often been accused of corruption: "Why not take him from his home, his kindred and his friends, and after promising him safety in the State of Illinois, shoot him like a dog, and leave his body (as did the ghouls in Louisiana) for birds and beasts of prey to feed on." The author conceded, of course, that he was being facetious; Republicans did not practice such barbarities. But, he said, "this slaughtering of human beings because of their political principles, . . . this is what the *Defamer*, with the copperhead Democrats of the North, calls justice!"[17]

Far from Vermont in the American West, rival Republican and Democratic newspapers debated the Twitchell story. In a series of articles in September and October 1879, the California *Bodie Standard* and the *Virginia City Territorial Enterprise* defended Twitchell and attacked ex-Nevada Congressman William Woodburn for his role in whitewashing the Louisiana White League. The *Virginia City Evening Chronicle* came to Woodburn's defense. An ex-Louisiana resident, "Coushatta," joined the fray on Twitchell's side. With respect to Twitchell's character, Coushatta wrote, "I consider him the peer of ex-Congressman Woodburn in integrity, and much his superior in brains and courage."[18]

In the midst of this journalistic skirmishing, *Sunny South*, an Atlanta literary magazine, serialized Mary E. Bryan's *Wild Work: The Story of the Red River Tragedy*, which then appeared in book form in 1881. Bryan was a former editor of the *Natchitoches Times* who had lived in Springville, on the outskirts of Coushatta, from 1868 to 1874. She obviously knew Twitchell, Thomas Abney, Julius Lisso, and most of the other participants in the Coushatta troubles. *Wild Work*, she says in her preface, was written "while the scenes it reproduces were fresh in the author's mind." Of the pivotal chase episode in which the six Republican officials are run down and murdered, she writes: "The circumstances . . . are almost word for word as they were told me by one of the men who accompanied the prisoners as a guard." Still later, she writes: "I was in the very heart of the tragedy and had exceptional opportunities to find out all about it." *Wild Work* is a roman a clef, that is, the book's

17. Ibid.
18. Ibid.

characters are based on real people. Indeed, the fictional names in the novel closely approximate real names and places. Captain Marshall Twitchell is Captain Marshall Witchell; Homer Twitchell is Omar Witchell; Adele Coleman is Adelle Holman; Thomas W. Abney is Colonel Alver; the Lisso brothers are the Lisson brothers; Captain Jack is Captain Dick. Similarly, Coushatta is Cohatchie; Lake Bistineau is Lake Wisteneau; and Brush Valley is Mossy Valley. Marshall Twitchell read the book with interest, if not pleasure. Inside the flyleaf of his personal copy is a handwritten key identifying all the characters and their real-life counterparts.[19]

While Mary Bryan purports to tell the true story of Coushatta, she admits that some of the incidents in her novel are fictitious, that "a thread of romance is interwoven with the warp of fact." We first meet the "soldierly figure" of Captain Witchell, for example, in the act of rescuing Adelle Holman, whose boat has drifted into the path of an oncoming steamer on the Red River. This rescue never happened. However, as in real life, the author has Adelle making a midnight ride to save her lover. And as actually happened, the carpetbagger marries the planter's daughter, only to have the young woman die tragically young. The author's claims to historicity notwithstanding, when her story line departs from the known facts about the historical Twitchell and Coushatta, the "thread of romance" runs away with the book.

Dedicated to Confederate vice-president Alexander H. Stephens, *Wild Work* is surprisingly ambiguous in its treatment of its subject. On the one hand, Mary Bryan deplores Captain Witchell's "carpet-bag dynasty," with its nepotism, reliance on ignorant Negro voters, and its "success makes right" ethics. On the other hand, she clearly admires the carpetbagger protagonist. He is manly, bold, and intelligent. Men follow him; women fall in love with him. Not only does he save Adelle from the steamboat, he nurses her brother during a yellow fever outbreak. Later, he rescues young white men from the wrath of a black mob. He engineers the creation of a new parish and the rise of Cohatchie. He is a good administrator who sponsors public improvements. He is popular with poor white farmers as well as freedmen. He is "the best of our carpetbag masters," one character remarks. "I want to con-

19. *Wild Work*, v–vii, 315; Mary E. Bryan to Mercedes Garig, 31 October 1907, Melrose Collection.

ciliate [whites]," Witchell says, "and gain their confidence and esteem. I want them to feel that I am one of them—that I have their interests at heart, as I have." In these passages, Bryan's Witchell sounds very much like the real Twitchell of the early 1870s.

Not content with wealth and power in northwest Louisiana, Witchell wants to be governor.[20] His ambition consumes him and undoes the good he has done. Although his young wife is gravely ill, he sends the dying woman away from him so that he can complete his senate work in New Orleans: "He had quieted his conscience by assuring himself that his wife was not dangerously ill, and that she would be better out of the city; but, when he carried her into her state-room, and, shutting the door behind stood looking at her as she lay, so pitiful in her youth, her faded loveliness, her death-like whiteness, the battle in his heart had to be fought over again." As he prepares to leave her, the poor woman reaches out to him: "You wouldn't send me away without you, would you, dear Marshall?" The boat bell rings, and the guilt-ridden man slips away. "He's a cold-hearted wretch," cries his wife's friend. A few days later, the dying wife has a terrible dream: "I saw Marshall swimming in a bloody sea, with a bloody mist above and around him. All at once, as he swam, both his arms dropped away, and the cloud shut him from me."

Witchell's ambition destroys the family he loves. After his brother Omar's murder, he cries out: "My brother, my brother! I would to God I had died in your place!" Still later, an embittered Witchell rides alone through the streets of Cohatchie: "All that had been soft in his nature hardened into iron now." He "was a stern and smileless man, whose eye had the cold flash of a bayonet, whose brow never relaxed, whose voice uttered only necessary words in hard, metallic accents." In Bryan's pages, Captain Witchell, like Robert Penn Warren's Willie Stark (modeled after Huey Long), almost becomes a tragic hero.

Conversely, the author has little good to say about Red River redeemers. Witchell's nemesis Colonel Alver (Thomas W. Abney) is a sinister, devious figure. Although seemingly gracious and well mannered, his eyes are cold and there is "a false ring in his voice." He hates Witchell because Alver aims to be "the big man of the town, the great mogul." He resents his merchant rivals the Lissons because their alli-

20. No evidence suggests that Twitchell ever seriously entertained such a notion.

ance with Witchell draws "the Negro trade—an important item" in Cohatchie, "where darkies handle so much money—to Lisson's store." Alver has an adulterous affair with a woman who had first offered herself to Witchell. Egged on by his embittered and unscrupulous lover, Alver organizes the White League and brings on the Cohatchie massacre. The novel's other villain is a crazed fire-eater name Richard Lanier (Captain Dick), who is Adelle Holman's fiancée before Witchell takes her away from him. You "saint-faced piece of falseness," the rejected man screams at Adelle when she returns his ring. Later, Lanier lies in wait for Witchell and his brother-in-law on the bank of the Red River. Laughing shrilly, his "wild hair" streaming from his head, the "madman" guns them down.

The White League followers of Colonel Aver and Captain Dick are misguided vigilantes, not noble redeemers. The justice of the Cohatchie massacre is lynch-law justice. To be sure, the murdered Republicans are members of Witchell's ring, but they are innocent of insurrection. The "hideous plot of blood"—of which they are accused—exists only in the fevered imagination of their enemies. Why, one of the heroines asks, would the radicals "wreck their own cause" with such a foolhardy scheme? Only one of Bryan's radicals, the mulatto Levi Adams (Levin Allen), lives up to "Tragic-Era" legend. "My pretty one," the Negro warns the white heroine, soon "this house will swarm with men— *niggers*, you call them—mad, drunk, furious, ripe for anything." "Kneel to me," he commands. "Seize my hands here in your soft palms, hug my knees with your arms, look up in my face with tears dropping from your eyes." Shortly thereafter, the would-be rapist is shot down in the woods by avenging whites. (The historical Levin Allen was killed because he had defended himself against a mounted white man who had tried to ride him down.)[21]

Bryan's first novel, *Manch*, had gone through two printings in its first year and become a traveling stage play. Although *Wild Work* was less successful, her publisher D. Appleton and Company was a major New York house with distribution all over America and in England. Twitchell probably purchased his copy of the novel off the shelf in Kingston. (A second edition appeared in 1893.) According to family tradition, Marshall Twitchell tried to persuade the U.S. government to

21. Bryan, *Wild Work*, 1–9, 14, 19, 36, 51, ff.

suppress the novel. How is unclear, and the author of this biography
has seen no evidence to support the claim. Still, family tradition no
doubt reflects Twitchell's opinion of the book: he did not like it.[22]

Judged solely on its literary merits, *Wild Work* has little to recommend it. No one is apt to mistake Mary Bryan's prose for Willa Cath-
er's or Edith Wharton's. As history, however, the novel offers valuable
insights into Twitchell and his times. Suffice it to say that when a later
generation of southern writers turned to the Reconstruction period for
inspiration, they would imitate neither Mary Bryan's admiration for an
ambitious carpetbagger nor her disdain for the brutal means of his destruction.

In the meantime, another story was unfolding in Louisiana, a story
whose outcome was to do Twitchell far more material damage than the
journalistic skirmishing in the Green Mountains and the Sierra Nevada.
In this last battle of Coushatta, the arena was the court.

Rumors of schemes to divest Twitchell of his Red River properties
had surfaced within months of the 1874 White League uprising. In the
summer of 1876, after Twitchell had headed North with his dying sister, the rumors became reality. Twitchell had not been back in Vermont
a month when John T. Yates filed a lawsuit against him in Coushatta.
Twitchell had forced Yates, the first sheriff of Red River Parish, out of
office for padding his travel expenses. Coushatta Democrats brought up
his name repeatedly during the Vance-Woodburn inquiry as one of
those "personal enemies" who might have shot Twitchell. (Deputy
Stockton had carried a warrant for Yates in his 1874 Coushatta raid.)
In his 1876 petition, Yates claimed that before Frank Edgerton's death,
Edgerton had acted as a business agent for both Yates and Twitchell. In
the winter of 1874, Edgerton reputedly had shipped eighteen bales of
Yates's cotton, the proceeds of which had ended up in Twitchell's New
Orleans bank account. Edgerton, being dead, could shed no light on the
transaction. Yates claimed that Twitchell owed him $800 plus interest.
Because Twitchell had left the parish and was unlikely to return, Yates
asked the court to attach his assets to satisfy the debt. Twitchell doubted

22. Mary E. Bryan published a dozen novels as well as stories and other works in her
career. Her writing and editing earned her a place in the *National Cyclopaedia of American
Biography* and in the *Dictionary of American Biography*. Twitchell appears in neither.

anyone in Coushatta actually believed Yates's story; nonetheless, he was not surprised when the ex-sheriff won his case. The first legal domino had fallen.[23]

Although Twitchell owned land in three parishes, the bulk of his holdings were in Red River. He hoped to save these lands as a legacy for his son and orphan nephews. The Yates case was a warning, and he heeded it. In April and June 1877, he sold 3,476 acres of Red River Parish real estate to his mother, Elizabeth, for $16,100. This included 130 acres within the town limits of Coushatta, Starlight Plantation, a 1,080-acre plantation formerly owned by George King, and more than 1,500 acres of land purchased at a tax sale that formerly belonged to a resident of Rapides Parish named L. A. Stafford. Transferring property to a wife or other kinsman was a standard way of protecting it from creditors. Thomas Abney and other Red River businessmen had employed the same stratagem. In this instance, there was an added advantage. Because Elizabeth Twitchell was a resident of Vermont, there was a good chance of getting any litigation into the federal courts, where the chances of weathering a legal storm were far better than in the state courts.[24]

Part of Twitchell's dilemma was his inability to work his property. There was no one he could trust to run the King place. The Stafford land, purchased in July 1874, a month before the massacre, remained uncultivated. In the past three years, he had not spent more than thirty days in the parish. His agents, Helen Twitchell (Mrs. Willis), William Mudgett, and John Harrison had tried leasing the lands, but in the prevailing political and economic climate, leasing had obvious pitfalls. In short, these extensive properties, instead of producing revenue, produced unpaid bills and property taxes.

Even Starlight was in trouble. After Helen's death, the on-site management was taken over by Mudgett and Harrison. Mudgett drank too much and made costly mistakes. A routine but essential item of equipment at harvest time, for example, was burlap bagging and cord, used to wrap and tie the heavy cotton bales. In August 1877, Twitchell learned from his commission merchant that the "bagging and ties sent up the river" had been shipped back to New Orleans. This was "one of

23. *John T. Yates for the Use of Love and Scheen v. M. H. Twitchell*, 12 August 1876, MHT Papers; A. F. Coleman to MHT, 14 April 1880, MHT Papers.

24. MHT Papers; MHT to L. B. Watkins, 30 July 1877, MHT Letterbook.

those unfortunate blunders," he wrote disgustedly, "for which Mudgett seems to be remarkable."[25]

As his difficulties mounted, Twitchell was profoundly ambivalent about spending money to defend his interests, as he put it, in "a country where there is no law and where it would be a special act of right and justice in the eyes of most of the community to destroy anything that belonged to me or mine." In mid-1877, he urged Harrison to ship as much cotton as possible from Starlight before the next session of the district court, because, "no one but the devil himself, in whose confidence I am not, knows what these people will do."[26]

In November 1877, five months after Twitchell transferred his Red River property to his mother, Carolyn Gillespie, the principal owner from whom he had purchased Starlight, sued to recover the plantation in the Red River Parish district court. Her attorneys were James and Joseph Pierson, both former members of the White League who in 1874 had been on Deputy Stockton's arrest list. The district judge was David Pierson, the brother of Gillespie's attorneys and an ex-member of the Natchitoches White League. James Pierson had already acted as Yates's attorney against Twitchell. Although unprovable, collusion between Gillespie and the Piersons seems likely. Judge Pierson set a trial date a year hence.

Carolyn Gillespie had inherited Starlight in 1862 from her first husband. Six years later she remarried. In December 1869 Twitchell offered the lady and her new husband, Charles Gillespie, $21,000 for the plantation. Secondary issues, none of which affected Twitchell's bid except that they required him to make his final offer at a sheriff's sale, complicated the purchase. He appeared the day of the sale and bid the amount agreed upon. The distribution of the sale money, paid in three installments, seemed to satisfy both Carolyn Gillespie and her husband. The Gillespies used the proceeds for a down payment on another property called the Turner Place.[27]

During the negotiations and transfer of property, Twitchell had formed a low opinion of Charles Gillespie, an opinion that Carolyn

25. MHT to [John W. Harrison], 20 August 1877, MHT Letterbook.

26. MHT to [John W. Harrison], 23 August 1877, MHT Letterbook.

27. Red River Parish District Court, *Gillespie v. Twitchell*, 15 February 1878, MHT Papers; *Louisiana Annual Reports* 34: 288–300.

Gillespie evidently soon came to share, because a year or so later, she filed for divorce. While the divorce was in progress, she named none other than John T. Yates "as her lawful agent and attorney." When Carolyn Gillespie filed suit to recover Starlight, Charles Gillespie had not been seen in the region for two years, partly, one suspects, because his name, like so many others, was on Deputy Stockton's arrest list.[28]

As the trial drew near, Harrison, in contrast to Mudgett, showed promise of becoming a plantation manager. His elderly sister, who moved from New York to manage the household, aided him. Harrison expressed confidence in attorney L. B. Watkins of Minden and believed the lawsuits were going well. He even managed to work out a settlement in a case he thought Twitchell was certain to lose. He claimed to have made a good impression on the local community: "I firmly believe I can beat Pierson and Co. right here with the help of a jury." He believed his actions had shaken the Piersons' confidence: "I am now all most as popular as if I had helped to rob you and your family." He urged Twitchell to trust him and give him a stronger power of attorney, one that would allow him to sell property and buy provisions from New Orleans. If we both do our parts, he said, "I have no fears for the future."[29]

In mid-September 1878, less than two months before Starlight went to trial, Harrison, his sister, and Mudgett were finishing up a Saturday's work at the plantation store. A bullet shattered the window behind Harrison, and he pitched forward into the arms of sister, dead from a shot through the back of his head. Once again, Coushatta made the New York and Chicago newspapers.[30]

Harrison's death was a hard blow to the Starlight defense. Twitchell could not return for the trial and was forced to present evidence through sworn depositions. A week after Harrison's death, lawyer Watkins wrote Twitchell a long, anxious letter, urging him to prepare his depositions with great care. Watkins wrote with one eye on getting the cases transferred to the Fifth U.S. Circuit Court: "State clearly that the sales made by you to your mother . . . were in *good faith*. . . . State further

28. *CV*, 123–25; Caroline Gillespie's power of attorney to John W. Yates, 11 January 1872, Miscellaneous Records, Red River Parish Courthouse.
29. John W. Harrison to Mother, 3 April 1878, MHT Papers; Harrison to MHT [1878], incomplete letter, MHT Papers.
30. *CV*, 201–2; *New York Times*, 27 September 1878; MHT Scrapbook.

that the price named was actually paid by you to Mrs. E. Twitchell, through her agent, J. W. Harrison. State further . . . that your mother (being then and now a citizen of Vermont) took possession and control of the property sold through J. W. Harrison, Agent." The fact that Twitchell had been crippled by the loss of both arms lent credibility to his claim that he was no longer able to care for the lands himself. "Spare no pains, care or expense," Watkins, advised. "This is particularly necessary since the *unfortunate* death of JW Harrison. We have lost an important witness by his death."[31]

During the trial, Carolyn Gillespie contended that her husband and Twitchell had entered into a "fraudulent conspiracy" to rob her and her children of their property. She had not been allowed to be a party to the negotiations. Her acquiescence in the sale resulted from ignorance and coercion. Furthermore, she had never received any of money from the "pretended sale." As to her signatures on the documents, her statements were contradictory. She initially claimed the signatures were forgeries, but later conceded: "I have no recollection of signing these receipts. I suppose I did sign them, as the signature appears to be mine." Twitchell refuted Mrs. Gillespie's allegations in a sworn deposition. He said she "seemed to be the more anxious of all the parties to make the trade." Her husband had at first rejected his $21,000 offer, and when he refused to go higher, she entered the negotiations, informing him "emphatically that she accepted it."[32]

J. B. Elam—Twitchell's Democratic opponent in the 1874 senate race and one of the most respected lawyers in De Soto Parish—had handled the original sale for the Gillespies. In a sworn deposition, Elam said he knew of no "unlawful advantage" taken of Mrs. Gillespie by Twitchell or her husband: "She never urged any objection to the suit, judgement or sale." Nor was there any doubt in his mind that she had received her share of the money from the sale. The ex-sheriff of De Soto Parish, as well as other Democratic officials, also said there was no evidence of fraud or conspiracy in the sale. Finally, there was the undisputed fact that the Gillespies used the sale money they received

31. L. B. Watkins to MHT, 24 September 1878, MHT Papers.
32. Red River Parish District Court, *Gillespie v. Twitchell*; Watkins brief, Supreme Court of Louisiana, No. 1348, MHT Papers; MHT interrogatory, Case 193, MHT Papers; *Louisiana Annual Reports*, 34: 288–300.

from Twitchell to buy the Turner place, on which Carolyn Gillespie still lived at the time of the trial. Despite the evidence, the jury awarded Starlight and court costs to Carolyn Gillespie and her children.

The Twitchells appealed. The financial strain was heavy. In January 1879 Watkins wrote Twitchell: "Captain, you must send me $700.00 dollars. I have made the fight for you against all odds, prejudice, politics, fraud and and avarice combined. I have never flinched for one moment in the full discharge of my whole duty." The cases require constant vigilance, the lawyer wrote: "I cant tell who to trust." Twitchell clearly had difficulty finding the money. In February, Watkins wired him in Kingston repeatedly: "Will you pay Cash required briefs must be filed Monday"; "Nothing but the cash will answer wont proceed without it"; "Will proceed no further until seven hundred dollars are paid Briefs are not filed." A month later, the lawyer was still demanding his $700. Marshall wired him to take the money out of the lands. Watkins shot back: "To this I do not ascent for the reason that your agents have sold all the crops, stock, farming utensils and have collected the money and deny [having] a cent." Somehow, Twitchell found a way to come up with the money, because Watkins labored on. The Twitchells remained in possession of Starlight until 1882, when the state supreme court upheld the trial verdict.[33]

The companion case to the Gillespie suit was *Stafford, Executor, v. Twitchell et al.* L. A. Stafford was a resident of Rapides Parish who owned 1,518 acres of Red River Parish real estate. The taxes on this land went unpaid from 1871 though 1873, despite frequent notices of the delinquency. In the latter year, Twitchell had helped pass a new law allowing the lands of delinquent taxpayers to be sold at public auction. In July 1874, Twitchell and an associate, Jesse Steel, purchased the Stafford lands at a sheriff's auction, bidding the amount of unpaid taxes, $1,197. By law, Stafford had six months to reclaim the lands by paying the buyers the amount of their purchase. He failed to do so. Steel later sold his interest to Twitchell.

As it turned out, L. A. Stafford was dead. His heir and executor was George A. Stafford. The latter's lawyers made much of the fact that the

33. L. B. Watkins to MHT, 27 January, 9 March 1879, Watkins telegrams to MHT, 1, 11, 15, 23, February 1879, MHT Papers; *Gillespie v. Twitchell*, eviction order, 30 March 1882, MHT Papers; *Louisiana Annual Reports*, 34: 288–300.

tax notices had been sent to "L. H." not "L. A." Stafford. In other words, the landowner (or in this instance the former landowner's heir) was never properly notified. Although his actions were legal, Twitchell's acquisition of the Stafford lands was not calculated to play well in court. The tax collector who levied the taxes was Twitchell's brother. The law required the land to be auctioned in 40-acre plots. Twitchell swore in a deposition that the land was sold in "legal subdivisions of forty acres." At the public auction other parties could have bid on portions of the property. Given the hard times, though, the public resentment of taxes, Judge Pierson on the bench, and a defendant who was now widely regarded as the Prince of Darkness, the jury's verdict in favor of Stafford was inevitable. Again, the Twitchells appealed, but in 1881 the state supreme court upheld the verdict.

Watkins had repeatedly appealed the cases to the United States courts and repeatedly been turned down. The Stafford and Gillespie lawyers in each instance argued that the transfer of property to Elizabeth Twitchell was a "simulated transfer." In 1881 the U.S. Supreme Court turned down the last appeal in the Stafford case.[34]

Between 1876 and 1882, everything Marshall Twitchell owned in Red River Parish, three plantations, his Coushatta lots, and less valuable properties, were lost. Land not taken directly by the courts had to be sold to pay heavy legal expenses. For another decade Twitchell dreamed of recovering his Louisiana lands. At one time he had estimated the value of his Red River properties at $100,000. The figure is not excessive, and it made him by modern standards a millionaire. As late as 1893, he corresponded with lawyer Albert Leonard in New Orleans about suing to recover Starlight, only to back off.[35]

That it was Albert Leonard to whom Twitchell wrote about Starlight was ironic. Twenty years earlier, Leonard had been the principal owner and editor of the *Shreveport Times,* the most influential White League newspaper in all of north Louisiana, perhaps in the state. In a brutal 1874 editorial called the "True Policy," Leonard's paper mentioned

34. Louisiana Supreme Court, *Geo. A. Stafford, Executor, v. M. H. Twitchell et al., Louisiana Annual Reports* (1881), 33: 520–32; MHT interrogatory, case 187, MHT Papers; R. B. Forman brief, Supreme Court of the United States, October term 1881, MHT Papers.

35. Oscar D. Scott to MHT, 1 October 1893, A. H. Leonard to MHT, 14 October 1893, MHT Papers.

Twitchell and a half-dozen other Republican leaders by name and *literally* called for their assassination. Several years later, however, Leonard switched parties, became a Republican, and in 1878 accepted a federal job from President Hayes. That the man who was virtually "Mr. White League" should have turned scalawag and offered to file suit in Twitchell's behalf stands as one of the most stunning apostasies of the period. The historian of Leonard's career has argued that much more than the prospect of a federal job motivated his remarkable conversion. Perhaps so. On the other hand, Major Lewis Merrill may have called it right when he described Leonard as a "reckless but shrewd man . . . with only one hope—that in a storm he may come to the surface."[36]

36. *Shreveport Times*, 15 November 1874; Vandal, "Leonard's Road," 55–76; *House Reports*, 43d Cong., 2d Sess., No. 101, pt. 2, p. 68.

SIXTEEN

KINGSTON

KINGSTON, the "Limestone City," rises on a rocky peninsula at the northeastern end of Lake Ontario where the Saint Lawrence River begins. In the 1840s when it was briefly the Canadian capital, it was a city of great economic and political promise. Then, the capital moved to Toronto, the Saint Lawrence Canal reduced its trade, and the Grand Trunk Railroad bypassed it. By the time Twitchell became consul in 1878, Kingston had become a stately backwater, a modestly progressive town of fifteen thousand inhabitants, graced by some of the most impressive public buildings in Canada. A summer resort city, gateway to the "thousand islands" of the Saint Lawrence and a day's journey from Vermont, it was a good location for Twitchell.

The man whom Twitchell replaced as consul was an Illinois politico named James M. True. In his autobiography, Twitchell describes True "as a natural product of the spoils system," whose goal was to get as much profit out of the consulate as possible, and, said Twitchell, "I do not think he ever let an opportunity escape him." True had annoyed his Foreign Service superiors and made enemies of both of Kingston's daily newspapers. His strained relations with Kingston's commercial establishment were auspicious for Twitchell, because with only modest effort the new consul made his presence seem a welcome improvement.[1]

The American consulate was on Ontario Street in the heart of the city's import-export district. Twitchell looked after the interests of American citizens in Kingston and kept the State Department posted on local politics. Such duties were rarely taxing given Canada's civilized public life and the good relations between the United States and its northern neighbor. Most of the paper that crossed Twitchell's desk each day concerned trade and navigation: customs collections, shipping, tariffs, agricultural policy, and the affairs of transportation, mining, and lumber companies. "Colonel" Twitchell, as the newspapers christened him, approached these matters with a tact and fairness that had been missing in the administration of his predecessor, earning him the admiration and praise of Kingston's business elite.[2]

Twitchell was adept at the consul's ceremonial role. He was a symbol and spokesman of the United States on Canadian soil. When a new mayor was inaugurated, when a visiting English or American dignitary stopped in the city, Twitchell invariably attended the banquet and made appropriate remarks about the strong ties between Canada, the British Empire, and the United States. In 1887 when the U.S. Congress created the Interstate Commerce Commission, Kingston's principal newspapers, the *British Whig* and the *Daily News*, looked to Twitchell for an explanation of the law's ramifications. On a more somber note, the newspapers interviewed him after President James A. Garfield's assassination. Twenty years later Twitchell would comment on the deaths of Queen Victoria and another slain American president, William McKinley.[3]

Twitchell was in his element. Canada enjoyed dominion status in the British Empire. The English-speaking people of Ontario deemed themselves loyal subjects of the British Crown. This allegiance bridged ethnic, class, and geographic lines. It was the underlying basis of political community and patriotism. The bond with England manifested it-

---

1. *CV*, 200; True's official correspondence with the State Department is notably brief. Generally confirming Twitchell's negative assessment, however, is James M. True to Assistant Secretary of State F. W. Seward, 14 July 1877, SDR, M-T472.

2. MHT Scrapbook.

3. Ibid.

self in many ways, in the names of colleges—Queen's University and the Royal Military College—the names of hotels—the Windsor, the British Empire, and the British-American—and in the name of the city's oldest and largest-circulation newspaper, the *British Whig*. A "British subject I was born," said Kingston's most famous citizen, John A. MacDonald, in 1891, and "a British subject I will die." Like many New Englanders, Twitchell was a natural-born Anglophile. This, plus the political skills learned in Louisiana, made him the right man in the right place. He talked easily and sincerely of the economic, political, and religious freedoms of the "two great English-speaking nations." He once toasted "the civilized nations of the world; there are but two of them."[4]

In 1882 the State Department summoned Twitchell to Washington and offered him the post of U.S. minister in Lisbon, Portugal. In that day, a minister was the highest-ranking diplomatic representative of the United States in any foreign country. He talked with the secretary of state, and Senator Kellogg introduced him to President Chester A. Arthur, who was momentarily discomforted by Twitchell's inability to shake hands. After being assured that he could keep his Kingston job if he declined the promotion, Twitchell expressed his heartfelt thanks but nonetheless chose to remain where he was. The reason he gave was the excellence of the Kingston schools.[5]

Twitchell bore the burden of educating four children. There was his oldest son by Adele, Marshall Coleman, who was in secondary school and would soon be old enough to attend Queen's University. Marshall and Henrietta had a two-year-old son named Emmus George (their first child had died) who would be starting school in a few years. Then there were his nephews Burt Holland and Homer King, whom he and Henrietta had taken in. In Lisbon he would have to hire tutors for the four children. Would he be able to find good tutors, and at what cost? Then there was his mother, Elizabeth, who lived with him and Henrietta. Almost certainly, Elizabeth did not want to spend what might be her last years on earth in Portugal.

4. Macdonald was the main author of the British North American Act of 1867 and the first prime minister of the Dominion of Canada. Desmond Morton, *A Short History of Canada*, 2d rev. ed. (Toronto, 1994), 142; MHT Scrapbook.

5. MHT Scrapbook.

Other considerations doubtless influenced his decision. Although he was only forty-two years old, he was no longer in the prime of life. Physically and emotionally, he was older than his years. His dreams of wealth and position had brought him only death and disability. Except for his mother, he alone had survived the family's Louisiana ordeal. In a reckoning measured in the lives of his brother Homer and his three sisters—and their husbands—he had failed as the head of family. How many times he must have asked himself: Why am I the only survivor? There was no answer to the riddle. It had just happened that way. Still, if the past was irredeemable, the present and the future were in some measure within his control. He could meet his new family responsibilities, provide for Henrietta, for his two children, and for the orphans of his slain kinsmen. He could ensure that the boys received a good education, including college, a head start denied to most Americans of that age. This he could do best by remaining in Kingston.

His disability was another consideration. By 1882 he was settled in Kingston, his routine fixed; he was known and respected. Lest we forget, he depended on other people to do almost everything. To go to Lisbon and struggle with Portuguese would be a much bigger adjustment for Twitchell than for most men. In all probability, he did not want to make the adjustment. He wanted to be settled in one place, to have a sense of belonging, to be close to Vermont. All this he had in Kingston.

A political calculation likely influenced his decision, too. Like all consuls, Twitchell served at the pleasure of the president of the United States. Just as his predecessor was a product of the spoils system; so too was he. If a Democrat won the next presidential election, a distinct possibility, Twitchell probably would be dismissed from his post, whether in Kingston or Lisbon. The thought of moving to Portugal and then, after only two years, moving back to Vermont was unsettling. He may also have calculated that under a Democratic administration he would stand a better chance of hanging onto the Kingston consulate than the Lisbon ministry, a much higher-profile appointment.

His concerns about presidential patronage proved well founded. In 1884 Democrat Grover Cleveland won the White House. "Is Twitchell still in office?" north Louisiana newspapers asked after the new president's inauguration. The entire Louisiana congressional delegation was soon demanding his dismissal. The Kingston consulate, one congressman wrote Cleveland, was a reward for Twitchell's Louisiana villainy:

He "was one of the most corrupt of the carpet bag members of the legislature" and "made himself odious to the best people of North Louisiana." For Twitchell, one of the pleasures of Kingston must have been that the word *carpetbagger* was seemingly denied entry by Canada's protective tariff. Neither of the city newspapers—nor the Montreal or Toronto papers—ever applied the term to him. On the contrary, they praised him as one of the best consuls in Canada.[6] The *British Whig* on one occasion called him the "Louisiana hero."[7]

In the winter and spring of 1885, Kingston rallied to his defense. In an impressive display of support, both newspapers, civic leaders, and the heads of Kingston's leading manufacturing, mining, and shipping companies appealed to President Cleveland for Twitchell's retention. The Grand Army of the Republic (GAR) backed him, too. Even with such support, Twitchell probably would have lost his place except that his likely replacement Vice Consul Mathew H. Folger, a Democrat, spoke up on his behalf. "Col Twitchell," Folger wrote, "is universally popular with the large number of American Citizens here, an exceedingly efficient officer, and . . . having lost both of his arms . . . is dependent on this position for the maintenance of himself and family." Folger's letter resonated with sincerity: "My democratic principles and good wishes . . . exceed my desire for the Office, and I would for this reason prefer Colonel Twitchell should retain it, than I should gain it." Had Twitchell gone to Lisbon, the outcome almost certainly would have been different. Of three dozen U.S. foreign ministers around the world, only one survived the new president's patronage ax.[8]

Eight years later, Twitchell ran the patronage gauntlet again when Cleveland, after being defeated in 1888, won a second term in 1892. In fact, any of the Gilded Age presidents could have dismissed him. In 1897 he worried over the inauguration of William McKinley, once again marshaling his support in Kingston and from the GAR. It was six months into McKinley's administration before he learned that he would be kept on.[9]

6. Ibid.

7. Ibid.

8. Ibid.; MHT appointment file, SDR, NA; Mathew H. Folger to T. F. Bayard, 2 April 1885, SDR, M-T472; William Barnes and John Heath Morgan, *The Foreign Service of the United States* (1961; reprint, Westport, Conn., 1978), 140.

9. MHT Scrapbook.

The years in Kingston slipped by. Periodically he heard from old Republican comrades that he had known in Louisiana. Kellogg kept in touch and was always available to write a letter of support to new presidents. "After the downfall of the Republican Party in La," one old Unionist judge wrote Twitchell, "I took Greeley's advice and went West . . . in the search of an Eldorado." The judge was practicing law in Colorado Springs and looking after his children and grandchildren. He looked forward to seeing Twitchell again: Our friendship "was made & ripened in times when they tried mens souls."[10]

In 1890 Twitchell corresponded with Andy Bosley, asking about his former landholdings in Red River Parish and about old friends and enemies. Starlight, Bosley replied, had passed to new owners. Up until his death two years before, the former White Leaguer Joseph Pierson, one of Carolyn Gillespie's attorneys, had owned the Homer Twitchell house in Coushatta, centerpiece of the imaginary 1874 Negro rebellion. Another old enemy, John T. Yates, had died the past fall. Their former ally, the black preacher Benjamin Perrow, was still living in the parish and doing well. William Mudgett was living at Bayou Pierre, but Bosley said nothing about how Starlight's onetime business manager was faring. The letter closed: "Your true Friend Andy Bosley address Coushatta La."[11]

Twitchell's salary was about $1,500 a year, plus fees—a substantive supplement—for consular services in Kingston and outlying stations. The combined income, salary and fees, provided Twitchell and his wife a comfortable middle-class existence. It enabled Twitchell to make modest investments in the Whitewater Railroad Company in southern Vermont and to enter into a partnership in a dry-goods and millinery store in Saint Albans, F. F. Twitchell, & Co., with his cousin Fred. Formed in 1882, the partnership lasted into the twentieth century.[12]

Each morning, from a rental house in a residential neighborhood, Twitchell took the tram into the consulate. Marshall Coleman went to Queen's University and in 1893 graduated from the University of Vermont Medical College. Emmus George, a decade younger than his

10. William H. Heistand to MHT, 5 January 1890, MHT Papers.
11. Andy Bosley to MHT, 18 February 1890, MHT Papers.
12. Stock certificates, MHT Papers; Fred W. Twitchell letters, MHT Papers.

half-brother, grew up in Kingston. As a child, Emmus was curious about his father not having arms. He knew from things adults said in his presence that his father's disability was connected with a faraway place named Louisiana where terrible things happened. The particulars, however, were a mystery to him. His father never talked to him about Louisiana.

Years later, after his father's death, Emmus recorded some of his childhood memories. When he was very small, he recalled, "Mother would put me on father's shoulders for him to take me down to the dining room. My mother would walk behind him to see I did not fall off. I suspect my father enjoyed this as he could not touch me except with his head." Father, he said, "very often put his face on my head. The only gesture of affection he could make. I remember once with the brutality and non-understanding of childhood I said, 'Don't wipe your nose on my head.' I do not think he ever told my mother or I would have been punished severely." Father's "feelings must have been badly hurt."

If "father had a cold," Emmus explained, "a towel was tied on the newel post upstairs so he could wipe his nose and not have to ask someone to take out his handkerchief." Emmus remembered a small bronze panther with erect tail, which was kept on the mantel shelf over the fireplace: "Father would move this around with his nose until the tail was headed towards him and then scratch one ear and then the other on the tail." Father "could put on his own rubbers using the other foot, open a latched door but could not turn a knob. He could write if a pen was put in his hand, sign his name or even write a short letter. He never complained and only when necessary would he ask for help. We all generally knew what he wanted before he had to ask." When he went shopping, Emmus's father would tell the clerk the things he needed: "The clerk would take money from his pocket, return any change. The package was put in his pocket or delivered. Everyone knew him and would open doors for him." On one occasion, Emmus climbed "up a metal fire escape ladder at the back of the house. I had gone up two or three rungs when father discovered me, ran out and leaned against me so I could not go up any further nor fall down. He yelled for the housekeeper who ran out and took me down."

As a schoolboy, Emmus said, "I used to give him his meals, sitting across the corner of the table from him and fed myself at the same time. If I got over-enthusiastic feeding myself he would give me a nudge with his knee and I would promptly get back to him." Another of Emmus's duties was the lowering and raising of flags at the consulate: "Father was very punctilious about having the U.S. Consulate flag up when indicated for half mast or full mast," and equally punctilious about the British flag.

Kingston civic leaders frequently hosted lavish banquets honoring visiting English and American dignitaries. Emmus's father invariably attended and made remarks appropriate to the occasion. "When I was old enough I went with him," Emmus recalled. "He never ate anything but did have to drink the toasts and I held the glass for him. Each place was set with different glasses for the various wines. They were kept filled. Once I decided the red wine at my place looked good and started to drink it. I was promptly reprimanded by my father and never tried it again."

When he was older and a student at Queen's University, Emmus became a clerk in the consulate. He recalled the 1901 visit of the duke of York (the future king of England George V) and his duchess. At the reception, said Emmus, "Father and I were in line (I had to take off his hat). When he passed the reception line he had to explain to the Duke why he could not shake hands. The Duke held him in conversation for quite a while."[13]

In mid-February 1898, news of the sinking of the battleship *Maine* in Havana Harbor reverberated through Kingston and around the world. Two months later on 25 April, the United States and Spain went to war over Cuba. A few weeks later, a battalion of New York volunteers stopped over in Kingston en route to the war zone. The soldiers were feted and dined at the Hotel Frontenac. The high point of the banquet—at least from the perspective of the press—was Colonel Twitchell's remarks depicting Spain's presence in the Western Hemisphere as a "festering sore." The war's outcome was not in doubt, he said, because the "liberation of Cuba" was "divinely ordered." He praised Great Britain's neutrality in the war and looked forward to the day, he said, when England and America, "the dominant race of the world, united by blood and civilization, will be by themselves a concert

13. Undated "EGT" [Emmus George Twitchell] narrative in possession of Mary Twitchell, Burlington, Vt.

of powers to protect the weak, liberate the oppressed and carry the civilization of the cross to every part of the world."[14]

The day after Twitchell's speech the Kingston newspapers reported the capture of two Spanish spies, one at Tampa and the other at Key West. The man arrested at Key West was a Spanish naval officer. The man detained in Tampa was a Canadian named "Frank Miller" (an alias) who falsely claimed to be an ex-member of the Northwest Mounted Police. Had he not been bound by secrecy, Twitchell in his speech at the Frontenac Hotel could have shed much light on these spy stories and riveted his audience's attention far more than he did with his jingoist remarks about Spain.[15]

In late April, when the United States and Spain broke diplomatic relations, the Spanish ambassador and his staff left Washington and moved to Canada. In the weeks that followed, Ramon de Carranza, the Spanish naval attaché, organized a spy ring out of Montreal to report on American army and naval movements. Aware of the threat, a special unit of the U.S. Secret Service shadowed Carranza and his known operatives. On 7 May, the Secret Service arrested one of Carranza's agents in Washington, D.C. Ten days later, the case broke wide open in Twitchell's office.

A young man named Prenter showed up unannounced at the consulate. As Twitchell described him, Prenter was "bright, intelligent, well-dressed, and fully loaded with Whisky." He rendered a British soldier's smart salute and asked to see Twitchell in private. Once seated in the consul's office, he launched into a rambling narrative. He said that he was an ex-British soldier who had been stationed at nearby Fort Henry and knew Twitchell by sight—indeed, had often saluted him. He confessed that he had become involved in something very foolish and hazardous. Under the influence of liquor, he had made an agreement with agents of the Spanish government and accepted money from them. He wanted to get out of the deal, but he had spent all of the money and could not even pay his hotel bill. In the course of this monologue, the young man kept pulling things from his pockets, army discharge papers, playing cards, trinkets, a train ticket to San Francisco, even a medal. He was *very* drunk. Twitchell heard Prenter out, then escorted him to the door with instructions to return the next day. The consul then investi-

14. *Kingston British Whig,* 25 May 1898.
15. Ibid., 26 May 1898.

gated the items left on his desk. Soon afterward he telegraphed the State Department. The assistant secretary of state promptly ordered copies of Twitchell's wire sent to the War and Navy Departments and the Secret Service.

The next day Prenter returned, unable to remember everything that he had said the day before, but very much aware that he had left many of his personal effects in Twitchell's office. The full story now came out. After his army discharge, Prenter had taken a job with the Pabst Brewing Company in Montreal. When the war broke out, two Spanish agents calling themselves "Haynes" and "Miller," had contacted him. The two men spent money freely and after feeling Prenter out, hired him as a spy. They gave him one hundred dollars for a train ticket to San Francisco and a large silver ring bearing the inscription "Confienza Augustina" on the inside. According to his instructions, once he reached San Francisco, he was to enlist in an American army unit heading for the Philippines, whereupon he would amass information about the American forces. In the battle zone, he would desert or allow himself to be captured. The silver ring with its hidden inscription would identify him to the Spanish commander as a spy. He would then report all that he had learned. Prenter believed other ex-British soldiers had been employed for similar missions.

Although this spy plot sounds like something Tom Sawyer and Huck Finn might have dreamed up, it was a real threat. The Secret Service traced the silver ring to a Montreal jeweler who had made five identical rings, all with same hidden inscription. The real identities of "Haynes" and "Miller" were uncovered and their connections to Carranza traced. Both were arrested in Tampa, Florida. The principal of the pair, Frank Mellor, was the "Frank Miller" mentioned in the news edition that reported Twitchell's Kingston speech. Carranza was later expelled from Canada. Twitchell was understandably gratified by his role in the case. The State Department thanked him profusely and gave him his own telegraphic cipher code and special operations fund. It "made me feel," Twitchell said, "that notwithstanding my physical condition, I had perhaps been able to do as much for the benefit of my nation as I would have done if I had taken the field."[16]

16. *CV*, 203–5; MHT to Assistant Secretary of State J. B. Moore, 17, 21, 31 May 1898, SDR, M-T472; Rhodri Jeffreys-Jones, *American Espionage: From Secret Service to CIA* (New York, 1977), 29–33.

Twitchell was acutely conscious of history. He joined the Kingston Historical Society and after being elected president, commissioned a city
history. "Thirty years ago," he wrote his old friend from the 109th
USCT Charles W. Smith, who was still living in Indianapolis, "we were
engaged in making history and now until we pass off the stage I think
it our duty to correct mis-statements which are likely to be formed into
history and thereby mislead others yet to come." He was active in 109th
USCT reunions (the 1899 meeting was in Kingston). He gave public
talks on the Civil War before church groups, the Kingston YMCA, at
festivals, and veterans meetings. His favorite theme was one he developed in an 1894 Memorial Day speech to a Montreal GAR post. On
this day, as in years past, he said, we commemorate the great war for
the Union and absent comrades: "In imagination we again drink our
coffee from the blackened cup" and "fry our meat in the half canteen."
He celebrated the heroic conduct of Vermont's citizen-soldiers in the
Battle of the Wilderness. The Green Mountain boys and their brothers
in blue, he claimed, were molded from "superior clay."[17]

Exactly when the idea came to him to write his autobiography is unknown. It probably germinated in his mind over many years. His role
in breaking the Carranza spy ring may have spurred his confidence in
thinking of himself as a historical figure. His age was another factor. He
was nearly sixty at the time of the Spanish-American War. His father,
his brother and sisters, and many old army comrades were already dead.
His mother died in 1899. Henrietta was ill. Twitchell himself had a her-
nia and wore a truss (he would later undergo surgery). If he was going
to write about his life, it was time to do so. Sometime around the turn
of the century, he began dictating the story, probably to a clerk in the
consulate, perhaps his son Emmus.

Whatever the conscious motivation behind the manuscript "Autobiography of Marshall Harvey Twitchell," the deeper motivation, one
suspects, was emotional closure. In a way that few Americans have ever
experienced, his life had been ripped apart in the prime of his years. A
quarter-century is a long time to a youth of twenty, but to a man in his
late fifties it can seem like yesterday. The pain of personal tragedy such
as Twitchell had experienced is with a person always. Indeed, as applied

17. MHT to Charles W. Smith, 1 October 1890, Smith Papers; MHT Papers; MHT
Scrapbook.

to Twitchell, the phrase "personal tragedy" is almost a euphemism. Counting Adele and her baby, nine members of his family—all young and vital people—had died in the three-year span 1873–1876, four of them brutally murdered. Twitchell himself had been horribly maimed and later stripped of his property. Short of a Job or Saint Francis, no human being could have avoided severe and permanent psychological trauma. Such wounds would scab over, the pain diminish, but they would never truly heal. Twitchell compensated well. He remarried, raised another family, and became a highly successful consul. Still, not a day passed, perhaps not a waking hour, in which his thoughts did not dwell on Coushatta. There were always his missing arms to remind him.

Many years before, in 1875 when he was still a whole man and first engaged to Henrietta, he had written her about a disturbing dream. In the dream, he stood in a room with his weeping sisters, crying over their murdered husbands. Bent upon vengeance, he tried to leave, but Henrietta appeared before him in the doorway. He tried to go around her, once, twice, even three times; each way he turned, she blocked the way. He assured Henrietta at the time that the dream was most unusual; indeed, he rarely dreamed at all, he said. The latter statements are highly suspect. When he wrote the letter, he was newly engaged and afraid for his life and property. A man beset by such woes was apt to see himself as a poor marriage risk and fearful of his fiancée changing her mind. (He mentioned releasing Henrietta in the letter.) In other words, Twitchell likely felt a compelling need to tell Henrietta about the torturous dream, while at the same time reassuring her that such dreams were infrequent, lest she think him mentally disturbed. (The word "madman" appears in his description of the dream.) One suspects the truth was otherwise, that in his distraught mental state, the dreams came to him often, three and four nights a week, and perhaps became even more agonizing after he lost his arms and Helen died in Indianapolis. Even in the 1890s, now and again in his sleep, he likely revisited the dark and bloody ground of Red River Parish.

His autobiography, then, was an effort to come to terms with his violent past. The work began with historiography: "There is no part of the history of the United States of which in a few years so little will be known as that portion which may be designated as the 'Reconstruction period' of the Southern states. There is no equal time of which so much was published that was false and so little that was true." Twitchell's historiographical prediction was prescient. William A. Dunning, the founder of the "Dunning School," was just beginning his career as the foremost Reconstruction scholar of his generation. For the next half-century the ideas of Dunning, his graduate students, and like-minded scholars—John W. Burgess, Claude G. Bowers, E. Merton Coulter, and many others—would dominate Reconstruction historical writing. In the Dunning tradition, Reconstruction is a sordid tale of corruption and abuse of power. Ignorant and barbaric black men, carpetbag villains, and turncoat scalawags seize power in the southern states and run roughshod of the rights of the southern people, i.e., southern whites. These racketeering Republican politicos loot state treasuries, rob white southerners of their lands, rights, and dignity, and bequeath a legacy of racial enmity that lasts for decades.

Twitchell had probably never heard of Dunning, much less read his *Essays on the Civil War and Reconstruction*, but he did not need to be a scholar to catch the direction of the wind. Years before Dunning published his first book on Reconstruction, the basic ideas of Dunningism were already in place in untold thousands of newspaper editorials and Democratic campaign speeches dating back to the 1860s. And before Dunning finished his second book or any of his graduate students published their dissertations, the dark legend of Reconstruction was already becoming a staple of popular fiction. About the time Twitchell began work on his autobiography, Thomas Nelson Page's *Red Rock*, followed in 1902 by Thomas Dixon's *The Leopard's Spots*, became best-sellers. The plot climax of each of these novels is the rape of a lovely white girl by a brutal, apelike black man, followed by the overthrow of Reconstruction. Dixon used the same formula in a sequel, *The Clansman*, which in 1905 was the fourth best-selling book in America and later became the basis of the famous silent film *The Birth of a Nation*. By the early 1900s, in other words, what modern historians call Dunningism was already enshrined in historical myth, above and below the Mason-Dixon Line.

Upon completion, Twitchell's autobiography was 248 legal-size typescript pages. He devoted about a third of the work to his experiences as a soldier. As the letter he wrote Charles Smith, mentioned above, shows, he believed his generation had saved the Union and carved a permanent place in the nation's history. While he was working on the autobiography, he received an invitation to the consecration of the Anglican bishop of Kingston. Academics and churchmen came in full regalia. Military and other government officials wore elegant uniforms. One of the last photographs of Twitchell is in a Civil War officer's uniform—tailored for the occasion—which he wore to the ceremony.

Most of the autobiography is about Reconstruction. This carpetbag version of the postwar era turns the "tragic legend" of Reconstruction—so dear to the white South—on its head. In Twitchell's simple morality tale, young northerners such as himself were the natural leaders of the Republican coalitions in the South. They were courageous, candid, and honest men, he claimed, "who zealously worked for nearly ten years to substitute the civilization of freedom for that of slavery." The so-called "redeemers," on the other hand, were a wicked lot, "reared under the demoralizing influence of slavery, traitors to their government for four years and then gamblers and barroom loafers." Addicted to whiskey and violence, Twitchell believed, southern Democrats employed murder as just another tool of the political trade. Given what happened to himself and his family, Twitchell's bitterness is understandable. Still, his narrative distorts history far less than those of Page or Dixon or the Dunning School. However biased in tone, his account of Reconstruction's overthrow in the Red River Valley, especially the body count, is basically factual; something that cannot be said of the Dunning School. It is doubtful, though, that the facts made the ghostly shadows of Coushatta easier to live with. The bitter motif that runs through the entire work suggests that words could never erase the heartbreak of those years.

After a long illness Henrietta died in 1902. Her long life with Twitchell, in the same household with his mother, is basically a mystery. None of her letters have survived, and her husband's autobiography tells us virtually nothing of their life together. In the tradition of nineteenth-century memoirists, he wrote about his public life. His private life was private. In 1905 Twitchell had been in Kingston for twenty-seven years. He had now served longer in one place than any consul in the U.S. Foreign Service. That summer, he took his annual holiday in Vermont. Only a few days after his return to Kingston, he suffered a stroke. Three days later on 21 August at four o'clock in the morning, without ever regaining consciousness, he died with his sons Emmus and Marshall Coleman at his bedside.[18]

Glowing obituaries appeared in both of Kingston's newspapers. The *Ottawa Globe* said he was one of Kingston's most honored citizens "Whose Death is Mourned Throughout Canada." Consul Twitchell, said the paper, "was a soldier and a patriot, a gentleman and a scholar, in the fullest sense of the terms, and was above all a kind-hearted man who gave ungrudgingly of his time and talents to every worthy cause." Flattering obituaries also appeared in the *Montreal Daily Star* and other Canadian papers, in Vermont, Boston and the upper Midwest. The *Detroit News-Tribune* aptly described him as "A Man of Battles," the *Kingston British Whig* perhaps wrote the best epitaph: "he served his country in war and peace, and was faithful unto death."

After a Kingston funeral, Emmus and Marshall Coleman, both men now doctors, shipped their father's body home to Townshend, Vermont. He was buried in a cemetery outside of town less than a mile from where he had been born sixty-five years before. He lay with Henrietta, his mother and father, and the "dust of kindred."[19]

The scales of history are calibrated in many ways. Marshall Twitchell was never truly a famous man, and if he had never lived, the North would still have won the Civil War—Reconstruction would still have ended as it did. Twitchell, though, was a more interesting man, and a better man, than many of those to whom Americans have raised monuments. In the long and troubled history of American race relations, he lived his life more on the side of the solution than the problem, no small achievement when one recognizes that during Twitchell's lifetime, a majority of his countrymen came to regard the oppression of African Americans as akin to social improvement or reform. And if he did not perform epic deeds, he was an actor in epic events—the Peninsula campaign, Gettysburg, the Wilderness, the USCT, the Freedmen's Bureau, and both the beginning and the end of Radical Reconstruction. His life was a Yankee odyssey of the Civil War era. Finally, during the overthrow of Reconstruction on the upper Red River, the "Time of Blood," he achieved epic stature through suffering. The inhuman scale of his

18. Peggy Twitchell Scrapbook.
19. Ibid.

ordeal haunts the imagination. Twitchell becomes a metaphor for the
real tragedy of Reconstruction, the crushing of the closest thing to liberal democracy the South had ever known—or would know again for
a hundred years—and the blighted hopes of millions of black people.
Twitchell's story speaks to the white South's stubborn persistence in the
1870s, as in 1861, in choosing the road that guaranteed the greatest suffering for the greatest number of its people.[20]

20. MHT Scrapbook.

BIBLIOGRAPHY

PRIMARY SOURCES

Manuscripts

Baker Library, Harvard Business School, Cambridge, Mass.
   R. G. Dun & Co. Collection.
Cammie G. Henry Research Center, Northwestern State University of Louisiana, Natchitoches, La.
   Roach Collection.
   Ellen L. Nachman Collection.
   Melrose Collection.
   Judge R. B. Williams Collection.
Indiana Historical Society, Indianapolis, Ind.
   Charles W. Smith Papers.
Louisiana State Archives, Baton Rouge, La.
   State Commission Books, 1868–1877.
   HRS, State Department of Education Records.
National Archives, Washington, D.C.
   RG 15: Civil War Pension Files.
   RG 59: State Department Records.
   RG 60: Department of Justice Records. Microfilm M-940, reel 2.
   RG 94:
      Adjutant General's Office, Bureau of Colored Troops.
      Adjutant General's Office M-666.
      Carded Medical Records, Fourth Vermont Regiment and 109th USCT.
      Compiled Military Service Records.
      Fourth Vermont and 109th USCT Regimental Books and Papers.

USCT Register of Applications, 1863–1865.

U.S. Military Posts, 1800–1916. M-617, reel 258.

RG 105: Bureau of Refugees, Freedmen, and Abandoned Lands.

RG 393:

United States Army Continental Commands.

Military Division of Western Louisiana.

Coushatta Post Records.

District Upper Red River.

Prescott Memorial Library, Louisiana Tech University, Ruston, La.

Marshall Harvey Twitchell Papers.

Private Collections

Clark Holland Letters. In the possession of Clark Holland, Medfield, Mass.

Twitchell Family Scrapbook. In the possession of Peggy Twitchell, Burlington, Vt.

Twitchell, Marshall Harvey. Papers in the possession of Mary Twitchell, Burlington, Vt.

Tulane University

Pierson Family Papers, Kuntz Collection

Vermont Historical Society.

Rufus Kinsley Diary.

Civil War Letters of Peter M. Abbott.

Timothy Kieley Diary.

Courthouse Records

Bienville Parish Conveyance Records, Bienville, La.

Red River Parish Conveyance Records, Coushatta, La.

Government Documents

Acts of the State of Louisiana.

Annual Report of the State Superintendent of Public Education. New Orleans, 1869–1876.

Records of Louisiana Confederate Soldiers and Louisiana Confederate Commands. Compiled by Andrew B. Booth. 3 vols. New Orleans, 1920.

Digest of the Laws of the State of Louisiana, in Two Volumes. New Orleans, 1870.

HRS, "County-Parish Boundaries in Louisiana," New Orleans, 1939.

Louisiana House Debates.

Louisiana House Journal.

Louisiana Senate Journal.

Official Journal of the Proceedings of the Convention for Framing a Constitution for the State of Louisiana. New Orleans, 1868.

Report of the Joint Committee of the General Assembly of Louisiana on the Conduct of the State Elections. New Orleans, 1869.

Statistics Relating to the Soldiers and Expenses of the Town of Townshend, Vt. Brattleboro, Vt., 1874.

U.S. Bureau of the Census. Federal Manuscript Census, Population, 1850, 1860, 1870, 1880.

U.S. Bureau of the Census. Federal Manuscript Census, Agriculture, 1850, 1860, 1870, 1880.

Revised Roster of Vermont Volunteers, 1861–1866. Montpelier, Vt., 1892.

Revised United States Army Regulations of 1861, updated 1863. Washington, D.C., 1863.

Congressional Documents: Serials

1435. "Louisiana Contested Elections." *House Miscellaneous Documents,* 41st Cong., 2d Sess., No. 154, pts. 1–2.

1629. Louisiana Affairs, 1874–1875. Senate Executive Documents, 43d Cong., 2d Sess., No. 13.

1629. "Affairs in Louisiana." 1874. *Senate Executive Documents,* 43d Cong., 2d Sess., No. 17.

1657. "Affairs in Louisiana." *House Reports,* 43d Cong., 2d Sess., No. 101, pts. 1–2.

1660. "Louisiana Affairs." *House Reports,* 43d Cong., 2d Sess., No. 261.

1716. "Federal Officers in Louisiana" and "Coushatta Affair." *House Reports,* 44th Cong., 1st Sess., No. 816.

1735–1737. Louisiana in 1876. *Senate Reports,* 44th Cong., 2d Sess., No. 701, 3 vols.

1735. Army in the South. *House Executive Documents,* 44th Cong., 2d Sess., No. 30.

1765–1767. Presidential Election Investigation, 1876. *House Miscellaneous Documents,* 44th Cong., 2d Sess., No. 34, pts. 1–6.

1840. "Louisiana and South Carolina in 1878." *Senate Reports,* 45th Cong., 3d Sess., No. 855, pts. 1–2.

1864–1865. "Presidential Election Investigation" (Potter Commission). *House Miscellaneous Documents,* 45th Cong., 3d Sess., No. 31, pts. 1–4.

1896. "Spofford v. Kellogg." *Senate Reports,* 46th Cong., 2d Sess., No. 388.

1899–1900. "Negro Exodus from Southern States." *Senate Reports,* 46th Cong., 2d Sess., No. 693, pts. 1–3.

Newspapers

Alexandria Louisiana Democrat
Atlanta Constitution
Bienville Messenger
Bossier Banner
Brattleboro Vermont Phoenix
Chicago Inter-Ocean

Chicago Tribune
Coushatta Citizen (special historical edition, 17 June 1938)
Coushatta Times, (MHT Papers)
Indianapolis Journal
Indianapolis Sentinal
Natchitoches People's Vindicator
New Orleans Crescent
New Orleans Picayune
New Orleans Republican
New York Times
New York Tribune
Opelousas Courier
Shreveport Times
Sparta Times (MHT Papers)
West Baton Rouge Sugar Planter

Published Documents, Contemporary Documents, Memoirs

Appleton's American Annual Cyclopaedia and Register of Important Events (1862–1877). New York, 1863–1878.

Berlin, Ira et al., eds. *Freedom: A Documentary History of Emancipation, 1861–1867.* Series 2, The Black Military Experience. New York, 1982.

Bryan, Mary E. *Wild Work: The Story of the Red River Tragedy.* New York, 1881.

Brooks, Noah. *Washington, D.C., in Lincoln's Time.* Edited with new commentary by Herbert Mitgang. Chicago, 1971.

Catalogues of the Officers and Students of Leland Seminary. Bellows Falls, Vt., 1853–1860. Archives of the Vermont Historical Society, Montpelier, and the University of Vermont, Burlington.

Commager, Henry Steele, ed. *The Blue and the Gray: The Story of the Civil War as Told by Participants.* New York, 1950.

A Compilation of the Messages and Papers of the Presidents, 1789–1897 . . . Compiled by James D. Richardson. 10 vols. Washington, D.C., 1896–1899.

Thomas W. Cutrer and Michael Parrish, eds. *Brothers in Gray: The Civil War Letters of the Pierson Family.* Baton Rouge, 1997.

De Forest, John W. *A Union Officer in the Reconstruction.* Edited by James H. Croushore and David M. Potter. Hamden, Conn., 1968.

Dodd, Ira S. *The Song of the Rappahannock: Sketches of the Civil War.* New York, 1887.

Eisenberg, Albert C. " 'The 3d Vermont *has won a name*': Corporal George Q. French's Account of the Battle of Lee's Mills, Virginia," *Vermont History*, 47 (1981): 223–31.

Fish, Hamilton. Diary. Library of Congress, Washington, D.C.

Fleming, Walter L., ed. *Documentary History of Reconstruction.* 2 vols., 1906–1907. Reprint, New York, 1966.

Greeley, Horace. *Recollections of a Busy Life.* 1868. Reprint, Miami, 1969.

Hyde, Thomas F. *Following the Greek Cross: Or Memories of the Sixth Corps.* Boston, 1894.

Johnson, Robert Underwood, and Clarence Clough Buel, eds., *Battles and Leaders of the Civil War.* 4 vols. (1887–1888). Reprint, with new introduction by Roy F. Nichols, New York, 1956.

Keen, W.W. "Military Surgery in 1861 and in 1918," *Annals of the American Academy of Political and Social Science*, 80 (1918): 11–22.

King, Edward. *The Great South.* Edited by W. Magruder Drake and Robert R. Jones. Reprint, Baton Rouge, 1972.

Livermore, Thomas L. *Days and Events, 1860–1866.* Boston, New York, 1920.

Lockett, Samuel H. *Louisiana As It Is: A Geographical and Topographical Description of the State.* Edited and with an introduction by Lauren C. Post. Baton Rouge, 1970.

MacDonald, George A., ed. "The Bloody Seven Days' Battles," *Vermont Quarterly*, n.s., 15 (1947): 230–35.

Moore, Frank, ed. *The Civil War in Song and Story, 1860–1865.* New York, 1889.

Murdoch, James E., ed. *Patriotism in Poetry and Prose.* Philadelphia, 1866.

Reid, Whitelaw. *After the War: A Tour of the Southern States, 1865–1866.* Edited by C. Vann Woodward. New York, 1965.

Post, Marie Caroline, ed. *The Life and Memoirs of Comte Régis de Trobriand . . . by His Daughter. . . .* New York, 1910.

Rosenblatt, Emil, ed. *Anti-Rebel: The Civil War Letters of Wilbur Fisk.* Croton-on-Hudson, N.Y., 1983.

Riling, Joseph R. *Baron von Steuben and His Regulations.* Philadelphia, 1966.

Stevens, George T. *Three Years in the Sixth Corps.* 1866. Reprint, Alexandria, Va., 1984.

Tourgée, Albion W. *A Fool's Errand.* Edited by John Hope Franklin. 1879. Reprint, Cambridge, Mass., 1961.

Tunnell, Ted, ed. *Carpetbagger from Vermont: The Autobiography of Marshall Harvey Twitchell.* Baton Rouge, 1989.

Warmoth, Henry Clay. *War, Politics, and Reconstruction: Stormy Days in Louisiana.* New York, 1930.

Wheeler, Richard, ed. *Sword over Richmond: An Eyewitness History of McClellan's Peninsula Campaign.* New York, 1986.

SECONDARY ACCOUNTS

Books and Essays in Books

Aldrich, Lewis Cass. *History of Franklin and Grand Isle Counties.* Syracuse, N.Y., 1891.

Anderson, Eric, and Alfred A. Moss Jr., eds. *The Facts of Reconstruction: Essays in Honor of John Hope Franklin.* Baton Rouge, 1991.

Ashkenazi, Elliott. *The Business of Jews in Louisiana, 1840–1875.* Tuscaloosa, Ala., 1988.

Barnes, William, and John Heath Morgan. *The Foreign Service of the United States.* 1961. Reprint, Westport, Conn., 1978.

Barra, Allen. *Inventing Wyatt Earp: His Life and Many Legends.* New York, 1998.

Bearse, Ray, ed. *Vermont: A Guide to the Green Mountain State.* 2d rev. ed. New York, 1966.

Bellesiles, Michael A. *Revolutionary Outlaws: Ethan Allen and the Struggle for Independence on the Early American Frontier.* Charlottesville, Va., 1993.

Benedict, George G. *Vermont in the Civil War.* 2 vols. Burlington, Vt., 1886–1888.

Bienville Parish Historical Society. *History of Bienville Parish.* Bienville, La., 1984.

Biographical and Historical Memoirs of Northwest Louisiana. Nashville and Chicago, 1890.

Boatner, Mark M. *The Civil War Dictionary.* New York, 1959.

Braudel, Fernand. *Civilization and Capitalism, 15th–18th Century: The Wheels of Commerce.* New York, 1982.

Burlingame, Roger. *March of the Iron Men: A Social History of Union through Invention.* New York, 1938.

Burnham, W. Dean. *Presidential Ballots, 1832–1892.* 1955. Reprint, New York, 1976.

Carleton, R. L. *Local Government and Administration in Louisiana.* Baton Rouge, 1935.

Carrigan, Jo Ann. *The Saffron Scourge: A History of Yellow Fever in Louisiana, 1796–1905.* Lafayette, La., 1994.

Carter, Dan. T. *Scottsboro: A Tragedy of the American South.* Rev. ed. Baton Rouge, 1979.

Cash, Wilbur J. *The Mind of the South.* New York, 1941.

Catton, Bruce. *Mr. Lincoln's Army.* New York, 1951.

———. *Glory Road.* New York, 1952.

Coddington, Edwin B. *The Gettysburg Campaign: A Study in Command.* New York, 1968.

Coleman, J. P. *The Robert Coleman Family: From Virginia to Texas, 1652–1965.* Ackerman, Miss., 1965.

Cornish, Dudley Taylor. *The Sable Arm: Negro Troops in the Union Army, 1861–1865.* 2d ed. New York, 1966.

Current, Richard N. *Those Terrible Carpetbaggers.* New York, 1988.

Currie-McDaniel, Ruth. *Carpetbagger of Conscience: A Biography of John Emory Bryant.* Athens, Ga., 1987.

Cutler, Howard Walden. *History of Leland and Gray Seminary*. Bellows Falls, Vt., 1927.

Davis, William C. *Lincoln's Men: How President Lincoln Became Father to an Army and a Nation*. New York, 1999.

Dawson, Joseph G. *Army Generals and Reconstruction: Louisiana, 1862–1877*. Baton Rouge, 1982.

Degler, Carl N. *The Other South: Southern Dissenters in the Nineteenth Century*. New York, 1974.

Duncan, Russell. *Freedom's Shore: Tunis Campbell and the Georgia Freedmen*. Athens, Ga., 1986.

Elting, John R. et al. *A Dictionary of Soldier Talk*. New York, 1984.

Evans, Eli. *The Provincials: A Personal History of Jews in the South*. 1973. Reprint, New York, 1997.

Fisher, Ernest F., Jr. *Guardians of the Republic: A History of the Noncommissioned Officer Corps of the U.S. Army*. New York, 1994.

Foner, Eric. *Reconstruction: America's Unfinished Revolution, 1863–1877*. New York, 1988.

Franklin, John Hope. *Reconstruction: After the Civil War*. Chicago, 1961.

Fox, William F. *Regimental Losses in the American Civil War, 1861–1865*. 1889. Reprint, Albany, N.Y., 1985.

Gillette, William. *Retreat from Reconstruction, 1869–1879*. Baton Rouge, 1979.

Glatthaar, Joseph T. *Forged in Battle: The Civil War Alliance of Black Soldiers and White Officers*. New York, 1990.

Hair, William Ivy. *Bourbonism and Agrarian Protest: Louisiana Politics, 1877–1900*. Baton Rouge, 1969.

Hardin, J. Fair. *Northwestern Louisiana: A History of the Watershed of the Red River, 1714–1937*. 3 vols. Louisville, Ky., and Shreveport, La., 1939.

Harris, William C. *The Day of the Carpetbagger: Republican Reconstruction in Mississippi*. Baton Rouge, 1979.

Hattaway, Herman, and Archer Jones, *How the North Won: A Military History of the Civil War*. Urbana, Ill., 1983.

Hemenway, Abby M., ed. *Vermont Historical Gazetteer*. 5 vols. Burlington, Vt., 1868–1891.

Hertzberg, Stephen. *Strangers within the Gate City: The Jews of Atlanta, 1845–1915*. Philadelphia, 1978.

Higginbotham, A. Leon, Jr. *Shades of Freedom: Racial Politics and Presumptions of the American Legal Process*. New York, 1966.

Holbrook, Stewart H. *The Yankee Exodus: An Account of Migration from New England*. New York, 1950.

Hunter, Louis C. *Steamboats on the Western Rivers: An Economic and Technological History*. Cambridge, Mass., 1949.

Hutton, Paul Andrew. *Phil Sheridan and His Army*. Lincoln, Neb., 1985.

Jellison, Charles A. *Ethan Allen: Frontier Rebel*. Syracuse, N.Y., 1969.

Kaplan, Benjamin. *The Eternal Stranger: A Study of Jewish Life in the Small Community*. New York, 1957.

Kaczorowski, Robert J. *The Politics of Judicial Interpretation: The Federal Courts, Department of Justice, and Civil Rights*. New York, 1985.

Kniffen, Fred B. *Louisiana: Its Land and People*. Baton Rouge, 1968.

Korn, Bertram Wallace. *The Early Jews of New Orleans*. Waltham, Mass., 1969.

Kousser, J. Morgan, and James M. McPherson, eds. *Region, Race, and Reconstruction: Essays in Honor of C. Van Woodward* (New York, 1982).

Leech, Margaret. *Reveille in Washington, 1860–1865*. New York, 1941.

Loewen, James W. *Lies across America: What Our Historic Sites Get Wrong*. New York, 1999.

Mattie, Joan. *100 Years of Architecture in Kingston: John Power to Drever and Smit*. Public Archives, Ottawa, Canada, 1986.

McPherson, James M., ed., *The Atlas of the Civil War*. New York, 1994.

———. *Battle Cry of Freedom: The Civil War Era*. New York, 1988.

———. *For Cause and Comrades: Why Men Fought in the Civil War*. New York, 1997.

———. *Ordeal by Fire: The Civil War and Reconstruction*. 2d ed. New York, 1992.

McFeely, William. *Yankee Stepfather: General O. O. Howard and the Freedmen*. New Haven, Conn., 1968.

Melville, Herman. *His Fifty Years of Exile (Israel Potter)*. 1855. Reprint, New York, 1957.

Meeks, Harold A. *Time and Change in Vermont: A Human Geography*. Chester, Conn., 1986.

Mika, Nick and Helma. *Kingston: Historic City*. Belleview, Ontario, 1987.

Mitchell, Reid. *Civil War Soldiers*. New York, 1988.

Moneyhon, Carl H. "The Failure of Southern Republicanism, 1867–1876." In *The Facts of Reconstruction*, 99–119.

Morris, Robert C. *Reading, 'Riting, and Reconstruction: The Education of Freedmen in the South, 1861–1870*. Chicago, 1981.

Morrissey, Charles T. *Vermont: A Bicentennial History*. New York, Nashville, 1981.

Morton, Desmond. *A Short History of Canada*. 2d rev. ed. Toronto, 1994.

Nevins, Allan. *The Emergence of Lincoln*. 2 vols. New York, 1950.

Newton, William Monroe. *History of Barnard, Vermont, with Family Genealogies, 1761–1927*. 2 vols. Montpelier, Vt., 1928.

Nieman, Donald G. *To Set the Law in Motion: The Freedmen's Bureau and the Legal Rights of Blacks, 1865–1868*. Millwood, N.Y., 1979.

Norris, James D. *R. G. Dun & Co., 1841–1900: The Development of Credit-Reporting in the Nineteenth Century*. Westport, Conn., 1978.

Oates, Stephen B. *A Woman of Valor: Clara Barton and the Civil War.* New York, 1994.

Olsen, Otto H. *Carpetbagger's Crusade: The Life of Albion Winegar Tourgée.* Baltimore, Md., 1965.

Oubre, Claude F. *Forty Acres and a Mule: The Freedmen's Bureau and Black Land Ownership.* Baton Rouge, 1978.

Parsons, George W. *Put the Vermonters Ahead: The First Vermont Brigade in the Civil War.* Shippensburg, Penn., 1996.

Pfanz, Harry W. *Gettysburg: The Second Day.* Chapel Hill, N.C., 1987.

Powell, Lawrence N. "The Politics of Livelihood: Carpetbaggers in the Deep South." In *Region, Race, and Reconstruction, 315–47. New York, 1982.*

Pullen, John J. The Twentieth Maine: A Volunteer Regiment in the Civil War. New York, 1957.

Perman, Michael. *The Road to Redemption: Southern Politics, 1869–1879.* Chapel Hill, N.C., 1984.

———. "Counter Reconstruction: The Role of Violence in Southern Redemption." In *The Facts of Reconstruction.*

Rabinowitz, Howard N., ed. *Southern Black Leaders of the Reconstruction Era.* Urbana, Ill., 1982.

Rable, George C. *But There Was No Peace: The Role of Violence in the Politics of Reconstruction.* Athens, Ga., 1984.

Reardon, Carol. "The Other Grant: Lewis A. Grant and the Vermont Brigade in the Battle of the Wilderness." In *The Wilderness Campaign,* edited by Gary Gallagher, 201–36. Chapel Hill, N.C., 1997.

Rhea, Gordon C. *The Battle of the Wilderness: May 5–6, 1864.* Baton Rouge, 1994.

Sears, Stephen W. *Chancellorsville.* Boston, 1996.

———. *George B. McClellan: The Young Napoleon.* New York, 1988.

———. *To the Gates of Richmond: The Peninsula Campaign.* New York, 1992.

Seip, Terry L. *The South Returns to Congress: Men, Economic Measures, and Intersectional Relationships, 1868–1879.* Baton Rouge, 1983.

Simpson, Brooks D. *The Reconstruction Presidents.* Lawrence, Kan., 1998.

Stilwell, Lewis D. *Migration from Vermont.* Montpelier, Vt., 1948.

Sombart, Werner. *The Jews and Modern Capitalism.* Translated with notes by M. Epstein, 1911. Reprint, New York, 1969.

Stampp, Kenneth M. *The Era of Reconstruction, 1865–1877.* New York, 1965.

Steiner, Paul E. *Disease in the Civil War: Natural Biological Warfare in 1861–1865.* Springfield, Ill., 1968.

Summers, Mark W. *Railroads, Reconstruction, and the Gospel of Prosperity: Aid under the Radical Republicans, 1865–1877.* Princeton, N.J., 1984.

Sutherland, Daniel. *The Confederate Carpetbaggers.* Baton Rouge, 1988.

Symonds, Craig L. *A Battlefield Atlas of the Civil War*. Cartography by William J. Clipson. Annapolis, Md., 1983.

Taylor, Joe Gray. *Louisiana Reconstructed, 1863–1877*. Baton Rouge, 1974.

Thornton, J. Mills. "Fiscal Policy and the Failure of Radical Reconstruction in the Deep South." In *Region, Race, and Reconstruction*, 349–94.

Trelease, Allen W. *White Terror: The Ku Klux Klan Conspiracy and Southern Reconstruction*. New York, 1971.

Tunnell, Ted. *Crucible of Reconstruction: War, Radicalism, and Race in Louisiana, 1862–1877*. Baton Rouge, 1984.

Twitchell, Ralph Emerson. *Genealogy of the Twitchell Family: Record of the Descendants of the Puritan—Benjamin Twitchell. . . .* New York, 1929.

Vincent, Charles. *Black Legislators in Louisiana during Reconstruction*. Baton Rouge, 1976.

Warner, Ezra J. *Generals in Blue: Lives of the Union Commanders*. Baton Rouge, 1964.

White, Howard A. *The Freedmen's Bureau in Louisiana*. Baton Rouge, 1970.

Wiggins, Sarah Woolfolk. *The Scalawag in Alabama Politics, 1865–1881*. University, Ala., 1977.

Wiley, Bell I. *The Life of Billy Yank: The Common Soldier of the Union*. Baton Rouge, 1978.

Williams, Lou Falkner. *The Great South Carolina Ku Klux Klan Trials, 1871–1872*. Athens, Ga., 1996.

Wyatt-Brown, Bertram. *Southern Honor: Ethics and Behavior in the Old South*. New York, 1982.

Articles

Beers, Lorna. "The Sleeping Sentinel William Scott." *New England Galaxy* 7 (1965): 3–14.

Cox, John and LaWanda Cox. "General O. O. Howard and the 'Misrepresented Bureau.'" *Journal of Southern History* 19 (1953): 427–56.

Cox, LaWanda. "The Promise of Land for the Freedmen," *Mississippi Valley Historical Review* 45 (1958): 413–40.

Davis, Donald W. "Ratification of the Constitution of 1868—Record of Votes," *Louisiana History* 6 (1965): 301–5.

Dethloff, Henry C. "Paddlewheels and Pioneers on Red River, 1815–1915, and the Reminiscences of Captain M. L. Scovell," *Louisiana Studies* 6 (1967): 91–134.

Holt, Thomas C. "Georgia Carpetbaggers: Politicians without Politics," *Georgia Historical Quarterly* 72 (1988): 72–86.

Lestage, Oscar H. Jr. "The White League in Louisiana and Its Participation in Reconstruction Riots." *Louisiana Historical Quarterly* 18 (1935): 615–95.

Longacre, Edward G. "Black Troops in the Army of the James, 1863–1865," *Military Affairs* 45 (1981): 1–8.

May, Thomas J. "The Freedmen's Bureau at the Local Level: A Study of a Louisiana Agent." *Louisiana History* 9 (1968): 5–19.

Monaghan, Jay. "Civil War Slang and Humor," *Civil War History* 3 (1957): 125–33.

Rable, George C. "Republican Albatross: The Louisiana Question, National Politics, and the Failure of Reconstruction." *Louisiana History* 23 (1982): 109–30.

Rushing, Fred J. "The Assassination of Judge T. S. Crawford, Bitter Fruit of the Tragic Era." *North Louisiana Historical Association Journal* 7 (1976): 131–34.

Small, Sandra E. "The Yankee Schoolmarm in Freedmen's Schools: An Analysis of Attitudes." *Journal of Southern History* 45 (1979): 381–402.

Suarez, Raleigh A. "Chronicle of Failure: Public Education in Antebellum Louisiana." *Louisiana History* 12 (1971): 109–12.

Swinney, Everette. "Enforcing the Fifteenth Amendment, 1870–1877." *Journal of Southern History* 28 (1962): 202–18.

Vandal, Gilles. "The Policy of Violence in Caddo Parish, 1865–1884," *Louisiana History* 32 (1991): 159–82.

———. "Albert H. Leonard's Road from the White League to the Republican Party: A Political Enigma," *Louisiana History* 36 (1995): 67–69.

Vazzano, Frank P. "The Louisiana Question Resurrected: The Potter Commission and the Election of 1876." *Louisiana History* 16 (1975): 39–57.

UNPUBLISHED PAPERS, DISSERTATIONS, AND THESES

Cook, Philip C. "Ante-bellum Bienville Parish." Master's thesis, Louisiana Polytechnic Institute (now Louisiana Tech University), 1965.

Pope, Ida Waller. "The Coushatta Massacre." Master's thesis, McNeese State University, 1968.

Powell, Lawrence N. "Centralization of Local Government in Reconstruction Louisiana: Democratic Contradictions and Republican Factionalism." Paper presented at Louisiana Historical Association Meeting. March 1989.

Snyder, Perry A. "Shreveport, Louisiana, during the Civil War and Reconstruction." Ph.D. diss., Florida State University, 1979.

Shoalmire, Jimmy G. "Carpetbagger Extraordinary: Marshall Harvey Twitchell, 1840–1905." Ph.D. diss., Mississippi State University, 1969.

Sipress, Joel M. "The Triumph of Reaction: Political Struggle in a New South Community, 1865–1898." Ph.D. diss., University of North Carolina at Chapel Hill, 1993.

Yount, David Adams. "Erastus Fairbanks: Vermont's First Civil War Governor." Master's thesis, University of Vermont, 1968.

INDEX

Abney, Thomas: as founder of Coushatta, 141–42, 176, 184; as leader of anti-Twitchell faction, 159–60, 187; gets yellow fever, 178; as merchant, 184, 186–87; as White League leader 159–60, 192, 194–95, 217–18, 230; in Coushatta massacre, 197–99, 201–5, 207–8, 211–12; *U.S. v. T. W. Abney et al.*, 220, 222, 225, 259–60; leaves Louisiana, 259 n; depicted in *Wild Work*, 281–83

Ackerman, Amos T., 235
Allen, Ethan, 9–10, 21, 30
Allen, Levin, 207, 283
Anderson, James E., 274–76
Anderson, Thomas C., 272
Antoine, Caesar C., 234
Arthur, Chester A., 294
Austin, Private Narcisse, 100–2
Antietam, 57–58
Ashkenazi, Elliott, 155–56

Beckwith, James, 219–20
Baird, Absalom, 108
Bartholomew, Colonel Orion A., 82–83, 267
Battle of Canal Street, 213–15
"Battle of Liberty Place." *See* Battle of Canal Street
Bayliss, Dr. Jeremiah, 265–67

Bienville Parish, 92–94, 97, 99, 103, 105, 107, 120, 140, 170, 227, 255
Blackburn, W. Jasper, 123–24
Blacks: in Reconstruction legend 2, 3–4, 304; and USCT, 74–76, 82–86; as occupation troops in north Louisiana, 94, 99–103; and Freedmen's Bureau, 92, 94–99; and Freedmen's Bureau schools, 103–5, 107–8; *gens de couleur*, 121–22; in constitutional convention, 121–24; in 1868 election, 129–33; in Red River Parish, 143–52, 169–70, 297; and Colfax massacre, 173–74; intimidated, 226–27, 242, 243, 263; and Black League, 190–91, in Coushatta massacre, 199–203, 207–8, 211; in Louisiana legislature, 128, 234; testify before Coushatta subcommittee, 253–54; mourn Twitchell, 247; and Hayes, 273; in *Wild Work*, 283; mentioned, 13–14, 80, 93, 113, 114, 118

Bosley, Andy: and Twitchell, 144–45,147, 188, 297; and Coushatta massacre, 211; testifies before Coushatta subcommittee, 253–54
Bosley, Ida, 144–45
Bossier Parish, 107–8, 140
Boult, D. H., 193–94
Boyd, Francis A., 85–86
Bradley, Joseph, 219–18

Bridges, John J., 186
Brown, William G., 149–50
Bryan, Mary E.: 150–51; writes *Wild Work*, 280–84
Bull Run: First Battle of, 21; Second Battle of, 56
Brush Valley, La., 110–16 *passim*, 228, 281
Burnside, General Ambrose: 57; at Fredericksburg, 62–63; Mud March, 63–64
Butler, General Benjamin F., 83–84, 251
Byles, Valmont, 150

Caddo Parish, 107–8, 140, 147, 205
Canby, General E. R. S., 203–4, 212
"Captain Jack": in Coushatta massacre, 203–8, 220, 224; sends warning to Starlight, 240–41 n; attack on King and Twitchell, 242–45, 259, 264; as hero, 271; in *Wild Work*, 281, 283; mentioned, 217–18
Carnes, John H., 254
Carpetbaggers: legend of, 1–6; defined, 2 n; origins of term, 124–28
Carranza, Ramon de, 300–1
Carroll, Mrs. Elizabeth A., 141, 158
Carson, Dr. William C., 245–47, 262
Cawthorn, George, 222
Chancellorsville, Battle of, 66–67
Cleveland, Grover, 295–96
Coleman, Adele. *See* Adele Coleman Twitchell
Coleman, Augustus (Gus), 109, 111–12, 118, 255
Coleman family, 109–13
Coleman, Judy, 109, 113, 115, 118, 180
Coleman, Isaac, 109–13, 115, 117–18, 140, 228, 255
Coleman, Luella, 110, 113–15, 181
Coleman, Richard. *See* "Captain Jack"
Colfax: massacre in, 173–74; mentioned, 211, 227
Commodore, Frank, 196–97
Cone, Gilbert, 202–3
Conway, Thomas W., 92, 95, 148

Cook, Sergeant John F., 51–52
Cosgrove, James H., 196, 220, 223
Coushatta: 116, 136, 138; founding of, 141–42; governance, 140, 142–47, 184; prosperity in, 150–54, 160; and Colfax massacre, 174; economic decline, 185–87; yellow fever in, 198–99, 233–34; massacre in, 197–209, 212–13, 218–19, 226, 233–34, 257; Camp Coushatta, 217–18, 234, 240, 247; arrests in, 222–25; and 1874 election, 225–27; attack on King and Twitchell in, 240–45, 259–62, 271; investigation of Twitchell-King shooting in, 251–58; as symbol, 239, 261, 271; depicted in *Wild Work*, 150–51, 281–83
Coushatta Bar, 153–54, 196
Coushatta Chute. *See* Coushatta
Coushatta Times, 146, 184, 212, 271
Cushman, Reverend Chester L., 15, 232, 271
Custom House faction, 170–71
Crawford, Thomas S., 175
Cruikshank, William, 219, 260. *See United States v. Cruikshank*
Cunningham, M. J., 194

Darrall, Chester B., 272
Day, Henrietta Nancy. *See* Henrietta Day Twitchell
Delaney, Patrick, 242
De Russey, Gus, 196
De Soto Parish, 107–8, 139–40, 192, 193, 203–4, 226–27
Dewees, Edward (W.): as Twitchell's political partner, 134, 139–40, 188, 194, 213, 217; buys share of Starlight, 136 n; and Coushatta massacre, 208–9; death of, 247
Dewees, Robert: friendship with Twitchell, 136, 188; run out of De Soto Parish, 193; victim in Coushatta massacre, 196, 199, 202–3, 206, 208
Dickson, John, 200, 201, 203
Dixon, Thomas, 2–3, 304
Dunn, Oscar J., 234

Dunning school, 2, 4, 303–4
Dunning, William A. *See* Dunning school

Earp, Wyatt, 209–10
Edgerton, Frank: joins Twitchell's Yankee colony, 136; becomes sheriff of Red River Parish, 185; and White League, 195–99; victim in Coushatta massacre, 202, 254, 284
Elam, J. B., 229, 288
Emory, General William H., 213, 216, 220, 229

Fish, Hamilton, 235
Fredericksburg, Battle of, 62–63
Fort Sumter, 20
Fourth Vermont Infantry: organization, 23–25; in Washington, 25–27; at Camp Advance, 27–28; at Camp Griffin; 30–36; sickness in, 31–34, 46–48; at Dam No. 1, 39–44; at Garnett's Farm, 49–50; at Savage's Station and White Oak Swamp, 53–54; at Malvern Hill and Harrison's Landing, 54–56; at Fredericksburg, 63; in the Wilderness, 77–79
Flood, Colonel Martin, 107–8
Floyd, Thomas, 197–98
Folger, Mathew H., 296
Fullerton, General James S., 95, 97

Gibson, Randall Lee, 251–52, 255
Gillespie, Carolyn, 135, 286–89, 297
Gillespie, Charles K., 135, 286–87
Gillem, Newt, 185
Godfrey, Lieutenant Edward L., 174, 265
Goggle-Eyed Man. *See* "Captain Jack"
Gone with the Wind, 2–4, 7
Grand Army of the Republic, 296
Grant Parish, 139
Grant, Ulysses S., 76, 82, 129, 132, 171, 212, 215–16, 235
Greeley, Horace, 12–13, 21, 171, 297
Green Mountain Boys: Revolution, 9–10, 21; nickname for Vermont's Civil War soldiers, 29–30

Hammond, Colonel John, 82
Harris, A. B., 175
Harris, Wallace, 99–103, 241
Harrison, John W.: joins Twitchell's Yankee colony, 136, 240–41; defends Twitchell, 245, 262; as Starlight manager, 272, 285–87; murdered, 287–88
Hayes, Duke H., 158, 243
Hayes, Rutherford B.: 261; in 1876 election, 266, 268; restores "home rule," 270; appoints Twitchell consul, 272–74
Holland, Burt, 294
Holland, Clark: joins Twitchell's Yankee colony, 136; as officeholder; 140; victim in Coushatta massacre, 201–6
Honneus, William H., 130, 135–36
Hooker, General Joseph: 57, 64; at Chancellorsville, 65–66
Howell, William: as parish attorney, 158, 185; victim in Coushatta massacre, 202–3, 206

Jews: in Louisiana, 155; in Red River Parish, 155–59
Johnson, Andrew, 95, 119–20
Johnson, Lewis, 200, 207–8

Keeting, Charles W., 189–90
Kellogg, William Pitt: elected Louisiana governor, 171–72; attack on, 174–75; and postwar debt, 175, 181–82; and Coushatta troubles, 195–96, 208–9; and Battle of Canal Street, 213–16; and Banditti affair, 229–30; and Wheeler compromise, 230–31, 236; impeachment of, 236–40, 261; and Twitchell shooting, 258–59, 261; aids Twitchell with appointments, 272, 294; mentioned, 220
Kent, J. Ford, 140
King, George A.: joins Twitchell's Yankee

colony, 136; officeholder, 140, 241, 256;
remarries, 241; during Coushatta
troubles, 203, 211; killed, 242–43, 245,
251, 265; mentioned, 285
King, Homer, 294
Kingston, 274, 292–306 *passim*
Knights of the White Camellia, 1, 129–32,
191
Ku Klux Klan, 129, 191, 220, 235

Lake Bistineau, 93, 117, 134–36, 281
Lake Bistineau Navigation Company,
134–35
Langhorne, Moses, 130
Leland Seminary, 14–17
Leonard, Albert (H.), 189–90, 221,
290–91
Lillie, Captain Daniel, 56; 66–67, 72 n–74,
78
Lincoln, Abraham, 38, 56, 62, 92
Lisso Bros., 186–87
Lisso family, 155–58
Lisso, Paul, 158, 187, 197
Lisso, Julius: as a founder of Coushatta,
141, 160; as leader of pro-Twitchell
faction, 155–59; as merchant, 157–58,
186–87; turns against Twitchell,
187–88, 192–93, 217, 253; arrest
warrant issued for 220, 222; describes
attack on Twitchell, 243; depicted in
Wild Work, 281–83; mentioned, 224,
242
Lisso, Marks, 141, 155–59, 178, 187,
281–83
Lisso, Michael, 155–56, 158
Lisso, Samuel, 158, 187, 197, 242
Little Big Horn, 265
Longstreet, James, 213
Louisiana: Reconstruction in, 5–6, 120,
128–34, 175–76, 189; constitutional
convention in, 121–24; carpetbaggers
in, 124–27; Republican feuding in,
170–72; as Republican albatross,
171–72, 213, 230; postwar debt, 175–77,

181–82; reputation for corruption,
278–79
Love, Leander E., 159, 253
Ludeling, John T., 238

McClellan, General George B., 37–38, 40,
43, 50, 62
MacDonald, John A., 294
McEnery, John D., 171, 220
McFadden, Lieutenant Colonel Orrin, 102
McIntosh, Lieutenant Donald, 222–25
McKinley, William, 296
Mac Veagh, Wayne, 270, 272–73
Marston, Ben W., 184, 190, 192, 253
Mason, E., 153, 178
Meadows, William, 130
Mellor, Frank, 300–1
Mercantile Agency, 154, 156–57, 159,
169–70, 185–86
Merrill, Mrs. E. J., 243–44
Merrill, Major Lewis: 192; and District of
the Upper Red River, 220–21; and
Coushatta arrests, 224–25; testifies
about White League, 230–31, 236;
opinion of Albert Leonard, 221, 290
Meyers, Captain Charles A., 103
Meyers, Henry C., 193–94
Miller, John P. 200–1, 211
Mitchell, Margaret, 2–4
Mudgett, William S.: wants to court-
martial Twitchell, 102; joins Twitchell's
Yankee colony, 136, 240; defends
Twitchell, 241, 245, 252, 254; as
Starlight manager, 285–87; remains in
Coushatta, 297

Nash, Christopher Columbus, 173–74
Natchitoches, Freedmen's Bureau in, 107;
opposes Red River Parish bill, 139;
White League in, 193–95; arrests in,
222–23; in 1874 election, 226
New Orleans: Reconstruction in, 92, 133;
Battle of Canal Street, 213–15;
Returning Board meets in, 227–228;
Banditti affair, 229–30; corruption in,

278; mentioned, 86, 94, 135, 181, 187, 192, 233, 255

Nicholls, Francis R. Tillou, 268–70, 272

Ogden, H. N., 256

Ord, General Edward O. C., 84

Packard, Stephen B.: as U.S. marshal, 170–71, 195–96, 214, 223; in 1876 election, 268–71

Page, Thomas Nelson, 2, 304

Paxton, Thomas, 158, 187, 193, 199, 205, 219

Pease, Captain Henry R., 103

Peck, William, 145, 188

Peninsula campaign: 37–38; Lee's Mill (Dam No. 1), 39–44; Williamsburg, 44–45; Chickahominy River, 45–49; Garnett's Farm, 49–50; Savage's Station, 50–54; White Oak Swamp, 54; Malvern Hill, 54–55; Harrison's Landing, 55–56; Seven Days' Battle, 55

Penny, Orin S., 158, 197

Pennypacker, Galusha, 245 n

Perrow, Benjamin, 145, 297

Pickens, A. O. P., 184, 187–88, 193

Pierson, David, 286, 290

Pierson, James, 253, 286–87

Pierson, Joseph, 194–95, 197, 201, 220, 286–87, 297

Porter, Henry, 145

Porter, Prior, 145

Potter Commission, 274–79

Potter Clarkson D. See Potter Commission

Prenter. See Spanish spy

Rawles, E. W., 243

Reconstruction Act, 119–20

Red River Parish: creation of, 138–41; governance, 142–46, 155–60, 256–58; violence in, 147; black schools in, 148–49, 263; population of, 141, prosperity in, 150–52, 160, 175; economic decline in, 176–78, 179–81,

185–87; yellow fever in, 178–79; White League in, 176–77, 253; alleged corruption in, 185, 187, 255–58

Red River, 141, 152–54, 177–79

Red River raft, 92–93

Red River Valley, 177–78, 189

Returning Board, 169, 171–72, 216, 227, 236

Ringgold, La., 120

Roach, P. E., 145

Sabine Parish, 149–50, 152, 226

Sams, Dennis, 242, 244–45

Sandiford, John L., 184, 192

Scanland, J. M., 110

Scott, Henry: joins Twitchell's Yankee colony, 136; in Coushatta massacre, 201–4; as U.S. deputy marshal, 222, 225

Scott, William (the Sleeping Sentinel), 27, 35

Scheen, John H., 121, 253

Sheridan, General Philip, 108, 129, 229–30

Sherman, John. See Sherman letter

Sherman letter, 275–76

Shoalmire, Jimmy, 5

Shreveport: 93; yellow fever in, 178, hard times in, 177–79; as headquarters, District of the Upper Red River, 220–22; mentioned, 102, 103, 104, 106, 204

Shreveport Times, 151, 153, 189–90, 192, 290–91

Smith, General William F. ("Baldy"), 28–29, 40, 42

Smith, Charles W., 262, 263

Snead, W. H.:, 186

Spanish-American War, 299–301

Spanish spy, 300–1

Sparta (Bienville Parish) La., 93–94, 100–112 passim, 121

Springville, La., 141

Stafford, George A., 289–90

Stafford, L. A., 289–90

Starlight Plantation, 135–36, 138, 142, 180, 206, 211, 233, 240–41, 286–89

Stearns, Captain Leonard A., 23, 28, 34–35, 49, 53–56

Stephens, John F., 141, 159, 176, 184, 220

Steuben, Baron Friedrich von, 59–60

Stockton, J. B., 222–25, 252, 286–87

Stoughton, Colonel Edwin H., 24, 26, 31–32

Stringfellow, H. C., 206

Studer, Major E. J., 106

"Ten Per Cent" Plan, 92

Thomas, Julia M., 104–8

Tooke, Jerry, 145

Trobriand, General Régis de, 229–30

True, James M., 292–93

Twitchell, Adele Coleman: courtship and marriage with Marshall Twitchell, 109–18 *passim*, 294; suffers from tuberculosis, 115–16, 118; death, 180–81; depicted in *Wild Work*, 281–83; mentioned, 7

Twitchell, Benjamin, 10

Twitchell, Daniel, 10–11

Twitchell, Daniel (baby), 182

Twitchell, Elizabeth Scott, 11–12, 22, 136, 232, 267, 285, 287–90, 294

Twitchell, Emmus George, 294, 297–298–99, 305

Twitchell family, 10–11 n, 14, 22–23

Twitchell, Fred F., 297

Twitchell, Harvey (baby), 118

Twitchell, Harvey Daniel, 11–13, 19, 22–23, 116

Twitchell, Helen (Mrs. Willis): 11, 22, 136, 205, 233, 242, 285, 295; nurses Marshall Twitchell, 245–46; death of, 262–65, as political symbol, 265–67

Twitchell, Henrietta Nancy Day, 15, 232–33, 268, 297–98, 303, 305

Twitchell, Homer: birth, 11–12; joins Yankee colony, 136; officeholder, 149, 176; in Coushatta massacre, 199–208,

224, 255–56, 295; in *Wild Work*, 281, 282; mentioned, 22

Twitchell, Joseph, 10

Twitchell, Isabelle Hannah, 11, 22, 136, 140, 241, 295

Twitchell, Kate Francis, 12, 136, 204–5, 233–34, 295

Twitchell, Lottie, 211

Twitchell, Marshall Coleman, 5, 118, 267, 294, 297–98, 305

Twitchell, Marshall H.: early years, 11–13; education, 14–17, 19

as soldier: enlistment in Fourth Vermont Infantry, 21–25; army experiences in Washington and northern Virginia, 25–28, 30–32, 34–36; at Fort Monroe, 38; at Dam No. 1, 39–44; at Williamsburg, 44–45; at Golding's Farm, 48; at Garnett's Farm, 49–50; at Savage's Station, 53–54; at White Oak Swamp, 54; at Harrison's Landing, 55; at Crampton's Gap, 56–57; at Antietam, 57–58; at Fredericksburg, 63; Mud March, 63–64; at Chancellorsville, 66–67; at Gettysburg, 68–69, 72–73; in the Wilderness, 77–78; wounded, 78–81; recovery from wound, 81–82; as first sergeant, 58, 59–62, 67; reenlistment, 70–71; applies to USCT, 74–76, 267; at Louisville, Ky., 82; with 109th USCT in Virginia, 76, 82–84; with 109th USCT in Texas, 84–86

as Freedmen's Bureau agent: 86; early days in Bienville Parish, 92–96; apprenticeship policy, 96; attitudes toward freedmen, 94–97; daily routine, 97–98; settling disputes, 98–99; killing of Wallace Harris, 99–103; freedmen's schools and conflict with teachers, 103–8; leaves bureau, 108

as politician: beginnings in Bienville

Parish, 120–21; in constitutional convention, 121–24; in 1868 election, 130–34; testifies before congressional committees, 131; as organizer of Coushatta town and Red River Parish, 138–60 *passim;* and postwar debt, 180–81; as political leader in Red River Parish, 174, 184–88; and Colfax, 174; and White League, 189–97, 201, 204, 208–12, 227–28; and Battle of Canal Street, 213–15; investigates Coushatta massacre, 216–20; arrests in Coushatta, 221–24; and Returning Board, 227, 229; as senate leader, 234–36, 258–59, 273; and Kellogg impeachment, 236–40; alleged corruption of, 235–36, 252–58, 251–58, 267, 275–80; attempted assassination of, 240–45, 251, 271; recovery from wounds, 245–47, 267–68; prosthetic arms, 268; Coushatta prosecution bills, 259–61; and Vance-Woodward subcommittee, 251–58, 267; in 1876 disputed election, 268–71; and death of sister Helen, 262–65; and Potter Commission, 274–80; depicted in *Wild Work,* 280–84
as U.S. consul: appointment of, 272–74; duties, 292–94; declines Lisbon ministry, 294–96; and family in Kingston, 297–99; and Spanish-American War, 299–300; and Spanish spy ring, 300–1
and Adele Coleman Twitchell, 109–18 *passim,* 180–81
and Henrietta Day Twitchell, 15, 232–33, 268
as founder of Yankee Colony, 135–36; 151, 189
as cotton planter and businessman, 116–18, 134–35, 142, 180, 253
loses Starlight and other properties, 284–90

character and values, 15–19, 61–62, 64
interest in history, 301–4
autobiography, 5–7, 302–5
as carpetbagger, 1–2, 4–5, 127–128, 141, 281–84, 296
attitudes toward South and white southerners, 38, 111, 112, 113, 114–15, 128, 305
and blacks, 94–97, 143–150, 247, 253–254, 263, 273
death of, 305–6
Twitchell, Ralph Emerson, 11 n

United States Colored Troops: origins of, 74–76; 109th Regiment, 76, 82–86; Sixty-first Regiment, 94, 99; Eightieth USCT, 99, 102
United States v. Cruikshank, 260–61

Vance, John Luther, 252–55, 267, 284
Vermont, 8–10; Puritan heritage, 17–19
Vermont Brigade: 1, 7, 32; organization and reputation, 28–30; in the Peninsula campaign, 39–44, 46; at Savage's Station, 51–55; at Antietam, 57–58; at Fredericksburg, 63; in Mud March, 63–64; winter of 1863, 64–65; at Chancellorsville, 66–67; at Gettysburg, 68–70

Waite, Morrison R., 260
Wardell, Mary E., 103–8
Warmoth, Henry Clay: elected governor, 126, 128; as carpetbagger, 127; and 1868 election, 132–33; centralizes government, 133–34; and Twitchell, 134, 139, 171; as centrist, 143; and Republican feuding, 169–72; and Louisiana debt, 175; and Kellogg impeachment, 238
Washington, D.C., 25–27
Watkins, L. B., 287–89
Weber, Don, 274–77
Weber, Emile, 269, 274–78
Wells, James Madison, 227, 230, 272

West, J. Rodman, 235
Wester, Z. T., 252–53
Wheeler compromise, 230–31, 235
Wheeler, William A., 230–31
Wheelock, Lieutenant Edwin M., 104
White, Edward D., 236
White League: origins in Louisiana
    188–89; in Opelousas, 189; in
    Shreveport, 189–90; in Red River
    Parish, 190–93, 195–96; in
    Natchitoches, 193–95; and Coushatta
    massacre, 196–212, 255–56; in New
    Orleans, 213–17
White Line strategy, 188, 279

Williams, Paul, 200, 207–8
Willis, Helen. *See* Helen Twitchell
Willis, Monroe C.: joins Twitchell's
    Yankee colony, 136; as officeholder,
    140; killed in Coushatta massacre,
    205–6; mentioned, 262
Wolfson, Ben, 194, 223, 243
Woodburn, William, 252–55, 267, 280,
    284
Wordlaw, W. W., 186
Wynn, Daniel, 197–98

Yates, John T., 158, 185, 284–85, 297
Young, David, 148